Melville's Science

GARLAND STUDIES
IN NINETEENTH-CENTURY
AMERICAN LITERATURE
(VOL. 3)

GARLAND REFERENCE LIBRARY
OF THE HUMANITIES
(VOL. 1710)

Garland Studies in Nineteenth-Century American Literature
(General Editor: Benjamin F. Fisher)

Melville's Complaint: Doctors and Medicine in the Art of Herman Melville, by Richard Dean Smith

Grim Phantasms: Fear in Poe's Short Fiction, by Michael L. Burduck

Melville's Science: "Devilish Tantalization of the Gods!," by Richard Dean Smith

The Language of Stephen Crane's Bowery Tales: *Developing Mastery of Character Diction,* by Alan Robert Slotkin

Melville's Science

"Devilish Tantalization of the Gods!"

Richard Dean Smith

GARLAND PUBLISHING, INC. • NEW YORK & LONDON
1993

Library of Congress Cataloging-in-Publication Data

Smith, Richard Dean, 1931–
Melville's science : "Devilish tantalization of the gods!" / by Richard Dean Smith.
p. cm. — (Garland reference library of the humanities ; vol. 1710. Garland studies in 19th-century American literature ; vol. 3)
Includes index.
ISBN 0–8153–1308–X
1. Melville, Herman, 1819–1891—Knowledge—Science. 2. Literature and science—United States—History—19th century. 3. Science in literature. I. Title. II. Series: Garland reference library of the humanities ; vol. 1710. III. Series: Garland reference library of the humanities. Garland studies in 19th-century American literature ; vol. 3.
PS2388.S35S63 1993
813'.3—dc20 93–17405
CIP

Printed on acid-free, 250-year-life paper
Manufactured in the United States of America

To

Gretchen
myn hertes Ledye

May it not possibly be, that as Burns perhaps understood flowers as well as Linnaeus, and the Scotch peasant's poetical description of the daisy, "wee modest, crimson-tipped flower," is rightly set above the technical definition of the Swedish professor, so in Art, just as in nature, it may not be the accredited wise man alone who, in all respects, is qualified to comprehend and describe.

Herman Melville: "Statues in Rome."

Contents

Series Editor's Preface

Nearly a century ago, science was in no way as we envision it today. Looking back, we might think that the world had not moved far beyond a kind of witch-doctor plane in the life of science. The present book provides companion reading to Smith's study of doctors in Melville's works, published as the first volume in this series. Interestingly, as Dr. Smith informs us, the term "scientist" was not coined until well into the nineteenth century. His introductory chapter gives us a concise review of origins and developments in the history of science to Melville's day. This section of the book is as studded with fascinating information as good as a Christmas pudding would be.

Melville's own interests in science are not so evident in his first two novels as they are in later books, but an attentiveness to science appears in those leadoff works, nonetheless, in allusions that bring in machine-in-the-garden motifs, the Elgin Marbles, Belzoni, Buffon, and Cuvier. These books prepare for what is to come in the Melville canon.

Mardi gives us Melville's concerns with science in a major way. The ideas of Linnaeus, Sir Thomas Browne (one of Melville's favorite writers), Benjamin Franklin and electricity, lore from astronomy are deftly worked into the dense texture of this novel. More significantly, however, Smith's section on the possibilities for creating life suggest (to me) a kinship between Melville's book and *Frankenstein*. *Mardi* has been a quarry for much else among Melville devotees, and here is another turn of the screw in literary linkages. The dream psychology that also infiltrates *Mardi* provides affinities with the visionary elements in Mary Shelley's novel. Both features relate to matters of the individual's place in nature that pepper pages of the novel.

A lull in incorporations of scientific theory occurs in *Redburn* and *White-Jacket*, only to resurface in full force in *Moby-Dick*. The relationship of the individual human to God makes for all sorts of ramifications into pathways of science, with two different views of nature (as paradise, as battlefield) emerging. A compelling explication of "The Whiteness of the Whale" also enlivens this chapter. *Moby-Dick* indicates a need to balance hard scientific outlooks with spiritual sustenance.

Pierre reminds us, time and again, of inconsistencies in existence that defy scientific explanations. Human nature is "unknowable," we read in the conclusion to this chapter. In the short stories and *Israel Potter*, we encounter variations on themes that run through preceding works. *The Confidence-Man* strikes out into new pathways, specifically those involving current theories of biology. Some of these ideas recur in the poetry, where shades of Darwinism, Positivism, and other biological investigations and hypotheses loom in important ways. Finally, in *Billy Budd*, a "fusion" of what had appeared in previous works is achieved, and the notion that mankind is not naturally depraved comes to the fore. The concluding chapter gives an overview of Melville's attitudes toward science, arguing persuasively for his basic skepticism about "advances."

I have given an outline of what awaits readers of the following pages because I wanted to indicate the breadth of knowledge that has gone into this book. There is more, I might add, because this is the type of book that suggests as much as it defines. Melville's relationship with science ranks him with many other literary figures of the nineteenth century, for example, Coleridge, the Shelleys, Bryant, Poe, Hawthorne, and Tennyson. Melville also adumbrates a twentieth-century writer like Frost, whose skeptical stance he probably would have admired. As has been the case when scientific contexts are brought to bear on the writings of these authors (and many more: Chaucer, Shakespeare, Browne), stimulating readings come forth. Dr. Smith furnishes us with plenty of those kinds of readings.

Benjamin F. Fisher
The University of Mississippi

Acknowledgments

I wish to acknowledge the valuable assistance received from the libraries of the University of California, Los Angeles, San Francisco State University, Stanford University, California State Library, Harvard University, and the New York Public Library. I particularly appreciate the use of the invaluable collections of the Bancroft Library, University of California, Berkeley, and the Watson Library, University of Kansas.

To the incomparable book stores of Berkeley: Cody's Books and Moe's Books, I extend my thanks and appreciation.

A special debt of gratitude is owed to Helen Reyes, Librarian, John Muir Medical Center, Walnut Creek, California, for locating numerous obscure articles, books, and other materials essential to the successful completion of this work.

At Garland Publishing, I thank Carl Buehler who promotes harmony amongst divisions, establishes order out of chaos, and brings peace between beings, giving further evidence of the wisdom and beneficence of design over chance.

Any remaining error, inadvertence, *lapsus cerebri,* or impercipience is hereby acknowledged, and remains the sole responsibility of the author.

This work was supported by Richard D. Smith, M.D., Inc., and to it, I express my sincere appreciation.

Preface
Nature: the Art of God

The novels of Herman Melville reveal the conditions and events of the mid-nineteenth century, reflecting the enormous changes wrought by science, especially man's perception of himself, and the influence that discoveries in science would have on religious faith. Along with an ability to assimilate dry, uninteresting scientific reports, he makes literary use of contemporary scientific theories and trends in science. The interrelationship of science and religion is a prominent, if not the dominant, theme in Melville's literary art. The relationship between science and religion is one of the most basic, persistent problems in philosophy, critical to an understanding of the human experience.[1] The faith-imbued medieval and Renaissance world view persisted into the mid-nineteenth century, a view that is now virtually unknown.

The early nineteenth century saw the culmination of centuries of investigation of the natural world and its conflict with theology. Medieval Christian scholars debated how the image of man differed from the design of God and how the rift with God after the Fall of man might be repaired. Aristotelian philosophy, brought to a central position in theology by Saint Thomas Aquinas (1225-1274), held that nature could be studied logically. As a result, in the Condemnation of 1277, some of Aristotelian science was forbidden by the Roman church. Fourteenth-century scholastics circumvented this restriction by contending that God, with absolute power, could do all things. God had produced the world, a world which could not be moved in a straight line, abhorred vacuums, and was centered around a stationary earth. At the same time, by keeping to accepted views, philosophers were able to discuss other possibilities in a conceptual way without offending the church. The compromise, according to modern study, may have contributed to the development of the scientific revolution.[2]

A new sense of human dignity developed: Man, able to train his intellect, could add to the knowledge of himself and the natural world. A new awareness of the nobility of God's world led to the notion that man, as part of nature, must also be noble. The ability to appreciate the grandeur and beauty of nature became a human quality. Man took his place in nature, and human society was a part of the grand complex of the natural order, bound together by rational laws. The entire universe appeared intelligible and accessible to human reason; nature was seen as an orderly system instead of a mysterious, necessarily obscure phenomenon; and man, capable of understanding natural laws, saw himself as the center of the natural world, an awareness that gave twelfth century man confidence in human powers implicit in the humanistic and scientific movements to follow. Thierry of Chartres (d. ca 1150) said, "The world would seem to have causes for its existence, and also to have come into existence in a predictable sequence in time. This existence and this order can be shown to be rational."[3] If nature could be understood, nature could be manipulated and controlled to the benefit of man.

The twelfth century scientist, or cosmologist, urged scientific investigation of the natural world as the duty of a Christian, undertaken in gratitude for the magnificent gift of the cosmos. Reason could be a source of pleasure and happiness, and a means of celebrating the glory of God's work. Stiefel says the ultimate purpose of reason was not the acquisition of scientific knowledge for its own sake, but to help man achieve a higher understanding of the Creator.[4] Man, in the egocentric view of medieval Christianity, was the supreme accomplishment of God; man existed in both material and spirit. In the thirteenth century, the aim of natural science was not simply to accept the statement of authority, but to investigate causes at work in nature. The beauty and the design of nature were accepted by theologians and scientists alike (then called natural philosophers). This precept was restated in the seventeenth century by Sir Thomas Browne, "for nature is the Art of God." From the second half of the seventeenth century into the nineteenth century, Isaac Newton's (1642-1737) studies of motion dominated science. Newton's laws of physical movement, unrelated to spiritual order, made science useful in everyday, practical application.

In the eighteenth and nineteenth centuries, the pre-eminent scientists were the naturalists and biologists whose work was eagerly received by the public. Increased education and literacy made it possible for the average person to follow the developments of scientific discovery. At the end of the eighteenth century, the Renaissance theological doctrine of the 'Great Chain of Being' or 'Scale of Nature,' a fixed, rigid scheme, prevailed in natural philosophy. The Scale of Nature ran from minerals by degrees to man, and beyond man to spiritual existences. Religious dogma forbade any implication of phylogenetic relationship or transformation and denied the possibility of extinction of species. Ape placed next to man in the Scale of Nature was of no consequence because of belief in the immutability of species and the special nature of man. The world was assumed by scientists and theologians to be static and unchanging according to God's design. The age of the earth was established according to Biblical generations as only a few thousand years, hence allowing little time for change in the physical world or transformation of living creatures. The idea of design was stated by William Paley (1743-1805), English theologian, philosopher, and clergyman, in *Natural Theology, or Evidences of the Existence and Attributes of the Deity collected from the Appearances of Nature* (1802), "The marks of design are too strong to be gotten over. Design must have had a designer. That designer must have been a person. That person is God."[5]

During the first half of the nineteenth century, science produced many famous names, and many remarkable discoveries claimed the attention of the public. The natural sciences of geology, astronomy, zoology and physics challenged old ideas and threatened religious tenets. Gradually, evidence of extinct forms of life were found; however, man had traveled little about the world—supposedly extinct species surely existed elsewhere on some distant continent. By the beginning of the nineteenth century, however, extinction of species could no longer be doubted.

The term 'scientist' was coined in 1840 by William Whewell: "We need very much a name to describe the cultivator of science in general. I should incline to call him a scientist."[6] Prior to Whewell's definition, science was pursued by natural philosophers using "philosophical instruments" such as test-tubes, retorts, etc. By the beginning of the nineteenth century, metaphysical speculation was replaced by experiment and observation of natural events, or positivism. Positivism is confined to the data of experience and excludes a priori or metaphysical speculation, a philosophy particularly attributed to French philosopher,August Comte (1798-1857), who said human thought had passed from a theological to a metaphysical stage into a positive or scientific stage. Comte contended religious faith would withstand scientific examination of the natural world claiming an intellectual progression of ideas from the times of Sir Francis Bacon (1561-1626) to the philosophy of Immanuel Kant (1724-1804). Historians have maintained that the biblical view of the goodness of the created order, coupled with the Greek view of the rationality of the cosmos, contributed to the rise of science in the West; and the belief in the dependability of nature had to precede the attempt to study its regularities.[7] The application of science to technology made the nineteenth century the "century of hope" because it invented invention.[8]

The revelations of the new science reached their stunning culmination during the lifetime of Herman Melville, placing the revolutionary concepts of natural science in epic conflict with theology, a conflict prominent in most of his works. Mumford observed that as much as Melville was enriched by Elizabethan writers, it is science that separates him completely from the poets of that day.[9] Melville interweaves science, medicine, philosophy, religion, the classics, and much more into a complex intellectual and literary fabric.

Herman Melville was born in New York City, August 1, 1819, the second son and third child of Allan and Maria Gansevoort Melvill (the 'e' was added later). Both of his parents came from prominent New England families. His principal writings were during the decade of the 1850s, a period of great turmoil in science, religion and their interrelationship. This turmoil shaped his literary art as well as the general attitude of the people towards the study of nature and religion, and determined nearly every aspect of twentieth century Western culture. His references to science are often concise, containing the essence of theories and their significance, but requiring some elaboration.

Notes

1. Maurice A. Finocchiaro, *The Galileo Affair: A Documentary History*. Berkeley, Los Angeles, and London: University of California Press, 1989, p. 2.

2. Nicholas H. Steneck, "The Relevance of the Middle Ages to the History of Science and Technology." *Annals of the New York Academy of Sciences* 441: 21-28, 1985.

3. Tina Stiefel, "'Impious Men': Twelfth-Century Attempts to Apply Dialectic to the World of Nature," in "Science and Technology in Medieval Society" *New York Academy of Science* 441 (1985) 187-203.

4. Stiefel.

5. William Paley, *Natural Theology*. (1802) reprint. Editor Frederick Ferré. Indianapolis and New York: Bobbs-Merrill, 1963.

6. OED.

7. Ian G. Barbour, "Science and Religion Today." *Science and Religion: New Perspectives on the Dialogue*. Ian G. Barbour, editor, Harper and Row: New York, Evanston and London, 1968. p. 11.

8. Alfred Kazan, *An American Procession; The Major American Writers from 1830-1930—The Crucial Century*. New York: Vintage, 1985, p. 6.

9. Lewis Mumford, *Herman Melville*. New York: Literary Guild of America. Harcourt, Brace and Company. 1929, p. 192.

Introduction: *fides quaerens intellectum*

The practice of religion and belief in a deity appear to be almost universal, with the exception of modern Western man, who lives in a society of belief and unbelief; an exception that is often attributed to the rise of science. The enhanced understanding of the physical world is thought to have undermined the belief of many people in a spiritual reality.[1] The interaction of supernatural belief with the meaning of the natural world which seeks to find a purpose to the world and man's existence predates recorded history. On the Mediterranean island of Ionia, the first natural philosophers posed abstract questions about the primary form and functions of natural phenomena. Anaxagoras of Clazamoenae (500-428 B.C.) is credited by both Plato and Aristotle as being the first to attribute the apparent structural harmony and order in nature to some form of intelligent design rather than chance; the mindless chaos of infinitesimal particles was ordered by the influence of a cosmic 'mind' into a vortical motion that led to harmony and order. Thus, 'mind' was interrelated with 'matter' as an explanation of phenomena. Empedocles of Argigentum (492-435 B.C.), a Sicilian contemporary and a careful observer of nature, developed the concept that changes in physical processes occur according to the presence of order and design. Socrates (470-399 B.C.) and Plato (427-347 B.C.)

objected to purely materialistic explanations of natural events and attempted to show that material order arose not only from 'mind' but is also sustained by it; in the 'laws' is evidence of the gods. Plato conceived the universe as an organic and ordered structure. Diogenes (400-325 B.C.) commented on the beneficial and superficially purposeful contrivance of natural things towards man's well-being, such as the regular cycle of the seasons.[2] In Plato's *Timaeus,* the Creator is no longer free to work in an arbitrary manner. The world had a rational, logical and discoverable structure, and by the exercise of intelligence, man could discover it.[3]

Aristotle (384-322 B.C.) was the preeminent ancient proponent for the existence of God based on the assumption that order in the universe implies an orderer and that order cannot be a natural feature of the universe; that a final cause exists; that purpose and design are a part of, or are apparent, in nature. His argument was assimilated into the Judeo-Christian revelation by the Scholastic synthesis and indirectly shaped Western thought for nearly two millennia. Aristotle objected to the atomists who said that a thing is explained when one knows what it is made of, and he distinguished four distinct 'causes': material cause, or the material composition; formal cause, or the form or pattern of the material; efficient cause, or the agent that molds the material (which is the modern idea of 'cause'); and a final cause, which was the most important, the purpose for which the object exists. He conceived a spherical boundary with the earth at its center surrounded by a series of concentric shells that carried the sun, moon, and planets. The goal was to understand the final, end cause or ultimate meaning which would be perfect. However, he allowed that the "actual facts are not yet sufficiently made out" and theory must be abandoned if not consistent with indisputable results of observation. From the final cause came the idea of an internal perfecting principle directing events toward a point of harmony.[4]

The Stoics, founded by Zeno of Citium (334-262 B.C.), replaced Aristotle's steady-state universe with the idea of cyclic recurrences and cosmic design. Cicero (106-43 B.C.), in *De Natura Deorum* made a case for the existence of gods in a classic argument for design based on the discernable order and mutual harmony in nature rather than any anthropocentric purposes, an argument to be repeated regularly in subsequent centuries.[5]

The concept of nature, or *natura,* does not exist in ancient mythology, but was invented by the pre-Socratic Greek philosophers. The idea is that the great variety of phenomena that surround us could be considered under one name, as if a single object. The goddess of nature depended upon the development of an abstract concept of nature.[6] That nature was under a central authority was to a great degree influenced by the development of a society with strong central governments, and the picture of the universe as an ordered state subject to rules for human well-being. Practical needs of the society motivated many investigations into agriculture, navigation, and defense. A gradual metamorphosis occurred away from a belief in laws arising from the intrinsic character of an object toward an early monotheistic idea that laws were imposed upon nature by a Law-giver. Imposed law transcends the observation that laws of nature are merely a series of invariable events. To the ancient Greeks, law meant immutable, static, and perfect harmony.[7]

The Greek philosophers sought for a 'unifying principle' to make sense of the enduring, unchanging 'flux.'[8] Their great contribution is the concept of science as we know it today: an abstract, mental model of the whole working of the universe. It had little practical use, for they desired knowledge as a means of understanding and to realize the harmony and order of the world, preferring abstract principles to the practical measurements and descriptions that are the basis of science. Their greatest achievement was in geometry, by the exercise of pure reason.[9]

The Romans produced little in the way of lasting abstract ideas, yet Boethius's (470-525) *The Consolation of Philosophy*, which Chadwick regards as an essay of natural theology apart from revelation yet rests on Christian assumptions,[10] was one of the few contacts between classical learning and the Middle Ages and was the most widely read scholarly work of the medieval period. Although Boethius supports an anthropocentric doctrine of final causes, his model of the universe does not, for he saw man's astronomical position as infinitesimal and insignificant. Greek and Roman arguments for and against design were perpetuated by the Arabic schools, reaching a zenith in the tenth century, and diffused into European culture by Thomas Aquinas as easily as into the thought of early Muslim philosophers.[11] Neither Greece nor Rome produced innovation in technology.[12]

Although the Greeks were the originators of the scientific spirit and of almost all the science of classical times, their important work was finished by 150 B.C. After about 300 A.D., interest in natural science almost ceases: Christianity provided what they had been seeking. Nothing seemed important except to live well and know the divine truth. For centuries the learned world was busy confuting heresies and defining exactly what a Christian can believe without fear of error.[13] After four centuries of struggle and violence, churchmen framed a dogma in the Nicean Creed (325 A.D.) that was to survive to the present, safeguarding the faith. Reason was of no avail, and disagreement or heresy doomed men to eternal torment. Early Christian theological academies were not interested in examining nature since the end of the world was considered to be close at hand. Knowledge of nature became identified with paganism.[14]

With the exception of medicine and astronomy, the study of nature held a precarious position in ancient societies, serving neither practical purpose nor social usefulness. Lindberg states, "Christians regarded science as important only insofar as it served the faith; but at least it did, on occasion, serve the faith." Basil of Caesarea (ca 330-379) summoned as much evidence as available in defense of natural philosophy in the biblical account of Creation and a temporal cosmos: "At all events let us prefer the simplicity of faith to the demonstrations of reason." Saint Augustine (354-430 A.D.) expressed the most influential Christian attitude toward science by holding great esteem for human rational capacities; reason is a divine gift that distinguishes man from animals; reason is indispensable if faith is to be defended and its content understood; reason is also required if one is to grasp that portion of truth not revealed in the Scriptures. Few Christians regarded study of the natural world as having much importance, and next to salvation through faith, it was decidedly insignificant. The early church and Greek natural science coexisted (though occasionally at odds), but interacted with mutually transforming views of the world.[15]

The influence of Islam on western Europe in the twelfth century was enormous. Located between the trade routes linking East and West, Islam was the meeting point of Greek, Egyptian, Indian, and Persian influences, and the technology of China. The stimulation of science in Islam was due to translations of Greek, Indian, and Persian texts, the cultural force of the new religion, and the assimilation of non-Arabs. Translations were made possible by the ready availability of inexpensive paper produced by paper-making technology that came from China in the eighth century. Islamic science was further influenced by the shift from a nomadic to an urbanized culture.[16] Averroës of Cordova (1126-1198), an Islamic philosopher in Spain, opposed the Scholastic synthesis and wished to separate experimental science and logic from religion, claiming that it was unreasonable to say that all nature exists solely for the luxury of mankind. Maimonides (1135-1204) also sought to reconcile Aristotelian philosophy with his own religious heritage founded on the earlier work of Avicenna (980-1037) and objected to the anthropocentric teleology.[17]

The most renowned center of scientific activity from the mid-eleventh to the mid-twelfth century was the school at Chartres which emphasized the defense of secular studies, disciplines understandable by reason alone, and the reintroduction of the idea that nature obeys verifiable laws. Many new attitudes developed about nature, the first since antiquity. Nature had become God's vice-regent who transformed His divine plan into reality and presided over Creation. The absolute transcendence of Augustine's God was modified by the laws of the sublunary world. The reintroduction of Roman law became a powerful system for the analysis of nature. By the twelfth century, nature was no longer a primitive force to be shunned (as the German tribesmen had feared the great forests), but wild nature could at times be subdued and put to man's service. The universe was seen to be organized.[18] Adelard of Bath is said to have preferred the 'reason' of the Arabs to the 'authority' of the schools of Laon. Daniel of Morley protested against pouring over the minutiae of texts instead of seeking knowledge of the natural sciences. Both sought knowledge of things instead of books. Knowledge came from reason rather than from authority, although there was greater scope for reasoning in Scholastic studies than in the natural science of the Arabs: the general tendency of Scholastic thought was to enlarge the scope of nature.[19] The early Renaissance became the age of scientific exploration which was divided by the conflict between science and its opponents: superstition and the authority of traditional philosophy and theology.[20]

Christian philosophers did not obtain their world view from the Bible alone; from the beginning of the thirteenth century onward, a persistent effort to integrate Aristotelian natural philosophy with Christian theology occurred, a goal achieved with considerable struggle. In the end, Christianity took its basic categories of thought and much of its metaphysics and cosmology from Aristotle; in return, science received support and access to new perspectives that enriched and redirected it. However, certain aspects of Aristotelian natural philosophy, such as its determinism, or the doctrine that all events and facts, including human choices and decisions, follow natural, preexisting laws (the opposite of free will), and its denial of Creation, ultimately led to the Condemnations of 1270 and 1277. The Condemnations placed a limit on certain lines of scientific speculation while opening the door to others in a give-and-take between medieval theology and medieval science that continued until the nineteenth century. The early church chose a middle road between endorsing and resisting science.[21]

Science and theology were never more closely interrelated than in the Latin Middle Ages, yet theology remained dominant. As Stiefel remarks, the 'proto-scientists' tried to "impart to their contemporaries their trust in the basic rationality of the universe." The bold new emphasis on rational inquiry led by Adelard of Bath, Peter Abelard, William of Conches, and others marked an initial, and unsuccessful, attempt to separate science from theology. They proposed a rational investigation of nature that foreshadowed events four centuries later, and for which they endured ridicule and persecution.[22] By the early thirteenth century, the works of Aristotle and Greco-Arabic science had been translated into Latin from Arabic with an enormous impact on Western thought. During the late Middle Ages, science and mathematics were extensively applied to theological problems unrelated to the account of Creation in Genesis. The application of quantitative apparatus to examine nature in the fourteenth century changed the traditional methodology of theology to an emphasis on natural philosophy and mathematics. The Condemnation of 1277 marked the culmination of theological efforts to contain and control natural philosophy, i.e., science. With theologians in sole possession of scientific studies, the late Middle Ages were a relatively tranquil period in the relationship between religion and science.[23]

By the middle of the thirteenth century, Albert the Great (1207-1280) and Thomas Aquinas (1225-1274) had completed Aristotle's assimilation into Christianity with a vast unification of Aristotle's philosophy with the Judeo-Christian doctrine of the Catholic church. Scholasticism preserved a belief in the intrinsic intelligibility of nature and in the presence of an underlying rationality in an age full of magic and astrological influences. The Scholastics first used the term *theologia naturalis,* which proved to be a popular notion in the seventeenth and eighteenth centuries.[24] Albertus Magnus (1193-1280) was the first since Aristotle to seriously study biology, and more importantly, he understood that nature is to be seen directly, not read about in books. Albertus Magnus and St. Thomas Aquinas saw the desirability of learning from sources other than spiritual sources. In this they were opposed by most theologians who considered the only valuable knowledge was that which showed the way to heaven. Few were interested in science in the thirteenth century because religion was the center of their lives. Even medicine was not very important for it was better to die well than to live badly. At Oxford, Roger Bacon (1214-1294), philosopher, scientist, and educational reformer, devoted great energy to the pursuit of experimental science, and compiled a vast encyclopedia of all the known sciences. He studied lenses with great care, emphasized the need to perform experiments, and asserted the value of mathematics in interpreting nature—ideas that did not mature until the sixteenth century.[25] For instance, Robert Grosseteste (ca 1168-1253), also at Oxford, recognized the importance of the relationship of the natural world and theology: if God spoke through the things which He had created, then pursuing the meaning of created things was essential. In the Bible, all things—lions, serpents, rocks, seas—possessed meanings and lessons for mankind. When Grosseteste began teaching, he brought his extensive knowledge of science to the study of theology and the exploration of the natural symbols in the Bible: what nature is to science, the Bible is to theology.[26]

Unity of thought had been the unifying purpose of medieval philosophy: to harmonize pagan science and Christian religion, to reconcile authorities, and to explain contradictions and discrepancies.[27] Christianity was the major vehicle for the preserving and spreading of ancient science through the study of the quadrivium—arithmetic, geometry, astronomy, and music—that was often aligned with medicine.[28] The fundamental concept of modern science has been that of natural 'laws,' and that every event occurs in 'obedience' to them. In medieval science, the fundamental concept was of certain sympathies, antipathies, and strivings inherent in matter itself—a *kindly enclyning*. Chaucer says, "The see desyreth naturely to folwen' the Moon" ("The Franklin's Tale," *The Canterbury Tales*), and Francis Bacon says, "The iron in particular sympathy moveth to the lodestone" (*Advancement of Learning*). However, medieval thinkers attributed life, and even intelligence, to the stars alone. The common medieval view allowed four grades of terrestrial reality: mere existence (stones), existence with growth (vegetables), existence, growth, and sensation (beasts), and all of these with reason (man). The four properties of matter and the four elements, and a fifth element or "Quintessence, the aether," were found only above the moon.[29]

In the scheme of the Ptolomaic universe (second century A.D.), the central spherical earth is surrounded by a series of hollow, transparent spheres or heavens; in each of the first seven is fixed a single luminous body; in order from the earth are the seven planets (the Moon, Mercury, Venus, the sun, Mars, Jupiter, and Saturn); then the *Stellatum* which contains all of the invariable stars, and beyond is the *Primum Mobile*, of which Aristotle says, "Outside heaven there is neither place nor void nor time" (*De Caelo*), a pagan sentiment. In Christianity, what is outside the heavens becomes the 'very heaven,' *caelum ipsum*,' and full of God as described in Dante's *Paradiso* (xxx, 38); beyond the material universe is intellectual light. Numerous medieval thinkers attempted to estimate the size of the planet including Isadore in the sixth century, Maimonides in the twelfth, and Bacon in the thirteenth, and they even made some rough estimates of the distances to the planets. The medieval universe, though unimaginably large, was unambiguously finite, making the earth vividly small. The heavens were seen as an object in which the mind can rest, overwhelming in its greatness, but satisfying in its harmony, like a vast cathedral. Lewis says the modern view probably started with Giordano Bruno and appears in English poetry with Milton who may be the first writer to use 'space' in the modern sense. The heavenly spheres transmitted influences to the Earth, i.e., astrology, which was inherited from antiquity and passed on to the Renaissance. The church objected to astrology because of its lucrative and undesirable practices, astrological determinism that could exclude free will, and the worship of planets, persistent Pagan gods.[30]

The medieval world view is most clearly defined by Dante in the *Divine Comedy* with his concept of a series of spheres, one inside the other, and the motionless earth at the center. The ordinary matter, that substance below the moon, is humble and unstable, subject to change and decay. The rotating spheres of the heavens were of a different kind of matter, cut off from the earth, yet combined into a coherent cosmos. The elements are graded according to their virtue: earth the least noble, water, air, and finally fire, which rises the highest. Each "aspires" to its proper sphere where it finds stability and rest. The "life" and vitality of the universe is created by the mixture of these elements; an element out of its proper sphere was bound to be unstable, accounting for rain, lightning, and the elevation of land out of the sea, and making the world subject to dissolution and decay. Dante says the mountains have been drawn up by an influence of the fixed stars. The tales of travelers to Africa and other discoveries and the disproportionate amount of water on the surface of the earth led to the growing view that earth and water were not separate circles one above the other, but were interwoven into a single sphere. The moon and supralunar bodies were made of a fifth, incorruptible matter subject to separate "physical" laws. Only one circular motion is possible for them, except for the tenth sphere which is the empyrean heaven, the abode of God, and it is at rest. The ninth heaven is empty of planets but must exist, for it contained the *primum mobile* which turns itself and all the other spheres; it is more rapid than all the others because it next to the empyrean heaven. The original beauty of this essentially Aristotelian system was compromised by improvements in astronomical observation. Early in the Christian era, during the age of Ptolemy, and in the Middle Ages, both Arab and Christians astronomers accumulated new observations and introduced intricacies into the system, but were required to continue in some sort of circular system to account for aberrant behaviors, i.e., variation of speeds and apparent reversal of movement. The enormous number of circles and epicycles required to maintain the Ptolemaic system became unworkable, and long before Copernicus, it was known that the structure of crystalline spheres did not explain the observed movements of the planets. Numerous writers tried to explain the aberrant findings without success. Dante said the various spheres were moved by intelligences or spirits: through the intelligences, God indirectly shaped the material world. Human souls were created directly by God and were incorruptible, though still influenced by planets. The church struggled against this deterministic view of astrology. Dante said the planets may affect the lower dispositions of man, but God has given each a soul by which to rise above such influences. Others said the opposite, that the stars affect only the higher qualities of human activity, and that evil comes from man's own evil disposition. Dante's world owed more to Aristotle than to Christianity. Consequently, it was Aristotle, who often appeared as an obstruction to the progress of science, rather than the church that was overthrown during the sixteenth century.[31]

Medieval man was characteristically an organizer, codifier, and a builder of systems. In spite of turbulent activities, he formalized activities by distinction, definition, and tabulation from the art of heraldry to the rules of chivalry. Studies demanding ordering of diversity, such as law and moral theology, particularly flourished. He organized the whole of his theology, science, and history into a single, complex, harmonious mental "model of the universe" through a great, finely ordered multiplicity that attempted to harmonize all apparent contradictions. The model included Platonic, Aristotelian, and Stoical philosophy, as well as pagan and Christian elements; everything linked in a hierarchical ladder. According to Lewis, this model of the universe was not only a supreme medieval work of art, but was in a sense the *central* work in which most particular works were imbedded and from which they drew a great deal of their strength.[32] Dante's elaborate model of cosmology did not explain whether God is the lover or the beloved, or whether man is a marginal creature needing the Fall of man for redemption. This produced considerable disharmony in a medieval cosmos that was sublimely ordered:

> Historically as well as cosmically, medieval man stood at the foot of a stairway; looking up, he felt delight. The backward, like the upward, glance exhilarated him with a majestic spectacle, and humility was rewarded with the pleasures of admiration.... One had

> one's place, however modest, in a great succession; one need be neither proud or lonely.[33]

Lewis observes that few constructions of the imagination seem to have combined splendour, sobriety, and coherence in the same degree: "[Yet] it had a serious defect; it was not true."[34]

Science since the middle of the fifteenth century has been in continuous advance sustained by continuous interest. The desire for greater knowledge about the world came from a new study of ancient Greek learning, a growing dissatisfaction with the inaccuracy of and the small extent of man's knowledge of the world, and a growing interest attached to industry as its products became more socially important. The new study began in Italy about 1450, and at about the same time the art of printing developed, permitting a wide distribution and diffusion of Greek scientific authors. The readers of these texts found that ancient authors disagreed with traditional medieval sources, challenging their authority, and that the newly discovered facts of nature disagreed with both. A large, wealthy merchant class grew in Europe that was principally interested in scientific study for its application to industrial production. The known world was expanding through exploration, trade, and the discovery of previously unknown geography and biology.[35]

Nicholas Copernicus (1473-1543), the last of the Aristotelians and the forerunner of the mechanical model of the universe, had a negligible effect until the seventeenth century. His *De revolutionibus orbium celestium* (1543), was little read and was completely overshadowed by the Portuguese voyages of discovery of the same period. Although his world model was heliocentric, his world view remained anthropocentric in that man's displacement is very slight given the immense size of the cosmos; spherical configurations were appropriate for celestial motions, for the figure of the circle was the "most perfect of all." Copernicus' scientific successors, Galileo (1564-1642), and Kepler (1571-1630), held opposite views on the centrality of man. Galileo maintained that such ideas were human presumption, while Kepler saw the presence of order in the universe as evidence verifying his belief that God had created the universe for the benefit of man in accordance with a perfect mathematical or geometrical principles. Many sixteenth century scholars disagreed and contrived some of the most cogent objections to teleology since those of the ancient Greeks. Montaigne (1533-1592) parodied man's grand self-image with an ornithocentric teleology, arguing that we don't know for whom or what purpose the natural world exists with an argument similar to Cicero's *De Natura Deorum*. More emphatic was Francis Bacon (1561-1626), who claimed that theology and philosophy should remain completely separate; he was hostile to all Aristotelian science in favor of the early atomists. Bacon did not deny that nature may possess some divine purpose; he objected to the use of this belief in the empirical investigation of natural phenomena. The trend that began with Bacon continues to the present with scientists ignoring "ultimate" questions to concentrate on limited problems. Bacon identified several 'idols' that obstructed rational inquiry, especially the tendency to perceive a greater degree of order in nature than actually exists. Réne Descartes (1596-1650), a contemporary of Bacon's, was convinced that the primary qualities of the universe were mathematical causing him to reject final causation with its anthropocentric view, and its the presumption that man could unravel the purposes of God, a view reinforced by his belief that the universe was infinite. His view was 'deistic' in that order was inherent in the properties of inorganic material endowed at the moment of creation, but he claimed that whatever the design or ultimate purpose might be, it was beyond man's ability to know.[36] The latter half of the sixteenth century saw improvement in nearly every science with little systematic order or development of method. The ancients were no longer considered reliable authorities, yet a method of determining what was reliable and what was magic or fancy could not be established, for magic and science were mixed together, often by the same individual, such as Paracelsus and others.[37] Nevertheless, because of the immense optimism produced by the Renaissance, and in spite of great conflict and disharmony, the period produced great works of art. All the spiritual enemies contributed to one common quality—great energy.[38]

Until the seventeenth century, in almost all societies, the course of world events and human life was considered to be under the influence of a higher, more perfect metaphysical order, power, God, or world of supernatural beings. As early as the 1580s, Dominican friar Giordano Bruno noted that the sun-centered universe of Copernicus meant that the distinction between the earthly world below and the heavenly world above was no longer tenable, that the earth itself was a heavenly body, and that the universe appeared infinite with the possibility of a plurality of worlds and other inhabited planets. Thus, the universe had some of the attributes previously ascribed only to God: infinity, eternity, and creative fecundity, leading Bruno to merge God and the universe together. The universe was the one incarnate divine being, making revelation and divine intervention redundant. These views were stated more rigorously two generations later by Baruch Spinoza (1632-1677), a heterodox Jewish philosopher in Amsterdam.[39] The ancient and

Renaissance organic world views gradually gave way to a mechanical model. With it came a more enthusiastic 'eutaxiological' argument that the presence of order in the universe must have a cause, especially among the British physicists. Robert Boyle (1627-1691), became its most eloquent spokesman, saying that the deity initiated the primordial motion of atoms that remain in lawful and beneficent control, and that "the laws of nature bear the hallmark of design." Yet, he was consistently mechanical in his view and rejected the Aristotelian organic world view. Although Boyle admired many aspects of Descartes's work, he strongly disagreed with Descartes's exclusion of a final cause. Boyle's design argument came from the minute observation of flora and fauna, noting that "the eye of a fly seems a more curious piece of work than the body of the sun." The invention of the microscope allowed the observation of the intricacies of the smallest organisms and greatly contributed to design argument. In 1688, Boyle published *Disquistion about the Final Causes of Natural Things,* attempting to classify the ends of nature into four categories: the 'universal' or divine, 'cosmical' or celestial, 'animal' or anatomy and functional anatomy, and 'human' or mental and corporeal—each with its own argument for design. He argued that the world is like a mechanism—built for a specific purpose that can be ascertained by inspection of its inner workings. Although immediate efficient causes of phenomena were entirely mechanical in Boyle's physics, their ultimate and final causes were seen as entirely supernatural.[40]

The astronomers of the fifteenth and sixteenth centuries developed a new attitude, the attitude of a scientist: they observed for themselves, seeking ever greater accuracy; they abandoned preconceptions about the nature of the universe, and kept and published accurate records of their observations.[41] The belief in crystalline spheres was declining, allowing a study of the actual paths of the planets. Tycho Brahe (1546-1601) built the first large accurately-constructed observatory. Johannes Kepler (1571-1630), driven by an almost mystical religious fervor, a passion to uncover the "music of the spheres," took the earlier developments and undisciplined data of Tycho Brahe and added his mathematical genius. Kepler was especially interested in the nonuniform speed of the planets. After enormous intellectual effort, he discovered the elliptical nature of the orbit of Mars, although from ancient times astronomers had realized that planets did not move in regular circles. Yet, more vexing questions arose: if not held in their proper place by the spheres, then by what mechanism did any order exist? Why didn't the earth careen into other planets?

Kepler was able to appreciate the mathematical order of celestial movements, and was an advocate of a mechanical system—the first of the seventeenth century—in the faith that this was the highest glorification of God.[42] The shift was from myth to math, from animism to mechanism, and from explanation from above to that from here below. Secularized politics, economics, science, and technology outgrew and overwhelmed the sacred. In the seventeenth century, focus shifted from a God-centered religion to that of tending to see God only in Christ, who became the main object of devotion rather than God; Christ became accessible as a friend, an elder brother, and a human ideal.[43]

The trial of Galileo in 1633 is probably the most dramatic incident in the relations between science and faith, but it must be considered in historical perspective: Galileo was born in 1564—the last year of the Council of Trent, which set the tone of Catholicism until Pope John XXIII in the twentieth century. Political events of the sixteenth century added to the conservative stance of the church, producing a willingness to exchange freedom for the security of a regulated order. Galileo's observation of the phases of Venus and the satellites of Jupiter by the use of the telescope in 1609 gave evidence that geocentricism, one of the fundamental concepts of the church, was incorrect. The observations were far from conclusive, but they renewed the nearly forgotten debate over the heliocentrism of Copernicus. Galileo said the world consisted of mathematical qualities; these mathematical laws were discoverable in detail and with absolute certainty. He said the Word of God could be read in natural science as well as in Scripture. Both "books" were thought perfect, since God created both; nothing in Scripture could be contrary to reason, thus some things are beyond reason—nature executes the commands of the divine Word. As a result of Galileo's argument, Copernicus's *De Revolutionibus* was placed on the list of forbidden books. In 1630, Galileo completed his masterpiece, *Dialogue on the Two Chief World Systems,* and after many delays, publication was completed in 1632. Galileo was summoned to Rome to explain whether he presented the heliocentric theory of Copernicus as a fact or an hypothesis. Despite his vigorous denial of arguing in favor of the heliocentric theory, he was judged to have contravened the orders of the church, ordered to recant his error, and confined to his estate near Florence. *Dialogue* remained on the forbidden list until 1832. Galileo's condemnation was the result of untoward political circumstances, personal ambitions, and the wounded pride of powerful church authorities. Nevertheless, the result inhibited scientific inquiry for a time in Catholic countries.[44] The agreement of the heliocentric theory with rational natural philosophy was Galileo's most important contribution to the debate on cosmology: that the science of motion was the foundation of physics, and that physics and astronomy were in accord—Galilean mechanics complemented Copernican astronomy. As Heisenberg observes, nothing could have been more surprising to the scientists of the seventeenth century than their discovery that the same mechanical laws applied to celestial and terrestrial motions alike.[45]

The concept of "laws of nature" was first formulated in the optical studies of Roger Bacon (1210-1292) in *lex regula,* and was used by subsequent scientists, including Tycho Brahe (1546-1601), Descartes and Kepler, to prove the existence of God as a celestial Law-giver. Gradually, investigators found they had little need for a philosophy of science and were motivated primarily by the desire to uncover more of the regularities in nature. The method and meaning of science began to go separate ways, with no implication of an ultimate truth. Kepler was particularly successful in expressing the laws of nature in mathematical terms. Galileo went further than merely observing nature, manipulating nature in order to make the laws apparent. By rolling a ball down an inclined plane, he was able to slow down time so that gravity could be measured. He found that Aristotle's theories did not agree with experimental observation. Imaginary experiments (such as, the rate of fall of a body in a vacuum put forward by Galileo) were the beginning of the modern scientific method.[46]

While most scientists of the seventeenth century followed the direction of the church, some were very tolerant of the new science. Marin Mersenne (1588-1648) who supported Galileo and favored biblical criticism, was tolerant beyond the norm of the times, whether Catholic or Protestant. Descartes held that some issues of theology could be answered by reason alone, yet he was opposed to rational theology; matters of faith could be determined only by revelation, but matters of fact were understandable by observation and reason. Descartes objected to theological arguments taken from observing nature; the world was not a collection of signs of divine attributes nor did it indicate the way toward God, or that a final purpose in nature was discernible. His theory of the world of vortices was not Christocentric, the vortex did not hold salvation. Blaise Pascal (1623-1662), also a Catholic, asserted that the authority of Scripture and the church was the sole source of truth in theology, but in matters of reason and the senses, authority was useless and faith could not be demonstrated by reason. He cautioned that the study of nature might become a worship, or idolatry, of nature. Nicolaus Steno (1638-1686), born in Denmark and raised a Protestant, converted to Catholicism after starting a career in science, became a priest and eventually an archbishop in Italy, leaving the pursuit of science. Steno found no conflict in the study of geology and the biblical account of Creation. He discovered most of the principles of modern geology while remaining within the traditional religious framework. Steno came close to being one of the great scientists of history, but withdrew to concentrate on theological interests.[47]

At the beginning of the seventeenth century, Christianity was the principal influence on the character of the people and institutions of Europe. By the end of the seventeenth century, Christianity had lost its place to science. Science was the first serious challenge to the authority of the church; subsequently, Christianity became ever more displaced from the central position in European life by the reliance on science. Philosophers turned to science for inspiration, direction, and the criteria of truth. Although the change was influenced by many forces political, economic, and social, the most important affecting the position of Christianity was the intellectual challenge of science. The three scientists who were the most influential were Kepler, Descartes, and Newton, all with a deep religious commitment. Kepler may be remembered as well for his religious devotion as for his scientific accomplishments. Descartes, one generation later, was no less faithful a Christian. He discarded Kepler's notion of an ordered cosmos, saying instead that it began with "a chaos as confused as the poets ever feigned" to show instead that laws of motion must have formed the world in endlessly repeated vortices without intelligent planning. In Descartes's universe, mankind cannot know a final cause; he found no evidence of God in nature. He acquired God the Creator and Sustainer at the loss of God the Redeemer. Yet, Descartes did not question the greatest miracle of all, the incarnation.[48] In addition, Isaac Newton's works contain many statements of religious conviction. A theological tradition of two thousand years was being rejected, and like all scientists of the age, Newton was aware of the change. Westfall comments:

> [Newton] had repeated it in his own intellectual life by casting aside the Aristotelianism the university taught, to embrace the new mechanical philosophy. In him, though not solely in him, the step Descartes refused was realized. At his hand, Christian theology felt the touch of cold philosophy.[49]

Although Newton accepted the idea of the 'revealed word of God,' he did not see the Bible as the revelation of truths above human reason; Nature was the revelation of God as much as the Bible—perhaps more so.

Newton found God in the nature of the universe and did not seek Him elsewhere. By their immense genius, Kepler, Descartes, and Newton were in the vanguard of intellectual activity, yet the public did not become aware of them until generations later. Subsequently, the enchanted world of the medieval church began to dissolve in the light of science and rationalism; unquestioned faith was lost to Western man.[50]

Richard Bentley (1662-1742) gave the first Boyle lecture, entitled *Confutation of Atheism from the Origin and Frame of the World,* in which he demonstrated a deep understanding of Newton's mathematics and argued that design is most clearly demonstrated in the "elegant mathematical laws of a general and invariant character rather than by the specific, but relative, adaptations we see in the animal world," especially Newton's gravitational constant, which made the world model a mechanical watchworks.[51] The seventeenth century, in contrast to earlier ages, was a brilliant age of science, filled with startling discoveries and grand generalizations. By contrast, the eighteenth century seems less dramatic. The first three-quarters of the century were occupied by observations and experiments that provided an unspectacular foundation for the great age of scientific discovery to come, work that was carried on by enthusiastic amateurs, many clergymen, and a few physicians. Nevertheless, science was popularized in numerous books, encyclopedias, and periodicals written for the general public. The Newtonian system was the chief subject of interest to a public curious about the nature of the universe, made good and orderly by the Creator (especially in England and Germany), while others were led to believe in a vast inanimate machine (especially in France).[52] Hall describes the phenomenon:

> Christianity furnished the scientist with God as the First Cause of things. But if this First Cause had, so to speak, set the universe to run its course and endowed man with free-will to make his own destiny, the phenomena of nature could only be the result of determined processes, manifestations of a mechanistic design,...The only sort of explanation science could give must be in terms of descriptions of processes, mechanisms, interconnections of parts. Greek animism was dead. Appetites, natural tendencies, sympathies, attractions, were moribund concepts in science, too. The universe of classical physics, in which the only realities were matter and motion, could begin to take shape.[53]

The question gradually gaining attention over three hundred years, received an answer in the seventeenth century in the physics of Newton.

By the beginning of the eighteenth century, England had become a market society with the appearance of wealthy, politically powerful landed and commercial classes; religion was to address itself to tradesmen and merchants rather than cloisters. Jacobs says, "Newtonianism became an ideology that justified commercial capitalism, empire, scientific progress, and a new religiosity geared more to the vicissitudes of this world than the rewards of the next." In spite of Newton's intense Christian stand, the church-sponsored, science-based English Protestantism produced an attitude that was distinctly less that Christian. European intellectuals hostile to organized religion, such as Voltaire, eagerly embraced the Newtonian position. Voltaire arrived in England in 1726, and stridently opposed clerics, religious persecution, and most of organized religion. The integration of Newtonian science into Western philosophy produced the first generation of European scholars whose faith in the order of the universe was more satisfying than faith in doctrines and authority. By the middle of the eighteenth century, the growth of reason and materialism, the degeneration of public morality, and political corruption were thought to be the result of the new science-based liberal Anglicanism that was undermining all religion. In spite of the reaction against the corruption of society and the perception of debasing of the faith, no outstanding spokesman denouncing the science-influenced faith developed during the rest of the seventeenth century; the link between Newtonian science and liberal Christianity remained intact.[54] The mood of science had changed; the rebellious spirit of Galileo was not necessary since the works of Aristotle had been dropped from serious science and the scientific revolutionaries had gained respect. Science became fashionable, and the discoveries of science were presented as humble tributes to patronage instead of challenges to established philosophy.[55] It was called the *siècle des lumières* by the French, the "century of light," for its emphasis on reason as a source of knowledge.[56] Science flourished in America with many distinguished contributions, and in colonial colleges, science was esteemed and encouraged. The spirit of America tended to be commercial, and acquiring wealth and property took precedence over letters and science.[57]

In Britain, the middle and upper classes, impressed by the marvelous inventions of science and technology, and by the growing speed of movement and convenience of everyday activities, were able to afford an increasing amount and variety of material goods. They were convinced they were living in the best of all possible worlds, and what was more, a world getting better all the time. Science was the new revelation—the Industrial Revolution was the proof and justification of the religion of progress.[58] Science forged ahead in British society with a transfer from religious to naturalistic belief: a great part of the reverence once given to priests and to their stories of an unseen universe was transferred to the astronomers, geologists, physicians, and engineers—a shift of authority and prestige from one part of the intellectual nation to another that caused considerable conflict. Cambridge philosopher Henry Sidgwick called it "a great and prominent *social* fact."[59] The remaining Renaissance world view gave way to the continued progress of natural science in Europe.

The advance of science was felt in the American colonies also. The first two centuries of European settlement in America coincided with one of the greatest intellectual upheavals in history. The Pilgrims lived in a world designed by the ancient philosophers Aristotle and Ptolemy—a stationary home near the center of a finite cosmos. "God lived not very far away and often reminded the colonists of his power and presence—to say nothing of his displeasure—by sending lightning and earthquakes, comets and meteors, famine and disease. Frightened—and sometimes repentant—Americans fasted and prayed and clung to the Bible as the repository of spiritual and temporal truth."[60] By the end of the eighteenth century, mechanical philosophy had replaced the old ideas: reason replaced revelation as the guide to truth. Yet, only a minority experienced a lessening in faith and the harmonious relationship between faith and reason was maintained.[61]

From the seventeenth century well into the nineteenth century, the parson-naturalist and the academic clergyman-scientist played a major role in British science. This group included John Ray, Joseph Priestley, John Stevens Henslow, Adam Sedgwick, and William Whewell. Natural science and natural theology, the clerical and the scientific callings, were not simply compatible to them, but complementary. However, after the 1840s, this position became increasingly difficult. The naturalist's theories caused a deep rift between the existing reconciliations of scientific theory and revelation, or theology, straining the concept that the truth of revelation and the truth of science must be the same. The amateur's day as a man of science was drawing to a close. The clerical scientists were accused of dual loyalties. The emerging professional scientist considered "scientifical-geological-theologians," such as Hugh Miller and Adam Sedgwick, who continued to attempt to reconcile science and revelation, as public embarrassments and claimed that no clergyman could be a genuine man of science.[62]

Highet asserts that the tone of literature changed abruptly about 1850 (when Melville was at work on *Moby-Dick*) due to the remarkable conditions of the nineteenth century which included industrialism and the rise of applied science, a tremendous increase in the population of Europe and America, the move away from governments of inherited privilege, and the wider education of the masses of people in many countries. The shift was to a literature acceptable to the common people with poetry giving way to prose, less emphasis on style, specialization, and an unquestioned gain in "vigour [and] spiritual energy."[63] Science became an integral part of Victorian culture; geology texts sometimes outsold popular novels, giving science strength and prestige. However, science could not interfere with the religious and social conventions of the day, especially in Britain, where anything that might threaten the status of man as a spiritual being was still taboo.[64] Early nineteenth century geologists romanticized field exploration, which became a cult and obsession with the cry, "to the field!" Fieldwork became an explicitly religious experience, a spiritual re-creation, elevating geologists above the mundane world of utility and everyday duties to an arena where they could test their moral fiber in the presence of pristine nature. Humphry Davy claimed, "That part of Almighty God which resides in the rocks and woods, in the blue and tranquil sea, in the clouds and moonbeams of the sky, is calling upon thee with a loud voice: religiously obey its commands and come worship with me on the ancient altars of Cornwall."[65] The pursuit of natural history by the English middle class served to relieve boredom, promote health, contribute to a feeling of being useful (or potential profitability), and was uplifting.[66]

The principal reason Western society is as it is today can be attributed largely due to the rise of natural science. The external circumstances of our daily lives are almost wholly dependent upon science and technology.[67] The period of the 1830s and 1850s was critical to the formation of modern culture.[68] Thus, the shift occurred in the mid-nineteenth century from one to the other of two mutually exclusive views of God: from *theism*—the belief in God the creator and ruler of the universe including revelation; to *deism*—the belief in God as evidence of reason or nature alone with the rejection of revelation, a belief in a God who created the world but has since remained indifferent to it. The statement, *fides quaerens intellectum,* "faith seeking understanding," attributed to St. Anselm (1033-1109) still holds true.[69] The meaning of Creation and the importance of the creatures of the earth, the meaning of man and his existence on earth, have been central to man's beliefs in nearly all cultures, East and West. The beauty of nature, the availability of natural resources, regular cycles of night and day, the seasons, and many other natural phenomena appeared to prove that man had a special, privileged position with the Creator. There was no doubt about the Creator's existence. Divine design became integrated into the Western Judeo-Christian world view by the merger with Aristotelianism, and was fortified by the science of Copernicus, Galileo, and Newton, demonstrating the 'laws' of God and the providential design of nature. This view was to be thoroughly undermined by an awareness of the operation of atheistic chance in the workings of nature that occurred toward the end of the decade of the 1850s—the decade of Melville's major works.[70]. Melville, sensitive to these movements, included the turmoil of faith and doubt, and the controversy of science and its threat to religious faith in nearly all of his works. During the mid-nineteenth century, science appeared to carry the day, although the controversy is still very much unsettled at the end of the twentieth century (the "Anthropic Cosmological Principle" reactivates the argument of design and all of its attendant questions). Melville did not accept the great enthusiasm of the time, often called the Age of Science, that science had, or soon would, solve all the concerns of human existence. The decline of belief in the well-ordered, Renaissance world view took place gradually, although public awareness of the change occurred abruptly in the middle decades of the nineteenth century—the period of Melville's novels and stories.

Notes

1. John Polkinghorne, *One World: The Interaction of Science and Theology.* London: SPCK Holy Trinity Church, 1986, p. 1.

2. John D. Barrow and Frank J. Tipler, *The Anthropic Cosmological Principle.* Oxford: Oxford University Press, 1988, pp. 31-36.

3. Stephen Toulmin and June Goodfield, *The Architecture of Matter.* Chicago and London: University of Chicago Press, 1982, p. 45.

4. Barrow and Tipler, ref. 2, pp. 38-39.

5. Barrow and Tipler, ref. 2, pp. 42-44.

6. C. S. Lewis, *The Discarded Image: An Introduction to Medieval and Renaissance Literature.* Cambridge: Cambridge University Press, 1964, pp. 37-39.

7. John D. Barrow, *The World Within the World.* Oxford and New York: Oxford University Press, 1990, p. 31.

8. Toulmin and Goodfield, ref 3, p. 46-47.

9. F. Sherwood Taylor, *A Short History of Science and Scientific Thought: With Readings from the Great Scientists from the Babylonians Through Einstein.* New York and London: Norton, 1949, p. 20-21.

10. Henry Chadwick. *Boethius: The Consolations of Music, Logic, Theology, and Philosophy.* Oxford: Oxford University Press, 1981, pp. 251-252.

11. Barrow and Tipler, ref 2, p. 45.

12. Brian Stock, "Science, Technology, and Economic Progress in the Early Middle Ages." in *Science in the Middle Ages.* David C. Lindberg, editor. Chicago and London: University of Chicago Press, 1978, p. 23.

13. Taylor, ref. 9, p. 37.

14. Homer W. Smith, *Man and His Gods.* Boston: Little, Brown, 1952, p. 227.

15. David C. Lindberg, "Science and the Early Church." in *God and Nature: Historical Essays on the Encounter between Christianity and Science.* David C. Lindberg and Ronald L. Numbers, editors. Berkeley, Los Angeles, and London: University of California Press, 1986, pp. 27-41.

16. Stock, ref. 12, pp. 12-13.

17. Barrow and Tipler, ref 2, pp. 46-47.

18. Stock, ref. 12, pp. 41-44.

19. R.W. Southern, *Robert Grosseteste: The Growth of an English Mind in Medieval Europe*. Oxford: Oxford University Press, 1986, pp. 92-96.

20. Gilbert Highet, *The Classical Tradition: Greek and Roman Influences on Western Literature*. Oxford: Oxford University Press, 1949. reprint 1970, pp. 180-181.

21. David C. Lindberg and Ronald L. Numbers, "Introduction." in *God and Nature: Historical Essays on the Encounter between Christianity and Science.* David C. Lindberg and Ronald L. Numbers, editors. Berkeley, Los Angeles, and London: University of California Press, 1986, pp. 10-11.

22. Tina Stiefel, "The Heresy of Science: A Twelfth-Century Conceptual Revolution." *Isis* 68 (1977):350-362.

23. Edward Grant, "Science and Theology in the Middle Ages." in *God and Nature: Historical Essays on the Encounter between Christianity and Science.* David C. Lindberg and Ronald L. Numbers, editors. Berkeley, Los Angeles, and London: University of California Press, 1986, pp. 50-70.

24. Barrow and Tipler, ref. 2, pp. 47-49.

25. Taylor, ref. 9, pp. 59-60.

26. Southern, ref. 19, pp. 173-176.

27. A.R. Hall, *The Scientific Revolution 1500-1800: The Formation of the Modern Scientific Attitude*. second edition. Boston: Beacon, 1962, p. 52.

28. Stock, ref. 12, p. 34.

29. Lewis, ref. 6, pp. 92-95.

30. Lewis, ref. 6, pp. 96-105.

31. Herbert Butterfield, *The Origins of Modern Science 1300-1800*. New York: Free Press, 1957, pp. 29-36.

32. Lewis, ref. 6, pp. 10-12.

33. Lewis, ref. 6, p. 185.

34. Lewis, ref. 6, pp. 116-121, 216.

35. Taylor, ref. 9, pp. 71-72.

36. Barrow and Tipler, ref. 2, pp. 49-54.

37. Taylor, ref. 9, p. 82.

38. Highet, ref. 20, p. 179.

39. Don Cupit, *The Sea of Faith: Christianity in Change*. Cambridge: Cambridge University Press, 1984, pp. 14-15.

40. Barrow and Tipler, ref. 2, pp. 56-58.

41. Taylor, ref. 9, pp. 74-75.

42. Butterfield, ref. 31, pp. 75-78.

43. Cupit, ref. 39, pp. 31, 52.

44. William R. Shea, "Galileo and the Church." in *God and Nature: Historical Essays on the Encounter between Christianity and Science.* David C. Lindberg and Ronald L. Numbers, editors. Berkeley, Los Angeles, and London: University of California Press, 1986, pp. 114-133.

45. Hall, ref. 27, p. 114.

46. Barrow, ref. 7, pp. 58-60.

47. William B. Ashworth, Jr. "Catholicism and Early Modern Science." in *God and Nature: Historical Essays on the Encounter between Christianity and Science.* David C. Lindberg and Ronald L. Numbers, editors. Berkeley, Los Angeles, and London: University of California Press, 1986, pp. 138-148.

48. Richard S. Westfall, "The Rise of Science and the Decline of Orthodox Christianity: A Study of Kepler, Descartes, and Newton." in *God and Nature: Historical Essays on the Encounter between Christianity and Science.* David C. Lindberg and Ronald L. Numbers, editors. Berkeley, Los Angeles, and London: University of California Press, 1986, pp. 224-228.

49. Westfall, ref. 48, p. 232.

50. Westfall, ref. 48, pp. 232-235.

51. Barrow and Tipler, ref. 2, p. 61.

52. Taylor, ref. 9, pp. 153-154.

53. Hall, ref. 27, p. xvii.

54. Margaret C. Jacob. "Christianity and the Newtonian Worldview." in *God and Nature: Historical Essays on the Encounter between Christianity and Science.* David C. Lindberg and Ronald L. Numbers, editors. Berkeley, Los Angeles, and London: University of California Press, 1986, pp. 242-253.

55. Hall, ref. 27, p. 341.

56. Thomas L. Hankins, *Science and the Enlightenment.* Cambridge: Cambridge University Press, 1985, p. 2.

57. I. Bernard Cohen, "Some Reflections on the State of Science in America During the Nineteenth Century." *Proceedings of the National Academy of Science.*" 45 (1959):666-677.

58. David S. Landes, *The Unbound Prometheus: Technological Change and Industrial Development in Western Europe from 1750 to the Present.* Cambridge: Cambridge University Press, 1969, pp. 122-123.

59. Frank M. Turner, "The Victorian Conflict between Science and Religion: A Professional Dimension." *Isis* 69 (1978):356-376.

60. Ronald L. Numbers, "Science and Religion." *Osiris* Second Series 1 (1985):59-80.

61. Numbers, ref 60.

62. Turner, ref. 59.

63. Highet, ref. 20, pp. 255-257.

64. Peter J. Bowler, *Evolution: The History of an Idea*. Berkeley, Los Angeles, and London: University of California Press, 1984, pp. 104-105.

65. Roy Porter, "Gentlemen and geology: the emergence of a scientific career, 1660-1920." *The History Journal* 21 (1978):809-836. Cited by Sandra Herbert, "Darwin the Young Geologist." in *The Darwinian Heritage*. David Kohn, editor. Princeton, New Jersey: Princeton University Press, 1985, p. 496.

66. Lynn Barber, *The Heyday of Natural History 1820-1870*. Garden City, New York: Doubleday, 1980, pp. 16-22.

67. Taylor, ref. 9, p. 1.

68. Pietro Corsi, *Science and Religion: Baden Powell and the Anglican Debate, 1800-1860*. Cambridge: Cambridge University Press, 1988, p. 291.

69. Polkinghorne, ref. 1, p. 28.

70. Barrow, ref. 7, pp. 363-365.

Melville's Science

Chapter 1

Typee and *Omoo*: Belzoni's Egyptian catacombs

The early works of Herman Melville contain little science, but his method of employing science is apparent at the outset. His first two novels are fairly straightforward adventure stories based on his sailing experiences; science material contained in these books has detailed references to science and natural history, a method he was to use throughout his writing career. By citing specific explorers and scientists, scientific discoveries and controversies, he gains sanction for the rest of his narrative. The use of science is both broad and appropriate to its application, which is the exposition of his social and philosophical purposes rather than the mere recitation of scientific facts. The early books show little of the depth and complexity of his later works, but his method of accurately quoting authoritative sources is effective from the beginning.

Melville sailed on a whaling voyage to the South Seas in January 1841, returning to Boston in October 1844. At Nukuheva in the Marquesas Islands, an island inhabited by cannibals, Melville and a companion jumped ship. Their travels are related in *Typee: A Peep at*

Polynesian Life during a Four Month's Residence in a Valley of the Marquesas (1846), a tale of exotic adventure revealing little of the richness of his later works. The accuracy of his account was later challenged and, in fact, Melville was ashore little more than two weeks, not the four months he claimed in the story. After their escaping to the hills and tropical forest, and hiding from both the friendly natives of the coast and the cannibals of the interior of the island, the narrator develops a painful swelling of his leg. They are captured by the cannibal Typees and taken to their native village where the narrator is treated by thumping and pinching by an "old Hippocrates" (Ch 11). The confinement caused by the leg affliction allows the narrator to observe the customs and everyday life of the uninhibited natives. He mentions authoritative writers whom he often quotes; such as Porter's "Journal of the Cruise of the U.S. frigate Essex, in the Pacific during the late War"; Stewart's "A Visit to the South Seas" and Ellis's "Polynesian Researches" (Ch 1). He also mentions the explorers Cook, Carteret, Byron, Kotzebue, and Vancouver (Ch 24). The specific references to actual explorers add to the accumulation of detail that makes Melville's story believable, providing an additional dimension to the adventure narrative. Although the explorers were principally adventurers, their explorations and discoveries were extremely important to the study of natural history, particularly geography, botany, and biology.

While finding their way through the thick jungle, the narrator remarks that: "Belzoni, worming himself through the subterranean passages of the Egyptian catacombs, could not have met with greater impediments" (Ch 9). Giovanni Battista Belzoni (1778-1823) was an Italian showman, engineer, and explorer of Egyptian antiquities who discovered the Valley of the Kings and was the first to penetrate into the second pyramid of Giza (1818). A structure made of great stones reminds Melville's narrator of "Stonehenge and the architectural labor of the Druid" (Ch 21). The monuments were "doubtless the work of an extinct and forgotten race" and a feeling of awe came over him greater than "if I had stood musing at the mighty base of the Pyramid of Cheops" (Ch 21), suggesting the antiquity of the island. The enigma of the pyramids, both natural history and metaphysical, is used metaphorically in many of Melville's works. The idea of the extinction of races, or species, was a highly controversial issue that was dealt with later in *Mardi.*

One of the Typee natives was covered all over with tattoos "with a view of improving the handiwork of nature." The tattoos "completely spanned his physiognomy," a pseudoscience Melville uses effectively in later works; "...the entire body of my savage valet, covered all over with representations of birds and fishes, and a variety of most unaccountable-looking creatures, suggested to me the idea of a pictorial museum of natural history, or an illustrated copy of 'Goldsmith's Animated Nature'" (Ch 11). Oliver Goldsmith's *An History of the Earth and Animated Nature* was an eighteenth century popular work on science, reprinted numerous times in England and America, and used in many schools, compiled by a nonscientist for a general audience. Although based on the work of the leading scientists, it is notable for its many inaccuracies. Goldsmith reiterated the "Scale of Being" in a very popular and durable book.[1] Patterson calls Goldsmith's *Animated Nature* "hackwork," along with most of his other works. Goldsmith (1728-1774) wrote the eight volume *Animated Nature* during the last five years of his life, and it was first published three months after his death. It became the eighteenth and nineteenth century equivalent of today's best sellers, going through twenty-five editions, the last in 1876. Goldsmith was not a learned naturalist, but a compiler of material; his main source was Buffon's *Histoire Naturelle* (16 volumes), published in Paris from 1749 onwards and which he openly plagiarizes in some sections. Goldsmith said of his book that it "may be found an innocent amusement for those who have nothing else to employ them, or who require relaxation from labour."[2]

Melville contrasts the idyllic conditions of unspoiled nature in the Marquesas Islands with civilization in pointing out the beauty of Fayaway: "The easy unstudied graces of a child of nature like this, breathing from infancy an atmosphere of perpetual summer, and nurtured by the simple fruits of the earth; enjoying a perfect freedom from care and anxiety, and removed effectually from all injurious tendencies, strike the eye in a manner which cannot be pourtrayed" (Ch 11). He calls Mehevi a "noble savage" (Ch 12), and the Typees are a "humane, gentlemanly, and amiable set of epicures" even though they are cannibals. The Polynesian savage "surrounded by all the luxurious provisions of nature, enjoyed an infinitely happier, though certainly a less intellectual existence, than the self-complacent European" (Ch 17). Yet, in the taboo groves of the valley, "[b]eneath the dark shadows of the consecrated bread-fruit trees there reigned a solemn twilight—a cathedral-like gloom" (Ch 12) picturing nature as threatening, a conflict to dominate some of his later works: nature as both idyll and evil.

The threat of the machine and technology appears even in his description of the South Seas: "The fiend-like skill we display in the invention of all manner of death-dealing engines, the vindictiveness with which we carry on our wars, and the misery and desolation that follow in their train, are enough of themselves to distinguish the white civilized man as the most ferocious animal on the face of the earth" (Ch 17). The development of the machine was more than a physical threat of danger, but also the extension to a mechanistic depiction of nature and the remoteness of God.

The Typees are blessed with medicinal waters, the "Cheltenham of Typee," the site of saline mineral springs in England discovered in 1716, and a fashionable tourist community visited by royalty. The moisture of the rocks was thought medicinal and "sufficiently nauseous" to make a fortune if in civilization: "As I am no chemist, I cannot give a scientific analysis of the water," but he suspects the magical ingredients are due to common sand (Ch 21).

Melville includes a brief account of natural science in his first book. He discovers stone structures "of a very high antiquity" at the base of a mountain; his native authority on "matters of scientific research" attributed them to divine origin. The narrator thought they might have been the work of "an extinct and forgotten race," concluding that the natives were living in the valley three thousand years ago. These heterodox statements for extinction of species, or races, or the antiquity of man were not yet accepted by scientists or clergy. He speculates on the origin of coral islands, whether the result of the work of coral insects or volcanic action, and the mutability of the surface of the earth (Ch 21). Although Melville does not specify his source, he probably took his account from John R. Forster's *Observations Made During a Voyage Around the World* (1778)[3]:

> These remains naturally suggest many interesting reflections. They establish the great age of the island, an opinion which the builders of theories concerning the creation of the various groups in the South Seas are not always inclined to admit. For my own part, I think it just as probable that human beings were living in the valleys of the Marquesas three thousand years ago as that they were inhabiting the land of Egypt. The origin of the coral island of Nukuheva cannot be imputed to the coral insect; for indefatigable as that wonderful creature is, it would be hardly muscular enough to pile rocks one upon the other more than three thousand feet above the level of the sea. The land may have been thrown up by a submarine volcano is as possible as anything else. No one can make an affidavit to the contrary, and therefore I will say nothing against the supposition: indeed, were geologists to assert that the whole continent of America had in like manner been formed by the simultaneous explosion of a train of Etnas laid under the water all

> the way form the North Pole to the parallel of Cape Horn, I am the last man in the world to contradict them. (Ch 21)

He is critical of scientists and the reliability of their dry reports: "The fact is, that there is a vast deal of unintentional humbuggery in some of the accounts we have from scientific men concerning the religious institution of Polynesia" who get their information from retired old South Sea rovers: "his powers of invention increase with the credulity of his auditors. He knows just the sort of information wanted, and furnishes it to any extent" (Ch 24). He castigates the explorer and naturalist, or "scientific voyager," for lack of human understanding, returning home with a "collection of wonders" and dull, haphazard descriptions of native customs (Ch 24). In other instances he uses "science" in a pejorative sense: Mehevi dips his forefinger into a dish "giving it a rapid and scientific twirl" (Ch 10); Kory-Kory perceives Tommo to be in "one of my inquiring, scientific moods" while inspecting a large stone structure (Ch 24), and a pair of "scientifically cut pantaloons" (Ch 25).

In Chapter 29, Melville makes an attempt to describe the "natural history" of the Typee valley citing "Count Buffon and Baron Cuvier" and describing the dogs, cats, lizards, birds, insects and "the cocoa-nut tree" in a brief and nondescript way (Ch 29). He recalls the tame birds on the Galàpagos during his visit, and mentions Selkirk, who had a similar experience with the birds and lizards of the valley: "Its tameness, far from shocking me, as a similar occurrence did Selkirk, imparted to me the most exquisite thrill of delight I ever experienced; and with somewhat of the same pleasure did I afterwards behold the birds and lizards of the valley show their confidence in the kindliness of man" (Ch 29). Alexander Selkirk (1676-1721), whose name was actually Selcraig, was the prototype of Robinson Crusoe. He sailed with William Dampier on an expedition to the Pacific in 1703 and was put ashore on an uninhabited island at his own request after a falling-out with the captain in 1704. He remained there until found in 1709.[4]

In spite of the serious condition of his leg, Melville makes a daring escape by sea and is taken aboard the Australian whaleship *Julia*. His observations of native life, especially their uninhibited sexual practices, which both heightened interest in tales of the South Pacific and brought the criticism of Victorians. A growing awareness of science in the nineteenth century was important in the development of Melville's ideas as reflected in his writings. He had a better grasp of the basics of science than other nineteenth century writers, including Nathaniel Hawthorne, who considered scientists "evil magicians." Melville was self-taught in matters of science through reading popular magazines such as the *Edinburgh Review,* which carried lengthy reviews of scientific works, and the books in the library of the *United States* during his voyage 1843-1844. Hillway says any attempt to identify the source of Melville's science is complicated by several factors, especially "his cosmopolitan tastes in reading," his interest in "the controversy raging between religion and nineteenth-century science" and his "skepticism toward some of the major claims of science." He borrowed from the naturalists for the "puarkee nuee" hog as an "extraordinary specimen of zoology" (Ch 3), the breadfruit tree (Ch 15), and the narcotic effects of "arva," a root extract with medicinal properties used for treating "scrofulous infections" and syphilis (Ch 23).[5] As naturalists and explorers examined the book, calling attention to its inaccuracies, he was criticized for distorting the "truth" of his narrative. In July 1846, Richard Tobias Greene, Melville's companion on Nukuheva, publicly attested to the accuracy of *Typee,* quieting the criticism for a time. *Typee* was an immediate success since stories of the exotic South Seas were in great demand, and few were as interesting or as well written as Melville's first novel.

Melville's next book, *Omoo: A Narrative of Adventures in the South Seas* (1847), recounts events after boarding the Australian whaleship *Julia*, and his travels and adventures in Tahiti, the most famous and exotic of the South Sea islands. In the preface to *Omoo*, Melville carefully states that the book is factual, quoting other voyages to corroborate his statements, and mentions William Ellis's *Polynesian Researches* (1833). The title "Omoo," from the Marquesean dialect, means wanderer. He kept no journal, saying "every occurrence has been put down from recollection." He again states he was "suffering severely from lameness" without adding further details. Because of the sickness of the captain, the *Julia* heads for Tahiti. Melville becomes a travelling companion of "Doctor Long Ghost," the demoted ship's surgeon.

The mate was the navigator: "At noon, he brought out his quadrant, a rusty old thing, so odd-looking that it might have belonged to an astrologer." He was often intoxicated and staggered about the deck:

> How upon earth he contrived, on some occasions, to settle his latitude, is more than I can tell. The longitude, he must either have obtained by the Rule of Three, or else by special revelation. Not that the chronometer in the cabin was seldom to be relied on, or was any ways fidgety; quite the contrary; it stood stock-still; and

> by that means, no doubt, the true Greenwich time—at the period of its stopping, at least—was preserved to a second. (Ch 17)

This brief statement contains the essence of the difficulty and the first solution of the problem of determining longitude at sea. The method of "triangulation" required an accurate clock and astral measurements taken from three sites to calculate the ship's position. Since the chronometer had stopped, he suspects that only divine revelation can reveal a natural fact. Though used in a humorous sense, the conflict of the accuracy of man's measure of the natural world was placed in contradistinction to revelation. That time is not the same at different points of the earth is not obvious, and this becomes a complex philosophical dilemma in a subsequent book, *Pierre.*

The outlying islands of Tahiti are the Coral Islands. They are "numerous; mostly small, low, and level; sometime wooded, but always covered with verdure." Melville offers another theory on the formation of the coral islands, which is generally ascribed to the creative power of the "coral insect":

> According to some naturalists, this wonderful little creature, commencing its erections at the bottom of the sea, after the lapse of centuries, carries them up to the surface, where its labors cease. Here, the inequalities of the coral collect all floating bodies; forming, after a time, a soil, in which the seeds carried thither by birds, germinate, and cover the whole with vegetation. Here and there, all over this archipelago, numberless naked, detached coral formations are seen, just emerging, as it were from the ocean. These would appear to be islands in the very process of creation—at any rate, one involuntarily concludes so, on beholding them. (Ch 17)

In a footnote, he says this theory is popular, but an opposite theory was advanced that the islands were "merely the remains of a continent, long ago worn away, and broken up by the action of the sea" (Ch 17). The latter is the "uniformitarian" theory of geology of Hutton to be discussed later. Gradual change in the surface of the earth required vast expanses of time that was not possible in the few thousand years of biblical time. That the earth's surface underwent change over time was one of the most important concepts of the eighteenth and nineteenth centuries and would change nearly every aspect of man's perception of the natural world. According to Hillway, Melville probably took his statements from John Reinold Forster's *Observations Made During a*

Voyage Round the World (1778). He says Melville may have known of Forster's book as early as 1845 when writing *Typee,* where he conjectures that the island of Nukuheva "may have been thrown up by a submarine volcano" (Ch 21), an idea stated by Forster.[6]

In Chapter 18, the narrator describes the geography of Tahiti, which was probably taken from accounts of other voyagers and greatly enhanced by Melville. The many navigators who had visited the island are listed: "Quiros, the Spaniard...Wallis, Byron, Cook, De Bougainville, Vancouver, La Perouse, and other illustrious navigators." He notes the island's importance to science: "Here the famous Transit of Venus was observed in 1769." Since Venus is closer to the sun than earth, Venus's course takes it directly between the earth and sun at infrequent intervals, i.e., the eclipse of the sun by Venus. In 1761 and 1769, many scientific expeditions were organized to observe this phenomenon from distant places around the earth.[7] The Transit of Venus is also mentioned in Chapter 179 of *Mardi.* Because of its beauty, Tahiti is the most famous of all the islands of the South Pacific, drawing the attention of famous explorers and receiving more complete accounts of its natural history than any other island. Tahiti, as Melville points out, was the first tropical island to receive Protestant missionaries, and from Tahiti, successive missions were sent to neighboring islands.

The fluctuations of the tides in Tahiti are so small that they cause no inconvenience to ships entering the harbor. Melville says, "The Newtonian theory concerning the tides does not hold good at Tahiti; where, throughout the year, the waters uniformly commence ebbing at noon and midnight, and flow about sunset and daybreak" (Ch 27n). Interest in the tides is recorded by ancient Chinese, Arabic, and Icelandic authors, but not the Greeks or Romans since they lived by a nearly tideless sea. In the seventeenth century, Kepler recognized the tendency of the tides to move towards the sun and moon. Galileo attributed the tides to the motion of the earth. The modern theory of the tides was put forward by Newton in *Principia* (1687), stating that the tides are caused by the gravitational attraction of the sun and moon. He gave a geometrical analysis of the forces producing the tides, calculated their strength, and accounted for many of the properties of tides, such as the phenomena of springs and neaps, priming and lagging, diurnal and elliptic inequalities, in fact, nearly everything except taking into account the earth's rotation. In *Mécanique céleste* (1773), Pierre Laplace made additional studies of the tides to be followed by investigations and theories by many famous scientists.[8] The great forces and "exactness" of science fail in Paradise. Melville's knowledge of Newton may have come from his reading on the frigate *United States.* Its library listed the *Harper's Family Library,* which contained a number of scientific and semi-scientific books. One was David Brewster's *Life of Isaac Newton.*[9]

Opposed to the idyll of Tahiti's South Sea paradise stood man's invention: the machine, which Melville saw as a threat to their culture. He includes several negative references to the excitement of the age of mechanics. One of the sailors aboard the *Julia* was derided as a landlubber: "Regarded in the light of a mechanical power, whenever there is any plain, hard work to be done, he is put to it like a lever; every one giving him a pry" (Ch 14). The machine was the symbol of nineteenth century progress and the power of human inventiveness, used here to illustrate the dehumanized quality of the machine age. He chides the French for their ship's rigging: "But your Gaul is scientific about every thing; what other people accomplish by a few hard knocks, he delights in achieving by a complex arrangement of the pulley, lever, and screw" (Ch 29). In other words, mechanics had replaced the importance of man. Later in the book, he says machinery was sent from London to establish weaving in Tahiti: "The whiz of the wheels and spindles brought in volunteers from all quarters, who deemed it a privilege to be admitted to work: yet, in six months, not a boy could be hired; and the machinery was knocked down, and packed off to Sydney" (Ch 49). In Melville's words, the machine fails in paradise, and may imply a sentiment often stated in his works that the natives have a greater sense of propriety than the European or American settlers on their islands.

A scientific discussion occurs between one of the most clever and intelligent natives and "our learned Theban of a doctor" on the subject of time and geography. The natives are perplexed by the loss of a day when coming around Cape Horn, and that it is Sunday in Tahiti when it ought to be Saturday, a convention established by the ship *Duff* more than a half-century earlier. A "worthy old missionary" tries to shed some light on the subject, which the narrator describes:

> "Here," says he, "you see this circle" (describing a large one on the ground with a stick): "very good; now you see this spot here" (marking a point in the perimeter): "well; this is Beretanee" (England), "and I'm going to sail round to Tahiti. Here I go, then" (following the circle round); "and there goes the sun" (snatching up another stick, and commissioning a bandy-legged native to travel round with it in a contrary direction). "Now then, we are both off, and both going away from each other; and here you see I have

> arrived at Tahiti" (making a sudden stop); "and look now, where Bandy Legs is!"
>
> But the crowd strenuously maintained, that Bandy Legs ought to be somewhere above them in the atmosphere; for it was a traditionary fact, that the people from the Duff came ashore when the sun was high overhead. And here the old gentleman, being a very good sort of man, doubtless, but no astronomer, was obliged to give up. (Ch 42)

As early as the fifth century B.C. the Greek atomists Leucippus and Democritus visualized the universe as an infinite empty space occupied by an infinite number of minute indivisible particles, or atoms, moving in all directions; the earth was but one of many similar bodies formed by the chance aggregation of atoms. An alternate cosmology was suggested by Pythagoras later in the fifth century. He placed the invisible fire of the Altar of Zeus at the center. A century later, Heraclides of Pontus suggested the daily rotation of the earth rather than movement of the celestial sphere. He further postulated that the planets Mercury and Venus revolved in circles about the moving sun instead of around the earth. In the third century B.C., Aristarchus of Samos ingeniously theorized that the the sun was at the center of an immensely expanded sphere of the stars, and the earth moved in a circle about the sun.[10] Kuhn claims that man occupies a crucial intermediate position in a universe of hierarchical chain:

> Man's location, too, is intermediate: the earth's surface is close to its debased and corporeal center but within sight of the celestial periphery which surround it symmetrically. Man lives in squalor and uncertainty, and he is very close to Hell. But his central location is strategic, for he is everywhere under the eye of God. Both man's double nature and his intermediate position enforce the choice from which the drama of Christianity is compounded.[11]

The position of man in the universe was an open question in the mid-nineteenth century, although a central, stationary earth had been doctrinal for centuries. The belief in an abstract world view, one that is opposed to what seems common sense to the observer on earth, is a complex and unsettled issue which recurs in many of Melville's works.

In Chapter 48, "Tahiti As It Is," and Chapter 49, "Same Subject Continued," Melville applies his research to develop and authenticate his story of South Sea travel by discussing social conditions, examining Tahiti beyond his personal observations and giving detailed references to his sources. For example, he cites voyager Captain Wilson, who concurred with Melville that the islanders had "more refined ideas of decency than ourselves," and Vancouver on the same conditions in Hawaii (Ch 48). In addition, he cites reference books by Otto Von Kotzebue, the Russian navigator (Ch 48n), the Right Rev. M. Russell, Captain F.W. Beechey, Daniel Wheeler, Captain Wilson, Vancouver, and Ellis (Ch 48). Melville alludes to W.S. Ruschenberger, M.D., "an intelligent surgeon in the United States Navy" whose book, *A Voyage round the World, in the years 1835-36-37* (1838), describes the decimation of the population of the Hawaiian Islands (Ch 49n). Citing authority makes the observations of a beachcomber more believable.

The natives protest the supposed advance in their civilization when they see their society is being decimated by disease brought to their disease-free islands:

> The palm-tree shall grow,
> The coral shall spread,
> But man shall cease. (Ch 49)

The missionaries and explorers who settled in the Pacific islands brought with them diseases that decimated the native populations of many of the islands, especially Hawaii and Tahiti.[12]

The narrator and the doctor travel to nearby islands, working for a time on a plantation. His sleep is disturbed by mosquitoes, which were brought to the islands by foreigners. He tries "mathematical reveries" to induce sleep: "but finding the multiplication table of no avail, I summoned up a grayish image of chaos in a sort of sliding fluidity" (Ch 56). The doctor achieved some stature as a "learned laborer" and a "man of science," dreaming of building a small ship for commerce between the islands in spite of the difficult navigation of the shoals: "He enlarged upon the science of navigation; treated us to a dissertation on Mercator's Sailing and the Azimuth compass; and went into an inexplicable explanation of, the Lord only knows what plan of his, for infallibly settling the longitude" (Ch 60). Geradus Mercator (1512-1594), Flemish, was the greatest of the Renaissance geographers, best known for his world map in the Mercator Projection. In navigation, the azimuth is the arc of the horizon measured clockwise from the north point to the point where a vertical circle through a given heavenly body intersects the horizon. As exploration and commerce developed around the world, cartography and navigation achieved great importance. A method of determining longitude eluded navigators until the mid-nineteenth century. The doctor was held in considerable esteem: "they counted more upon his ultimate value to them as a man of science, than as a mere ditcher" (Ch 60). That Doctor Long Ghost was both scientist and humbug is no coincidence, a persistent theme of Melville's works. The book ends when the narrator signs aboard the whaler *Leviathan* and Doctor Long Ghost remains in Tahiti.

Notes

1. Tyrus Hillway, "Melville's Education in Science." *Texas Studies in Literature and Language* 16 (1974):421-422.

2. Colin Patterson, "Animated Nature." Review of *History of the Natural World* by Oliver Goldsmith. London: Studio Editions, 1990, in *Nature* 349 (1991):115-116.

3. Hillway, Tyrus. "Melville's Geological Knowledge." *American Literature* 21 (1949):232-237.

4. *Encyclopædia Britannica* 20 (1971):196.

5. Hillway, 1974.

6. Hillway, 1974.

7. *Encyclopædia Britannica* 7 (1971):906.

8. *Encyclopædia Britannica* 21 (1971):1126-1127; Isaac Newton. *Philosophiæ Naturalis Principia Mathematica*. (1687) translated by Andrew Motte in 1729. reprint Florian Cajori, editor. Berkeley, Los Angeles, and London: University of California Press, 1934, pp. 435-440.

9. Hillway, 1974.

10. Thomas S. Kuhn, *The Copernican Revolution: Planetary Astronomy in the Development of Western Thought.* Cambridge, Massachusetts: Harvard University Press, 1957, pp. 42-43.

11. Kuhn, p. 113.

12. Leslie Roberts, "Disease and Death in the New World." *Science* 246 (1989):1245-1247.

Chapter 2

Mardi: a fire in the brine

In *Mardi, and a Voyage Thither*, Melville's use of science progresses to a remarkable degree. He expanded his reading during the spring of 1848 to included travel writers Charles H. Barnard and Louis Bougainville (1729-1811), as well as such diverse authors as Shakespeare, Montaigne, Proclus, Seneca, Thomas Browne, Coleridge, and Rabelais.[1] Authorities cited in *Mardi* become a compilation of the famous scientists of the early nineteenth century. Melville gives full rein to his intellect in a large, two volume work; science receives emphasis in more than one-third of the 195 chapters. Science references are often brief and require explanation; at other times, science is almost descriptive, yet contains metaphysical overtones. In some citations the use of science is so subtle and closely woven into the great fabric of the story as to be nearly overlooked.

Mardi is set aboard a whaling ship in the South Pacific after passing the Galápagos Islands "which Dampier once trod" (Ch 1). William Dampier (1652-1715), English explorer and writer, was noted for voyages to the South Pacific, especially a famous voyage in 1699 along the coasts of Australia and New Guinea. Dampier's voyages were remarkable for his extraordinarily keen observations of natural phenomena; he was a pioneer of scientific exploration.[2] Melville capitalized on interest in the Galápagos Islands that resulted from many explorers' tales of the remarkable islands and the continuing interest in Darwin's *Journal of Researches* of the Galápagos Islands published in 1839. The ship has a dull pagan crew, "no soul a magnet to mine" (Ch 1). The captain is equally uninteresting. His library contained only two books: one by Nathaniel Bowditch (1773-1838), American mathematician, astronomer, and navigator. Bowditch edited J. H. Moore's *The Practical Navigator,* and in 1802 wrote *The New Practical Navigator* based on Moore's book. The *Navigator* soon became the standard reference for seamen, adopted as the official text of the United States Navy. He was particularly known for correcting and extending the work of other scientists, especially for his translation of Laplace's *Mechanique celeste,* thought to be the culmination of the Newtonian revolution. At the time, Bowditch lived an isolated scholarly life, for America had not yet developed an intellectual milieu.[3] Events of the age had effects on astronomy, for it was a period of voyages and explorations: fifty years before Copernicus's birth, Portuguese voyages of exploration along the African coast excited the imagination and avarice of Europeans. Exploration of the world created a demand for improved maps and navigation that depended to a great extent on a better knowledge of the heavens. Each voyage uncovered errors in ancient descriptions of the earth.[4]

The ship enters a calm; he recalls "Priestley on Necessity," a book he cites in subsequent works:

> If a reader of books, Priestley on Necessity occurs to him; and he believes in that old Sir Anthony Absolute to the very last chapter. His faith in Malte Brun, however, begins to fail, for the geography, which from boyhood he had implicitly confided in, always assured him that though expatiating all over the globe, the sea was at least margined by land....
>
> To his alarmed fancy, parallels and meridians become emphatically what they are merely designated as being: imaginary lines drawn round the earth's surface.
>
> The log assures him that he is in such a place; but the log is a liar; for no place, nor any thing possessed of a local angularity, is to be lighted upon in the watery waste.
>
> At length horrible doubts overtake him as to the captain's competency to navigate his ship. The ignoramus must have lost

> his way, and drifted into the outer confines of creation, the region of the everlasting lull, introductory to a positive vacuity. (Ch 2)

Joseph Priestley (1733-1804), an English chemist, author, and clergyman, wrote *Doctrine of Philosophical Necessity* (1777), stating that free will is undesirable. He is best known as the disputed discoverer of oxygen. Priestley's opinions disturbed Melville, for he subsequently criticizes his writings even though Priestley was a greatly respected scientist.

The concept of the vacuum had troubled philosophers since the ancient Greeks, as used as metaphor earlier, and the narrator subsequently deals with the idea of a vacuum saying: "Are not such well-ordered dispensations of Providence? filling up vacuums, in intervals of social stagnation relieving the tedium of existing?" etc. (Ch 11); and during the calm, "The silence was that of a vacuum. No vitality lurked in the air. And this inert blending and brooding of all things seemed gray chaos in conception" (Ch 16). The metaphysical place of the vacuum is further discussed in Chapter 135.

The narrator implies a strata of knowledge, listing more of the famous voyagers to the South Seas and including some of the terms of ancient astronomy:

> Then shall we list to no shallow gossip of Magellans and Drakes; but give ear to the voyagers who have circumnavigated the ecliptic; who rounded the Polar Star as Cape Horn. Then shall the Stagirite[5] and Kant be forgotten, and another folio than theirs be turned over for wisdom; even the folio now spread with horoscopes as yet undeciphered, the heaven of heavens on high. (Ch 3)

Cosmology, or the study of the origin of the universe, is a recurring theme in many of Melville's works, and in *Mardi* even the simple Jarl has his own theory, "'I have lived ever since I can remember.' And truly, who may call to mind when he was not? To ourselves, we all seem coeval with creation. Whence it comes, that it is so hard to die, ere the world itself is departed" (Ch 3). Jarl expands his notion of cosmology:

> According to his view of the matter, this terraqueous world had been formed in the manner of a tart; the land being a mere marginal crust within which rolled the watery world proper. Such seemed my good Viking's theory of cosmography. As for other worlds, he weened not of them; yet full as much as Chrysostom. (Ch 3)

That the sea was margined by land was an ancient Egyptian or Greek concept. The idea of plurality of worlds was a medieval concept.

The narrator and Jarl abandon the whaleship in a small whaling boat. At intervals, they encounter strange sea life swimming by, as described in Chapter 13, "Of the Chondroptergii, and Other Uncouth Hordes Infesting the South Seas." Melville commends an open boat to any student of ichthyology: "what strange monsters float by.... And nowhere are they found in the books of the naturalists.... And whoso crosses the Pacific might have read lessons to Buffon." He also mentions Sir Thomas Browne, who, while exploding "'Vulgar Errors,' heartily hugged all the mysteries of the Pentateuch" (Ch 13). At the close of the Babylonian captivity the Hebrews possessed a large body of folklore, legends, genealogies and fragments of history that eventually became the first five books of the Bible—the Pentateuch. This material, previously an oral history with many changing viewpoints and contradictions through the centuries, was finally edited about the time of Ezra (ca 400 B.C.). From the time of the Reformation, Christian scholars believed this literature to be divinely inspired and literally true until the nineteenth century when it came to be seen in an historical light and was questioned at every point.[6] Sir Thomas Browne (1605-1682), a prominent and respected physician in Norwich, England, wrote *Pseudodoxia Epidemica, or, Enquiries Into Very Many Received Tenents, and Commonly Presumed Truths, Which Examined Prove but Vulgar and Common Errors* (1646), more commonly called *Vulgar Errors*, to correct mistaken popular beliefs and superstitions. At the same time, Browne held to religious doctrine, the Pentateuch. Browne was one of the few writers to have a major influence on the development of Melville's metaphysics and literary style. Melville's love of classical and biblical allusions, comprehensive scholarship, appeal to authority, and stylistic parallels can be traced to Browne. Browne's recognition of the conflict of science and faith in the seventeenth century were in sympathy with Melville's ideas expressed in *Mardi*.[7]

The narrator was fascinated by the life in the sea, and says of man's willingness to distrust the shark and Jarl's claim to have murdered shoals of tiger sharks: "As well hate a seraph as a shark. Both were made by the same hand" (Ch 13). Melville discourses on the shark, referring to the work of classification by German naturalists Johannes Müller and Jacob Henle, who christened the sharks with the "most heathenish names" (Ch 13). Müller (1801-1858) German naturalist, recognized the important interrelationship between anatomy and physiology. Henle (1809-1885), a student of Müller's, was a great anatomist who did for microscopic anatomy what Vesalius in the sixteenth century did for gross anatomy, virtually creating the science of histology. Hillway reports that the 40-volume *The Naturalists Library* (1833-1845), discusses their monumental work on the shark, *Systematische Beschreibung der Plagiostomen* (1838-1841), and may have been known to Melville.[8]

Chapter 13 on the classification of sharks reflects the emphasis on axonomy, naming, and classification in the eighteenth and nineteenth centuries. Melville refers to Buffon; in later works, he also mentions the most eminent name in taxonomy—Linnaeus. Buffon and Linnaeus were the most famous names in science in the eighteenth century. Carolus Linnaeus (1707-1778), Swedish born, received a medical degree in Holland, was the foremost naturalist of the eighteenth century, a genius and phenomenon of the times, virtually the symbol of science. With great personal charm, Linnaeus received popular acclaim for his poetic gift of naming species of plants and animals: the binomial system of nomenclature still in use. Advanced technology and design of sailing ships permitted voyages of exploration to all parts of the world; the expeditions included naturalists, elegantly equipped and quartered, who returned to Europe with vast collections of new species for Linnaeus to classify and name. A strict definition of species was necessary for scientific analysis to maintain the concept of the beauty and order of nature. In his later years, he became aware of new varieties, aberrant plants developing from normal plants, and saw the possibility of new species arising through crossbreeding. Linnaeus's only rival for public acclaim with a worldwide reputation was Georges Buffon (1707-1788), French naturalist, who theorized a 'falling away' from one type of animal into another. He observed that within a given species, variations of form occur and an underlying similar structure occurs among quite dissimilar animals. Buffon sought natural explanations for the formation of the earth and for geological events, anticipating a time scale of the earth longer than the 4,000 years of biblical time. He accepted the unorthodox idea that certain species had become extinct. Buffon sensed the importance of the difference in world distribution of plant and animal species with their eternal imperfection and change.[9] Linnaeus was primarily a botanist and his system was most successful in botany, although *System Naturae* included the kingdoms of animals, vegetables, and minerals. References to God abound in Linnaeus's works. He saw the world as an orderly whole made by a wise creator, a concept to be found in Plato, or natural theology, and searching for the order of God was part of the challenge of taxonomy. In Linnaeus's lifetime, exceptions and variations in characteristics raised doubts about classification. Most of his contemporaries believed in the Great Chain of Being, whose central idea was theological, with some basis in observation, showing not only how things were arranged, but why. God, being complete in Himself, would necessarily create a varied and full world without any void or gaps in matter or creatures, i.e., the principle of plenitude, "nature makes no jumps." The discovery of coralline was particularly vexing since it is on the borderline between plants and animals. Louis Agassiz (1807-1873), in *Essay on Classification* (1859), restated the notion of preestablished harmony of an intelligent and understandable creator along the lines of established, separate classes. He was unable to account for the similarity of European faunas to those of North America, and to the faunas of Africa and South America, and postulated separate centers of creation for each region in order to maintain the uniqueness of species. Agassiz received the degree of doctor of philosophy from Erlangen, Switzerland, and doctor of medicine from Munich; in 1832, he received a professorship in Paris under Cuvier. Agassiz became a renowned scientist noted for his study and classification of fishes, *Reserches sur les Poissons Fossiles* (1833-1844). His greatest contribution was the study of fossil fishes of Europe and the discovery of extinct species of fish, giving great impetus to the study of extinct species. Agassiz studied the movement and effects of glaciers, and determined that in a recent geological period Switzerland was covered by one vast sheet of ice. He came to America in 1846, giving popular lectures attended by large and enthusiastic audiences; the lectures were reported in the newspapers and received wide attention. In 1848, Agassiz joined the faculty at Harvard where he continued his work in zoology and became an outstanding teacher. He retained the idea of divine order, saying that each species was "a thought of God."[10] The character of Azzageddi, or the 'devilish spirit' in Babbalanja, may have been based on Agassiz. Agassiz is cited in *Moby-Dick,* Chapter 68, "The Blanket": "I should say that those New England rocks on the sea-coast, which Agassiz imagines to bear the marks of violent scraping contact with vast floating icebergs..."

Subsequently, a system of classification by A. L. de Jussieu (1789), became accepted for its use of characteristics of primary importance and general value, especially the reproductive system, in a natural and workable system that made the artificial system of Linnaeus obsolete. The natural system was slow to gain acceptance in Britain, but was finally accepted largely due to John Lindley's *Introduction to the Natural System of Botany* (1830). The natural system was based on the principle that the affinity of plants are determined by considering all the points of resemblance between the "various parts, properties, and qualities." By the nineteenth century, long lists of names of plants and animals from many different classifications had to be included in the description. During the seventy years following de Jessieu and Linnaeus, the artificial system had been replaced by the natural system, but was still committed to a belief in the presence of order in nature. Some naturalists took this as evidence of divine design, while others considered the division into species artificial.[11]

Although a minor notation, the simple observation of waves arising from an unseen action takes on a noteworthy importance:

> On the second day of the calm, we unshipped the mast to prevent its being pitched out by the occasional rolling of the vast smooth swells now overtaking us. Leagues and leagues away, after its fierce raging, some tempest must have been sending to us its last dying waves. For as a pebble dropped into a pond ruffles it to its marge; so, on all sides, a sea-gale operates as if an asteroid had fallen into the brine; making ringed mountain billows, interminably expanding, instead of ripples. (Ch 16)

The idea of the effect of 'action at a distance' was a highly controversial conflict from the times of the ancient Greeks and discussed at length by Priestley in *A Free Discussion of the Doctrines of Materialism and Philosophical Necessity*.[12] The subject became particularly important with Newton's discovery of gravitation and the movement of planets.

An immense shovel-nosed shark swims near the boat accompanied by small 14-inch pilot fish, or "Remora" which Melville says are parasites: "it feeds upon what it clings to; its feelers having a direct communication with the esophagus" (Ch 18). Melville's use of science in the chapter on sharks is notable for its many inaccuracies. The remora attaches to the shark for transportation, but is not a parasite nor does it harm the shark. In addition, the remora attaches to the ventral or underside of the shark, not its dorsal side. Some of Melville's misinformation may have come from Oliver Goldsmith's *Animated Nature*, which states the remora "sticks to the shark, and drains away his moisture."[13]

After a number of days at sea, they meet a brigantine that appears deserted. Before boarding the vessel, the narrator is wary because of certain superstitions about abandoned ships, but Jarl is practical about her: "Wherein, he resembled my right reverend friend, Bishop Berkeley—truly, one of your lords spiritual—who, metaphysically speaking, holding all objects to be mere optical delusions, was, notwithstanding, extremely matter-of-fact in all matters touching matter itself" (Ch 20). George Berkeley (1685-1753), Anglican bishop, is most famous for his dictum "*esse es percipi*" ("to be is to be perceived"), i.e., color means something seen: the external world exists only in the mind and its sensations. *An Essay Towards a New Theory of Vision* (1709), develops his ideas on the perception of space as being largely psychological, a concept which greatly influenced subsequent philosophers, especially Hume, Kant, and J. S. Mill.[14]

On boarding the ship, they find an oak box "much battered and bruised like the Elgin Marbles, all over inscriptions and carvings..." (Ch 20). The Elgin marbles were pieces of Greek sculpture of the Fifth Century B.C., brought to England by Thomas Bruce, Earl of Elgin (1766-1844) in large numbers (1803-1812), sold to the English government, and placed in the British Museum. Two Polynesians, a man with a mutilated arm and a woman, hiding in the main-top rigging, climb down the mast when discovered by the narrator and Jarl (Ch 21). They say that the rest of the crew was killed during an attack while in port, and part of the crew was on shore when they escaped to sea. Samoa and the woman, Annatoo, were the only survivors. In Chapter 24, "Dedicated to the College of Physicians and Surgeons," Samoa amputates his own arm using a serrated shell in a scene of black humor leading to a metaphysical inquiry: "But which of the writhing sections of a ten times severed worm is the worm proper" (Ch 24)? The example is a combination of the quandary caused by the question of the origin of parasitic worms and the regenerative power of the hydra, or fresh water polyp. When cut into sections, the hydra regenerates a complete new individual organism from each section, a process discussed at some length in Chapter 155.

The narrator says the ship *Etna* was struck by lightning: "But almost as potent as Moses' rod, Franklin's proved her salvation" (Ch 28). Benjamin Franklin (1706-1790), American diplomat, scientist, and inventor noted for his investigation of electricity and lightning, is credited with inventing the lightning rod. Annatoo steals articles from the ship stores and hides them about the ship like "the inscrutable penguins building their inscrutable nests, which baffle all science, and make a fool of a sage" (Ch 31). Penguins and the South Pole defied nineteenth century explorers. Although its coast was explored, the continent remained a mystery. Antarctica was explored by sailing ships of three expeditions between 1838 and 1843. The first person to sight land was probably U.S. Navy officer Charles Wilkes in 1840. No ships visited Antarctica until 1892, except for a single voyage in 1874.

The Indian swordfish is known as the billfish, "while for those who love science and hard names, be it known, that among the erudite naturalists he goeth by the outlandish appellation of 'Xiphius Platyperus'" (Ch 32). The narrator prefers the name "the Chevalier," for the fish is known to attack and spear ships. An English ship was struck by a swordfish, he says, and on its return to London, the sword in its timber was removed "like a fossil" and is still preserved, an event alluded to in Chapter 7 when he ponders the fate of the *Arcturion*: "Sunk she silently, helplessly, into the calm depths of that summer sea, assassinated by the ruthless blade of the swordfish. Such things have been" (Ch 7). He further claims a "Chevalier" stabbed the *Rousseau* of Nantucket, and withdrew its blade. The *Rousseau* managed to make port to "have her wound dressed by a ship-surgeon with tar and oakum" (Ch 32), a story probably based on Frank Debell Bennett's *Narrative of a Whaling Voyage Round the Globe* (1840) describing swordfish attacking ships.[15] Hillway points out that the Indian swordfish is the sailfish, *Istiophorus gladius*. The swordfish's sword imbedded in a ship's hull on museum display is the spearfish, genus *Tetrapturus*. The triangular poniard does not belong to the swordfish, but to the sailfish or spearfish.[16]

Melville records the popular theory that the ocean possesses a "special purifying agent" in its salts. He says, "But I build no theories," probably paraphrasing Newton's *hypotheses non fingo,* "I build no theories,"[17] yet he proposes an alternate theory (Ch 34). During a quiet, moonlit night, the sea becomes afire with luminescence: "Faraday might, perhaps, impute the phenomenon to a peculiar electrical condition of the atmosphere" but it is attributed to animal waste by the sailors. The narrator observes that the water retains its phosphorescence when drawn in a bucket, but soon subsides with standing:

> But after all, this seeming ignition of the sea cannot be wholly produced by dead matter therein. There are many living fish, phosphorescent; and, under certain conditions, by a rapid throwing off of luminous particles must largely contribute to the result. Not to particularize this circumstance as true of divers species of sharks, cuttlefish, and many others of the larger varieties of the finny tribes; the myriads of microscopic mollusca, well known to swarm off soundings, might alone be deemed almost sufficient to kindle a fire in the brine.
>
> But these are only surmises, likely but uncertain.
>
> After science comes sentiment. (Ch 38)

Darwin wrote on phosphorescence of the sea, his first entry in his *Zoological Diary* aboard the *Beagle,* 6 January 1832, was on the "Luminous Sea": "The sea was luminous in specks & in the wake of the vessel, of an uniform slightly milky colour.—When the water was put into a bottle, it gave out sparks for some minutes after having been drawn up.—When examined both at night & next morning. it was found full of numerous small (but many bits visible to naked eye) irregular pieces of (a gelatinous?) matter.—The sea next morning was in the same place equally impure." And 10 January 1832, "sea very luminous. chiefly from a crustacean animal. which gave a very green light retaining for some time after having been taken out of water."[18] Including Michael Faraday (1791-1867) in a discussion of phosphorescence seems inappropriate, except that his probable source, Bennett, supposes the phenomenon to be due to "a peculiar electrical condition of the atmosphere." Faraday, one of the greatest physicists of all time, was noted for his researches in electricity. Darwin's *Journal of Researches* (1839), also suggested that a disturbed electrical condition of the atmosphere contributed to phosphorescence of the sea.[19] The "French naturalist" he cites is probably Georges Cuvier (1792-1832); Melville borrowed *Animal Kingdom* (1827-1835), volume 10 of Cuvier, from his brother Allan on January 1, 1851, three years after completing *Mardi.* [20] Georges Cuvier (1769-1832), a naturalist born in Switzerland, was the foremost ichthyologist of his time, especially known for his study of structure and classification of mollusca, the comparative anatomy of fishes, and the study of fossil mammals and reptiles. His work shifted attention from fossil shells to fossil bones. He accepted the notion of extinction of species and stratification of time from the study of rock formations of Paris extensively quarried during the First Empire. Cuvier was able to determine the appearance of ancient animals from examining their fossil remains; i.e., reconstruct the entire form and outward appearance of an extinct creature from examining a single bone by the principle of "the correlation of parts" — as the function of an organ changes, so will its structure. Whether Melville was familiar with the book or other works of Cuvier when he composed *Mardi* is not known. Cuvier discusses the firefly, saying the phosphoric brilliance emitted by females is a sexual attractant, as Melville states.[21] Later in the book, the Milky Way is used as a metaphor (Ch 188) for the phosphorescent glow of a ship's wake in the tropical seas.

Annatoo is swept overboard during an intense storm and lost at sea. Jarl, Samoa, and the narrator travel through the islands of the mythical archipelago of Mardi. They are accompanied by King Media (the mind),

Yoomy (poetry), Babbalanja (philosophy), and Mohi (history); numerous other symbolic characters appear during their travels. Melville assumes the name Taji, meaning "little prince" in Persian which usually means a voyager or adventurer. Most of the names of the characters in the Mardian archipelago were taken from Persian places and characters in Herodotus and from Arabic words in Lane's translation of *The Arabian Nights*.[22] Although *Mardi* is regarded a metaphor for the countries of the world, certain descriptions suggest that all of the islands of Mardi are based on the islands of the Galápagos. Melville gives the exact location of the ship, "sixty degrees west of the Galápagos," the location of the Ellice, Gilbert, and Marshall Islands.[23]; he gives the location of ship as in the Ellice's group (Ch 3). As they approach land, their boat is met by an old priest and his sons who have an albino young woman in captivity. The young woman, named Yillah, is to be offered as a blood sacrifice. On the wrinkled brow of the old priest "were characters still more mysterious, which no Champollion nor gypsy could have deciphered" (Ch 40). Jean Francois Champollion (1790-1832) was a French Egyptologist mentioned occasionally by Melville. Yillah was revealed to the priest in a dream, called home by spirits "and plunging into a vortex" to well up in an island fountain (Ch 43). Melville's reference to the vortex, a mathematical and physical phenomenon advanced by Descartes, receives treatment in subsequent books.

How did Yillah, with an anomaly of skin pigment, regard Samoa's amputation? At first, she shrank from him, but regarded him as harmless "May be, she held him a being of spontaneous origin" (Ch 47). Spontaneous origin, or spontaneous generation of life from inorganic material of certain lower forms was accepted by naturalists beginning with Aristotle until the advent of the microscope. Francesco Redi (ca 1626-1697), Italian naturalist, was the first to show that the appearance of larvae on meat required the presence of adult forms. Nevertheless, the concept remained a fervent topic which challenged the theological doctrine of divine Creation and suggested the sudden appearance of bizarre animals and variation of life forms. The controversy did not abate until Louis Pasteur showed conclusively in the mid-nineteenth century that putrescence required the presence of living organisms. Proponents of spontaneous generation believed that "some living entities may arise suddenly by *chance* from matter independently of any parent."[24]

The narrator says the colorless Yillah is an albino or "Tulla" "As a race, the Tullas die early. And hence the belief, that they pertain to some distant sphere, and only through irregularities in the providence of the gods, come to make their appearance upon earth: whence, the oversight discovered, they are hastily snatched" (Ch 49). Melville's discussion of the phenomenon of albinism and its significance to native belief can be traced to Bennett's *Narrative of a Whaling Voyage Round the Globe* (1840). Bennett describes an albino child, a girl about five years old, varying his character from Bennett's.[25] Albinism stirred considerable interest in the developing theories of inheritance and natural occurrence of aberrant forms in the "war of nature," since albinos die young. After a fight with the natives, Yillah is freed from captivity and saved from death, but she soon eludes the travelers. The remainder of *Mardi* is a mythical search for the albino goddess Yillah. The symbolism of Yillah has been treated at great length and usually considered an allegorical search for truth and happiness.

The Mardian Isles are described in terms of astronomy in both threatening and idyllic terms:

> Far and wide was deep low-sobbing repose of man and nature. The groves were motionless; and in the meadows, like goblins, the shadows advanced and retreated. Full before me, lay the Mardian fleet of isles, profoundly at anchor within their coral harbor. Nearby was one belted round by a frothy, luminous reef, wherein it lay, like Saturn in its ring. (Ch 58)

The arrangement of the coral reefs around the central island was the clue that Darwin observed that helped to develop his theory of the formation of reefs and the origin of coral islands.

A notion fundamental to the medieval world was the idea of influences: God exerted a continuous influence upon his creatures on earth, sometimes directly, but chiefly through the heavenly bodies, and above all through the sun. Everything on earth was linked to various heavenly bodies. Man was subject to these influences, but not fatalistically bound to them. Through free will, man coped with the evil influences of the planets as best he could. This general system of man's world view received little dispute or changed little before the sixteenth century.[26] The influence of stars and the theme of plurality of world is a troubling and recurring theme in the works of Melville:

> From earth to heaven! High above me was night's shadowy bower, traversed, vine-like, by the Milky Way, and heavy with golden clusterings. Oh stars! oh eyes, that see me, wheresoe'er I roam: serene, intent, inscrutable for aye, tell me Sibyls, what I am.—Wondrous worlds on worlds! Lo, round and round me,

> shining, awful spells: all glorious, vivid constellations, God's diadem ye are! To you, ye stars, man owes his subtlest raptures, thoughts unspeakable, yet full of faith. (Ch 58)

That the motion and nature of celestial bodies affected the behavior of sublunar, animate and inanimate bodies was generally accepted based on what was considered to be overwhelming evidence. The sun's cyclic rising in the sky and retreat was essential for life, as well as the moon's effect on the tides, the humors of animals, the star's effect on diseases, etc.; other planets as well were assigned important causative powers. Only human intellect and will, which were independent of material influence, were exempt from their influence. The supremacy of the human intellect and will over celestial influences was stated in a popular medieval dictum, *Vir sapiens dominabitur astris*, (which literally means "wise men will be dominated by the stars," but has been interpreted to mean "a wise man will dominate the stars").[27] To Augustine, consulting the stars for information about future events was as irrational as consulting the entrails of animals, and was an affront to divine Providence and human liberty; besides, he said, it didn't work. Nevertheless, despite Augustine's antipathy to astrology, the theological objection crumbled. However, the forecasting of a particularly dangerous planetary conjunction predicted to occur in 1186 brought about elaborate and careful preparations in laying up of food and spiritual preparation, yet the crops were abundant and nothing of note happened: a disappointment that would hound astrologers the rest of the Middle Ages.[28]

In a seemingly offhand remark, the narrator states one of the observations that was to dramatically influence biology toward the end of the decade: "A noteworthy circumstance, observable in these regions, where islands close adjoining, so differ in their soil, that certain fruits growing genially in one, are foreign to another" (Ch 63). The close relationship between species in a genus was initially thought to be a formalized part of God's plan, but the similarities were so striking that naturalists had to consider whether a genus might be formed by the gradual splitting of a single original form into a number of closely related ones. Linnaeus originally strenuously denied this possibility. However, he came to accept that a multiplication of species within a genus could occur due to different environments, tacitly threatening the traditional distinction between species and varieties. In some conditions, the effect produced was so great that a variety might become a distinct new species raising the question of which species were the original creations of God.[29] The effect of locality on the growth of plants and animals precipitated an enormous change in man's perception of himself. In addition, though nature was perceived as paradise and evidence of the benevolence of an all-powerful deity in the tropical idyll, evidence was mounting to the contrary. The narrator describes this in the story of the change of the larva into a butterfly—does it imply a similar miraculous change in man after death?:

> No; for the analogy has an unsatisfactory end. From its chrysalis state, the silkworm but becomes a moth, that very quickly expires. Its longest existence is as a worm. All vanity, vanity, Yoomy, to seek in nature for positive warranty to these aspirations of ours. Through all her provinces, nature seems to promise immortality to life, but destruction to beings. Or, as old Bardianna has it, if not against us, nature is not for us. (Ch 69)

Thus, he argues against the millennia of attempts to demonstrate the presence and affirmation of the Creator in the works and wonders of nature, which Locke called the "Book of God's Works." He makes a heterodox statement, a deistic concept, that nature may be indifferent to the welfare of man rather than seeing man's place as one of special creation and privilege. This is a theme Melville pursues at length in later works, especially in *Moby-Dick*.

In Chapter 75, "Time and Temples," Melville's writing expands with a distinct maturing in style and depth. This remarkable chapter surely was influenced by Sir Thomas Browne, although Davis says the chapter may have had its genesis from seven lectures on astronomy by John P. Nichol during January and February 1848, and reported in the *New York Tribune*.[30] Melville names the most famous chroniclers of discovery voyages from Europe to Asia and the South Seas. Their discoveries of ancient temples introduce a philosophical discourse on the emerging new concept of time: "In the Oriental pilgrimage of the pious old Purchas, and in the fine old folio voyages of Hakluyt, Thevenot, Ramusio, and DeBry,..." (Ch 75). He elaborates the importance of time in geology, cycles of time, the age of the universe of six thousand years, and the "fullness" of nature:

> Nor was Virginia's Natural Bridge worn under in a year; nor, in geology, were the eternal Grampians upheaved in an age. And who shall count the cycles that revolved ere earth's interior sedimentary strata were crystalized into stone.... Yea, with uttermost reverence, as to human understanding, increase of dominion seem increase of power; and day by day new planets are being added to elder-born

> Saturns, even as six thousand years ago our own Earth made one more in this system; so, in incident, not in essence, may the Infinite himself be not less than more infinite now, than when old Alderbaran rolled forth from his hand. And if time was, when this round Earth, which to innumerable mortals has seemed an empire never to be wholly explored; which, in its seas, concealed all the Indies over four thousand five hundred years; if time was, when this great quarry of Assyrias and Romes was not extant; then, time may have been, when the whole material universe lived its Dark Ages; yea, when the Ineffable Silence, proceeding from its unimaginable remoteness, espied it as an isle in the sea. And herein is no derogation. For the Immeasurable's altitude is not heightened by the arches of Mahomet's heavens; and were all space a vacuum, yet would it be a fullness; for to Himself His own universe is He.
>
> Thus deeper and deeper into Time's endless tunnel, does the winged soul, like a night-hawk, wend her wild way; and finds eternities before and behind; and her last limit is her everlasting beginning....Thus, then, though Time be the mightiest of Alarics, yet is he the mightiest mason of all. And a tutor, and a counselor, and a physician, and a scribe, and a poet, and a sage, and a king. (Ch 75)

Rome was more a center of literature, history, and law than of science, and declined greatly after its sack by the Alaric, king of the Visgoths, in 410 A.D. When Roman knowledge of Greek died out in the fifth century, so did most ancient science, for very little science was translated into Latin.[31] Melville's exquisite chapter shows the influence of Browne on his style: reference to classical antiquities, biblical sources, an extraordinary vocabulary, compound sentences, ornamented phrases, abundant and varied punctuation, and very long paragraphs to produce a depth and richness of thought that would characterize Melville's future writings. He encounters the controversies in the intellectual circles of Europe and America: the earth's biblical age of 6,000 years, natural changes in the surface of the earth, exploration of the remote areas of the globe, geological strata, origin of the planets, growth and imperfection of nature, infinite time, and the power of time to produce vast changes in the earth. He implies that the earth is solid to its core, an error he corrects in later works. The age of the earth was calculated by James Ussher (1581-1656), the archbishop of Armagh, according to the generations of the Bible in *Annales Veleris et Novi Tentamenti*. He concluded that man was created by the Trinity on October 23, 4004 B.C. Ussher wrote numerous works of profound and extensive learning, but regrettably he is known today as the man who estimated man's antiquity. Ussher was at Oxford for a time and is buried in Westminster Abbey.[32]

Melville expands the theme of time in Chapter 78, "Babbalanja Solus," discussing eternity including elements of recent findings in geology and astronomy, and also including metempsychosis:

> But dead, and yet alive; alive, yet dead;—thus say the sages of Maramma. But die we then living? Yet if our dead fathers somewhere and somehow live, why not our unborn sons? For backward or forward, eternity is the same; already have we been the nothing we dread to be. Icy thought!...Nothing abideth; the river of yesterday floweth not today; the sun's rising is a setting; living is dying; the very mountains melt; and all revolve:—systems and asteroids; the sun wheels through the zodiac, and the zodiac is a revolution. Ah, gods! in all this universal stir, am *I* to prove one stable thing? (Ch 78)

He notes the importance of fossil bones and paleontology:

> Grim chiefs in skeletons, avaunt! Ye are but dust; belike the dust of beggars; for on this bed, paupers may lie down with kings, and filch their skulls. *This*, great Marjora's arm? No, some old paralytics? *Ye*, kings? *Ye*, men? Where are your vouchers? I do reject your brotherhood, ye libelous remains. But no, no; despise them not, oh Babbalanja! Thy own skeleton, thou thyself dost carry with thee, through this mortal life; and aye would view it, but for kind nature's screen; thou art death alive; and e'en to what's before thee wilt thou come. Aye, thy children's children will walk over thee: thou, voiceless as a calm. (Ch 78)

Nature's deception of the senses made many difficulties for the philosopher as well as the scientist, a subject to reappear often in Melville's works, especially *Moby-Dick*. Fossil bones were the clue to the past "like vouchers." The interest in fossil bones produced a lively trade in fossils between professional scientists and amateurs because the professional anthropologists and geologists were often dependent on amateurs for bones. Fossil bones were also bought and sold, sometimes bringing large sums, depending on what bones were in the most demand. Davis says the finding of anonymous bones and their meaning may be influenced by Browne's beautifully written *Hydriotaphia. Urne Buriall; or, a Discourse of the Sepulchrall Urnes Lately Found in*

Norfolk.[33] A few chapters later, Melville reiterates the problem of time: "'Oh Time, Time, Time!' cried Yoomy —'it is Time, old midsummer Time, that has made the old world what it is'" (Ch 89). The problem of time and its multiple dimensions was discussed by philosophers and scientists in the eighteenth and nineteenth centuries. The enigma of time becomes an important theme in *Moby-Dick* and *Pierre*.

In Chapter 84, "Taji Sits Down to Dinner with Five-and-Twenty Kings, and a Royal Time They Have," Melville introduces a pseudoscience he will use a number of times, the kings were arrayed: "as the rows of lips, eyes and ears in Johann Casper Lavater's physiognomical charts. Nevertheless, to a king, all their noses were aquiline" (Ch 84). An aquiline nose, according to Lavater's charts, indicates power to rule, act, overcome and destroy. Lavater (1741-1801) was a Swiss writer, patriot, Protestant minister and the founder of physiognomy. Physiognomy claims character or personal characteristics are determined by the form and features of the body, especially the face. Lavater, in *Essays on Physiognomy* (1789-1798), which achieved considerable reputation, believed that the interrelationship of mind and body was part of the healing ministry of Christ.[34]

Yoomy, the poet, relates a verbose legend receiving a counter argument from Mohi, the historian. Yoomy disputes the historian saying he has not told the truth. Babbalanja says, "truth is in things, and not in words: truth is voiceless...for things visible are but conceits of the eye: things imaginative, conceits of the fancy." Mohi demands, "what is truth?" Yoomy replies, "The old interrogatory; did they not ask it when the world began?...that question is more final than any answer" (Ch 93). The silence of God was the essence of the claim for design in nature as the proof of the existence of God, that God spoke to man through nature as stated by Paley in 1802:

> "No man hath seen God at any time" (John I:18). And this, I believe, makes the great difficulty....The Deity, it is true, is the object of none of our senses; but reflect what limited capacities animal senses are....Wherever we see marks of contrivance, we are led for its cause to an *intelligent* author.[35]

The idea that truth, whether in matters of faith or in matters of the world in natural history, i.e., science, cannot be known with certainty is a persistent Melvillian theme. The best that one can hope for is to persist in the search knowing that the goal of "truth" cannot be found on earth and requires faith whether in theology or science. The voice of God is silence, as silent as the interior of the pyramids where the idea of

Jehovah was conceived. What appears as material truth is merely the reflection of its outer surface. The deeper meanings must be sought by everlasting searching, a motif to become more important in his later works, especially *Moby-Dick.*

Borabolla and Jarl were as dissimilar as chemicals, "...hence the affinity. But as the affinity between those chemical opposites chlorine and hydrogen, is promoted by caloric; so the affinity between Borabolla and Jarl was promoted by the warmth of the wine that they drank at this feast" (Ch 95). In a controversy with Claude Berthollet (1748-1822), Joseph Louis Proust (1754-1826) supported a hypothesis that substances always combine in the same proportion by weight, forming specific compounds in the "rule of definite proportions" (1799). The controverly was ended by the appearance of the atomic theory, which encompassed the rule of definite proportions.[36] In the 1780s, Lavoisier and associates attempted to reform the nomenclature of chemistry to conform with philosophical principles free from any speculations about the nature of matter. Newly discovered elements were named according to their properties, i.e., hydrogen meant the generator of water, and oxygen the generator of acids.[37] In the early years of the century, John Dalton (1766-1844) introduced the atomic theory in chemistry, which gave a theoretical basis for definite proportions. J. J. Berzelius (1779-1848) in Sweden during the second decade of the nineteenth century made atomism more secure with 'isomerism' of chemical elements and 'isomorphism' of atoms in crystals. With the introduction of the principle of conservation of energy by Helmholtz in 1847, the whole range of physical sciences progressed more securely and began the age of "classical physics" with the extension of the principle to as many areas as possible and unifying many separate disciplines.[38] By the work of Priestley, Cavendish, and Lavoisier, the elemental water of the poets was demonstrated to be a compound of two gases. Lavoisier's great contribution to chemistry was to expand the known list of four "elements" of the Greeks to thirty-three in his 1789 textbook of chemistry. His list included oxygen, hydrogen, phosphorus, carbon, copper, and zinc. Humphry Davy, mentioned in several of Melville's works, was disabled for a time by an explosion while studying compounds of hydrogen and chlorine.[39] Earlier in *Mardi*, while adrift in the sea, the narrator notes that money is as worthless as "charcoal or diamonds. Nearly one and the same thing, say the chemists;...Ah! but these chemists are liars, and Sir Humphry Davy a cheat" (Ch 19).

Samoa was adept at surgery and replaces a severely fractured skull bone of an injured diver with a piece of "cocoa-nut shell." While all present admire Samoa's artistic skill, and Samoa complacently regards his workmanship, the diver is found to be dead. "The bystanders loudly lamented; but declared the surgeon a man of marvelous science" (Ch 96). Jaffe notes the source for Samoa's surgery is probably William Ellis's *Polynesian Researches* (1833). Ellis describes the operation of trepanning fractured skulls and replacing the removed bone with coconut shell.[40]

In many instances, Melville casts doubt on the reliability of the senses and the potential error of human reason:

> The higher the intelligence, the more faith, and the less credulity: Gabriel rejects more than we, but out-believes us all. The greatest marvels are first truths; and first truths the last unto which we attain. Things nearest are furthest off. Though your ear be next door to your brain, it is forever removed from your sight. Man has a more comprehensive view of the moon, than the man in the moon himself. We know the moon is round; he only infers it. It is because we ourselves are in ourselves, that we know ourselves not. And it is only of our easy faith, that we are not infidels throughout; and only of our lack of faith, that we believe what we do. (Ch 97)

Thus, point of view is as important as any feature of the observed. He implies that faith and reason are complementary and mutually exclusive qualities, concepts of modern physics discussed in Chapter 10. Babbalanja doubts the story, because if true, human reason could be put into a pig:

> I have long thought, that men, pigs and plants, are but curious physiological experiments; and that science would at last enable philosophers to produce new species of beings, by somehow mixing, and concocting the essential ingredients of various creatures; and so forming new combinations. My friend Atahalpa, the astrologer and alchemist, has long had a jar, in which he has been endeavouring to hatch a fairy, the ingredients being compounded according to a receipt of his own. (Ch 98)

Hybrids of man and animal were postulated by some naturalists and taken seriously. Such statements were heretical, defying the uniqueness of species and the special status of man. Ellis was probably also the source for the example of the brain transplant. In *Polynesian Researches*, Ellis relates that native surgeons have a pig ready in case the man's brain as well as bone has been injured; the surgeon has "taken out the pig's brains, put them into the man's head, and covered them up. They persist in stating that this has been done; but add, that the persons always became furious with madness and died."[41] The passage embodies Melville's skepticism towards the pretensions of science. According to Sealts, "Atahalpa" was a product of Melville's reading of Browne's *Religio Medici*; in the edition borrowed by Melville from Evert Duyckinck in 1848, a footnote to Part the First, Section XXXVI, referring to Paracelsus, cites Benjamin D'Israeli, who said:

> Paracelsus...offered to give birth to a fairy, and has sent down to posterity the recipe....fixed in a phial in fuming dung, will in due time settle into a full-grown fairy, bursting through its vitreous prison...There was a greatness of mind in Paracelsus, who, having furnished a recipe to make a fairy, had the delicacy to refrain...[42]

The idea of the scientist creating life was both preposterous and remotely possible. Newtonian theory unified the physical sciences, but not the life sciences. 'Vitalism,' prevalent in the later half of the eighteenth century, adhered to the notion that laws of living things were independent of the physical and chemical interrelations of nonliving things. Vitalism distinguished animate from inanimate matter; living organisms were not subject to the laws of physics. Chemical substances produced by living organisms were thought to be fundamentally different from organic matter a scientist could synthesize in a retort. Wöhler's synthesis of urea in 1812 destroyed the presumption of the uniqueness of life-substances and ended the idea of vitalism by showing that living creatures obey the same chemical laws as inorganic materials. Thereafter, the Newtonian method of mechanics was applied to the investigation of life processes seeking cause and effect relationships in living organisms. In medicine and physiology, with the idealization of Newton's mechanics as the method for all science, the body was likened to a complicated machine dependent on the movement of the smallest particles.[43] Samoa's "science" of surgery fails in paradise.

In 1836, the *Somerset County Gazette* published the remarkable experiment of Andrew Crosse, who was working with artificial crystals from silica and electricity. Crosse claimed life had been created when mites crawled from the apparatus, leading to an international sensation and accusations of Crosse as "a reviler of our holy religion." The event, the creation of life by electricity, was covered by *The Times* of London, then by hundreds of newspapers, magazines, and journals. In 1837, confirmation was attributed to Michael Faraday, although Faraday had not even attempted the experiment. He did his best to disassociate himself from the report to no avail; he was still invoked in this connection as late as 1879. Crosse was advised not to meddle further in his "obstetrico-galvanic apparatus."[44] The appearance of fully developed organisms such as algae, fungi, insects, parasitic worms, and bacteria, arising from inorganic matter, 'abiogenesis,' or arising from organic matter, 'heterogenesis,' was a crucial distinction in the debate of 'vitalism,' and whether it took place continuously or only in the distant past. The *chance* occurrence of new life implied an unlawful, accidental event which was antithetical to the concept of the universality of deterministic natural laws. In the seventeenth and eighteenth centuries, common sense observations held that spontaneous generation was a fact: eels from mud, fleas and lice appeared on the bodies of men, and parasitic worms arose internally. Yet, by the end of the seventeenth century, spontaneous generation was incompatible with the new scientific philosophy of mechanism. Belief in spontaneous generation collapsed. Previously, the mechanical philosophy of Descartes claimed that all that was necessary was to add heat, acting on putrefying matter, to form new organic life. Paracelsus had said that milk was the "mysterium" forming cheese, and cheese was the "mysterium" of maggots and worms; each in turn derived from the "Mysterium Magnum." The theory was strongly attacked by English naturalist John Ray (1627-1705) in *Wisdom of God manifested in the works of creation* (1691); once the origin of animal form reverted to God, any spontaneous generation was an act of God, yet creation ceased on the seventh day of Creation, so spontaneous generation was inconceivable on theological as well as scientific grounds. The role of worms in the spontaneous generation controversy was immense until the mid-nineteenth century. The triumphant return of spontaneous generation occurred during the first three decades of the nineteenth century, especially the spontaneous generation of infusorians and parasitic worms, particularly by the teaching of the German Romantic philosophers in the doctrine of *Naturphilosophie*, whose main proponent was Ernst Haeckel, seeking unity in nature. The idea of 'unity' in all of nature had profound implications: if nature is conceived as one vast and infinite life, an absolute death becomes inconceivable. Thus, spontaneous generation was a necessary element in *Naturphilosophie* whether from unorganized matter or matter from a living or dead organism. In spite of opposition in Britain, spontaneous generation was generally accepted until the life cycle of parasitic worms was dramatically demonstrated in 1851.[45] The confusion of generation of life is illustrated when the narrator says, "Wherefore it was, that many ignorant Mardians, who had not pushed their investigations into the science of physiology, sagely divined, that the Taparians must have podded into life like peas, instead of being otherwise indebted for their existence" (Ch 127).

Juxtaposed to a funeral, the idyll of the luxuriant grow of nature is set beside the scene of death: "Doth not all Nature rejoice in her green groves and her flowers" (Ch 99)? Blindness becomes a symbolic death in a deistic argument challenging his faith and doubt[46]:

> All, all is chaos! What is this shining light in heaven, this sun they tell me of? Or, do they lie? Methinks, it might blaze convictions; but I brood and grope in blackness; I am dumb with doubt; yet, 'tis not doubt, but worse: I doubt my doubt. Oh, ye all-wise spirits in the air, how can ye witness all this woe, and give no sign? Would, would that mine were a settled doubt, like that wild boy's,[47] who without faith seems full of it. The undoubting doubter believes the most. Oh! That I were he. (Ch 109)

The argument of design is followed by the argument of theism: "Gods glance in the eyes of birds, and sparkle in the crests of the waves; gods merrily swing in the boughs of the trees, and merrily sing in the brook. Gods are here, and there, and everywhere; you are never alone for them" (Ch 110). And he searches for man's place in the universe: at the temple of Oro (God), a boy is commanded to declare himself the "vilest creature that crawls." The boy replies:

> I love great Oro, though I comprehend him not. I marvel at his works, and feel as nothing in his sight; but because he is thus omnipotent, and I a mortal, it follows not that I am vile. Nor so doth he regard me. We do ourselves degrade ourselves, not Oro us. Hath not Oro made me? And therefore am I not worthy to stand erect before him?...But Oro knows my heart, which I cannot speak. (Ch 112)

The incomprehensibility of God, who is silent, can only be known in his 'works,' a deistic concept; man is degraded by a Calvinist God. The deception of the senses is repeated in Babbalanja's story of the blind men and the banyan tree (Ch 114).

In Chapter 118, Taji learns that Jarl and Samoa are dead. His human traveling companions—Annatoo, Jarl and Samoa—all dead, Taji continues his search in the company of his mythical wayfarers.

In the nineteenth century, the development of new units of measure and definition of elemental bodies produced a need for advanced mathematics. The exaggerated claims of progress and the mathematician's inflated jargon Melville reduces to absurdity. Media asks if Babbalanja has a statistical table: "...there must be at least three billion trillion of quintillions." "A mere unit!" said Babbalanja. "Old man, would you express an infinite number? Then take the sum of the follies of Mardi for your multiplicand; and for your multiplier, the totality of sublunarians," etc. (Ch 110). Mathematical statistics were founded on the work of Pierre Simon Laplace (1749-1827), French astronomer and mathematician, and Karl Friedrick Gauss (1777-1855), German astronomer and mathematician. A number of long standing algebraic equations were solved in the early nineteenth century by the work of many mathematicians.

In a number of instances, Melville utilizes metempsychosis for philosophical purposes and includes a generous amount of science at the same time. Beginning with astronomy and geology, the narrator muses:

> [L]ike a frigate, I am full with a thousand souls;...Shoals, like nebulous vapors, shoreing the white reef of the Milky Way, against which the wrecked worlds are dashed; strowing all the strand, with their Himmaleh keels and ribs....
>
> Sometimes, when these Atlantics and Pacifics thus undulate round me, I lie stretched out in their midst: a land-locked Mediterranean, knowing no ebb, nor flow. Then again, I am dashed in the spray of these sounds: an eagle at the world's end, tossed skyward, on the horns of the tempest....
>
> In me, many worthies recline and converse....
>
> Yet not I, but another: God is my Lord; and though many satellites revolve around me, I and all mine revolve round the great central Truth, sun-like, fixed and luminous forever in the foundationless firmament. (Ch 119)

Yet, he may be eternal like the sun in many resurrections, but concludes, "my own mad brood of eagles devours me," alluding to the myth of Prometheus, the hubris of man to control nature for his own ambition; fever runs through his brain "like lava," not to be envied in this heliocentric example.

In Chapter 121, "They Regale Themselves with Their Pipes," Melville presents a taxonomic discussion of pipes and tobaccos, naming many types of each, with historical items, and fanciful sources of tobacco. They digress into the origin of amber, such as "gold fishes brains," then follow with a discussion of ambergris. Davis observes that the satire of ambergris is a close parallel of Ephraim Chambers's *Cyclopedia: or, An Universal Dictionary of Arts and Sciences* (1742). Chambers mentions Pliny and Boerhaave, whose names Melville changed to "Ancient Plinnee" and "Borhavo." Herman Boerhaave (1668-1738) was a physician at Leyden, the most famous teacher of medicine in Europe, best known for his *Aphorismi*, or *Aphorisms on the diagnosis and treatment of diseases*.[48]

In Chapter 122, "They Visit an Extraordinary Old Antiquarian," who goes by the name Oh-Oh, "by reason of the delighted interjections, with which he welcomed all accessions to his museum." Oh-Oh has a remarkable nose and a humped back. In his museum reside a strange assortment of bones, skeletons, shells, "Mermaids Hair," "Files, Rasps, and Pincers, all bone, the implements of an eminent Chiropodist, who flourished his tools before the flood." Oh-Oh's penchant for minute scientific observation, according to Melville, is not only useless, but destructive: "[his] famous telescope, by help of which, he said he had discovered an ant-hill on the moon. It rested in the crotch of a breadfruit tree; and was a prodigiously long and hollow trunk of a Palm, a scale from a sea-kraken its lens," undoubtedly a reference to the remarkable telescope of William Herschel discussed in *Moby-Dick* (Chapter 74). "[A] bamboo microscope, which had wonderfully assisted him in his entomological pursuits" and "scientific purposes" confirms divine design as well as its folly:

> "By this instrument,...in the eye of a dragon-fly there are precisely twelve thousand five hundred and forty-one triangular lenses; and in the leg of a flea, scores on scores of distinct muscles....And one of the greatest consolations I draw from these studies, is the ever-strengthening conviction of the beneficent wisdom that framed our Mardi...."
>
> "But Oh-Oh," said Babbalanja, "what other discoveries have you made? Hast put a usurer under your lens, to find his conscience? or a libertine, to find his heart? Hast yet brought your microscope to bear upon a downy peach, or a rosy cheek?"
>
> "I have," said Oh-Oh, mournfully; "and from the moment I so did, I have had no heart to eat a peach, or salute a cheek."
>
> "Then dash your lens!" cried Media.
>
> "Well said, my lord. For all the eyes we get beyond our own, but minister to infidelity. The microscope disgusts us with our Mardi; and the telescope sets us longing for some other world." (Ch 122)

If the seventeenth century marked the birth of modern science, the invention of the telescope about 1608 in Holland is the prototype of modern scientific instruments, the first to extend human senses.[49] The scientist is portrayed as ugly and misshapen. Melville says science debases beauty with its absurd quantifying and counting. The microscope fails to aid in human concerns.

The Isle of Fossils looks like a black whale's hump in blue water fringed with ferns sprouting from clefts and thin soil gradually washing into the lagoon much like the Galápagos Islands where Melville visited aboard the whaleship *Acushnet* in 1841. In 1835, Darwin visited the Galápagos Islands creating interest in the islands when he published *Journal of Researches* (1839). The book was in the library of the man-of-war *United States* when Melville was a member of the crew in 1843-1844.[50] The voyage of the *Beagle* was not entirely the pursuit of scientific specimens, but also to gain geographical and meteorological knowledge necessary for the possession of sea power.[51] In the listing of fossils and relics in a long procession to "guanos, serpents, tongueless crocodiles" (Ch 132), Melville acknowledges the extinction of species suspected by Linnaeus at the end of the eighteenth century, but the theory did not gain acceptance until later in the nineteenth century. The philosopher says these are the "leaves of the book of Oro," (i.e., words or works of God). In the fossils we read how worlds are made, along with the rise and fall of nature's kingdoms, the start of man's furthest histories, and the secret memoirs of times past: "tombs burst open by volcanic throes; and hither hurled from the lowermost vaults of the lagoon. All Mardi's rocks are one wide resurrection" (Ch 132). The stone fossils record the antiquity of man's treachery: "a monarch fossilized in very act of murdering his guest" at a stately banquet. The study of natural history had shifted from fossil shells to fossil bones of vertebrates, and here to the fossils of man. On another side of the island the travelers are asked to settle a dispute of the origin of a three-toed fossil footprint (Ch 132):

> Upon a long layer of the slaty stone were marks of ripplings of some now waveless sea; mid which were tri-toed foot-prints of some huge heron, or wading fowl.
>
> Pointing to one of which, the foremost disputant thus spoke, "I maintain that these are three toes."
>
> "And I, that it is one foot," said the other. (Ch 132)

The dispute becomes became a contentious argument; Babbalanja says, "Is not this the very question concerning which they made such dire contention in Maramma, whose tertiary rocks are chiseled all over with these marks" (Ch 132)? The Tertiary period of geology corresponds to a period one million to 70 million years ago characterized by the introduction of mammals other than man, whales, and flowering plants. The term was used by Lyell and Brongniart in 1801 for fossil deposits of the Paris basin. The fossil remains produce a circular argument employing mathematics, a jibe at scientist's attempts to explain natural phenomena and the alteration of the surface of the earth.

The origin of the coral islands puzzled naturalists as they explored the South Seas. Here, the narrator gives a fable that might solve the mystery:

> In old times of genii and giants, there dwelt in barren lands, not very remote from our outer reef, but since submerged, a band of evil-minded, envious goblins, furlongs in stature, and with immeasurable arms; who from time to time cast covetous glances upon our blooming isles. Long they lusted; till at last they waded through the sea, strode over the reef, and seizing the nearest islet, rolled it over and over, toward an adjoining outlet. (Ch 69)

And he gives another fable-explanation: that the island lagoons of Ohonoo were made by the genii who saw the wickedness of the people and knocked the top of the mountains off as he went. "These here and there fell into the lagoon, forming many isles, now green and luxuriant; which, with those sprouting from seeds dropped by a bird from the moon, comprise all the groups in the reef" (Ch 90). Babbalanja explains how Mardi was formed by including the geological controversy of the nineteenth century: the formation of coral islands taken from the "leaves of the book of Oro" in fossils, and the theory of Vulcanism:

> The coral wall which circumscribes the isles but continues upward the deep buried crater of the primal chaos. In the first times this crucible was charged with vapors nebulous, boiling over fires volcanic. Age by age, the fluid thickened; dropping, at long intervals, heavy sediment to the bottom; which layer on layer concreted, and at length, in crusts, rose toward the surface. Then, the vast volcano burst; rent the whole mass; upthrew the ancient rocks; which now in divers mountain tops tell the tale of what existed ere Mardi was completely fashioned. Hence many fossils on the hills, whose kith and kin still lurk beneath the vales. Thus

> Nature works, at random warring, chaos a crater, and this world a shell. (Ch 132)

Marine fossils found on mountaintops were a perplexing phenomenon, but they were thought to be evidence of the great flood of Neptunism. Prior to the nineteenth century, geological observations, largely restricted to Europe, were haphazard and infrequent. By the seventeenth century, hints of geological antiquity arose. Ray suspected that the rise of the mountains, if not present at Creation, must have taken much longer than a few thousand years of biblical time, and cautiously speculated that certain fossil shells may be the remains of extinct species. If the age of the earth was correct, changes present in the world must have occurred by great upheavels, or catastrophes under supernatural control. The concept of "catastrophism" allowed the expansion of the world's time without offending the church. Catastrophism held that life was recreated after each global catastrophe. Nicolas Desmarest (1726-1815), French geologist, found evidence of extensive volcanic activity in Europe and that rock associated with volcanic activity was basalt of igneous origin (i.e., from molten magma).[52] Geological discoveries in the eighteenth century, such as the finding of the fossil remains of extinct animals, cast doubt on the creation myth of the origin of the earth and its inhabitants. As Enlightenment materialist philosophers became bolder in their attacks on traditional religion, they searched for explanations on how life began on earth without supernatural origin. The only plausible explanations available to them were spontaneous generation and the transmutation of existing forms due to environmental causes.[53]

Darwin was greatly impressed by the destructive effect of the 1835 earthquake in Concepcion, Chile, and noted at the same time that the coastline rose ten feet from its original level; beaches still lined with shells were raised above sea level, and that fossils of the Tertiary period similar to living species were present but covered with a considerable thickness of overlying rock which showed that they had been carried to great depth. Over extended time, such events could raise and lower the surface of the earth to a significant extent, and could cause large scale changes including the building of a mountain range. He proposed a theory on the formation of coral reefs (1842) by the gradual subsidence of the ocean floor. Coral is formed by minute sea creatures that can live only in fairly shallow water—no more than about 150 feet. Darwin assumed that reefs are formed as the land subsides and must occur gradually if the coral organisms are not to be killed by submersion.[54] The theory of the origin of coral islands occurs again in *Moby-Dick* when the whaleboat is swamped: "There we sat up to our knees in the sea, the water covering every rib and plank, so that to our downward gazing eyes the suspended craft seemed a coral boat grown up to us from the bottom of the ocean" (Ch 48).

The first scientist to visit linear island groups in the Pacific was James Dwight Dana in 1838-1842. Darwin had crossed the Pacific a few years earlier, but stopped only at the non-linearly arranged Galápagos Islands and at Tahiti. Dana observed that the Society, Samoan, and Hawaiian islands are all in lines trending towards the northwest, and each shows a progression with age, then barrier reefs, and beyond were atolls of still greater age. When Dana reached Australia, he learned from a newspaper account that Darwin had just announced in London his now-celebrated theory of the origin of atolls. Dana had found the entire Darwinian age sequence in a single linear archipelago—from active volcano to atoll! Dana proposed that these island chains were arranged along a fault, presumably caused by some widespread break in the earth's crust. Darwin's theory of the origin of atolls has been proved by drilling, the discovery of guyots, or "drowned ancient islands" by Harry H. Hess, and evidence from dredging of the atolls' sea floor during the early 1960s. Darwin had only deduced the existence of guyots, but by 1960 guyots were found to be widespread. The theory of sea floor spreading was finally proven in 1965.[55]

Neptunism, the other principal theory of the formation of the earth, opposed to Vulcanism, had wide support in Britain at the beginning of the nineteenth century, but the formation of the Royal Geological Society in London in 1807 stimulated empirical study, eventually leading to the theory of catastrophism. Few could believe that earthquakes could raise a mountain range, or that a river could erode a large valley. Thus, the catastrophists proposed sudden upheavals to explain the raising of mountain ranges, and tidal waves capable of immense erosion in great floods. Not until the 1840s did an alternative explanation based on the study of glaciers occur.[56]

Benoit de Maillet (1656-1738), a French government official and not a scientist, published a fanciful book on the natural world pursuing the discovery of fossils of species no longer in existence, *Telliamed* (published in 1748, but probably written between 1692 and 1718). He suggested a "retreating ocean" theory that gained wide popularity in the eighteenth century, but few compromised their belief in Genesis because the process required a vast prehuman time span.[57] De Maillet speculated that the finding of marine fossil shells on mountaintops was possibly due to a universal flood. Fossils, he said, were "the most Ancient Library in the World"; Melville calls fossils the "leaves of the book of Oro," i.e., that fossils are the evidence of God in the development of nature. According to de Maillet, the shrinking water of the world occurred by Descartes's theory of vortices. He challenged the belief that life in the sea cannot be transformed into life on land and thought that the transformation was continuous. He considered that life on land duplicated life in the sea, although certain species of amphibians may be transitional between the two. Similarly, Melville says, "And slow sailing overhead were flights of birds, a wing in the air for every fin in the sea" (Ch 48). Browne wrote in *Vulgar Errors*, "That all animals of the land, are in their kind in the sea," but he argues against the idea.[58] De Maillet postulated the mutability and change of the surface of the earth. The book was popular in England and, though fiction, may have stimulated inquiry into his unorthodox ideas. About this time, the importance of vertebrate bones replaced the study of fossil shells. Melville's nebulous vapors from volcanic fires of primal chaos probably refers to the Cartesian theory of the origin of the earth from a vortex of cosmic matter.

Cuvier's study of fossil bones from remote parts of the world (1812) became the foundation of modern paleontology. The wooly mammoth from Siberia, and the mastodon from America—a strange type of elephant whose teeth resembled those of the hippopotamus—were at the center of the controversy. These creatures were thought to still exist somewhere in the world, but eventually were acknowledged as extinct species. The search for fossil bones extended over most of the world leading to the discovery of fossils in successive geological layers according to time: the older were found in the deeper layers of earth strata. Cuvier and Alexandre Brongniart used marine invertebrates to establish distinctions between successive formations; the older the deposits the more bizarre the vertebrate fossils and less similar they were to present-day forms. Ancient species proved to be just as complex and well-balanced in their structure as living forms, confirming Cuvier's idea that each species is a functional whole that cannot tolerate significant variation. In addition, French expeditions to Africa returned with mummified animals thousands of years old that were identical to living species, which established to Cuvier the stability of species and the extinction of ancient forms. Exploration of the Paris basin revealed an alternating of deposits caused by fresh and salt water flooding indicating a series of major changes in the relative positions of the land and sea that appeared to be abrupt, supporting the concept of catastrophism by geological upheavals as the cause of extinction. Cuvier allowed that supernatural creation may have occurred at the beginning of the Tertiary period when he supposed that all mammals were introduced simultaneously, but he remained implacably opposed to transmutation of species.[59]

James Hutton (1726-1797), Scottish geologist who studied medicine in Edinburgh and Paris, published *Theory of the Earth* (1785), applying the idea of infinite space in astronomy to the concept of time. Hutton challenged the doctrine of the great flood; instead, he postulated that dynamic forces in the earth elevated new lands from the ocean while exposed surfaces were subjected to erosion. Thus, the world itself is a living earth, decaying and renewing. He concluded, "...we find no vestige of a beginning,—no prospect of an end," a position in direct opposition to catastrophism; changes in the earth occur independent of supernatural influence. Hutton's genius was not recognized until much later. His reward was animosity, charges of heresy, and eventually, silence. Hutton's ideas were expressed in such a convoluted and prolix style, he would have been forgotten had not his friend John Playfair presented Hutton's works in an elegantly written treatise in 1802. Charles Lyell (1797-1875), a lawyer who became a geologist, wrote *Principles of Geology* (1835), incorporating the possibility of unlimited time and natural forces in geology; over enough time, changes in the earth could occur without global catastrophes. The concept of 'struggle for existence' was developed by Lyell, who observed that unhealthy plants are choked and destroyed by healthy plants. Melville's account incorporates both the gradual formation of the earth, or uniformitarianism, and catastrophism. Catastrophism adhered more closely to religious views since events could be compressed into the few thousand years of biblical time.[60]

Melville's theory of the changing earth has a long history. Thales of Miletus (?640-550 B.C.), an astronomer, was the first to attempt a purely naturalistic interpretation of the cosmos. He proposed that the sun and moon were not gods, but fiery bodies. He proposed that behind the multiplicity of phenomenon was one universal material—water—from which all things metamorphosed. By predicting the eclipse of the sun on May 28, 585 B.C., he excited the Greeks to a curiosity in the art of calculation and a respect for numbers. The school of *physiologoi* (from the "nature of knowledge") was formed. His young associate, Anaximander (611-547 B.C.), conceived that life had been formed in the water and driven onto land where it underwent further change. Thus, the phenomenon of 'change' was fundamental to nature. The order of nature, the forces that kept the stars in their courses and maintained harmony of motion, was attributed to *logos*, which led to the physical idea of 'natural law.' That a cause, or causality, was required was first explicitly stated by Leucippus of Miletus (ca 450 B.C.), or by necessity according to the nature of the thing. Democritus of Thrace (ca 470 B.C.) framed the doctrine of causality in terms of natural 'laws' by distinguishing between a substance and its qualities, (such as color, taste, temperature) and consisting of indivisible, eternal atoms immersed in an infinite void or vacuum. He conceived of a universe where worlds are born, grow, decay and perish. The *physiologoi* dismissed the gods as barbaric superstition, and were branded as atheists. Many were banished. In 399 B.C., Socrates was executed for denying the existence of the gods. Pythagoras, a mathematician, along with Thales, is supposed to have contributed much that appears in the first six books of Euclid. Mathematics became a medium for establishing communion with the gods; the mathematician-priests of Egypt and Babylonia were the chief spokesmen for the divinities. That Aristotle should call Pythagoras a 'theologian' shows that the Greek heavens were no exception. Pythagoras established the importance of 'limit' in numbers that are the essence of limit and order. Lucretius's *De Rerum Natura* was called the most rationalistic document of ancient times, but was condemned in favor of the worship of gods.[61]

In several instances, the narrator refers to a developing geological concept in a metaphorical sense: Jarl consumed Indian weed (tobacco), the bottom was compacted with a dark variety, "fossil-marked, like the primary stratum of the geologist" (Ch 17); and refers to "Donjalolo, absolute monarch of Juam—the husk-enhusked meat in a nut;...the ensphered sphere of spheres" (Ch 79); leading to the second theory of the origin of the earth which takes into account the rapid discoveries in geology during the end of the eighteenth century and the beginning of the nineteenth century: "the celebrated sandwich System," i.e., rock strata as a result of a universal flood:

> "Nature's first condition was a soup, wherein the agglomerating solids formed granitic dumplings, which, wearing down, deposited the primal stratum made up of a series, sandwiching strange shapes of mollusks, and zoophytes; then snails and periwinkles...And next, my lord, we have the fine old time of the Old Red Sandstone sandwich, clapped on the underlying layer, and among other dainties, imbedding the first course of fish...Now comes the New Red Sandstone sandwich: marly and magnesious, spread over with old patriarches of crocodiles and alligators..."
>
> "What next?" cried Media.
>
> "The Ool, or Oily sandwich:—rare gormandizing then; for oily it was called, because of fat old joints, and hams, and rounds, and barons of seabeeves and walrusses, which then crowned the

> stratum-board.... And all these sandwiched right over all that went before.... Next the Chalk, or Coral sandwich...eocene, miocene, and pliocene. The first was wild game for the delicate...The second side-course—miocene—was out of course, flesh after fowl:—marine mammalia.... The third side course, the pliocene, was goodliest of all:—whole-roasted elephants, rhinoceroses, and hippopotamuses... We Mardians famish on the superficial strata of deposits; cracking our jaws on walnuts, filberts, cocoa-nuts, and clams."
>
> "And bravely done it is. Mohi tells us, that Mardi was made in six days; but you, Babbalanja, have built it up from the bottom in less than six minutes."
>
> "Nothing for us geologists, my lord. At a word we turn you out whole systems, suns, satellites, and asteroids included." (Ch 132)

The Old Red Sandstone undoubtedly makes reference to Hugh Miller's *The Old Red Sandstone* (1841), a collection of articles, describing his geological discoveries in Cromarty, Scotland. Miller was a stone mason and lay theologian who studied the Old Sandstone formations which captured the attention of Murchison at Oxford, and Agassiz, who was still in Switzerland. He was even more famous for his *Footprints of the Creator* (1849), an enthusiastic and amateurish work on the design and fixity of species. The Old Red Sandstone formation is one of the least interesting geological formations to be found, but Miller's lucid, homely style made his book known in every Victorian parlor and made geology lively and sensuous.[62] The Neptunian theory of the great flood was supported by many prominent authorities, especially Abraham Werner. The theory was later discarded, but it had strong adherents, including Goethe, because it pictured nature as serene, complete, and perfect from the beginning of time. The Neptunian theory of Buffon, and later Hutton, was the basis of the "Sandwich system" Melville used humorously in *Mardi.* Melville's account of the theory is amazingly accurate, placing the fossils in the correct rock strata. He uses the same terminology as Lyell, although he skips some of the layers to shorten the "banquet," yet he uses all of the characteristic rocks of each geological period with only two errors: placing the "seabeeves and walruses" in the Oolite period. The error was probably due to his source, since it agreed with Cuvier and other reputable geologists. Lyell corrected his mistake after the rocks were reclassified by Sir Richard Owen. The error was still present in Chambers's *Vestiges* in 1846. The second error was placing the Eocene, Miocene, and Pliocene periods in the Secondary division of geological time when they are properly included in the Tertiary period.[63]

Abraham Gottlob Werner (1750-1817), a German geologist and founder of the Neptunian theory of the origin of rocks (1777), whose interest in geological layers provided a background for William Smith (1769-1839), who introduced the concept that rock strata can be identified by the fossils imbedded in the layers of rock, and that in superimposed strata, the deeper levels are the oldest. Smith, a surveyor and engineer in great demand in the industrialization of England for constructing canals, became a "practical field geologist." Smith observed that each strata contains distinct organic ingredients. He outlined them in *The Strati-graphical System of Organized Fossils* (1817), but to avoid offending religious orthodoxy, maintained that each layer must have been formed by a catastrophe. The result was to effectively expand the concept of time—one of the most radical changes in man's outlook ever to occur. The two main theories of Creation, then, were the Neptunian—the great flood, and the Plutonian—the coalescence of a fireball. Melville's humorous allusions to the serious and most publicized scientific discoveries of the century illustrate his irreverence for the bland scientists and their exaggerated claims of progress. He refers to specific geological periods and the succession of development of more complex species in the more superficial, recent strata, or more recent time; the appearance of new species occurring with passage of time was contrary to the accepted concept that all creatures were formed at once at Creation. In the following chapter, Melville alludes to mutability of species, "...at last your Mardian lions lose their caudal horns" (Ch 133). John Mason Good's *The Book of Nature* (1836), may have been his source of geology, and the refutation of the Plutonian view used in *Mardi*. Both the Plutonian and the Neptunian theories were included in Good. In addition, Robert Chambers's *Vestiges of the Natural History of Creation*, as shown by Hillway, may have been a source of Melville's stratum theory. Chambers, who was not a professional scientist, put together the isolated parts of Hutton, Smith, and Cuvier and stated his idea of organic as well as cosmic development. The "Leaves of the Book of Oro" probably came from Chambers, for passages are very similar, with Melville adding humor.[64] Whewell had referred to the rocks of the world as the "geological alphabet." Once the succession of strata was found to be universal, English geologists quickly concluded that earth strata held the "records of creation," and fossils were valued as markers of past forms of life. In 1843, Murchison concluded: "...from the dawn of existing races, we ascend through successive deposits gradually becoming more analogous to those of the present day, until at length we reach the bottoms of oceans so recently desiccated, that their shelly remains are indistinguishable from those now associated with Man, the last created in this long chain of animal life in which scarcely a link is wanting!—all bespeaking a perfection and grandeur of design, in contemplating which we are lost in admiration of creative power." [65]

Later in the book, Yoomy, the poet, reflects on the new concepts of the heavens and earth—astronomical infinity, and new stratigraphic discoveries in geology: "Now, heaven over heaven in the skies; now layer under layer in the dust" (Ch 170); the philosopher points out that the poet is not qualified in "sciences" (Ch 171). William Smith was the first to observe the unvarying sequence of fossils, that the descent into the earth is a descent into the earth's remote history, and that each strata has its characteristic fossils: "the earth is formed as well as governed, like the other works of its great Creator, according to regular and immutable laws, which are discoverable by human industry and observation." He was unaware of his break with the creation account of Genesis. He saw each layer and its fossils as made by God, but unrelated; each an act of separate creation, not a single biblical Creation. By degrees, geology became autonomous and secular, and the biblical account came to have less and less explanatory significance. Still, life had a separate, mysterious significance that could only have been brought about by a supernatural agent, and man transcended nature.[66]

The travelers ask the philosopher what lies beyond the ocean. He replies that there may be other regions unknown to Mardians:

> Braid Beard, those strangers, that came to Mondoldo prove isles afar, as a philosopher of old surmised, but was hooted at for his surmisings. Nor is it at all impossible, Braid Beard, that beyond their land may exist other regions, of which those strangers know not; peopled with races something like us Mardians; but perhaps with more exalted faculties, and organs that we lack. They may have some better seeing sense than ours; perhaps have fins or wings for arms. (Ch 133)

Benoit de Maillet provided one of the theories to dispense with creation and the deluge. He postulated a version of the germ theory as the beginning of life with gradual modification into the species observed on the earth. The first members of each species had to be an aquatic form, and evolved into a terrestrial form once land formed; he claimed external conditions had an effect upon a species. He eliminated the miracles and partly circumvented the design argument.[67]

The travelers doubt his crazy hypothesis; the philosopher replies, "and are all inductions vain?...Have we mortals naught to rest on, but what we see with our eyes? Is no faith to be reposed in that inner microcosm, wherein we see the charted universe in little, as the whole horizon is mirrored in the iris of a gnat" (Ch 133)? He doubts man's ability to solve the puzzle of the universe with his senses, or the concept of the positivism of Auguste Comte discussed in a later chapter. The idea of the conversation about the inner microcosm surely was derived from Browne's *Religio Medici* (1635). Browne said, "...there is all Africa and her prodigies within us"; a theme Melville later states as "deep diving" or introspection.

While becalmed, one of the crew meets with a serious accident falling from the crow's nest to the deck without inducement or volition; they wonder what brought such a careless being into Mardi:

> "A long course of generations. He's some one's great-great-grandson, doubtless; who was great-great-grandson to some one else; who also had grandsires."
>
> "Many thanks then to your highness; for you establish the doctrine of Philosophical Necessity."
>
> "No. I establish nothing; I but answer your questions."
>
> "All one, my lord; you are a Necessitarian; in other words, you hold that everything takes place through absolute necessity." (Ch 135)

An accident seems inexplicable, except by fate, or determined by inheritance. Melville's argument includes Priestley's *The Doctrine of Philosophical Necessity* (1777). In addition to science, Priestley wrote on experimental investigation, the history of science, philosophy, education, and political theory. In philosophy, his *Disquisitions Relating to Matter and Spirit* (1777) emphasized the importance of matter in spiritual considerations. *The Doctrine of Philosophical Necessity*, opposed the idea of free will as theologically objectionable, metaphysically incomprehensible and morally undesirable. He denied the existence of a human soul separate from the body, rejected the doctrines of the divinity and preexistence of Christ, and of atonement. Davis suggests that the parody of *Philosophical Necessity* was provoked by the conflict over Priestley's ideas between David Hartley's *Observations on Man,* and Coleridge's *Biographica Literaria.*[68] Babbalanja explains:

> ...Fatalism presumes express and irrevocable edicts of heaven concerning particular events. Whereas, Necessity holds that all events are naturally linked, and inevitably follow each other, without providential interposition, though by the eternal letting of Providence. (Ch 135)

Watters argues that Melville's fatalism implies a process toward a predestined end, or miraculous supernaturalism, with necessitarianism being a process from an initial cause or scientific determinism: "In their absolute form both, on different premises, deny free will." Watters concludes that Melville favored necessitarianism, or scientific determinism, because he could see no evidence of a final purpose.[69] Yet, Melville was a critic of science and scientists, arriving at no conclusion: as Babbalanja says, the closest one can get to the meaning of human life is that the question itself is "more final than any answer" (Ch 93). He continues with a restatement of an Aristotelian world view:

> Then, if that be absolutely so, Oro is not merely a universal onlooker, but occupies and fills all space; and no vacancy is left for any being or any thing but Oro. Hence, Oro is *in* all things, and himself *is* all things—the time-old creed. But since evil abounds, and Oro is all things, then he cannot be perfectly good; wherefore, Oro's omnipresence and moral perfection seem incompatible. Furthermore, my lord, those orthodox systems which ascribe to Oro almighty and universal attributes every way, those systems, I say, destroy all intellectual individualities but Oro and resolve the universe into him. But this is a heresy; wherefore, orthodoxy and heresy are one.
>
> ...Let us be content with the theology in the grass and the flower, in seedtime and harvest. Be it enough for us to know that Oro indubitably is. (Ch 135)

Melville appears to be stating the Renaissance world view of the goodness of nature and that nature is the evidence of the existence of God as stated by Paley in 1802:

> ...if one train of thinking be more desirable than another, it is that which regards the phenomena of nature with a constant reference to a supreme intelligent Author....The world thenceforth becomes a temple, and life itself one continued act of adoration. The change is no less than this: that whereas formerly God was seldom in our

> thoughts, we can now scarcely look upon anything without perceiving its relation to him.... Under this stupendous Being we live. Our happiness, our existence, is in his hand.... We have no reason to fear, therefore, our being forgotten, or overlooked, or neglected.[70]

The argument is one of theism, that God is ever-present and ever-caring.

Babbalanja illustrates the conflict of necessity versus fate and free will with a curious story after further discussion, "Your Highness," said Mohi, "this whole discourse seems to have grown out of the subject of Necessity and Free Will. Now, when a boy, I recollect hearing a sage say that these things were reconcilable." For instance, a king had a fool who strictly obeyed the king, but thought himself free. The fool says he wishes to walk on his hands: "But soon, his bottled blood so rushed downward through his neck, that he was fain to turn a somerset and regain has feet. Said he, 'Though I am free to do it, its not easy turning digits into toes; I'll walk, by gad! which is my other option'" (Ch 135). Physiology or anatomy are not entirely subject to free will, and limit choice.

Yoomy startles from a dream after a heavy meal; the philosopher is puzzled by his alarm and says:

> Do our dreams come from below, and not from the skies? Are we angels, or dogs? Oh, Man, Man, Man! thou art harder to solve, than the Integral Calculus—plain as a primer; harder to find than the philosopher's-stone—yet ever at hand; a more cunning compound, than an alchemist's.... (Ch 136)

Dreams play an important role in Melville's novels. In this instance, Melville stands apart from the dream to wonder about the nature of man. Is man another atomic, mathematically divisible being, or a spiritual creature defying both science and superstition? Until the nineteenth century, man was a spiritual as well as a physical being; the examination of nature produced evidence to prove the design of God. But with the description of units of matter and new measuring techniques introduced by men whose names are immortalized by the units named after them—Volta, Gauss, Ampere, Faraday, etc.—and the advance of mathematics linked more closely to natural science, some scientists claimed to have found the very main spring of the universe—that man had at last discovered God and that man was a mere physical being.[71] The philosopher's stone was a dream of the alchemists, an imaginary substance or preparation believed to be capable of transmuting baser metals such as lead, into gold, or silver, or into substances that prolong life. The integral calculus, capitalized to give it an inflated significance, was developed independently in the seventeenth century by Leibniz and Newton.

Babbalanja suggests that the world would be the same with or without God, similar to the argument that whether two and two would be four did not depend on the existence of a deity, saying:

> My lord, nature is an immaculate virgin, forever standing unrobed before us. True poets but paint the charms which all eyes behold. The vicious would be vicious without them. (Ch 137)

The narrator suggests that the earth cannot accommodate all of its inhabitants (which has important social and philosophical implications), saying:

> And well knowing this, nature has provided this jolly round board, our globe, which in an endless sequence of courses and crops, spreads a perpetual feast. Though, as with most public banquets, there is no small crowding, and many go away famished from plenty. (Ch 55)

He continues this theme by noting that the Isle of Diranda, according to Mohi the historian, was divided between two kings who calculated by "a sort of arithmetical progression," because of the fertility of the people, that the island would become so crowded the people would "inhale choke-damp for air and have not a private corner to say thy prayers." One king was concerned that overpopulation might "denude of herbage his portion of the island" (Ch 138). The kings were content with the tranquil times and did not relish picking war with their neighbors "and running its risks, in order to phlebotomize his redundant population." An advisor to the king urged patience, that "haply a pestilence may decimate the people....But no pestilence came. And in every direction the young men and maidens were recklessly rushing into wedlock; and so salubrious was the climate that the old men stuck to the outside of the turf, and refused to go under." A "Machiavel of a philosopher" suggested the object of war might be achieved without going to war—games so violent as to voluntarily kill off participants peaceably and stabilizing the population without troubling the kings. Babbalanja, the philosopher, continues the argument:

> "Come on, I say, for who shall stay ye? Come on, and healthfulize the census!...Cracked our crowns by nature, and henceforth forever, cracked shall they be by hard raps."
>
> "And hopelessly cracked the skull, that hatched such a tirade of nonsense," said Mohi. (Ch 138)

Thomas Malthus (1766-1834), English clergyman and economist, said in *Essays on the Principles of Population* (1798), that a population will tend to outrun its growth of food production because population increases geometrically and production arithmetically. He postulated a "struggle for existence" and artificial selection of species through selective breeding, ideas that greatly influenced nineteenth century naturalists. The old idea of a static, harmoniously designed balance of nature was being replaced by the concept of the ecological "niche" that each species exploits within its environment, which changes over time. The environment could not be uniform over a large area, thus species could not be adapted perfectly to a given area. Darwin saw that one area might favor one species over another, while a short distance away another species might be favored, and in between the two may be struggling to occupy territory open to either species, an idea taken from Lyell. Lyell quoted botanist Alephonse de Candolle, that all species in a given area are at war with one another. He concluded the most bitter competition in nature is not between a species and its food supply or its predators, but between a species and its closest ecological rivals.[72] Mohi, the historian, insists the warring of man to be natural and will not cease until the arms of war are removed. The kings dealt with the Malthusian notion of overpopulation by war games since the natural forces of fertility, longevity, and lack of disease accelerated the problem. The 'cracked' ideas of the Machiavellian philosopher were soundly denounced by Mohi, the poet.

The "war of nature," as conceived by Lamarck and Erasmus Darwin, was a fundamental idea leading to the concept of adaptation of animals to their environment. Extending the "war of nature" to man was a statement few naturalists were courageous enough to make. Jean Baptiste Lamarck (1744-1829), French naturalist who studied medicine in Paris, theorized that physiologic need will stimulate new organs or alter old ones; disuse will promote their loss. Change, or adaptation, occurred for the purpose of perfecting Creation. A change in need changes behavior which alters habits and by slow degrees alters body structure; thus, a "striving" of the organism for adjustment and toward perfection. Organic divergence was thought circumscribed about a norm, preserving the belief in fixity of species. Lamarck stated, "...it is the stronger and the better equipped that eat the weaker, and that the larger species devour the smaller." Lamarck and Erasmus Darwin (1731-1802) proposed the concept of the persistent adjustment of the animal to its environment in a "war of nature" (Ch 132) as noted by Melville.[73]

In Chapter 143, "Wherein Babbalanja Discourses of Himself," a humorous masterwork of philosophy, Babbalanja points to the rising sun and says:

> ...the astronomers maintain that Mardi moves around the sun; which I, who never formally investigated the matter for myself, can by no means credit; unless, plainly seeing one thing, I blindly believe another. Yet even thus blindly does all Mardi subscribe to an astronomical system, which not one in fifty thousand can astronomically prove. And not many centuries back, my lord, all Mardi did equally subscribe to an astronomical system, precisely the reverse of that which they now believe.... And thus, my lord, is it, that the mass of Mardians do not believe because they know, but because they know *not.* And they are as ready to receive one thing as another, if it comes from a canonical source. (Ch 143)

The reliability of the senses was emphasized by the positivism of Comte, but Melville observes that the senses can deceive and that interpretation requires an inference. Aristotle was able to adduce the spherical shape of the earth by observing the varying position of stars, the stars that never set, and the shadow cast by the earth in eclipse of the moon, yet it contradicted the 'common sense' observation that the earth is flat. By measuring the altitude of a star from different latitudes, he was able to estimate the circumference of the earth by simple arithmetic; his estimate was too great by a factor of two, but he demonstrated that such calculations were within the reach of mathematical science, and that science was able to demonstrate conclusions completely opposed to common sense.[74] Copernicus's *De revolutionibus orbium caelestium* (1543) became a revolutionary work in that it stimulated a new focus of inquiry. In the preface he says he came to conceive such motion of the earth, contrary to the impression of the senses. Yet, his system is no more accurate nor simpler than Ptolemy's. Copernicus's most important contribution is his painstaking detail in his mathematical, technical study of the motions of the earth. Critics of the Copernican system quoted the biblical citations Ecclesiastes 1:4-5 "the earth abideth forever" and "The sun also ariseth, and the sun goeth down, and hasteth to his place where he arose." Calvin, in *Commentary on Genesis,* cited the 93rd Psalm "the earth also is stablished, that it cannot be moved." Biblical citation became the favored anti-Copernican argument. Cosmology, morality, and theology had been woven into a complex fabric of Christian thought: the vigorous criticism of Copernicus persisted for three centuries because his proposals raised serious problems for the believing Christian. In 1611, John Donne acknowledged that Copernicanism may be true, and conceded the probability of the earth's motion in the impending dissolution of traditional cosmology in the poem *Anatomy of the World,* which is specifically derived from Copernicanism.[75] Among the arguments against the Copernican system reflected in traditional beliefs were epistemological, philosophical, theological, religious, physical, mechanical, astronomical, and empirical objections, especially the argument called "the objection from the deception of the senses." That the senses are in error about such a basic phenomenon as the state of rest or motion of the earth was a fundamental change in thinking; that the earth is in motion was in direct contradiction with sense experience and confounded the common sense idea that the senses are the best instruments to test reality. The idea advanced by Copernicus was vulnerable to a number of counter arguments and counter evidence. To think the earth in motion contradicted the ordinary sense observation that the earth is stationary; the astronomical evidence could not be proven; it seemed to contradict the most fundamental mechanical phenomena; it seemed to violate the principles of physics of the day; and it contradicted the words of the Bible and the interpretation of the church.[76]

Babbalanja expresses the Aristotelian theme of the living nature of all things on the earth:

> Trust me, there are more things alive than those that crawl, or fly, or swim. Think you, my lord, there is no sensation in being a tree? feeling the sap in one's boughs, the breeze in one's foliage? think you it is nothing to be a world? one of a herd, bison-like, wending its way across boundless meadows of ether? In the sight of a fowl, that sees not our souls, what are our own tokens of animation? That we move, make a noise, have organs, pulses, and are compounded of fluids and solids. And all these are in this Mardi as a unit. Daily the slow, majestic throbbings of its heart are perceptible on the surface in the tides of the lagoon. Its rivers are its veins; when agonized, earthquakes are its throes; it shouts in the thunder, and weeps in the shower; and as the body of a bison is covered with hair, so Mardi is covered with grasses and vegetation, among which, we parasitical things do but crawl, vexing and

> tormenting the patient creature to which we cling. Nor yet hath it recovered from the pain of the first foundation that was laid. Mardi is alive to its axis. When you pour water, does it not gurgle? When you strike a pearl shell, does it not ring? Think you there is no sensation in being a rock?—To exist is to be; to be is to be something; to be something is— (Ch 143)

This Aristotelian concept, favored through the Middle Ages and Renaissance, was to receive its downfall in the physics of Isaac Newton and the science of the eighteenth and nineteenth centuries. Babbalanja, the philosopher whose name Melville perhaps contrived to mean "babbling angel," discourses on the bewildering inconsistencies of life in Chapter 143 similar to Browne in *Religio Medici*: "I hold that God can doe all things, how he should work contradictions I do not understand, yet dare not therefore deny."[77] Melville debates fate, in the form of instincts, and free will in trying to define human existence. He speaks through his 'babbling angel' who Melville likens to a "crack'd archangel."[78] Babbalanja says, "...we are air, wind, breath, bubbles; our being is told in a tick." Media says, "You everlastingly travel in a circle":

> "And so does the sun in heaven, my lord; like me, it goes round, and gives light as it goes. Old Bardianna, too, revolved. He says so himself. In his roundabout chapter on Cycles and Epicycles, with Notes on the Ecliptic, he thus discourseth:—'All things revolve upon some center, to them, fixed; for the centripetal is ever too much for the centrifugal. Wherefore, it is a perpetual cycling with us, without progression; and we fly round, whether we will or no. To stop were to sink into space. So, over and over we go, and round and round; double-shuffle, on our axis, and round the sun.' In another place, he says:—'There is neither apogee nor perigee, north nor south, right nor left; what to-night is our zenith, to-morrow is our nadir; stand as we will, we stand on our heads; essay to spring into the air, and down we come; here we stick; our very bones make glue.'"
>
> "Enough, enough, Babbalanja," cried Media. "You are a very wise Mardian; but the wisest Mardians make the most consummate fools."
>
> "So they do, my lord; but I was interrupted. I was about to say that there is no place but the universe; no limit but the limitless; no bottom but the bottomless." (Ch 143)

The wandering stars, or the solar planets, moved in relation to the fixed stars of the heavens, and in time, five planets in addition to the sun and moon were recognized such that the universe of crystalline spheres was beginning to get crowded. The order of the planets could be arranged with the earth at the center, and in each orbit somewhat farther from the earth, in order, were the moon, sun, Venus, Mercury, Mars. In the second century B.C., the order was changed to the moon, Mercury, Venus, Sun, Mars, Jupiter, Saturn and finally, the stellar sphere, an ingenious arrangement of homocentric spheres that proved to be an immensely powerful concept in astronomical research. It solved many questions, but did not allow for the irregular movement of the planets. The concept of concentric spheres remained at the center of astronomy and cosmology until the early seventeenth century. The origin of the concept that replaced homocentric spheres is not known, but the early investigations of Apolonius and Hipparchus from mid-third century to end of the second century B.C. led to the epicycle-deferent concept to explain the motion of the planets in respect to the fixed stars. Claudius Ptolemaeus (2nd century A.D.), or Ptolemy, was a celebrated astronomer, geographer, and mathematician who performed most of his studies in Alexandria. He devised an ingenious solution to reconcile the inconsistencies in the Greek concept of the universe: heavenly bodies revolve around a stationary and fixed earth; the earth was the center of the universe; the stars move in a series of 'shells' or upside-down bowls over the earth; heaven was beyond the highest of the shells. The Ptolemaic system of cosmic dimensions was an ingenious mixture of philosophy, spurious geometry, planetary theories, and naked eye estimates, though inaccurate, were plausible and ingenious and came to occupy an important place in the cosmology of Moslem astronomers and Christian scholars.[79] Although Ptolemy's concept did not account for all observed events, his theory of the heavens was accepted for more than a thousand years—through the Middle Ages. According to Lovejoy, the geocentric, or earth centered, view is often thought to place man at the center of the universe, but the reverse is true:

> For the centre of the world was not a position of honor; it was rather the place farthest removed from the Empyrean, the bottom of the creation, to which its dregs and baser elements sank. The actual centre, indeed, was Hell; in the spatial sense the medieval world was literally diabolocentric.[80]

Since man was much closer to hell than to heaven, geocentric cosmography humiliated rather than exalted man; redemption could be obtained only by devotion to God. The Copernican heliocentric, or sun centered, view of the cosmos of the sixteenth century was opposed in part because it tended to elevate man to a lofty and too dignified position away from hell, and distanced man from the necessity of religious service. However, the acceptance of the idea of infinity in the heavens of the sixteenth and seventeenth centuries by the discovery of many other planetary systems was devastating to man's perception of his place in the order of the universe. Man became insignificant in a vast, remote, and unknowable cosmos. Ptolemy's great contribution of cycles, epicycles, and deferent was to resolve not only the motions of the sun and moon, but also the quantitative regularities and irregularities of the seven planets. His theory, put forward in *Almagest,* the greatest achievement in ancient astronomy, was the first systematic mathematical treatise of the celestial motions. So influential was Ptolemy's system that his successors added refinements, but did not seek fundamental modifications. So extensive were his mathematical computations that all the data needed by Copernicus are contained in *Almagest*. Copernicus did not attack the spherical universe of the ancients, but the mathematical minutiae of the Ptolemaic system. The universe of crystalline spheres could not be upset without overturning physics and religion based on its assumptions, both of which had become part of a larger body of thought. During the thirteen centuries between Ptolemy and Copernicus, no important modification of Ptolemaism developed.[81]

Aristotle's writings include a fundamental unity of man and the universe that had an immense influence. The Aristotelian universe contained all space within the sphere of the stars of the outer surface of the celestial sphere, which could tolerate no holes or vacuums. Outside the sphere was nothing—neither space nor matter. There could not be a plurality of worlds. He proposed a total of fifty-five crystalline spheres, but the concept of deferent and epicycles did not fit with the Aristotelian crystalline spheres. Aristotle, whose authority was foremost in all questions of science and cosmology, declared the earth to be immobile. Astrology may have been the most important force binding astronomers to the concept of the earth's uniqueness; it was linked with astronomy from the second century B.C. for 1800 years. With its strict determinism, astrology was suppressed by the church whose doctrine required the existence of freedom of the will.[82]

Bardianna may well have been based on Isaac Newton, who defined the phenomena of centripetal and centrifugal in *Principia* (1687), meaning, respectively, "center-seeking" (def. V) and "center-fleeing" (Section II, Prop. IV, Scholia). Both concepts were necessary for the theory of maintenance of celestial orbits. According to Cajori, the purpose of the preface in the second edition of *Principia,* written by Roger Cotes (1713), was to counteract the philosophy of the vortex proposed by Descartes which was accepted in England soon after its appearance in 1644 with the idea that motion in a circle is as natural as motion in a straight line.[83] The cycles and epicycles of Ptolemy gave way to the orbital theories of Copernicus, Kepler, and Newton. In fact, Newton gives the same example as Melville; circular orbits require that the centripetal and centrifugal forces be equal. As stated by Newton: "[In the radius of the circle] This is the centrifugal force, with which the body impels the circle; and to which the contrary force, wherewith the circle continually repels the body towards the centre, is equal."[84] The concept of the lack of an absolute frame of reference and the discussion of limit and limitless, or infinity, used as reciprocal ideas or complementary relationships, become important in twentieth century physics and is discussed in Chapter 10.

On one of the islands, sorcerers were employed by individuals to settle disputes by casting spells and counter-spells. The satire is on lawyers, yet Melville includes science in their tricks: "when interrogated concerning their science, would confound the inquirer by answers couched in an extraordinary jargon, employing words almost as long as anacondas" (Ch 144). The sorcerers were a closed brotherhood who did not invoke their spells on each other. While barratry seems a more appropriate word, Melville describes their methods as science.

In Dominora (England), they meet starving men and women leading to a scathing attack on industrialism, although many thought the machine was the salvation of the age:

> "The magician [the machine] hath turned us out from our glen, where we labored of yore in the days of the merry Green Queen. He has pinioned us hip and arm that we starve. Like sheep we die off with the rot.—Curse on the magician. A curse on his spell."
>
> Bending our steps toward the glen, roaring down the rocks we descried a stream from the mountains. But ere those waters gained the sea, vassal tribute they rendered. Conducted through culverts and moats, they turned great wheels, giving life to ten thousand fangs and fingers, whose gripe no power could withstand, yet whose touch was soft as the velvet paw of a kitten. With brute force, they heaved down great weights, then daintily wove and spun; like the trunk of the elephant, which lays lifeless a river-horse, and counts the pulses of a moth. On all sides, the place seemed alive with its spindles. Round and round, round and round;

> throwing off wondrous births at every revolving; ceaseless as the cycles that circle in heaven. Loud hummed the loom, flew the shuttle like lightning, red roared the grim forge, rung anvil and sledge; yet no mortal was seen.
>
> "What ho, magician! Come forth from thy cave!"
>
> But all deaf were the spindles, as the mutes, that mutely wait on the Sultan. (Ch 148)

The dehumanizing effect of machinery on the spiritual potential of man was contrary to the mood of the nineteenth century and the theory of progress through technology, a theme expanded in Melville's short stories written a decade later.

King Bello, the satirical name for King George, king of England from 1760 to 1820, is a choleric, kyphotic old monarch. Melville likens the burden of dominion to a humpback: "Against which calamity to guard, his medicos and Sangredos sought the hump's reduction." The hump could not be reduced, so the nobles rallied about the hump of dominion; though King Bello may long lean, would never fall:

> "Nevertheless, he who doctors Verdanna [Ireland, or part of the dominion] aright, will first medicine King Bello; who in some things is himself a patient, though he would fain be a physician. However, my lord, there is a demon of a doctor in Mardi, who at last deals with these desperate cases. He employs only pills, picked off the Courouptia Guianenesis tree."
>
> "And what sort of a vegetable is that?" asked Mohi.
>
> "Consult the botanists," said Babbalanja. (Ch 152)

On consulting the botanists, the *Encyclopedia Britannia Micropedia*, the species *Courouptia Guianensis* is a soft wooded tree of the family *licidacia mertalis*, native of the northeast section of South America, which produces spherical, woody fruit up to eight inches in diameter; the hard shell resembles a rusty cannonball.[85] *C. Guainensis* is also called the 'cannon-ball tree.' Melville uses Linnaeus's binomial system of naming species in his political allegory of the threat of war in America against King George.

While the party has wine, philosophy and science intermingle. Mohi says wine opens his heart and glorious visions are born in his brain, "...it is then that I have all Mardi under my feet, and the constellations of the firmament in my soul": "Aye," cried Media, "the study of astronomy is wonderfully facilitated by wine. Fill up, old Ptolemy, and tell us should you discover a new planet...." (Ch 151)

The travelers head for Porpheero (Europe) for a brief visit. Media says: "Babbalanja! here you will find food for philosophy...Here you will find science and sages; manuscripts in miles" (Ch 153). Enroute to Vivenza (United States), Babbalanja tells of one of his students: "Ay, keep moving is my motto; but speaking of hard students, did my lord ever hear of Midni the ontologist [or metaphysician] and entomologist" (Ch 155)? Midni thought daylight vulgar and toiled only at night, reading in the woods by the light of a glowworm. However, he rarely accomplished a thought, spending the night chasing more glowworms, since their light span was brief. One of the travelers, in uncontrolled laughter, says he could not help himself. Babbalanja observes how earnestly he struggled to suppress his mirth:

> Our souls belong to our bodies, not our bodies to our souls. For which has the care of the other? which keeps house?...Simpletons show us, that a body can get along almost without a soul; but of a soul getting along without a body, we have no tangible and indisputable proof. My lord, the wisest of us breathe involuntarily. And how many millions there are who live from day to day by the incessant operation of subtle processes in them, of which they know nothing, and care less? (Ch 155)

The bizarre anatomical and physiological discourse on ontology reflects the ideas of Christian Wolff (1679-1754), a German mathematician and natural philosopher, introduced the term 'ontology,' meaning a branch of philosophy dealing with the theory of being, i.e., what really exists in contrast to what only seems to exist, what exists permanently in contrast to what exists temporarily, etc. Ontology has been replaced by the more general term: metaphysics.

The ontological discussion continues after the occurrence of paraplegia (paralysis of the legs). Neuroanatomy and physiology made great advances in the early nineteenth century through the work of Francois Magendie (1783-1855) in France, Müller (1801-1858) in Germany, and Sir Charles Bell (1774-1842) in Scotland. In 1811, Bell proposed the law that bears his name, that the anterior spinal roots are motor nerves, and the posterior roots are sensory.[86] In Melville's novel, a philosopher was angry with his body, and "seizing a cudgel" struck himself across the shoulders; one of his thwacks injured his spinal cord. He had no voluntary use of his legs:

> But a huge wasp happening to sting his foot, not him, for he felt it not, the leg incontinently sprang into the air, and of itself, cut all

> manner of capers....But all commands, volitions, and persuasions, were as nought to induce his limbs to carry him home. (Ch 155)

The metaphysical Babbalanja expands concerning "still more perverse bodies than Grando's," the fresh water polyp:

> "In some things science cajoles us. Now, what is undeniable for the Polyp some physiologists analogically maintain with regard to us Mardians; that forasmuch, as the lining of our interiors is nothing more than a continuation of the epidermis, or scarf skin, therefore, that in a remote age, we too must have been turned wrong side out: an hypothesis, which, indirectly might account for our moral perversities: and also, for that otherwise nonsensical term—'the coat of the stomach;' for originally it must have been a surtout, instead of an inner garment."
>
> "Pray, Azzageddi," said Media, "are you not a fool?"
>
> "One of a jolly company, my lord; but some creatures besides wearing their surtouts within, sport their skeletons without: witness the lobster and turtle, who alive, study their own anatomies."
>
> "Azzageddi, you are a zany."
>
> "Pardon, my lord," said Mohi, "I think him more of a lobster; it's hard telling his jaws from his claws." (Ch 155)

Abraham Trembley (1710-1784) discovered the hydra, or the fresh water polyp (classified a plant by Leeuwenhoek who observed that they reproduced by budding), caught food with tentacles and delivered it to their stomachs, reacted to touch, and could move using a primitive foot which made them animals of the lowest form, possibly a transition between plants and animals. When cut into pieces, he observed that each piece grew into an entire new polyp. When turned inside out, the polyp grew a new outside on what had been the inside, findings he published in 1744. These experiments produced a major philosophical dilemma: if the parts of an animal could regenerate an entire new animal, then where is the "soul" or organizing principle? Crabs and salamanders long had been known to regenerate lost parts, but unlike the polyp, the lost part died.[87] The argument is similar to that of the severed arm of Samoa (Ch 24).

La Mettrie (1748) was fascinated by Trembley's discovery. He considered that life was an inherent property of matter, and if so, the whole traditional idea of souls and vital forces could be replaced by pure materialism—man becomes a machine—in a belief of 'hylozoism'—

that matter itself is in some primitive way alive or aware. La Mettrie's *L'homme machine* (1748) first claimed the life-force of the body came not from the "soul," but that life is the product of the organization of the material of the body itself: a conclusion supported by several scientific discoveries including Trembley's and Albrecht von Haller's work on the "irritability" of organic tissue. Matter was no longer the passive substance of Descartes's mechanism, but possessed an active principle in itself. All of these developments led to the belief that the mind was merely a physical activity of the physical body.[88] Melville's awareness of the polyp may have occurred through his acquaintance with the theories of Agassiz. Hillway, however, says the story of the polyp probably comes from *Animal Kingdom* vol 14, "Cuvier." The reference, occasionally noted by Melville, which describes the hydra that can turn itself inside out like a glove.[89]

The metaphysics, or ontology, grows even more zany, yet incorporates more natural science including the study of fossils and development:

> Yes, Braid-Beard, I am a lobster, a mackerel, any thing you please; but my ancestors were kangaroos, not monkeys, as old Boddo erroneously opined. My idea is more susceptible of demonstration than his. Among the deepest discovered land fossils, the relics of kangaroos are discernible, but no relics of men. Hence, there were no giants in those days; but on the contrary, kangaroos; and those kangaroos formed the first edition of mankind, since revised and corrected. (Ch 155)

Stratigraphic findings of geology applied to the concept of time allow the philosopher to speculate on the origin of man, for the deepest, or oldest, fossils are kangaroos, not man. Human fossils are not found in the deeper, older strata. Adaptation to civilization removed the tails of frogs and kangaroos, i.e., the theory of the inheritance of acquired characteristics of Lamarck. At the time, Melville's suggesting the mutability of species by adaptation was a daring statement. He even goes so far as to suggest plants may have some advantages over man, who was thought to be God's 'perfection.'

Among the many astronomical phenomenon cited by Melville, the comet makes a transient but important appearance: "Long absent, at last the red comets have returned. And return they must, though their periods be ages. And should Mardi endure till mountain melt into mountain, and all the isles form one tableland; yet, would it but expand the old battle plain" (Ch 161). Comets fascinated their observers from antiquity. They developed a vast lore and were seen as omens of plague, famine, war, or the end of the world. Edmund Halley added to the fear of comets when he suggested that the biblical deluge was caused by a comet (1694). Comets were a problem for the concept of crystalline spheres of Aristotle and Ptolemy. In the Middle Ages, comets were seen as terrestrial exhalations, "material enough to explain their transience, ethereal enough to serve as vehicles of heavenly wrath." The observations of Brahe demonstrated that comets were above the lunar sphere, and if so, were able to penetrate the supposedly impenetrable crystalline spheres contributing to the downfall of the ptolemaic system. The periodic nature of comets was discovered by Halley, who predicted that a particularly bright comet would return in 1758, and it appeared in 1759.[90] Melville uses the comet to establish the notion of vast periods of time required to produce changes in the surface of the earth, i.e., the theory of uniformitarianism advanced in the early nineteenth century by Hutton and Lyell.

In Vivenza (United States), they visit a great temple, the head of Saturnia (usually interpreted as Daniel Webster) showed above the mob: "Gall and Spurzheim! saw you ever such a brow?—poised like an avalanche, under the shadow of a forest! woe betide the devoted valleys bellow! Lavater! behold those lips,—like mystic scrolls!" Babbalanja cautions, "We must measure brains, not heads, my lord; else, the sperm-whale, with his tun of an occiput, would transcend us all" (Ch 158). Melville cites the famous names of the pseudoscience phrenology—Franz Joseph Gall, Johann Casper Spurzheim, and Johann Casper Lavater—using their names as exclamatory interjections, jestingly giving the phrenologists an inflated authority. The travelers hear a long dissertation on political freedom; including the growth and decay of nations, time theory, overpopulation, and "transmigration of souls" among other references: "Then, your great experiment might have proved an explosion; like the chemist's who, stirring his mixture, was blown by it into the air" (Ch 161), a reference that could apply to many chemists, but probably to Humphry Davy who was disabled for a time by an explosion. They discuss the many anomalies of the residents of Vivenza who "are only warlike in opposing war" and a biological analogy to politics: which is the individual, the whole or the parts? The union of Vivenza, modeled on "nature's planning" is compared to the "mollusca of the Tunicata order—in other words, a species of cuttlefish abounding at the bottom of the lagoon?" and Babbalanja says:

> "Ah! my lord king, we should not cut off the nervous communication between our eyes, and our cerebellums."

> "What were you about to say concerning the Tunicata order of mollusca, sir philosopher?"
>
> "My very honorable lord, I hurry to conclude. They live in a compound structure; but though connected by membranous canals, freely communicating throughout the league—each member has a heart and stomach of its own; provides and digests its own dinners; and grins and bears its own gripes, without imparting the same to its neighbors. But if a prowling shark touches one member, it ruffles all. Precisely thus now with Vivenza...."
>
> "Babbalanja, you yourself are made up of members:—then, if you be sick of a lumbago,—'tis not *you* that are unwell; but your spine....[A philosopher says] 'Who put together this marvelous mechanism of mine; and wound it up, to go for three score years and ten; when it runs out, and strikes Time's hours no more? And what is it, that daily and hourly renews, and by a miracle, creates in me my flesh and blood? What keeps up the perpetual telegraphic communication between my outpost toes and digits, and that domed grandee up aloft, my brain?—It is not I; nor you; nor he; nor it. No; when I place my hand to that king muscle my heart, I am appalled. I feel the great God himself at work in me. Oro [god] is life.'" (Ch 163)

In Babbalanja's metaphor, the whole is greater than the sum of its parts, the 'organism' of the nation of Vivenza is not a Newtonian mechanism any more than the toadstool, with a generous use of anatomy and physiology to illustrate his point.

In Chapter 169, "Sailing On," Melville makes a summary statement employing an astronomy metaphor: "And as in Orion, to some old king-astronomer,—say, King of Rigel, or Betelgeuse,[91]—this Earth's four quarters show but four points afar; so, seem they to terrestrial eyes, that broadly sweep the spheres" (Ch 169).

The narrator's motivations remain obscure, the earth but a planet among the stars that move as if by divine influence according to Newton's laws of motion and gravitation of planets. The planets follow a path independent of God, yet, Newton did not draw the conclusion of the absence of God's influence in natural phenomenon. He did not foresee that a mathematical interpretation of nature would separate man from God. In this instance, Taji is moved by "some mystical influence," or pre-Newtonian cosmology probably implying astrology. The "chartless" voyage is unaided by science, the great truth of the Mardian isles remains undiscovered by the searchers and naturalists.

They may as well stay ashore, for the shore is the only certainty and the only safety.

The narrator moves from the inflated language of philosophy to Doxodox, the "Wise One," an incomprehensibly verbose so-called wise man on one of the islands of Mardi, and a satire of the language of science and logic: "Then, if thou comprehendest not my nomenclature:—how my science?" illustrated by the "Shark-Syllogism" in abstract and esoteric metaphysics (Ch 171). The discussion probably comes from Thomas Taylor's translation of *The Six Books of Proclus*...(1816). Davis points out the similarity of the "Shark-Syllogism" to an entry in Ephraim Chambers's *Cyclopaedia: or, An Universal Dictionary of Arts and Sciences* (1741), noting the observation of a woman begging a crocodile to release her son.[92] Words and rhetoric outrun reason, and reason conflicts with faith.

The travelers land on the Isle of Cripples, Hooloomooloo, ruled by their own competent but deaf and dumb monarch: "At last we halted before a tenement of rude stones; crooked Banian boughs its rafters, thatched with fantastic leaves. So rambling and irregular its plan, it seemed thrown up by the eruption, according to sage Mohi, the origin of the isle itself" (Ch 174). The cripples were isolated to keep them out of sight of the rest of society and they see no "normal" people. The travelers themselves are taken for cripples by the "King of the Cripples" who asks if there are any "Comparative Anatomists" among them. On Hooloomooloo, a monarch died whose closest companion had been a chimpanzee who also died and was buried in the same vault as the king, scandalizing the people of the island "that a baseborn baboon should share the shroud of their departed lord," and resolved to build a separate vault:

> But at the disinterring, a sad perplexity arose. For lo! surpassing Saul and Jonathan, not even in decay were these fast friends divided. So mingled every relic,—ilium and ulna, carpus and metacarpus;—and so similar the corresponding parts, that like the literary remains of Beaumont and of Fletcher,[93] which was which, no spectacles could tell. Therefore they desisted; lest the towering monument they had reared, might commemorate an ape and not a king.

Babbalanja says:

> I could weep that Comparative Anatomists are not so numerous now, as hereafter they assuredly must become; when their services

> shall be in greater request; when, at the last, last day of all, millions of noble and ignoble spirits will loudly clamor for lost skeletons; when contending claimants shall start up for one poor, carious spine; and doglike, we shall quarrel over our own bones. (Ch 174)

The systematic study of animals had its beginning in the numerous bestiaries, or collections of actual and mythical stories and fables of animals, of the Middle Ages. They were derived to some extent from the ancient and anonymous *Physiologus*, originally written in Greek and translated into Latin, dating from the second century A.D. which probably originated in Alexandria.[94] Modern comparative anatomy had its beginning in 1555 by the work of Pierre Belon who demonstrated that the skeletons of man and birds are constructed of similar elements in a similar arrangement. Later, it was discovered that all animals have similarly arranged anatomical elements, which had a great influence on biology in the nineteenth century.

Chapter 175, "A Book from the 'Ponderings of Old Bardianna,'" is a *tour de force* of nineteenth century science and philosophy, and the conflict of science and faith. After the travelers have a banquet of deformed, shapeless, and grotesque food with "mishapen Mardians," they sail away from the Island of the Cripples. Babbalanja cites Diloro, a mythical philosopher, who discourses extensively on a number of current problems in the interrelationship between science, philosophy, and religion beginning with the arbitrariness and uncertainty of human knowledge and the plurality of worlds:

> "But I am, as I am; whether hideous, or handsome, depends upon who is made judge. There is no supreme standard yet revealed, whereby to judge of ourselves;...'Our very axioms, and postulates are far from infallible.' 'In respect of the universe, mankind is but a sect,' saith Diloro: 'and first principles but dogmas.' What ethics prevail in the Pleiades? What things have the synods in Sagittarius decreed?"
>
> "...Thus saith the sage in Book X. of the Ponderings, 'Zermalmende,' the title; 'Je pense,' the motto:—'My supremacy over creation, boasteth man, is declared in my natural attitude:—I stand erect! But so do the palm-trees; and the giraffes that graze off their tops. And the fowls of the air fly high over our heads; and from the place where we fancy our heaven to be, defile the tops of our temples. Belike, the eagles, from their eyries look down upon us Mardians, in our hives, even as upon the beavers in their dams,

> marveling at our incomprehensible ways. And cunning though we be, some things, hidden from us, may not be mysteries to them....We inhabit but a crust, rough surfaces, odds and ends of the isles; the abounding lagoon being its two-thirds, its grand feature from afar; and forever unfathomable.
>
> "'What shaft has yet been sunk to the antipodes? What underlieth the gold mines?" (Ch 175)

Man's growing hubris is expressed in his confidence in controlling the natural world to his advantage. The theme of the plurality of worlds is woven into the entire chapter, as well as the new awareness of the knowledge of the surface of the earth being a "crust." He introduces one of the most pervasive theories created by human intellect:

> "'Oh men! fellow men! we are only what we are; not what we would be; nor every thing we hope for. We are but a step in a scale, that reaches further above us than below. We breathe but oxygen. Who in Arcturus hath heard of us? They know us not in the Milky Way. We prate of faculties divine: and know not how sprouteth a spear of grass; we go about shrugging our shoulders: when the firmament-arch is over us; we rant of etherealities: and long tarry over our banquets; we demand Eternity for a lifetime: when our mortal half-hours too often prove tedious....our mortal lives have an end; but that end is no goal: no place of repose. Whatever it may be, it will prove but as the beginning of another race. (Ch 175)

The narrator refers to the *scala naturae,* the Scale of Nature, the Ladder of Perfection, best known as the Great Chain of Being. The Great Chain of Being is one of the oldest principles attempting to establish a relationship of man to the design of God with its beginning at least two millennia past in the philosophy of Plato and possibly had its origin with Homer in the golden chain extending from earth to heaven.[95] The Great Chain of Being, with three supporting ideas of fullness, plenitude, and sufficient reason, together produced one of the major concepts of Occidental thought. The result was a world view accepted through the Middle Ages and into the nineteenth century by most men of science. Indeed, most educated men and philosophers accepted it without question. The infinite number of links of the chain ranged from the meagerest existence to the *ens perfectissimum* to the absolute being; each differing from the nearest beings by the least possible degree of difference. Faith in the Great Chain of Being grew in the face of the spirit of patient, empiric inquiry into nature and the triumphant march of science; the assumptions on which it depended were not derived from experience and were difficult to reconcile with the known developing facts of nature. Nevertheless, writers of all disciplines accepted the general scheme and drew bold new implications from it. Next to the word 'nature,' 'Great Chain of Being' was the sacred phrase of the eighteenth century. The conviction that there was a continuous chain of creatures produced a search for missing species, or missing links, in the chain, and greatly stimulated naturalists and microscopists of the early eighteenth century. By the end of the eighteenth century, one of the few great changes in man's standard of values took place; a profound change in man's concept of nature: the ideal of a single uniform excellence gave way to the principle of diversity. This produced vast changes in all aspects of human thought and endeavor—social, theological, scientific, artistic, philosophical, etc. and a temporalization of the Great Chain of Being, incorporating change over time. The Great Chain of Being was one of the most "grandiose enterprises of the human intellect," but failed to show an absolute rationality or design of the cosmos. According to Lovejoy, the failure of the Great Chain of Being was not in vain: "erroneous hypotheses are often the avenues to truth;" as Melville later says in *Pierre*, "though Folly be our teacher, Sense is the lesson she teaches" (Bk IX pt 1). The Great Chain of Being lost its influence through the advance of natural science, especially with the discovery by Cuvier that animals could not anatomically belong to a single ascending system. Although Melville was familiar with the writings of the most important advocates of the Great Chain of Being, he only briefly includes it in his writings of philosophy, science, and religion. The theory had been largely discarded by the mid-nineteenth century, but was surely known to him since it was the dominate theme of Goldsmith's *Animated Nature*, which he often used as a reference, and was treated at some length by Browne in *Religio Medici*.[96] French philosopher Jean-Baptiste Robinet (1725-1820) did not believe that the chain of being could be divided into links, or species, but was more like a rope with no clear divisions: species do not exist in nature, only individuals corresponding to every possible point along the chain. The concept of God's design was still widely held well into the nineteenth century in spite of gradually accumulating scientific data; it would receive a serious challenge within the decade of the 1850s. Buffon, in his early works, also argued against Linnaeus on the occurrence of genera and species, saying that only individuals exist in a complete spectrum of variations, making classification impossible. By 1749, however, he wrote of distinct, fixed species, a view he maintained with some modification the rest of his life.[97]

The mythical philosopher continues by including more current theories and astronomical findings:

> The thick film is breaking; the ages have long been circling. Fellow men! if we live hereafter, it will not be in lyrics; nor shall we yawn, and our shadows lengthen while the eternal cycles are revolving....Other worlds differ not much from this, but in degree. Doubtless, a pebble is a fair specimen of the universe. (Ch 175)

In 1815, spectrographic studies of stars revealed the heavens to be composed of the same elements as earth; the stars lost their mystery and supernatural meaning. The crystalline spheres had given way to the idea of infinity in space, although the idea of depth of space was put forth in the nineteenth century by astronomer William Herschel. When Copernicus placed the fixed stars at immeasurable distances away from earth, he was often associated with the idea of infinity in the universe, and Giordano Bruno went so far as to speak of a plurality of worlds and ask if the human beings in other worlds need redemption, more appearances of Christ, atonement. For this and other heresies, Bruno was burned at the stake in 1600, for he intensified the fears provoked by the Copernican system.[98] The philosopher reaffirms the glory of nature, and natural explanations replaced supernatural miracles:

> We point at random. Peradventure at this instant, there are beings gazing up to this very world as their future heaven. But the universe is all over a heaven: nothing but stars on stars, throughout infinities of expansion. All we see are but a cluster. Could we get to Boötes, we would be no nearer Oro, than now; he hath no place, but is here. Already, in its unimaginable roamings, our system may have dragged us through and through the spaces, where we plant cities of beryl and jasper. Even now, we may be inhaling the ether, which we fancy seraphic wings are fanning. But look around. There is much to be seen here, and now. Do the archangels survey aught more glorious than the constellations we nightly behold? Continually we slight the wonders, we deem in reserve. We await the present. With marvels we are glutted, till we hold them no marvels at all. But had these eyes first opened upon all the prodigies in the Revelation of the Dreamer, long familiarity would have made them appear, even as these things we see. Now, *now*, the page is outspread: to the simple, easy as a primer; to the

> wise, more puzzling than hieroglyphics. The eternity to come, is but a prolongation of time present: and the beginning may be more wonderful than the end. (Ch 175)

Time continues to perplex the philosopher, and Oro (God) has been replaced by reason:

> The soul needs no mentor, but Oro, and Oro, without proxy. Wanting Him, it is both the teacher and the taught. Undeniably, reason was the first revelation; and so far as it tests all others, it has precedence over them. It comes direct to us, without suppression or interpolation; and with Oro's indisputable imprimatur....Fellow-men, the ocean we would sound is unfathomable, and however much we add to our line, when it is out, we feel not the bottom. Let us be truly lowly, then; not lifted up with a Pharisaic humility. We crawl not like worms; nor wear the liveries of angels.
>
> ...Curiosity apart, do we really care whether the people in Bellatrix [the third brightest star in the Orion constellation] are immortal or no?" (Ch 175)

The position of man was radically disturbed from the egocentric medieval world view due to the rapid occurring discoveries in natural philosophy, neither worm nor angel, but ambiguously placed, but denying a Pharisaic, sanctimonious salvation—displaced by a phenomenal discovery in astronomy:

> There was a time, when near Cassiopeia, a star of the first magnitude, most lustrous in the North, grew lurid as a fire, then dim as ashes, and went out. Now, its place is a blank. A vast world, with all its continents, say the astronomers, blazing over the heads of our fathers; while in Mardi were merry-makings, and maidens given in marriage. Who now thinks of that burning sphere? How few are aware that ever it was?...
>
> [We] must go, and obtain a glimpse of what we are from the Belts of Jupiter and the Moons of Saturn, ere we see ourselves aright. The universe can wax old without us; though by Oro's grace we may live to behold a wrinkle in the sky. (Ch 175)

He refers to the astronomical phenomenon of a 'supernova' which had been observed by the ancient Chinese and recorded by Hipparchus (ca 190-ca 125 B.C.), but the first to arouse great interest in Europe was reported by Brahe. In 1572, at the beginning of his career in astronomy, Brahe observed a new celestial body in the constellation Cassiopeia, raising distressing questions about the mutability of the fixed stars and the celestial spheres. It was so bright that it could be see in broad daylight for six months, then grew progressively dimmer and disappeared entirely in early 1574. It could not be a comet for it had no tail and did not appear to move in relation to the fixed stars. If it was a star, the heavens had changed, casting doubt on the basic contrast between the superlunary heavens and the corruptible earth; and if a star, the earth may be conceived as a planet, for the transitory character of terrestrial life had been discovered in the heavens. Astronomers were unable to place it below, or anywhere near, the lunary sphere, concluding that it was among the stars since it appeared to move with the stars. Brahe was also able to show that comets were above the lunary sphere because they did not produce measurable parallax, also suggesting change in the heavens.[99] The death of a star led to the concept of a black hole, so important to modern physics. The black hole concept is attributed to the English clergyman John Mitchell in 1783. He assumed that gravity acts upon light and matter in a similar manner, and pointed out the possibility of the existence of large quantities of hidden material in the universe, and that black holes could be detected by searching for their effects in binary stars systems where one was visible and the other a black hole[100].

> We Mardians talk as though the future was all in all; but act as though the present was everything. Yet so far as, in our theories, we dwarf our Mardi; we go not beyond an archangel's apprehension of it, who takes in all suns and systems at a glance. Like pebbles, were the isles to sink in space, Sirius, the Dog-star, would still flame in the sky. But as the atom to the animalculae, so Mardi to us. (Ch 175)

The importance of God is questioned. Whether the creator interferes in terrestrial events cannot be proven by science, and our understanding and reason can never be more than relative, or as Melville subsequently says in *Pierre,* "provisional."

The long-standing idea of our universe being but one of many possible worlds has been coupled with Leibniz's claim that ours is the "best of all possible worlds," particularly by Maupertuis. Such universes may have different constants of nature. If the universe is infinite (which present astronomical data suggest), then any conditions can occur somewhere (actually, infinitely often). Further, if a universe of fifteen billion light years is necessary for observers to evolve, there must be an infinite number of conditions similar to our observed universe unless the universe is proven to be finite. A type of universe with a change in the values of the constants of nature, or other values that would constrain the outcome of the laws of nature, such as variations in Newton's gravitational constant in time and space, implies a simultaneous existence of an infinite number of equally real worlds that are more or less causally independent.[101]

Galileo's *The Assayer* was the manual that taught a new language; that with aid of the telescope, the universe could be read like a book. This opposed the whole tradition of Scholastic thought and led to intense controversy over the physics of phenomena of nature perceptible to the senses. In the times of the seventeenth century, the world was populated by a collection of invisible signs. In 1837, Friedrich W. Bessel (1784-1846), German mathematician and astronomer, was able to measure the earth's motion relative to the fixed stars.[102] The triumph of theology over natural philosophy came with the Condemnation of 1277, with the objectives of exalting God's absolute and unpredictable power, and damning natural philosophers, placing a limit on their power and their appeals to rational demonstration. It also declared that it was possible for God to make several worlds. As a consequence, it became respectable during the fourteenth century (as it was not before 1277) to contemplate the possibility of simultaneous existence of other worlds.[103] In 1854, Whewell published *Dialogue on the Plurality of Worlds*, suggesting the hypothetical inhabiting of other worlds by arguing that the sun is not a typical star; the sun, moon and the solar planets seemed uninhabitable, that the earth is unique, and so, therefore, was man, which was in line with the teachings of the church. David Brewster replied in *More Worlds than One: the creed of the philosopher and the hope of the Christian,* relying on the uniformity of nature using analogy and the theory of classification.[104] The discovery of the "mutability of the heavens" in the discovery of a new star in 1572 by Brahe and comets that moved through what had been the crystalline spheres gave continuing evidence of superlunary change.[105]

The story of the cripples, or outcasts, and the arbitrariness of human judgement exhibit Melville's concern for the unfortunate, deformed natives of Hooloomooloo, or Hawaii, who were horrible victims of the effects of civilization brought by missionaries, causing disfigurement by diseases previously unknown in Hawaii, also mentioned in *Omoo*.[106] He satirizes the comparative anatomists for their morbid, pecuniary pursuit of bones. Deformity breeds deformity on the island of Hooloomooloo, reflecting the argument in genetics of the time, i.e., the inheritance of acquired characteristics of Lamarck. In Chapter 175, the awareness of the extinction of stars, infinity in space, and the possibility of infinite time are incorporated into Melville's metaphor of need for improvement on earth: "Here, *here*, fellow-men, we can better minister as angels, than in heaven, where want and misery come not" (Ch 175). Kepler's theory dislodging the sun from the central position in the universe displaced man into cosmic insignificance; the death of a star and its life goes unnoticed in man's quarrels on earth. Fate is the ultimate master, and he chides the childlike scientist:

> All we discover has been with us since the sun began to roll; and much we discover, is not worth the discovering. We are children, climbing trees after birds' nests, and making a great shout, whether we find eggs in them or no. But where are our wings, which our forefathers surely had not? Tell us, ye sages! something worth an archangel's learning; discover, ye discoverers, something new. Fools, fools! Mardi's not changed: the sun yet rises in its old place in the East; all things go on in the same old way; we cut our eye-teeth just as late as they did three thousand years ago. (Ch 176)

Babbalanja says: "Oh, my lord! though we galvanize corpses into St. Vitus' dances, we raise not the dead from their graves! Though we have discovered the circulation of the blood, men die as of yore..." (Ch 176). Electrophysiology of muscle was pioneered by Luigi Galvani (1737-1798), physiologist and professor of surgery and anatomy at Bologna, Italy. In 1791, he found that electrical stimulation of the crural nerve of a frog caused a violent muscular contraction; atmospheric electricity also caused a strong contraction. He conceived the theory of 'animal electricity.' Galvani's electrophysiological studies were extended by Leopoldo Nobili (1784-1835) who developed a galvanometer able to measure the electrical effects of muscular contraction. Thus, Melville's passage of "galvanizing corpses into St. Vitus dances" is based on the work of distinguished scientists. Galvani's observation that two different metals placed together produced an electrical potential led to the invention of the battery by Alessandro Volta (1745-1827), in 1800. Volta rejected the notion of animal electricity.[107] In addition, as Babbalanja notes, the discovery of the circulation of blood in 1628 is attributed to William Harvey (1578-1657), English physician.

In several instances, the narrator makes use of the theory of metempsychosis, the rebirth of the soul at death into another body: "In some universe-old truths, all mankind are disbelievers. Do you believe that you lived three thousand years ago" (Ch 97)? This and a further digression on metempsychosis were probably influenced by Browne.[108] Later, the narrator applies a similar idea to inheritance:

> We are full of ghosts and spirits; we are as graveyards full of buried dead, that start to life before us. And all our dead sires, verily, are in us; *that* is their immortality. From sire to son, we go on multiplying corpses in ourselves; for all of which, are resurrections. Every thought's a soul of some past poet, hero, sage. (Ch 180)

In a subtle shift of emphasis, he alludes to the theory of preformation, one of the two most important theories of embryology in the nineteenth century: "Giants are in our germs; but we are dwarfs, staggering under heads overgrown. Heaped, our measures burst. We die of too much life" (Ch 180). Preformation theory claimed that a fully-formed individual exists in miniature in the egg and grows to adulthood by the stimulation of sperm. Consequently, all future generations exist in the egg. Sheer numbers made this theory difficult to defend. Proponents of epigenesis, the other important theory, were in sympathy with spontaneous generation, i.e., each new organism was a new formation, and extended to the idea that any organic substance could spontaneously generate into a living organism, a theory formulated by Pierre Louis Maupertuis and Buffon in France, and John Turberville Needham in England. Buffon and Needham attacked preformation theories taking note of evidence of the contribution of both sexes to the offspring. Buffon objected to the necessity of an infinity of beings present in the germinal cells. He theorized that the organic particles were absorbed and employed in developing the parts according the *moule intérier* or mold; at puberty when growth stops, the excess particles passed to the reservoirs—the testes and ovaries. The generative power of the hydra seemed to suggest that nature had an innate capacity to form organic beings. Needham's experimental evidence in support of spontaneous generation became important support for the new materialism. Thus, defense of preexistence and the attack on spontaneous generation became a central tenet of Christian faith. Living material was thought imbued with a "vital spirit" in order to maintain living integrity. The concept took opposite courses in Germany and France. In Germany, the chief spokesman was Casper Wolff. To him, nature was unified by a process of development and became one of the important aspects of *Naturphilosophie*.[109] The theory of preformation solved two difficult problems: the existence of Original Sin and the origin of the embryo, and it removed the need for continuous spontaneous generation.[110]

In the early nineteenth century, the atomic theory of the Greeks was revived by the work of many famous scientists. Melville works the theory into his allegory *Mardi*. The man-made pyramids seek to challenge nature and imitate the grandeur of God:

> Oh! could Mardi but see how we work, it would marvel more at our primal chaos, than at the round world thence emerging. It would marvel at our scaffoldings, scaling heaven; marvel at the hills of earth, banked all round our fabrics ere completed.—How plain the pyramid! In this grand silence, so intense, pierced by that pointed mass,—could ten thousand slaves have ever toiled?—ten thousand hammers rung?—There it stands,—part of Mardi: claiming kin with mountains;—was this thing piecemeal built?—It was. Piecemeal? Atom by atom it was laid. The world is made of mites. (Ch 180)

Full of wine, perhaps overcome by the risk of death, he tries to accept fate:

> Go, Yoomy: go study anatomy: there is much to be learned from the dead, more than you may learn from the living, and I am dead though I live; and as soon dissect myself as another; I curiously look into my secrets: and grope under my ribs. I have found that the heart is not whole, but divided; that it seeks a soft cushion whereon to repose; that it vitalizes the blood;...But so the great world goes round, and in one somerset, shows the sun twenty-five thousand miles of a landscape! (Ch 183)

The remarkable arrangement of anatomy was surely part of God's design: Giovanni Battista Morgagni's famous book, *On the Seats and Causes of Diseases as Disclosed by Anatomical Dissections* (1761), founded the discipline of gross pathology. Improvements in the microscope in the first half of the nineteenth century confirmed the cellular nature of disease. Rudolf Virchow's *Cellular-pathologie* (1858) was a landmark in the development of microscopic pathology.[111] Harvey, in *De Motu Cordis* (1628), said, "Thus Nature, perfect and divine, making nothing in vain, has neither added a heart unnecessarily to any animal nor created a heart before it had a function to fulfil, but by the same steps in the formation of every animal...she secures perfection in the individuals."[112] Adding the circumference of the earth is a detail that lends an aura of expansiveness and grandeur to his introspection.

The concept of time in Chapter 176 is not the same as expressed elsewhere: "In the books of the past we learn naught but of the present; in those of the present, the past. All Mardi's history—beginning, middle, and finis—was written out in capitals in the first page penned" (Ch 176). The statement of 'circular time' and recurring events is an ancient concept opposed to 'linear time' of the Judaic and Christian concept of progress.[113] Earlier, Melville gives Mardi's age, or the Earth's age, in agreement with biblical time according to orthodox religious dogma of a few thousand years. He states a new estimate of man's age in Mardi of fifty million years. Earth's age was debated between the geologists and physicists in the second half of the nineteenth century with estimates of 25 to 100 million years, which Melville anticipated. John Jacob Astor's will published in the New York *Herald* on April 5, 1848, is used in his satire in Bardianna's last will and testament dated "anno Mardis 50,000,000 O.S." (Ch 177). A time scale of fifty million years, though vastly greater than biblical time, became a constraint to later developments in geology and biology.

After sailing all night, the sun rises while they are at sea; the narrator becomes more daring in expanding the concept of time: "Five hundred thousand centuries since," said Babbalanja, "this same sight was seen" (Ch 184), i.e., fifty million years. In 1862, thirteen years after the publication of *Mardi,* William Thompson, Lord Kelvin (1824-1907), English physicist and mathematician, read his first paper on the age of the earth determined by its rate of cooling. He estimated the age of the earth could be as much as 400 million years. In 1868, before the Geological Society of Glasgow, he placed the limit at no more that 100 million years and most likely 24 million. This became the accepted estimate until the end of the nineteenth century and was not challenged until 1904 by Ernest Rutherford (1871-1937) at Cambridge, England, applying new theories of radioactive decay.[114]

The discovery of numerous planetary systems prodded speculation that other planets in addition to earth may be inhabited by plant and animal life. Taji extends the idea of Browne's metempsychosis to the inhabitants of the heavens. The development of the concept of infinity in astronomy had a powerful influence on the mind of man; no longer did he reside on a God-imbued special creation; man saw the earth as an insignificant sphere wandering in the vastness of space. Small wonder at the turmoil in the minds of men, the conflict with the teachings of the church, and the sensation of the idea that man had found the formulas of God. That the age of the earth is only a few thousand years was refuted in 1838 by Bessel, who recorded the first accurate determination of a distant star. By measuring parallax (change in apparent position as seen from earth at different places in its orbit around the sun) of the star 61 Cygni, he found its distance from earth was 10^{14} kilometers, and that its light would require a little more than ten years to reach earth. William Herschel had determined that the distances of some nebulae to be hundreds or thousands of times greater than 61 Cygni. In 1843, Marcel de Serres at the University of Montepellier, France, stated that some nebulae must be at least 230,000 light years away. Thus, at least *some* stars have existed for much longer than the biblical six thousand years. He also noted that if the entire universe had been created at once, Adam would not have seen any star other than the sun for ten years; then new stars would have appeared one by one as their light reached earth. Such a remarkable phenomenon could not have gone unnoticed, especially to the early seagoing peoples who relied on the stars for navigation. The appearance of a new star, such as the super nova that occurred in 1572, was such a rare event as to undermine Aristotle's cosmology would have been an everyday event.[115]

The bowsman falls overboard and is lost: "Ay, gone," said Babbalanja, "and whither? But a moment since, he was among us: now, the fixed stars are not more remote than he....Life is wearisome to all: the same dull round" (Ch 185). He debates man's ethical habit of attributing moral significance to physical phenomena in a narrow escape from a storm, the accident injuring one of the sailors, and a man lost overboard. Thus, all natural events are attributed to a temporary victory of either good or evil, or anthropomorphism of God or Satan, or their equivalent, in that physical events are not seen as natural causes, but the will of some higher being, deity or evil. The emerging science challenged the will of the supernatural, saying natural events occur by chance.[116]

The vortex is mentioned in several places in *Mardi* as a tantalizing, threatening phenomenon of nature:

> Nor would she say why it was, that she did so; until at length she yielded; and replied, that whatever false things Aleema might have instilled into her mind; of this much she was certain: that the whirlpool on the coast of Tedaidee prefigured her fate; that in the waters she saw lustrous eyes, and beckoning phantoms, and strange shapes smoothing her a couch among the mosses. (Ch 51)

It is also mentioned in Chapter 50, "by the vortex on the coast of Tedaidee." The enticing Hautia says, "I, the vortex that draws all in" (Ch 194); the concept of the vortex of Descartes, and its deterministic significance, implies that the vortex cannot be resisted, a concept that attains a great significance in *Moby-Dick*.

The astronomy and mythology of the star Arcturus appears throughout *Mardi*: in the beginning, he abandons the ship *Arcturion*; the sons of the murdered priest pursue him, guided by the star Arcturus; and at the end, their escape was observed by Arcturus. The references to Arcturus may be attributed to the magazine *Arcturus* published by his friends, the Duyckinck brothers, whose library Melville used while writing *Mardi*. The prologue of the first issue states that Arcturus looks keenly down upon men's follies and errors, or is an impartial observer of the world; Arcturus the 'negative' symbol complimentary to Yillah the 'positive' goal of peace and happiness. In addition, Arcturus represents a criticism of the ways of mankind, including man's science.[117] Davis says Melville's interest in astronomy was stimulated by attending the lectures of Professor William Mitchell from the Cincinnati Observatory and John Nichol from the University of Glasgow given in New York in December 1847 and January 1848. Babbalanja is the fictional character who expresses Melville's distrust of science. Babbalanja, like Browne, is caught in the conflict between science and religion.[118] At the end of the book, of all the stars, only red Arcturus shone. Through the gloom, "the breakers dashed ghost-white....Serenia [or the Christian ideal of heaven] is our haven." Through the straight of death, "no voyager e'er puts back.... And why put back? is a life of dying worth living o'er again?" The narrator darts through the strait into "the realm of shades!" (Ch 195) over an endless sea.

During the nineteenth century, the focus of the greatest interest in science shifted from astronomy to geology, and from physics to biology. Melville was aware of the change of attention and the implications of scientific discoveries on philosophical thought and religious belief. They attracted his interest, yet caused anguish as well, making his works more than romantic adventure, speculative allegory, or satire. He used the names of the important scientists from popular scientific works, especially Beale and Bennett, as though he were thoroughly acquainted with each. Certainly, Melville was interested in literary effect, not necessarily scientific credibility. Critics have made much of the errors in the science of *Mardi*, yet, nearly all of the inaccuracies can be traced to his sources rather than to inaccuracy on the part of Melville. Another source of scientific information he probably used was the forty-volume, *The Naturalists Library,* edited by William Jardine (1833-1845), which includes a memoir of Lacépède and references to Müller and Henle. Melville was also familiar with the *Edinburgh Review*, which printed reviews of scientific works. Most of the science references were popular works, with the exception of Beale's scientific *Natural History of the Sperm Whale.*[119]

In a number of instances in *Mardi*, Melville refers to the concept of infinity. During the seventeenth century in England, science created an obsession with the unlimitedness of space, the infinite varieties of life, and the possibility of an infinite number of inhabited worlds that possessed a spiritual nature inspired by infinity instead of the divine spirit. Nicolas of Cusa, a popular writer in the 1640s, dwelled on infinity as the chief attribute of God; God's center was "everywhere and nowhere," but his views had little influence on the old medieval cosmology. Tuveson says Giordano Bruno probably combined the radical concept of Cusa with the new discoveries in science: "The great traditional hierarchy of celestial spheres, through which divine influence was thought to be rayed down to earth from the empyrean, vanished like a cloud."[120] In 1646, Henry More further developed the idea that infinite space is an attribute of God, a basic position of Newtonianism rejected by Descartes because neither the divine essence nor infinity were subject to the imagination and could not be separated into parts, but were subject merely to reason. An infinite universe did not call for the presence of a Creator.[121] Locke embraced the concept of absolute space and time, which helped him resolve the problem of the absence of innate ideas. The problem of infinity occupied the greatest minds over the centuries. The great Renaissance concept of order had satisfied the deepest needs and longings of the human mind and heart. Within a few decades, with unbelievable rapidity, this work of art had been hopelessly shattered during the eighteenth century, gradually developing into an aesthetic view based upon the qualities of immensity, unlimitedness, and awe and leading to the concept of the "natural sublime"—a prominent theme in *Pierre.*[122] Nevertheless, Gauss in 1844 challenged the concept of infinity with the development of non-Euclidean geometry. Though the issue remains contested, some modern evidence supports the concept of a finite universe.[123]

Discoveries in geology and paleontology greatly disturbed religious views in the middle of the nineteenth century when Melville was at work on *Mardi,* polarizing his thinking—naturalism on the one hand and Christianity on the other. Wright says *Mardi* is Melville's earliest, longest, and most undisguised account of his search for the "full-developed man," his most important single work on one of his most important themes. The Mardian quest for this archetype is a continual oscillation between two extremes: the life of the head, self-centered as found by examining nature, and the life of the heart; i.e., science versus faith.[124]

The desire to understand the physical world at all times led to the question of how the world began. The best known is the vivid, primitive Hebrew explanation of the world as the creation of a powerful God.[125] The age of the cosmos was taken as nearly synonymous with the age of mankind. Browne said in *Religio Medici* (1633), "time we may comprehend; 'tis but five days older than ourselves." Many scholars made determinations of the age of the earth; all arrived at a calculation within a range of a few thousand years, including Newton, who estimated the date of Creation to be 3988 B.C.[126] The estimate of 4004 B.C. by Ussher is the best known through its adoption in the marginal notes of the seventeenth century King James Bible. This scholarly consensus was disturbed by the finding of greater antiquity in the records of Egyptian dynasties, and in the seventeenth century claims of even greater antiquity in China. Bruno described a cosmos without a center or boundaries, infinite, eternal, and possibly without creation, a concept Descartes tried to revive in the mid-seventeenth century by attempting to separate earth history from cosmic history. Numerous theories of the origin of the cosmos were put forward in the seventeenth and eighteenth centuries denying the literal interpretation of the Bible, eventually leading to Hutton's *Theory of the Earth* (1795), saying that the earth is, "without vestige of a beginning, without prospect of an end," and in Lamarck's *Hydrogeologie* (1802), extending the age of the earth to "millions of centuries." Digging through rock strata in the eighteenth century, workers found bones of exotic animals in the deeper layers, but no human remains. No evidence of the biblical Flood appeared in the rocks. The age of the earth was separated from the age of mankind, a long history without human records. The age of the earth was markedly lengthened by Buffon, though little known outside a small group of naturalists; rival cosmologies struggled to find a compromise between science and religion in a search for the meaning of a vast prehuman history. The abrupt change in fossils in adjacent strata led to the theory of catastrophism of Cuvier. Geology revealed an astonishing drama of vanished worlds inhabited by exotic, extinct creatures in a time scale that made human history insignificant. The public eagerly followed the drama that ran against tradition. In opposition to the self-styled 'scientific' geologists, a 'scriptural geology' emerged that reasserted the biblical chronology developed in the seventeenth and eighteenth centuries and retained the views of Genesis and the Pentateuch that were thought to be written by Moses under divine influence. 'Mosaic geology' was practiced by both erudite scholars and enthusiastic, poorly informed amateurs. Geological speculation was open to all until the mid-nineteenth century when the startling information from global exploration became increasingly esoteric and beyond the grasp of the amateurs, who remained attracted to Mosaic geology. Lyell said he was determined to "free the science from Moses," but maintained a pragmatic association with liberal Christians and scientific geologists. The static concept of design was dramatically enlarged by assuming divine providence had formed all the successive phases of the earth, including prehuman history, a concept that brought harmony to the two groups.[127]

During the middle decades of the nineteenth century, evidence had accumulated to support the idea that life developed progressively from 'lower' to 'higher' forms, independent of environmental change. Agassiz and Owen suggested that gradual development resulted in its culmination: the creation of man, an idea expanded by the amateur Chambers in *Vestiges of the Natural History of Creation* (1844). *Vestiges* was extremely popular and interfered with the boundary protecting the scientists and forcing them into the controversy. The Mosaic geologists responded by interpreting the new finds of geology in a biblical context in an equally popular book, *Footprints of the Creator* (1847), by Hugh Miller, the last popular work of biblical geology. The origin and antiquity of man could no longer be excluded from scientific geology and was debated into the late nineteenth century—not between science and religion, but between rival cosmologies, and particularly over the difference in antiquity between man and the rest of the animal world. Miller warned the churches that the principal challenge to faith was coming from natural science and not philosophy, claiming that the fossil record and the latest scientific knowledge were in accord with the book of Genesis. He was refuting Chambers's *Vestiges* in an incompatible blending of scientific and scriptural thought, claiming the author of the Bible and the author of nature are the same with analogies and correspondence between Scripture and nature, between the gospel of redemption and the facts of science.[128]

At the beginning of the nineteenth century, the 'Vulcanists' and 'Neptunists' debated the primary principle of fire and water in forming the earth, while the naturalists and theologians were in conflict over the finding of extinct fossils in earth strata. By 1830, the argument had to include an expanded biblical time scale and consider whether geological change had occurred gradually or catastrophically as in the Mosaic flood, i.e., naturally or miraculously; as well as whether the geological strata included a process of progressive development. The global Flood of Genesis had to be reinterpreted; geological time, or the history of earth, was unimaginably vast. The days of Creation, of Genesis, came to be seen as an accommodation to the views of ancient people—the text of Genesis could not be discovered by science. Geological explanation was thwarted at every turn by the Flood or by the objection to divine creation.[129]

By the middle of the century, Lyell's idea of limitless time was assimilated into most geological theories. Soon, the estimates of the rate of earth sedimentation and the determination of the rate of cooling of the planet more or less agreed on the figure of about 100,000 years as the age of the earth, constricting the likelihood of gradual change.[130] Melville's statement of "ten hundred thousand moons since there died the last of a marvelous race" (Ch 93), or 28 million years, is consistent with the expanded concept of time developed in the latter part of the nineteenth century.

Bacon (1605) warned that studying the Bible cannot be searched too far by either divinity or natural philosophy, "only let men beware...that they do not unwisely mingle or confound these learnings together." The doctrine of the 'two books,' nature, the book of God's works, and the Bible, the book of God's word, was a compromise which allowed freedom from harassment by interpreters of the Bible. For more than two hundred years, the "Baconian compromise" became the basis of cooperation between naturalists and the church, and was the chief sanction for the growth in volume and expertise of the scientific examination of nature, particularly in the English-speaking world. By the early nineteenth century, the Baconian compromise had been extended to the emerging science of geology, but it erupted into controversy over the ability of the geologists to interpret Genesis.[131]

Conjecture on the origin of life occupied a prominent position during the early nineteenth century and, without definitive authority, Chambers's *Vestiges* attracted undue attention.[132] The identity of the author was not known until 14 years after Chambers's death in 1871.[133] Chambers, one of many amateurs active in science, had the audacious idea that the implications of remote time and change found in geology, the ascending series of fossil remains, and the nebular hypothesis of astronomy could be shown to follow a fundamental principle or law of development, i.e., a simple, single law controlling all human knowledge—a law as basic as Newton's law of motion. The prevailing geological doctrine was formulated by John Woodward in *An Essay Towards a Natural History of the Earth* (1695), and Thomas Burnet in

The Sacred Theory of the Earth (1697); any theory of observed fact must be consistent with Scriptural accounts of Creation and the Deluge. At the time Chambers published *Vestiges*, the possibility of gradual change postulated by Lamarck and Cuvier attracted the attention of noted scientists and intellectuals. The theory, supported by findings in geology, embryology, and comparative anatomy, became conspicuous to the point that the idea of gradual change had to be taken seriously even by those most hostile to the idea. Embryonic change seemed plausible to Chambers, since both he and his brother were hexadactyls (having six digits on each hand and foot), which he took as living proof that embryos could be altered. The distinction between man and animal was held by most to be fundamental, an absolute. The mind, including reason and speech, constituted the uniqueness of man that was thought inexplicable in physiological terms. In the conventional view, since the form of the brain of ape and man are similar, the mind of man possessed a 'qualitative' difference, i.e., animals possess instinct and man possesses reason, or free will. Chambers challenged the idea of the 'immateriality of mind' citing the findings in the laboratory of electricity and magnetism: the twitch of a limb when stimulated by a Galvanic current suggested a commonality of electricity and free will.[134]

Vestiges was violently attacked by the highest authorities, and the populace in general; its detractors make a roll of the notables of the day. At a social gathering, Florence Nightingale, "got up so high into *Vestiges* that I could not get her down again, and was obliged to go off as an angel." Actress Fanny Kemble said, "Its conclusions are utterly revolting to me—nevertheless they may be true." Whewell, at Cambridge University, argued strenuously against *Vestiges* without specifically mentioning it. The condemnation added to the book's appeal and notoriety.[135] The concerted position of the average, commonsense religious opinion was a cry of revulsion against what was thought to be a noxiously wicked and extremely foolish book. Nevertheless, by 1850, *Vestiges* went through eight British and seven American editions. For fifteen years, *Vestiges* was the center of attention of the scientific and religious communities, and read widely by all levels of the public. On the other hand, a few were amazing generous to the book, acknowledging the basic ideas and considering its theological implications innocuous, or possibly valuable to science in stimulating reevaluation of theories and provoking useful discussion. *Vestiges* influenced many aspects of thought, including contemporary literature, for instance, Disraeli's *Tancread* (1847), Tennyson's poem "The Princess" (1847), and Schopenhauer's *Pararga und Paralipomena* (1850), owe much to the book.[136] The 1840s were pivotal in the history of science, and Melville, sensitive to these changes and aware of their importance, included much of Lyell's *Principles of Geology,* and Darwin's *Voyage of the Beagle,* in his early works. Melville does not mention Chambers or *Vestiges,* perhaps because it was immediately denounced by both the church and science. Nevertheless, he could not have missed Chamber's *Vestiges*, for it was the "rage of the decade."[137]

British scientists were especially hostile to the idea of spontaneous generation in their attacks on Chambers, who denied that non-living matter was created in a different manner from plants and animals. Chambers cited an experiment lasting over three years (1842-1845), applying an electrical current to a solution of potassium ferrocyanate and producing living ticks and mites. But the scientists were not convinced and stayed with the belief put forward by Paley, "There cannot be design without a designer; contrivance without a contriver; order without choice; arrangement, without anything capable or arranging; etc." Despite the optimism of the materialists, the concept of spontaneous generation was in disarray by the end the 1850s.[138] Paley's *Natural Theology* remains the best statement of what is generally recognized as the most highly respected theistic argument in its classical form.[139] More than any other, Paley made natural history popular with the middle classes in the early decades of the nineteenth century for its association with moral and religious justification without any awareness that natural history would become irreligious or anti-religious in the latter part of the century.[140] Chambers said that the unfolding of God's plan of creation was not dependent on a series of miracles, but that God had "programmed" the law of progression in the universe where it could unfold. Chambers was most criticized for arguing that man had to be included in this last step as the highest creature in the animal kingdom, and that man's character did not stem from a spiritual quality marking him distinctly from the animals, but from a direct extension of faculties that unfolded through biological development.[141]

Since the dawn of recorded history man has used the environment to his advantage. This led to the conclusion that the world in all its richness was designed for man alone. To a variety of cultures, nature appeared to have a special meaning and significance to the benefit of man, an idea nurtured by the religious and scientific beliefs of the times. Providential design was a key feature of Creation narratives of the early Hebrew writings that form the Old Testament, epic poetry, and prophetic writings. A partially anthropocentric universe with teleological aspects (because of the laws of causality, order must have a consequent purpose) in the basic fabric of Judeo-Christian world view is at the base of the growth of Western civilization. Early Greek science and logic generated a similar view that was eventually combined by the Scholastics with the poetic view of the Judeo-Christian tradition.[142]

During the Victorian age, churches were crowded with worshipers, most from the middle and upper classes. It was an age of church building, a great output of religious and theological literature, missionary zeal, and expansion. Multitudes of people had a simple unshaken devotion to the faith of their forefathers. Yet, beneath the surface was a turmoil of doubt and uncertainty. Their struggle for belief produced a vast literature of lost faith by the pressure of doubt: "It would be truer to say that the age was one of religious seriousness than of faith."[143] The discoveries in natural science, and the literary and historical criticism of the Bible, in addition to a revolt from the apparent immorality and inhumanity of the Christian scheme of salvation ("divine favouritism"), led to a decline in the belief in next-worldliness that seemed to deny the possibility of improving conditions in this world. Polkinghorne observes: "...people came to feel that they had no need of the hypothesis of God. The Enlightenment attitude had done its acid work and many people's faith dissolved away."[144] Religious belief in England was little disturbed by the developments in France and Germany in the first half of the nineteenth century in spite of a certain amount of agitation. In the 1850s, authorities still held to the age of the earth as 6,000 years, that the Genesis story of Creation was historical, and that innocence was lost in the Fall. The books of Lyell and Dean Buckland in the 1830s on geological succession of rocks and fossils were the first evidence to disturb the notion of the age of the earth which required a new explanation. But the greatest shock came with the publication of *Vestiges* in 1844.[145] On Christmas Eve, 1856, Hugh Miller, author of *The Old Red Sandstone* (1841), *Footprints of the Creator* (1849), and *The Testimony of the Rocks* (1857) which were immensely popular books that attempted to reconcile geology and faith, committed suicide, destroying the persuasive arguments of his books.[146]

In *Mardi*, Melville had mastered enough geology and paleontology to use with extraordinary accuracy the new discoveries of science proving the most threatening to religious faith: antiquity of the earth, gradual changes in biology and geology through natural events, rise and extinction of species, appearance in succeeding ages of related and higher forms of life, and the challenge to the doctrine of the fixity of species, which tended to discredit the idea of special creation of earth and man. Foster says, in addition to using science for humor, Melville's knowledge of geology did not disturb his tentative faith:

> Yet the story that the rocks had to tell of Nature, of the mindless, planless, fortuitous, and wasteful change and development in the material universe, could not lie comfortably in his courageous and open mind along with a creed of universal intelligence and benevolence....at the end of *Mardi*, Melville begins his long and agonizing search for a place for faith, and for the ethics of the Sermon on the Mount, in a heartless universe.[147]

Foster concludes no one source accounts for Melville's geological knowledge and takes exception to Hillway's suggestion of individual source material. Melville's description of geological events and use of geological terms could have originated from a number of contemporary books. His error in the origin of coral islands in *Omoo* cannot be readily attributed to a single source, nor can the volcanic origin of the island Nukuheva in *Typee* be attributed to any one authority. Foster offers alternative explanations for Melville's two opposing theories of the origin of the earth: the inclusion of specific fossils in the "sandwich" in the exact layers argues against Chambers as the basis of the account in *Mardi*, for some of the fossils included are in other popular books and not in *Vestiges*. Melville probably took the stratigraphic theory of the earth from Lyell. Foster says Melville's knowledge was "for a nonscientist, remarkably accurate, specific, and up-to-date" and derived from many sources including Lyell, Owen, and Darwin.[148] Melville had a large personal library, was a shareholder in the New York Society Library, and had access to the excellent libraries of publishers Evert and George Duyckinck and his father-in-law, Justice Lemuel Shaw. Since the house in New York was busy and crowded, Melville often visited the reading rooms of the many libraries of the city for solitude. Certainly he read Darwin's *Voyage of the Beagle* and must have been familiar with the works of Lyell and Chambers, although no direct evidence has been found of his owning or borrowing their works. In 1849, Melville took a step many scientists were reluctant to take: the possibility of creation and the appearance of human life as a long, slow process.

Notes

1. Merrell R. Davis, *Melville's Mardi: A Chartless Voyage*. New Haven and London:Yale University Press and Oxford University Press, 1952, p. 65.

2. *Encyclopædia Britannica* 10 (1971):148.

3. Nathan Reingold, "Two Grand Old Men." in *Science in Nineteenth Century America: A Documentary History*. Nathan Reingold, editor. Chicago and London: University of Chicago Press, 1964, pp. 11-14.

4. Thomas S. Kuhn, *The Copernican Revolution: Planetary Astronomy in the Development of Western Thought*. Cambridge, Massachusetts: Harvard University Press, 1957, p. 125.

5. Inhabitants of Stagira, birthplace of Aristotle.

6. Homer W. Smith, *Man and His Gods*. Boston: Little, Brown, 1952, p. 92.

7. Brian Foley, "Herman Melville and the Example of Sir Thomas Browne." *Modern Philology* 81 (1984):265-277.

8. Tyrus Hillway, "Melville's Education in Science." *Texas Studies in Literature and Language* 16 (1974):421-422.

9. Loren Eiseley, *Darwin's Century*. Garden City, New York: Doubleday, 1958, pp. 39-45.

10. David Knight, *Ordering the World: A history of classifying man*. London: Burnett Book, Andre Deutsch, 1981, pp. 71, 112-113; Davis, p. 67; Edward Lurie, *Louis Agassiz, A Life in Science*. Chicago: University of Chicago Press, 1960.

11. Knight, ref. 10, pp. 127-129.

12. Richard Price, *A Free Discussion of the Doctrines of Materialism, and Philosophical Necessity, in a Correspondence Between Dr. Price and Dr. Priestley.* (1778) London: J. Johnson and T. Cadell, Millwood, New York: Kraus Reprint, 1977, pp. 24-38.

13. Tyrus Hillway, "Melville as Amateur Zoologist." *Modern Language Quarterly* 12 (1951):159-164.

14. George Berkeley, *A New Theory of Vision and Other Writings*. Introduction by A.D. Lindsay. London: Dent, 1963. Sections CXVII to CXXXI and CLIV to CLVI.

15. David Jaffe, "Some Sources of Melville's *Mardi.*" *American Literature* 9 (1937):56-69.

16. Hillway, ref 13.

17. A. N. Whitehead, *The Function of Reason.* Princeton: Princeton University Press, 1929. reprint. Boston: Beacon, 1958, p. 51.

18. Duncan M. Porter, "The Beagle Collector and His Collections." In *The Darwinian Heritage*. David Kohn, editor. Princeton, New Jersey: Princeton University Press, 1985, pp. 980-981.

19. Hillway, ref. 13.

20. Merton M. Sealts, *Melville's Reading: Revised and Enlarged Edition.* Columbia, South Carolina: University of South Carolina Press, 1988, number 171, p. 68.

21. Hillway, ref. 8.

22. Tyrus Hillway, *Herman Melville.* Indianapolis: Bobbs-Merrill, 1979, p. 158.

23. Davis, ref. 1, p. 105.

24. John Farley, *The Spontaneous Generation Controversy from Descartes to Oparin.* Baltimore and London: The Johns Hopkins University Press, 1977, p. 1.

25. Jaffe, ref. 15.

26. F. Sherwood Taylor, *A Short History of Science and Scientific Thought: With Readings from the Great Scientists from the Babylonians Through Einstein.* New York and London: Norton, 1949, pp. 60-62.

27. Edward Grant, "Cosmology," in *Science in the Middle Ages.* David C. Lindberg, editor. Chicago and London: University of Chicago Press, 1978, pp. 288-290.

28. R. W. Southern, *Robert Grosseteste: The Growth of an English Mind in Medieval Europe.* Oxford: Oxford University Press, 1986, p. 106.

29. Peter J. Bowler, *Evolution: The History of an Idea.* Berkeley, Los Angeles, and London: University of California Press, 1984, pp. 62-63.

30. Davis, ref.1, p. 68.

31. Taylor, ref. 26, p. 52.

32. *Encyclopædia Britannica* 22 (1971):813.

33. Davis, ref. 1, p. 175.

34. Tyrus Hillway, "Melville's Use of Two Pseudo-Sciences." *Modern Language Notes* 64 (1949):145-150.

35. William Paley, *Natural Theology.* (originally published in 1802 as *Natural Theology, on Evidences of the Existence and Attributes of the Deity collected from the Appearances of Nature.*) Frederick Ferré, editor. Indianapolis and New York: Bobbs-Merrill, 1963, pp. 35-37.

36. Harold I. Sharlin, *The Convergent Century: The Unification of Science in the Nineteenth Century.* London, New York, Toronto: Abelard-Schuman, 1966, pp. 51-52.

37. Knight, ref. 10, p. 24.

38. David Knight, *The Age of Science: The Scientific World-view in the Nineteenth Century*. Oxford: Basil Blackwell, 1986, pp. 152-159.

39. David Knight, "Michael Faraday: The Use of Pure Science." in *Man Masters Nature: Twenty-Five Centuries of Science*. Roy Porter, editor. New York: George Braziller, 1988, pp. 108-109, 130.

40. Jaffe, ref. 15.

41. Jaffe, ref. 15.

42. Merton M. Sealts, Jr., "Melville's 'Friend Atahalpa.'" *Notes and Queries* 194 (1949):37-38.

43. Werner Heisenberg, *Philosophical Problems of Quantum Physics*. Woodbridge, Connecticut: Ox Bow Press, 1979, p. 82.

44. James A Secord, "The curious case of *Acarus crossii*." *Nature* 345 (1990):471-472.

45. Farley, ref 24, pp. 1-22, 32-56.

46. Joan Frederick, *Variations upon a Theme: The Use of Physical Disabilities in Melville's Fiction*. PhD. Dissertation, University of Tennessee, 1973, p. 94.

47. The "wild boy" is probably Peter the Wild Boy, also mentioned in *The Confidence-Man*.

48. Davis, ref. 1, p. 168n.

49. Albert Van Helden, *Measuring the Universe: Cosmic Dimensions from Aristarchus to Halley*. Chicago and London: University of Chicago Press, 1985, p. 163.

50. Hillway, ref. 8.

51. J. G. Crowther, *British Scientists of the Nineteenth Century*. London: Routledge and Kegan Paul, 1935, p. x.

52. Thomas L. Hankins, *Science and the Enlightenment*. Cambridge: Cambridge University Press, 1985, p. 153.

53. Bowler, ref. 29, p. 46.

54. Bowler, ref. 29, pp. 148-149; Charles Darwin, *The Structure and Distribution of Coral Reefs*. (1842) reprint. Tucson: University of Arizona Press, 1984. pp. 88-118.

55. H. W. Menard, *The Ocean of Truth: A Personal History of Global Tectonics*. Princeton, New Jersey: Princeton University Press, 1986, pp. 186, 195, 238-255.

56. Bowler, ref. 29, pp. 112-113.

57. Bowler, ref. 29, p. 29.

58. Thomas Browne, *Vulgar Errors*. Book 3, Ch 24.

59. Bowler, ref. 29, pp. 109-112.

60. Eiseley, ref. 9, pp. 69-75, 109.

61. Homer W. Smith, ref. 6, pp. 143-169.

62. Lynn Barber, *The Heyday of Natural History 1820-1870.* Garden City, New York: Doubleday, 1980, pp. 225-233.

63. Tyrus Hillway, "Melville's Geological Knowledge." *American Literature* 21 (1949):232-237.

64. Tyrus Hillway, "Melville and the Spirit of Science." *South Atlantic Quarterly* 48 (1949):78-88.

65. Roderick Murchison, "Presidential address." *Proceedings of the Geological Association of London.* 3 (1843) 65-151, cited by Sandra Herbert, "Darwin the Young Geologist." in *The Darwinian Heritage.* David Kohn, editor. Princeton, New Jersey: Princeton University Press, 1985, p. 488.

66. Don Cupit, *The Sea of Faith: Christianity in Change.* Cambridge: Cambridge University Press, 1984, pp. 60-63.

67. Bowler, ref. 29, pp. 65-66.

68. Davis, ref. 1, p. 65.

69. Reginald E. Watters, "Melville's Metaphysics of Evil." *University of Toronto Quarterly* 9 (1940):170-182.

70. William Paley, *Natural Theology.* Originally published in 1802 as *Natural Theology, on Evidences of the Existence and Attributes of the Deity collected from the Appearances of Nature.* Frederick Ferré, editor. Indianapolis and New York: Bobbs-Merrill, 1963, pp. 84-85.

71. René Taton, editor. *Science in the Nineteenth Century.* Basic Books, New York, 1965, p. 2.

72. Bowler, ref. 29, 1984, p. 151.

73. Eiseley, ref. 9, pp. 200-201.

74. Geoffrey Lloyd, "Aristotle: The Theory and Practice of Science." in *Man Masters Nature: Twenty-Five Centuries of Science.* Roy Porter, editor. New York: George Braziller, 1988, pp. 20-21.

75. Kuhn, ref. 4, pp. 171-194.

76. Maurice A. Finocchiaro, *The Galileo Affair: A Documentary History.* Berkeley, Los Angeles and London: University of California Press, 1989, pp. 17-25.

77. Thomas Browne, *Sir Thomas Browne: Selected Writings.* Geoffrey Keynes, editor. Chicago: University of Chicago Press, 1968, p. 34.

78. *Log* 1:273.

79. Van Helden, ref. 49, pp. 26-27.

80. Arthur O. Lovejoy, *The Great Chain of Being.* Cambridge, Massachusetts, and London: Harvard University Press, 1936 and 1964, pp. 101-102.

81. Lovejoy, ref. 80, pp. 108-109; Kuhn, ref. 4, pp. 52-77.

82. Kuhn, ref. 4, pp. 83-92.

83. Florian Cajori, *Isaac Newton's Mathematical Principles of Natural Philosophy and His System of the World. Translated into English by Andrew Motte in 1729. The translations revised, and supplied with an historical and explanatory appendix.* Berkeley, Los Angeles, London: University of California Press, 1934, pp. 629-632.

84. Cajori, ref. 83, pp. 3, 47

85. *The New Encyclopædia Britannica, Micropedia.* Chicago 1986, II, p. 807.

86. Taton, ref. 71, p. 411.

87. Hankins, ref. 52, pp. 131-133.

88. Bowler, ref. 88, pp. 73, 90.

89. Hillway, ref. 8.

90. Edward Harrison, "Nomads of the Sky." review of Donald K. Yeomans, *Comets: A Chronological History of Observation, Science, Myth and Folklore.* London: Wiley, 1991, in *Nature* 350 (1991) 521-522.

91. Stars in the Orion constellation.

92. Davis, ref. 1, pp. 66, 178n.

93. James B. Beaumont and John F. Fletcher (fl. ca 1607-1625) two popular English dramatists whose plays had a great influence on Restoration drama.

94. Jerry Stannard. "Natural History," in *Science in the Middle Ages.* David C. Lindberg, editor. Chicago and London: University of Chicago Press, 1978, pp. 430-433.

95. Homer, *Iliad* VIII 19; Plato, "Theatetus" I 153c.

96. Eiseley, ref. 9, p. 88; Browne, ref. 77, p. 39; Lovejoy, ref. 80.

97. Bowler, ref. 29, pp. 58-68; Hankins, ref. 52, p. 149-150.

98. Herbert Butterfield, *The Origins of Modern Science 1300-1800.* New York: Free Press, 1957, p. 69.

99. Kuhn, ref. 4, pp. 206-209; Bernard Jaffe, *Men of Science in America: The Role of Science in the Growth of Our Country.* New York: Simon and Schuster, 1944, pp. 480-481.

100. John D. Barrow and Frank J. Tipler, *The Anthropic Cosmological Principle.* Oxford: Oxford University Press, 1988, p. 347.

101. Barrow and Tipler, ref. 100, pp. 1-8.

102. Pietro Redondi, *Galileo: Heretic.* translated by Raymond Rosenthal. Princeton, New Jersey: Princeton University Press, 1987, pp. 51-53, 65.

103. Edward Grant, "Cosmology." in *Science in the Middle Ages.* David C. Lindberg, editor. Chicago and London: University of Chicago Press, 1978, p. 270.

104. Knight, ref. 10, p. 43.

105. Kuhn, ref. 4, p. 208.

106. Richard D. Smith, *Melville's Complaint: Doctors and Medicine in the Art of Herman Melville.* New York and London: Garland, 1991, p. 30.

107. Ralph H. Major, *A History of Medicine.* 2 vols. Oxford: Blackwell, and Springfield, Illinois: Charles C. Thomas, 1954, p. 622; Taton, ref. 71, p. 181.

108. R. D. Smith, ref. 106, p. 97.

109. Farley, ref. 24, pp. 22-31.

110. Hankins, ref. 52, p. 134.

111. Major, ref. 107, II 807.

112. Stephen Toulmin and June Goodfield, *The Architecture of Matter.* Chicago and London: University of Chicago Press, 1982, p. 146.

113. Morris Morris, Richard. *Time's Arrows: Scientific Attitudes Toward Time.* New York: Touchstone, Simon and Schuster, 1985, pp. 15-24.

114. Morris, ref. 113, pp. 86-95.

115. Stephen G. Brush, "Ghosts from the Nineteenth Century: Creationists Arguments for a Young Earth." in *Scientists Confront Creationism.* Laurie R. Godfrey, editor. New York and London: W.W. Norton, 1983, pp. 52-54.

116. Watters, ref. 69.

117. Gordon H. Mills, "The Significance of 'Arcturus' in *Mardi.*" *American Literature* 14 (1942):158-161.

118. Davis, ref. 1, pp. 67-68, 182.

119. Hillway, ref. 8.

120. Ernest Tuveson, "Space, Deity, and the 'Natural Sublime.'" *Modern Language Quarterly* 12 (1951) 20-38.

121. Stanley L. Jaki, *God and the Cosmologists.* Washington, D.C. Regnery Gateway, 1989, p. 7.

122. Tuveson, ref. 120.

123. Jaki, ref. 121, pp. 13-26.

124. Nathalia Wright, "The Head and the Heart in Melville's *Mardi.*" *PMLA* 66 (1951):351-362.

125. Hans Reichenbach, *The Rise of Scientific Philosophy.* Berkeley, Los Angeles, and London, 1951, p. 9.

126. John D. Barrow, *The World Within the World.* Oxford and New York, Oxford University Press, 1990, p. 66n.

127. Martin J. S. Rudwick, "The Shape and Meaning of Earth History." in *God and Nature: Historical Essays on the Encounter*

between Christianity and Science. David C. Lindberg and Ronald L. Numbers, editors. Berkeley, Los Angeles, and London: University of California Press, 1986, pp. 296-317.

128. Cupit, ref. 66, pp. 63-64.

129. Rudwick, ref. 127, pp. 315-317.

130. Moore, James R. "Geologists and Interpreters of Genesis in the Nineteenth Century," in Lindberg, David C. and Numbers, Ronald L. editors, *God and Nature: Historical Essays on the Encounter between Christianity and Science*. Berkeley, Los Angeles, and London: University of California Press, 1986, pp. 323-325.

131. Moore, ref. 130, pp. 322-325.

132. Eiseley, ref. 9, p. 11.

133. Milton Millhauser, *Just Before Darwin: Robert Chambers and 'Vestiges.'* Middletown, Connecticut: Wesleyan University Press, 1959, pp. 4-7.

134. Millhauser, ref. 133.

135. Eiseley, ref. 9, p. 39.

136. Millhauser, ref. 133, pp. 120-139.

137. James Robert Corey, *Herman Melville and the Theory of Evolution*. PhD. Thesis, Washington State University, 1968, p. 41.

138. Farley, ref. 24, p. 70.

139. Frederick Ferré, "Introduction." in William Paley, *Natural Theology*. (Originally published in 1802 as *Natural Theology, on Evidences of the Existence and Attributes of the Deity collected from the Appearances of Nature.)* Frederick Ferré, editor. Indianapolis and New York: Bobbs-Merrill, 1963, p. xxviii.

140. Barber, ref. 62, p. 22-26.

141. Bowler, ref. 29, pp. 136-138.

142. Barrow and Tipler, ref 100, p. 27.

143. Alec R. Vidler, *The Church in an Age of Revolution: 1789 to the present day*. Hammondsworth and New York: Penguin, 1961, p. 113.

144. John Polkinghorne, *One World: the interaction of science and theology*. London: SPCK Holy Trinity Church, 1986, p. 4.

145. Vidler, ref. 143, pp. 114-115.

146. Barber, ref. 62, pp. 237-238.

147. Elizabeth S. Foster, "Melville and Geology." *American Literature* 17 (1945):50-65.

148. Elizabeth S. Foster, "Another Note on Melville and Geology." *American Literature* 22 (1950):479-487.

Chapter 3

Redburn and *White-Jacket*: a scientific professor

After the extensive use of science in *Mardi,* Melville's next two novels, which were written in a matter of a few months, are notable for the near absence of references to science. Natural history had become a national craze and he may have felt that his satire of such a serious public interest had alienated his readers. *Mardi* was a publishing failure and received strong criticism which may have set Melville against employing science, although the actual reason is not known. *Redburn: His First Voyage. Being the Sailor-boy Confessions and Reminiscences of the Son-of-a-Gentleman in the Merchant Service* (1849), is a fictionalized story of his first ocean voyage to Liverpool in 1839. He mentions in passing a number of prominent names of science, some already noted, although they are not considered in reference to science in this work: d'Alembert (Ch 1), Jean le Rond d'Alembert (1717-1783), French mathematician and philosopher, developed the mathematical solution to the perturbations of the planets. Paracelsus and Campanella (Ch 49), Tommaso Campanella (1568-1639), Italian philosopher and poet, attempted to reconcile the natural philosophy of the Renaissance with theological orthodoxy; Bacon and Newton (Ch 50), and Lavater (Ch 54).

Redburn is bewildered by the many names of ropes on a ship; he suggests they could be simplified like the "classes of plants in botany....There is no counting the names, that surgeons and anatomists give to the various parts of the human body; which, indeed, is something like a ship....I should not be surprised, if there were a great many more names, than things in the world" (Ch 13). Classification was not limited to natural history, for the eighteenth and nineteenth centuries were great periods for schemes of classification and the urge to impose order in the more mundane aspects of life. Many believed that the main task of science was to classify nature in an exciting way and discovering how everything was arranged and worked together. Diseases were classified; stars were classified; even the sciences were classified in extensive tracts by Hegel, Kant, and Whewell. The organization of knowledge was compiled in *Encyclopedia Metropolitana* (29 volumes 1817 to 1845), mainly by the inspiration of Samuel T. Coleridge, in the *Encyclopedia Britannica* in the second half of the century, and in other similar collections of organized and classified knowledge.[1]

Melville, always alert to pretentiousness of the scientist, was skeptical of supposedly learned men, often remarking on the intelligence and wisdom of ordinary seamen. One of the sailors, Jack Blunt, recorded and interpreted his dreams according the "Bonaparte Dream Book" with tables "something like the Logarithm Tables at the end of Bowditch's Navigator," mentioned in *Mardi* (Ch 17). Blunt startles from a dream, calling for the men to "get the benches ready!" since the "Day of Judgement is coming!" for he had overheard the sailors debating whether mankind would sit or stand "at the Last Day." Homer Smith says Christianity "is an eclectic system drawn from the multiple morality of the Roman Empire, constrained to a monotheistic pattern and fired to urgent fervor by the impending advent of doomsday."[2] One concept of time prior to the end of the nineteenth century claimed that the birth of Christ was halfway in time, that the world would end in 4,000 A.D., implying that humanity had little time to change, and that it was much more important to prepare for eternity than to seek improvement during life on earth.

In Liverpool, "inquisitive old ladies" gaze at the sailors ashore "as at leopards in the Zoological Gardens" (Ch 34). The docks collect many blind, sick, and injured people who beg from the sailors, forming long lines of petitioners. One held a painted board with a picture of himself "caught in the machinery of some factory, and whirled about among spindles and cogs, with his limbs mangled and bloody" (Ch 38). The great enthusiasm for the machine and other new technology did not convince Melville of their infallible merit, a subject to occur again, especially in his short stories.

The narrator satirizes the philosophers and suggests that animals have a native intelligence, which caused revulsion when it was written in Chambers's *Vestiges* (1844):

> There are unknown worlds of knowledge in brutes; and wherever you mark a horse, or a dog, with a peculiarly mild, calm, deep-seated eye, be sure he is an Aristotle or a Kant, tranquilly speculating upon the mysteries in man. No philosophers so thoroughly comprehend us as dogs and horses. They see through us at a glance....But there is a touch of divinity even in brutes, and a special halo about a horse, that should forever exempt him from indignities. (Ch 40)

Although Immanuel Kant (1724-1804) is seldom mentioned by Melville, he was one of the most important figures in the history of science and its relationship with faith. Kant opened the way for nineteenth century developments by recognizing the significance of the natural laws of Newton combining the "starry heavens above and the moral law within" together in a single framework. He expanded Hume's argument that the observation of nature allows for probability in nature, but not in the uniformity of necessary law of nature. The final principles that rule the world cannot be understood by reason, yet experience becomes knowledge when organized by the mind. By reversing the order of knowledge, a fundamental change in thinking occurred including postulating a system of mechanical necessity, for many things lie outside the realm of the experience of the senses. Cragg says, "Insight is really more important than exact scientific knowledge, and Kant believed that what our moral experience discloses carries us far beyond the truths which phenomena reveal." He quotes Kant who says, "I have therefore found it necessary to deny *knowledge* in order to leave room for *faith*." By affirming the supremacy of the spirit, Kant bequeathed to the nineteenth century its chief philosophical problems.[3]

Melville's fifth book, *White-Jacket or the World in a Man-of-War* (1850), is based on his voyage on the frigate *United States* from August 1843 to October 1844. The book's name comes from a jacket the narrator made out of canvas for protection against the extreme weather rounding Cape Horn. The jacket was protection against wind and cold, but not rain because of its "capillary attraction" (Ch 1). Capillary attraction, due to surface tension of liquids, was investigated by numerous famous scientists, and was probably discovered by Leonardo da Vinci (1452-1519). Newton discussed it in the third edition of *Opticks,* calling attention to the local cohesion of particles. In 1802, John Leslie (1766-1832), Scottish mathematician and physicist, gave the first modern explanation of capillary attraction, explaining that a liquid rises in a tube due to an attraction of the solid for the surface of the liquid. In 1804, Thomas Young (1773-1929), English physician, physicist, mathematician, and Egyptologist, founded the theory of capillary attraction, or surface tension. Alexis Claude Clairaut (1808) was the first to call attention to the attractive forces of the fluid itself. Laplace applied mathematical studies to the phenomenon, further developed by Gauss in 1830.[4] Capillary attraction was one of the science concepts used extensively by Kant in his metaphysical speculations on natural phenomenon.[5]

Their duties and station affect the personality and temperament of the men. He suspects machinery and technology because "forced, interior quietude, in the midst of great outward commotion, breeds moody people. Who so moody as railroad-brakemen, steam-boat engineers, helmsmen, and tenders of power-looms in cotton factories" (Ch 12)? In addition to the danger of machinery, Melville was equally concerned about the dehumanizing effect of the machine on the operator. One of the quarter gunners took great pride in the care of the guns as if they were fragile "like glass retorts" (Ch 11). Retorts were early 'philosopher's instruments' used by alchemists to separate substances by heat. A retort is usually a glass bulb with a long tube extending from the top bent downward, also used for distilling. Science had the image of being detailed and accurate; the ship's cooking was the opposite: "Now the ships cooking required very little science" (Ch 15). John Mason Good's *Book of Nature* is mentioned in Chapter 41; the ship's library contains "Mason Good's Book of Nature—a very good book, to be sure, but not precisely adapted to tarry tastes" (Ch 41). Good, a conservative scientist, presented science in a way that supported religious doctrine.[6]

The deck was washed daily and thrashed with dry swabs: "After which an extraordinary implement—a sort of leathern hoe called a '*squilgee*'...I think something of drawing up a memoir, and read it before the Academy of Arts and Science" (Ch 22). Melville, however, resists taking an excursion into the realm of the scientist. Bland, the master-at-arms, proved to be a scoundrel, heading a smuggling ring aboard ship: "Phrenologically, he was without a soul" (Ch 44). The use of phrenology to emphasize evil character is a device Melville was to use often in later works. The magazine of gunpowder is lighted by lanterns "something like Sir Humphry Davy's Safety-lamp for coal mines" (Ch 31).

Serious accidents occasionally occur on navy ships; Baldy, one of the mizzen-top men, fell to the deck: "Surgeon Cuticle devoted all his science to this case" (Ch 46). The seaman soon recovers, one of the few cases of favorable outcome from medical treatment in Melville's novels. Surgeon Cuticle is described as "a gentleman of remarkable science, and a veteran practitioner....Like most old physicians and surgeons who have seen much service, and promoted to high professional place for their scientific attainments, this Cuticle was an enthusiastic in his calling" (Ch 61). He maintains a collection of "Morbid Anatomy," or pathology, in keeping with the fascination with collections of all sorts during the nineteenth century, including casts of specimens "often to be met with in the Anatomical Museums of Europe." The officers in the wardroom trick Cuticle into thinking a parcel is from "an eminent physician in Rio...to the scientific Senhor Cuticle—with the doctor's compliments—an uncommonly fine specimen of a cancer." Cuticle is enraged when he discovers it is only pudding. Yet, nothing exceeded his coolness in practicing his profession:

> Indeed, long habituation to the dissecting-room and the amputation-table had made him seemingly impervious to the ordinary emotions of humanity. Yet you could not say that Cuticle was essentially a cruel-hearted man. His apparent heartlessness must have been of a purely scientific origin. It is not to be imagined even that Cuticle would have harmed a fly, unless he could procure a microscope powerful enough to assist him in experimenting on the minute vitals of the creature. (Ch 61)

By stretching the necessity for surgery, Surgeon Cuticle performs an amputation on a sailor who had sustained a gunshot wound to the leg. One of the junior surgeons uses several anatomical names correctly, which Cuticle concedes; he comments:

> "For once, Surgeon Wedge, you use the only term that can be employed; and let me avail myself of this opportunity to say to you, young gentlemen, that a man of true science"—expanding his shallow chest a little—"uses but few hard words, and those only when none other will answer his purpose; whereas the smatterer in science"—slightly glancing toward Wedge—"thinks, that by

> mouthing hard words, he proves that he understands hard things." (Ch 63)

He derides Mexico for not having a navy and "has always been backward in furnishing subjects for the amputation-tables" of foreign navies: "The cause of science has languished in her hands." White-Jacket ponders:

> Life is more awful than Death; and let no man, though his live heart beat in him like a cannon—let him not hug his life to himself; for, in the predestinated necessities of things, that bounding life of his is not a whit more secure than the life of a man on his death-bed. (Ch 63)

Cuticle lectures the junior surgeons using detailed anatomical terms and making use of a skeleton "procured in person from the Hunterian department of the Royal College of Surgeons in London" (Ch 63). Richard Owen, after taking his medical degree in London in 1825, became the assistant curator of the museum of the Royal College of Surgeons, married the daughter of the curator, and soon was in charge of the museum. The museum was founded on the collections of John Hunter, an eighteenth century anatomist and surgeon, but Hunter's executor had destroyed all the labels of thousands of specimen jars. By 1830, Owen had sorted the specimens and was able to publish *Catalogue of the Hunterian Collections*, and under his supervision, the museum became the model for natural history museums.[7]

Master of science, venerable practitioner of surgery, Fleet Surgeon Cuticle's patient fares no better than the patient of the untrained Polynesian Samoa in *Mardi,* for Cuticle's patient dies immediately after the operation. One of the sailors is examined by Cuticle, and on "purely scientific grounds," he reprimands the sailor for not coming forward sooner with a long-standing pulmonary complaint. The sailor dies of tuberculosis. The tenderness and caring of the sailors toward their dying shipmate stands in sharp contrast to the callous "scientific" physician.

A school for midshipmen is presided over by "*The Professor*" who is in charge of "Science and Learning." He is equal in rank to the purser, surgeon, and other non-combatants: "Science and Learning were ennobled in the person of this Professor, even as divinity was honored in the Chaplain enjoying the rank of a spiritual peer." That science had achieved equal rank with religion was a phenomenon of the nineteenth century, though not in the belief of the general European mind until the end of the century. The professor took great pride in teaching the theory of gunnery, a pretentious affair "where mystical mathematical problems were solved." The professor's lecture included "the path a shot in vacuo," following a "parabolic curve" according to "the method pursued by the illustrious Newton in treating the subject of curvilinear motion" in a vain attempt to educate the midshipmen that developed into esoteric and polysyllabic humor (Ch 83). In *Principia*, Newton illustrated the effect of centripetal force and gravity citing the example of a cannonball: "It is by its gravity that it is drawn aside continually from its rectilinear course, and made to deviate towards the earth, more or less, according to the force of its gravity, and the velocity of its motion."[8]

An astronomy metaphor illustrates the mundane voyage of the *Neversink* as something of greater significance in Melville's tale in a deistic argument to complete his novel:

> As a man-of-war that sails through the sea, so this earth that sails through the air. We mortals are all on board a fast-sailing, never-sinking world-frigate, of which God was the shipwright; and she is but one craft in a Milky-Way fleet, of which God is the Lord High Admiral. The port we sail from is forever astern. And though far out of sight of land, for ages and ages we continue to sail with sealed orders, and our last destination remains a secret to ourselves and our officers; yet our final haven was predestinated ere we slipped from the stocks at Creation. (The End)

At the end of the cruise, White-Jacket reflects in Melville's philosophical bent on the microcosm of the man-of-war, reminiscent of the introspection of Browne. He says we are the repository of the secret whose mysteriousness we long to learn. No one knows better than we, "assuredly not the chaplain; even our professor's scientific surmisings are vain." We behold our dead shipmate, "sooner or later, the everlasting under-tow sweeps him toward our own destination" (Ch 94). Melville's concise resume heralds his masterpiece, *Moby-Dick.*

Notes

1. David Knight, *Ordering the World: A history of classifying man.* London: Burnett Book, Andre Deutsch, 1981, pp. 129-130, 145-147.

2. Homer W. Smith, *Man and His Gods.* Boston: Little, Brown, 1952, p. 187.

3. Gerald R. Cragg, *The Church and the Age of Reason: 1648-1789.* Grand Rapids, Michigan: Eerdmans, 1960, pp. 250-254.

4. René Taton, editor. *Science in the Nineteenth Century.* New York: Basic Books, 1965, pp. 102-103.

5. A. N. Whitehead, *Science and the Modern World.* New York: Macmillan, 1925, p.139.

6. Tyrus Hillway, "Melville's Education in Science." *Texas Studies in Literature and Language* 16 (1974):421-422.

7. Lynn Barber, *The Heyday of Natural History.1820-1870.* Garden City, New York: Doubleday, 1980, pp. 174-175.

8. Florian Cajori, *Isaac Newton's Mathematical Principles of Natural Philosophy and His System of the World. Translated into English by Andrew Motte in 1729. The translations revised, and supplied with an historical and explanatory appendix.* Berkeley, Los Angeles, London: University of California Press, 1934, p. 3.

Chapter 4

Moby-Dick: gospel cetology

Melville took the proofs of *White-Jacket* to London, sailing on the cargo ship *Southampton* October 11, 1849. In London, he visited the Zoological Gardens in Regents Park, and Greenwich Hospital. On November 28th, he took the boat to France. An accident occurred to one of the hands causing him to have reservations about technology and the great enthusiasm for mechanical inventions: "his foot was ruined in the machinery." He sailed for America on Christmas Day, 1849, arriving in New York on February 1, 1850, and soon began work on a new novel. *Moby-Dick; or, The Whale* was published in New York on November 14, 1851.

Two short sections at the beginning of *Moby-Dick*, often overlooked, examine the origin of the word 'whale,' and list a number of references to whales and whaling. The first section is titled "Etymology (supplied by a late consumptive usher to a grammar school)," i.e., tubercular. The book begins: "The pale Usher—threadbare in coat, heart, body, and brain; I see him now." The image of a sickly authority or scholar is unmistakable. He cites Richard Hakluyt (1553-1616), an early English travel writer, also cited in *Mardi*, and the dictionaries of Webster and Richardson on the origin of the word 'whale.' Melville establishes from the beginning the authority of statements to follow in the scientific exposition of *Moby-Dick*. The second section "Extracts (supplied by a sub-sub librarian)" a "painstaking burrower and grubworm of a poor devil" is presented as by a researcher, possibly a pejorative reference to the scientist as is the case in *Mardi*. "Extracts" provides an historical model for the development of the book with biblical, classical, poetic, and scientific origins. The eighty-five entries of "Extracts" are ordered in approximate chronology beginning with Genesis, "And God created great whales," progressing to the natural history of the nineteenth century. The wide range of authorities cited is much like the writings of Robert Burton and Sir Thomas Browne; he includes Oliver Goldsmith's *Natural History*, Charles Darwin's *Voyage of a Naturalist*, and his most useful scientific sources of Scoresby, Beale, Bennett, and J. Ross Browne. "Extracts" contains information on the physical attributes of the whale, its enormous size, an albino whale, and phosphorescence. The extract from Hamlet, "Very like a whale," according to Shuffelton, implies that the disturbing significance of the whale may be its symbolic potential as a sign of deeper, more terrible meanings rather than its physical attributes. The basis of the story in fact is given in "Extracts": "'My God! Mr. Chace, what is the matter? I answered, 'We have been stove by a whale.'" "Extracts" contains a few physiological estimates given by the famous scientists of the time, John Hunter's account of the dissection of a small whale, and entries from Paley's "Theology," and Baron Cuvier. The first "Extracts" connect God and whales through Creation; later "Extracts" show men viewing whales objectively from a distance. After the Romantic revolution at the end of the eighteenth century, as illustrated by "Extracts," the meaning of nature is prophesied *by* men, not *to* them. "Extracts" forms an history of human ideas grappling with the riddle of nature under the rubric of cetology. The author cannot present his "Extracts" as "veritable gospel cetology" because the truth about the natural world is in the process of unfolding new ideas. The history of ideas is the "long Vatican" from which "gospel cetology" will issue as man tries to come to terms with the natural world.[1] Thus, "Extracts" provides a solid framework in religious, classical, scientific, and topical reports for the story that follows, and to some extent, reflects the development of the conflict and heightened tension between science and faith in the mid-nineteenth century.

In the opening paragraph of Chapter One, "Loomings," the narrator takes the name Ishmael, or outcast. Nechas remarks on the beauty, complexity, and ambiguity of the language of *Moby-Dick* in Ishmael's mutually exclusive maladies. He says "some certain significance lurks in all things" (Ch 99), using synonymy, repetition, and restatement in each word and its synonyms expressing slightly different facets of the same concept.[2] In the 1840s, P. T. Barnum, the master showman, found Americans had developed a taste for the exotic and the strange, a reverence for violence and size, and a hankering for nature's monstrosities, abortions, and morbidities. He showed his attractions as "science and education"; that nothing is as wonderful as the grotesque or pitiable mistakes of nature. He adopted a style of deadpan elaboration of facts, an air of authenticity, and an unawareness of anything strange or fantastic in what he was showing; in other words, a style much like the naturalists. Chase says Melville may have intended something of a Barnum-like hoax at the beginning of *Moby-Dick* in "all the attending marvels of a thousand Patagonian sights and sounds" (Ch 1).[3] Man's traditional views were challenged by remarkable new discoveries and images:

> And still deeper the meaning of that story of Narcissus, who because he could not grasp the tormenting, mild image he saw in the fountain, plunged into it and was drowned. But that same image, we ourselves see in all rivers and oceans. It is the image of the ungraspable phantom of life; and this is the key to it all. (Ch 1)

Perception of natural phenomena had changed man's image of himself and his relationship to his God; those perceptions, says Ishmael, are all-important, a theme maintained throughout *Moby-Dick*. In looking at the Spouter Inn, he quotes "an old writer":

> 'In judging of that tempestuous wind called Euroclydon,[4]...it maketh a marvellous difference, whether thou lookest out at it from a glass window where the frost is all on the outside, or whether thou observest it from a sashless window, where the frost is on both sides, and of which the wight Death is the only glazier.'...Yes, these eyes are windows, and this body of mine is the house. What a pity they didn't stop up the chinks and the crannies though, and thrust in a little lint here and there. But it's too late to make any improvements now. The universe is finished; the copestone is on, and the chips were carted off a million years ago. (Ch 2)

The statement of time of a million years is opposed to the few thousand years of biblical time stated elsewhere in the book.

In New Bedford, at the Spouter Inn, Ishmael must share a room and bed with Queequeg, a tattooed harpooner (Ch 3). "But Queequeg, do you see, was a creature in the transition state—neither caterpillar nor butterfly" (Ch 4). Jaffe, referring to Charles Wilkes' *United States Exploring Expedition, 1838-1842...Under the Command of Charles Wilkes, U.S.N.* (5 volumes. 1844), based on a four-year voyage to the South Seas and the Antarctic, says the prototype of Queequeg was a friendly native chief in northern New Zealand and fits the character of the 'noble savage,' a prominent motif in the literature of world exploration.[5] "But who could show a cheek like Queequeg? which, barred with various tints, seemed like the Andes' western slope, to show forth in one array, contrasting climates, zone by zone" (Ch 5). This offhand remark probably came from Alexander von Humboldt, who was famous for his expedition to Central and South America (1799 to 1804). He returned from his explorations with a great number of plants and animals as well as geological data which he published in thirty volumes (1805-1830). On the mountain of Chimborazo in Ecuador, he noted the change in vegetation according to altitude is similar to the distribution of vegetation according to longitude: going vertically up the mountain was similar in natural history to going further from the Equator. Thus, geographic location was observed to be important in the development of plant and animal life.[6]

Queequeg becomes Ishmael's bosom friend; Ishmael regards him highly: "his head was phrenologically an excellent one" (Ch 10), reminding him of General Washington. He feels mysteriously drawn toward Queequeg: "And those same things that would have repelled most others, they were the very magnets that thus drew me. I'll try a pagan friend, thought I, since Christian kindness has proved but hollow courtesy" (Ch 10).

Ishmael attends the Whaleman's Chapel in New Bedford while a winter storm howls outside; tablets on the chapel wall record tragic accidents at sea. While waiting for the sermon, Ishmael ponders:

> Methinks we have hugely mistaken this matter of Life and Death. Methinks that what they call my shadow here on earth is my true substance. Methinks that in looking at things spiritual, we are too much like oysters observing the sun through the water, and thinking that thick water the thinnest of air. Methinks my body is but the lees of my better being. In fact take my body who will, take it I say, it is not me. (Ch 7)

Man's perception, like the oyster's, is distorted and spiritual truth cannot be understood by his senses, though scientific observation was creating an understanding of the heavens. Ishmael's revery resembles that of Thomas Vaughn (1621?-1666), British chemist and mystic, who wrote as Philalethes, expressed, Lovejoy says, in "Kantian terms":

> Transcendent knowledge is that which, reaching beyond all possibility of experience, strives to determine the nature of things as they are in themselves; immanent knowledge, on the other hand, is that which keeps within the confines of the possibility of experience, and consequently can tell us only of appearances. Thou, as an individual, endest at death. Only, this individuality of thine is not thy true, essential and ultimate being, but is, rather, a mere outward expression of it; it is not the thing-in-itself, but only its appearance, which is manifested in the form of time and consequently has a beginning and an end. This essence, in itself, on the contrary, knows ought of time, nor of beginning nor end, nor of the limitations of a given individuality; therefore it can be excluded from no individuality, but exists in each and all....for thy life is in *time*, thy immortality in *eternity*—it may accordingly be called an immortality without duration—which is once more, a contradiction.[7]

Father Mapple's sermon restates the Renaissance theistic concept of God in the hymn: "Awful, yet bright, as lightning shone / The face of my deliverer God." In the sermon, Jonah's sense perception is distorted by the swinging lamp that alarms and frightens Jonah in that the "contradiction of the lamp more and more appals him" (Ch 9). He concludes: "I leave eternity to Thee; for what is man that he should live out the lifetime of his God" (Ch 9)?

The mastheads on whaleships are manned in all weather without protection from storms and weather. He cites Captain Sleet, probably a satirical name referring to Scoresby's book, which contains a long, dull discussion of magnetism and the vagaries of the compass. The captain of the *Glacier* took his turn standing at the masthead and gave: "a very scientific account of his experiments" in this crow's nest on the compass, "counteracting the errors" from what is called the "local attraction" and learned opinions on "binnacle deviations," "Azimuth compass observations," and "approximate errors" (Ch 35). He says the Egyptians were great masthead standers "based on the general belief among archæologists, that the first pyramids were founded for astronomical purposes" (Ch 35). The guardians and priests of the ancient Egyptian temples were the first astronomers who predicted the flooding of the Nile by noting that Sirius, the Dog Star, rose just before dawn on the day of the flood. The river and the star were but manifestations of Osiris; by telling when the gods were to manifest themselves, the priests appeared to possess knowledge never before available: when to prepare the land for planting. The priest alone could mediate between men and gods because he alone knew the wishes of supernatural beings.[8]

The solitude and quiet of the masthead produces a dream-like state: "There you stand, lost in the infinite series of the sea, with nothing ruffled but the waves....the drowsy trade winds blow; everything resolves you into languor" (Ch 35). Melville develops the theme of the vortex: the sailors stand watch at the top of the mast-head "in due rotation," "The tranced ship indolently rolls," Ishmael stands his watch "With the problem of the universe revolving in me," "a gently rolling ship," and finally, over "Descartian vortices you hover" (Ch 35). Descartes advanced the theory of vortices, a concept held by de Maillet who connected the idea of cosmic and biologic change, and suggested a shrinking amount of water on the earth's surface based on Descartes' theory of vortices, or whirlpools, that exposed more and more of the earth's surface for animal habitation. Additional reference to the vortex occurs in Chapter 36, "The Quarter-deck," when one of the harpooners says the White Whale has many harpoons in him "all twiske-tee be-twisk...and screwing his hand round and round," twisted like cork-screws "all twisted and wrenched in him", the ship "heaved and rolled", and they pass the "charged flagon" that "spiralizes in ye." The use of the image of spiraling or revolving of a vortex increases the deterministic nature of the chase, or fate, directing the pursuit of Moby Dick.

Ishmael says his spirit becomes diffused through "space and time" (Ch 35) implying a relation between the two. The discovery of the wave propagation of light by Scottish physicist James Clerk Maxwell (1831-1879), and other advances in mathematics in the nineteenth century were to destroy the long held foundation of Euclidian geometry of the separation of time and space. Georg Friedrich Riemann (1826-1866), German mathematician, profoundly influenced mathematics and geometry; numerous methods, theorems, and concepts bear his name. The new ideas led to the concept of 'curved space' and other ideas strange to the Euclidian and Newtonian scheme of the universe.[9] Einstein gave credit to Riemann's concept of geometry which made possible the development of the general theory of relativity. The idea of the close relationship of space and time developed in contrast to the Newtonian concept of 'absolute' time separate from space and objects. According to John Locke (1687), "To conclude: expansion and duration do mutually embrace and comprehend each other; every part of space being in every part of duration, and every part of duration in every part of expansion." No major advance in the concept of the unity of time and space occurred until the twentieth century. In 1907, Hermann Minkowski (1864-1909) defined his revolutionary theory of 'space-time' based on the Einstein's theories of relativity. In 1922, Hermann Weyl (1885-1945) said that since history is a process going forward in time and takes place in space, change is not merely three-dimensional Euclidean space, but a fourth dimension linking space and time indissolubly, in a continuum which is neither time nor space. Einstein had a remarkable forerunner in the English mathematician W. K. Clifford, who in 1875 said that the theory of space curvature and the possibility of matter and motion are terms of 'extension' of one another. Shortly after the development of Einstein's theories of relativity, physicists developed the concept of "cosmic time" separate from relative "local time." E. P. Hubble in 1929 observed the red shift in optical wavelengths of galaxies as a Doppler effect indicating motion away from observation on earth due to an expansion of the universe, marking a major change in man's concept of the cosmos.[10]

Since the mid-nineteenth century marked a period in history when man's view of his universe was badly shaken by science, *Moby-Dick* contains contradictory statements about the natural world; Melville reflects both the old and new views. Two distinct views of nature develop: nature as paradise, and nature as battlefield. In the first chapter, the sea is regarded as the source of all life: it is the image of the "ungraspable phantom of life"; and this is the "key to it all." Melville returns to this theme at intervals throughout the novel. For instance, in "The Mast-Head," he says life comes from the sea: "borrowed from the sea; by the sea, from the inscrutable tides of God" (Ch 35), that life had its origin in the sea—the Neptunian theory of creation.[11] "The Mast-Head" chapter was probably taken from a single paragraph in J. Ross Browne's *Etchings of a Whaling Cruise,* greatly enlarged and enriched by Melville. Later in the novel, the sea is also a battlefield, as in the "universal cannibalism" of Chapter 58, "Brit." Melville warns the dreamy, idealistic transcendentalists in their pantheisitc revery to keep a sharp eye or miss the whales.[12]

Captain Ahab, pacing the deck dented like "geological stones" by his bone leg calls the crew together and offers a Spanish doubloon, an ounce of gold, to whoever first sights the White Whale and passionately convinces the crew to join him to hunt Moby Dick. Only Starbuck, the first mate, resists Ahab's monomaniac, destructive course; Starbuck possesses the sanity of mind that Ahab must overcome to carry out his insane mission. Ahab says Starbuck needs a little more explanation: "Starbuck; thou requirest a little lower layer." Starbuck says the whale "simply smote thee from blind instinct!" To be enraged at a dumb thing is "Madness!...blasphemous":

> Hark ye yet again,—the little lower layer. All visible objects, man, are but as pasteboard masks. But in each event—in the living act, the undoubted deed—there, some unknown but still reasoning thing put forth the mouldings of its features from behind the unreasoning mask. If man will strike, strike through the mask! (Ch 36)

The image of the pasteboard mask has received much comment and widely differing opinion as to what Melville intended. If man is to understand the world, he must look deeper than superficial appearances, i.e., deeper than the sense perception of the positivists. In a subsequent chapter, "On the Whiteness of the Whale" (Chap. 42), the importance of the superficial nature of things becomes more apparent.

Rothschild claims the ceremony of the "Quarter-Deck" uses the imagery of mesmerism, or "animal magnetism," popular in America during the 1830s and 1840s along with hypnotic trances, clairvoyance, and spirit communications; all following in the wake of phrenology. The scene also emphasizes interest in electricity, as in the Leyden jar, a simple device for storing an electrical charge, and its importance in mesmerism: "touch the axis" with crossed "radiating lances...suddenly and nervously twitched them." It seemed "he would fain have shocked into them the same fiery emotion accumulated within the Leyden jar of his own magnetic life"; "For did ye three but once take the full-forced shock, then mine own electric thing, that had perhaps expired from out me" (Ch 36). The scene continues with a pagan religious ceremony dominated by Ahab pledging with "murderous chalices" death to Moby Dick. The mesmeric force, i.e., animal magnetism, was thought to be inherent in man, and when transferred to another, causes a temporary loss in the mesmerizer, a peculiar loss of strength and general uneasiness, that if carried to an extreme would "drop ye dead." Rothschild says the imagery suggests both the divine and the horrible, since mesmerism appeared to be a new testimony to man's spiritual capacity and a hideous perversion of it.[13] Paracelsus (1493?-1541), in addition to being an alchemist, was the first 'magnetiser' and the first to attribute occult and miraculous powers to the magnet; he was convinced that the magnet was the philosopher's stone. A succession of magnetizers, principally in Germany, followed Paracelsus. In 1772, Maximillian Hell, a Jesuit professor of astronomy at the University of Vienna, became famous for his cures by applying magnetic steel plates to the naked body. In 1774, he instructed Anthony Mesmer (1734-1815), who studied medicine at the University of Vienna, and later founded the theory of 'animal magnetism.' Mesmer successfully treated a young woman suffering from periodic attacks of delirium and syncope. He concluded he could produce magnetism by his touch, which he termed "animal magnetism." The ceremony of Mesmer is similar to the ceremony performed by Ahab. Mesmer died unaware that the wild phenomenon of animal magnetism was the beginnings of hypnotism. Animal magnetism flourished in England and America into the early nineteenth century.[14] "The Quarter-Deck" becomes a turning point in the novel revealing the character and motives of the captain and the "conversion" of the crew. Ahab obtains the pledge of the crew to join his quest of Moby Dick.

Though Ahab is the 'rational man' even in his madness, he exclaims, "Gifted with the high perception, I lack the low, enjoying power; damned, most subtly and most malignantly! damned in the midst of Paradise" (Ch 37)! In this brief statement, Melville defines his dilemma: the fatal nature of a Faustian-greater understanding. He can no longer control events: "it's all predestinated" (Ch 39).

In Ahab's earlier encounter with Moby Dick, his whale boat was destroyed by the whale. In the struggle that followed, Ahab audaciously attacked the whale with his knife: "sweeping his sickle-shaped lower jaw beneath him, Moby Dick had reaped away Ahab's leg" (Ch 41). Many whales and dolphins with badly deformed jaws, or those entirely missing a lower jaw, appear to have good health; the deformity may result from prey-stunning.[15] Ahab is driven to revenge against the White Whale: "The path to my fixed purpose is laid with iron rails, whereon my soul is grooved to run....Naught's an obstacle, naught's an angle to the iron way" (Ch 37)! The choice is not Ahab's at this point; he is the victim of mechanical fate. The injury becomes the focus of all of life's evil: "for long months of days and weeks, Ahab and anguish lay stretched together in one hammock, rounding in mid winter that dreary, howling Patagonian Cape; then it was, that his torn body and gashed soul bled into one another; and so interfusing, made him mad" (Ch 41).

In the middle part of the novel, or the 'Cetological Center,' Melville reviews the study of the whale adding comments on science, zoology and taxonomy, beginning with classification, "a systematized exhibition of the whale in his broad genera,...The classification of the constituents of chaos, nothing less is here essayed. Listen to what the best and latest authorities have laid down" (Ch 32). He cites Beale's *Natural History of the Sperm Whale* on the difficulties of studying the whale: "Unfitness to pursue our research in the unfathomable waters." "Impenetrable veil covering our knowledge of the cetacea." "A field strewn with thorns." "All these incomplete indications but serve to torture us naturalists." He cites: "The Authors of the Bible; Aristotle; Pliny; Aldrovandi; Sir Thomas Browne; Gesner; Ray; Linnaeus; Rondeletius; Willoughby; Green; Artedi; Sibbald; Brisson; Marten; Lacépède; Bonnetierre; Desmarest; Baron Cuvier; Frederick Cuvier; John Hunter; Owen; Scoresby; Beale; Bennett; J. Ross Browne; the Author of Miriam Coffin; Olmsted; and the Rev. T. Cheever" (Ch 32). Melville refers to many authorities, but probably took nearly all of the information from Thomas Beale's *Natural History of the Sperm Whale*.[16] He cites Scoresby (1820), "No branch of Zoology is so much involved as that which is entitled Cetology." The authorities in "Extracts" are also given credit for writing about the whale; he credits two books as authoritative—Beale's and Frederick Debell Bennett's *Narrative of a Whaling Voyage Around the Globe*, "both in their time surgeons to English South-Sea whale-ships, and both exacting and reliable men" (Ch 32). He gives special credit to Scoresby who was "a professional harpooneer and whaleman." Cetology is a ponderous task, says Melville, "To grope down into the bottom of the sea after them; to have one's hands among the unspeakable foundations, ribs, and very pelvis of the world; this is a fearful thing." He cites Linnaeus in "Systems of Nature, A.D. 1766," separating whales from fish. Melville satirically classifies whales as he would books, by book, folio, octavo, and duodecimo according to the size of the whale. The narwhale, "sea-unicorn," has a long pointed horn, that in ancient times was regarded as an antidote against poison and brought a high price. In addition, it was distilled "to a volatile salts for fainting ladies" (Ch 32). "As yet, however, the sperm whale, scientific or poetic, lives not complete in any literature. Far above all other hunted whales, his is an unwritten life" (Ch 32). The understanding of the whale is further complicated: "For as the secrets of the currents in the seas have never yet been divulged, even to the most erudite research; so the hidden ways of the Sperm Whale when beneath the surface remain, in great part, unaccountable..." (Ch 41). Melville disagrees with experienced whalemen and learned naturalists on the nature of the whale's skin. A lengthy discourse on whale skin follows in Chapter 68, "The Blanket":

"I have had controversies about it with experienced whalemen afloat, and learned naturalists ashore" (Ch 68).

Although scholars differ on the 'central' or theme chapters of *Moby-Dick*, most consider Chapter 42, "The Whiteness of the Whale," important to the interpretation of the book. Ishmael introduces reasons that whiteness enhances beauty and possesses a special virtue, yet notes that whiteness may be awful and appalling. Moby Dick was distinguished by "a peculiar snow-white wrinkled forehead, and a high, pyramidical white hump" (Ch 41). White is the color of the dead and the color of ghosts:

> Is it that by its indefiniteness it shadows forth the heartless voids and immensities of the universe, and thus stabs us from behind with the thought of annihilation, when beholding the white depths of the milky way? Or is it, that in essence whiteness is not so much a color as the visible absence of color, and at the same time the concrete of all colors;...a colorless, all-color of atheism...And when we consider that other theory of the natural philosophers, that all other earthly hues...the sweet tinges of sunset skies and woods...and the butterfly cheeks of young girls; all these are but subtle deceits, not actually inherent in substances, but only laid on from without...the great principle of light, for ever remains white or colorless in itself, and if operating without medium upon matter, would touch all objects, even tulips and roses, with its own blank tinge. (Ch 42)

Although an albino whale was mentioned in "Extracts," Melville's references to albinism probably arose from P. T. Barnum, who featured albinos in his freak shows. In addition, the Albany *Evening Journal* on June 19, 1837, carried an account of an albino child exhibited at the Albany Museum for a few days where Melville may have seen the child, or at least the newspaper accounts of the exhibition.[17] Further, a description of an enormous albino whale called Mocha Dick appeared in *The Knickerbocker, New York Monthly Magazine* in May 1839, written by J. N. Reynolds. Melville uses contemporary theories of light to intensify the mystic whiteness of Moby Dick. Newton, using a prism, demonstrated that white sunlight consists of component colors, "the concrete of all colors." Galen quotes Demokritos that sensations are only conventions and that the qualities result from atomic collisions: "In reality, there is no whiteness or blackness or yellowness or redness;..."[18] In the thirteenth century, Grosseteste said:

> ...the penetrating power in virtue of which the mind's eye does not rest on the outer surface of an object, but penetrates to something below the visual image. For instance, when the mind's eye falls on a coloured surface, it does not rest there, but descends to the physical structure of which the colour is an effect. It then penetrates this structure until it detects the elemental qualities of which the structure is itself an effect.[19]

During the seventeenth century, a sharp distinction was drawn between the material body and the immaterial soul and mind, but Descartes put forward his theory that the body was a machine governed by laws of matter. Thus, the soul received its information about the world through the brain and senses that might be colored by the perceiving and transmitting mechanism, the body. As science conceived the phenomenon, only mathematically expressible properties of size, shape, and motion could be perceived, but not its color, luster, or beauty, which could not exist apart from the brain. However, size, shape and motion could, a view that has remained intact to the present. Taylor agrees with Melville, the objects of the scientist have:

> ...size, shape, motion, but there is no colour, scent, beauty in that world: there is no purpose, no emotion, no love. That is why it is so utterly dangerous to treat the world which the scientist has abstracted for study from what he perceives, as if it were the totality of things; and that is the fallacy of the materialist.
>
> Because science is so intelligible, works so perfectly, and gives us such power, we are tempted to treat its world as the real world, despite our knowledge that the things which are important in human life are not quantitative or extended and so can never enter into science.[20]

Kant, in his *Critique of Pure Reason* (1781), reversed the concept of perception in that the mind converts the chaos of "raw sense-experience" into an ordered cosmos—the ordered world we see is the creation of the mind for there is no other way to know it, but it does not connect the world to God, for God is not part of world of experience. According to Kant, the human mind not only discovers truth, but constitutes truth: The creative work of turning chaos into cosmos, ascribed in the past to God, is now seen as something that is necessarily done by the human mind.[21]

Great progress occurred in light theory during the nineteenth century by Thomas Young, Augustin Jean Fresnel (1788-1827), French physicist, and Lord Kelvin. The modern theory of electromagnetic wave propagation of light was formulated by Maxwell shortly after the publication of *Moby-Dick.* Matter has no inherent color, but only selectively absorbs certain wavelengths of light and reflects the unabsorbed light. White is the reflection of all color. Thus, white obscures the perceptions of the inward character of man and matter. The surface of beautiful things is deceitful; true meanings lie beneath, independent of the surface reflection, like the disfigured bronzed skin of a man "the palsied universe lies before us a leper" for there is no color unless light strikes an object. On the awful whiteness of the albatross, he says: "Not Coleridge first threw that spell; but God's great, unflattering laureate, Nature" which he says in a footnote he first saw during a prolonged gale in "waters hard upon the Antarctic seas" (Ch 42).

At night, Ahab methodically and "scientifically" studies ocean charts, currents, and sightings of whales, plotting the probable course of Moby Dick, giving the madness of the chase a base in rational planning in the "The Chart," Chapter 44. According to Vincent, Melville relied on Charles Wilkes's *Narrative* and Matthew Maury's *Explanations and Sailing Directions, etc.* (1851), for the information in "The Chart." Commodore Wilkes led the first large scientific expedition to Antarctica and the Pacific Ocean. Prior to his exploration, Polynesia was remote and unfamiliar to most Americans, except for the stories of Captain Cook (1728-1779). Melville owned Wilkes's book and probably borrowed from the essay, "On Currents and Whaling," for *Moby-Dick.* Melville added a footnote to *Moby-Dick* acknowledging the circular of Lieutenant Maury's of the National Observatory in Washington, charting of whale migrations and the location of the best whaling grounds which was published in 1851, just after the publication of *Moby-Dick.*[22] Matthew F. Maury (1806-1873), U.S. naval officer and hydrographer, whose oceanographic research received wide acclaim, was in charge of charts and instruments which became the navy observatory and hydrographic office; he advocated cooperation between nations on ocean meteorology which led to an international conference in Brussels in 1853 greatly benefiting navigation.[23]

After examining the charts night after night, sleepless, restless, and weary, Ahab's tormented dreams and pursuits fuse. Forced from his hammock by "exhausting and intolerably vivid dreams," he rushes from his cabin "a vacated thing, a formless somnambulistic being, a ray of living light, to be sure, but without an object to color, and therefore a blankness in itself" (Ch 44): a restatement of the theme of Chapter 42,

"The Whiteness of the Whale." Starbuck alone among the crew abhors Ahab's quest for the whale, but Ahab controls Starbuck's will:

> To accomplish his object Ahab must use tools; and of all tools used in the shadow of the moon, men are most apt to get out of order. He knew, for example, that however magnetic his ascendency in some respects was over Starbuck yet that ascendency did not cover the complete spiritual man any more than mere corporeal superiority involves intellectual mastership; for to the purely spiritual, the intellectual but stands in a sort of corporeal relation. Starbuck's body and Starbuck's coerced will were Ahab's, so long as Ahab kept his magnet at Starbuck's brain. (Ch 46)

The use of the metaphor of the magnet suited Melville's purpose to illustrate "force at a distance." Later, Ahab tells the captain of the *Samuel Enderby* of Moby Dick: "What is best let alone, that accursed thing is not always what least allures. He's all magnet" (Ch 100)!

On a cloudy, sultry afternoon, while weaving a sword mat with Queequeg, a strange dreaminess came over the ship:

> ...it seemed as if this were the Loom of Time, and I myself were a shuttle mechanically weaving and weaving away at the Fates....The straight warp of necessity, not to be swerved from its ultimate course—its every alternating vibration, indeed, only tending to that; free will still free to ply her shuttle between given threads; and chance, though restrained in its play within the right lines of necessity, and sideways in its motions directed by free will, though prescribed to by both, chance by turns rules either, and has the last featuring blow at events. (Ch 47)

In "The Mat-Maker," as well as "The Mast-Head" (Ch 35) and in "Time and Temples" (Ch 75) in *Mardi,* Melville explores the nature of time; time, fate, and science become inter-related, and again here in the "Loom of Time." Time in Babylonian, Greek, and Roman eras was thought to be cyclical, or measured by recurring seasonal and celestial events. According to Plato, time was a product of motion. Aristotle considered time dependent on observable physical phenomenon, such as the seasons or the human heartbeat, a concept that endured from the classical period through the Middle Ages. The idea of 'linear time,' or progression, arose from Judaism and Christianity: the flight from Egypt could not recur in cyclic time. St. Augustine in the fourth century A.D. said, "once Christ died for our sins; and rising from the dead, He dieth no more."[24] The death and resurrection of Christ is the principal event of Christianity and, if cyclical, would destroy the meaning of Redemption. St. Augustine divided time into six stages according to the six days of Creation. The last stage began with the birth of Christ and will end with the Last Judgement when God will end time. The dominant idea of time in the Middle Ages was the concept that the world was nearing its end. Consequently, man's goal was not betterment in this world, but preparation for eternity.

Man's awareness of time in the performance of music began earlier than the development of the clock; Gregorian chants, which originated in the ninth century, became more complex with separate, simultaneous melodies. An even greater advance occurred with the definition of the duration of 'rests,' or periods of omission of sound, a concept that was impossible up to the period of the Middle Ages. Thus, by the sixteenth century, a new perception of time in music had evolved, and Galileo, schooled in the quadrivium—arithmetic, geometry, astronomy, and music—began a revolution in human thought by applying time to the scientific measurement of physical events. He devised a method of lengthening the time required to cover vertical distance by allowing a brass ball to roll down planks of various lengths; he measured time by weighing the amount of water flowing through a narrow tube into a beaker. With this prosaic experiment, he discovered one of the enduring laws of nature: that time and the distance traveled by a falling body maintain a constant ratio no matter the height or length of the incline. Galileo recognized time as an independent dimension that could be used to measure motion. A half century later, Newton found the attraction of heavenly bodies varied according to the mass and inversely to the square of the distance between them; the path and position of the planets could be determined and, by extrapolation, the location of a planet could be calculated for any past or future time. If true of celestial bodies, man's past and future activities may also be determined by the same mathematical, mechanistic certainty of fate. Descartes did not share the notion of his contemporaries that the world would soon come to an end, and he was one of the first to pose the idea of progress of time. Hutton, the founder of modern geology, is also the founder of geological time, saying that there is "no evidence of a beginning [of the earth] or prospect of an end." Once the restraints were broken, the examination of time was greatly extended to the point that some scientists thought time was infinite. The Laplace 'demon' of determinism (a hypothetical superior intelligence knowing all of the forces acting in the universe and the positions and velocities of all atoms at any instant) may not exist, but arguments for the principle of indeterminism are not entirely convincing either. No one knows if there is just one possible future or many.[25] In 1936, Sir James Jeans said that before Einstein stated his Special Theory of Relativity in 1905, the ordinary man as well as the scientist regarded the passage of time like "the pattern of a tapestry is woven out of a loom" like the sword mat (Ch 47); no absolute distinction exists between present, past, and future; the 'tapestry' is already woven and we become aware of it bit by bit. The familiar concept of time as a vast advancing knife edge, as in "The Matt-Maker" (Ch 47), has been replaced by the unfamiliar Minkowski diagram, "a complex of advancing light cones in space-time, the track of each vertex being the world line of a potential observer."[26] Melville examines the complexities of time even more in his next book, *Pierre*. The dreaminess of the afternoon is broken by Tashtego calling out the first sighting of whales. Thus, the conflict of fate, free will and necessity remains unsolved by twentieth century science and the ideas expressed by Melville in "The Sword-Mat" are reasonable: that chance, free will, and fate each limit choice within certain bounds as expressed by twentieth century science in probabilities, not certainties.

In Chapter 55, "Of Monstrous Pictures of Whales," Melville criticizes naturalists for their inaccurate depiction of a whale which looks like "an amputated sow," and the "scientific drawings" taken from stranded whales. In Chapter 56 "Of the Less Erroneous Pictures of Whales," and Chapter 57 "Of Whales in Paint; in Teeth; in Wood; &c.," Ishmael says the artist is more accurate and reliable than the naturalist and scientist. On the London docks, a crippled sailor holding a painted board before him depicting the scene where he lost his leg to a whale was more representative of the whale than the drawings of the naturalists. Melville's source for these examples was probably the Jonathan Bourne Whaling Museum in New Bedford.[27] The whale was commonly regarded as a fish during the Middle Ages:

> Since the sight of a living whale was restricted to fishermen, among whom few *literati* normally would be included, reports of its great size became exaggerated in direct proportion to the distance from the coastline. Such reports, moreover, fitted nicely with the biblical account of Jonah and his misadventures. As a consequence, the whale became a popular subject, not only in bestiaries but in ecclesiastical art and sculpture as well.[28]

Ishmael says the whale has been pictured on shields, medallions, coins, etc., since the oldest Hindu, Egyptian, and Grecian sculptures: "ever since then has something of the same sort of license prevailed, not only in most popular pictures of the whale, but in many scientific presentations of him" (Ch 55):

> In the title-page of the original edition of the "Advancement of Learning"[29] you will find some curious whales.
>
> But quitting all these unprofessional attempts, let us glance at those pictures of leviathan purporting to be sober, scientific delineations, by those who know....
>
> Nor are the most conscientious compilations of Natural History for the benefit of the young and tender, free from the same heinousness of mistake. Look at that popular work "Goldsmith's Animated Nature."...
>
> Then, again, in 1825, Bernard Germain, Count de Lacépède, a great naturalist, published a scientific systemized whale book, wherein are several pictures of the different species of the Leviathan....
>
> But the placing of the cap-sheaf to all this blundering business was reserved for the scientific Frederick Cuvier, brother to the famous Baron. In 1836, he published a Natural History of Whales, in which he gives what he calls a picture of the Sperm Whale....Frederick Cuvier's Sperm Whale is not a Sperm Whale, but a squash. Of course, he never had the benefit of a whaling voyage (such men seldom have), but whence he derived that picture, who can tell? Perhaps he got it as his scientific predecessor in the same field, Desmarest, got one of his authentic abortions; that is, from a Chinese drawing....
>
> But these manifold mistakes in depicting the whale are not so very surprising after all. Consider! Most of the scientific drawings have been taken from the stranded fish; and these are about as correct as a drawing of a wrecked ship, with broken back, would correctly represent the noble animal itself in all its undashed pride of hull and spars....The living whale, in his full majesty and significance, is only to be seen at sea in unfathomable waters; and afloat the vast bulk of him is out of sight, like a launched line-of-battle ship;...In fact, as the great Hunter says, the mere skeleton of the whale bears the same relation to the fully invested and padded animal as the insect does to the chrysalis that so roundingly envelopes it....
>
> For all these reasons, then, any way you may look at it, you must needs conclude that the great Leviathan is that one creature in the world which must remain unpainted to the last. (Ch 55)

He says the English and American:

> ...whale draughtsmen seem entirely content with presenting the mechanical outline of things, such as the vacant profile of the whale; which, so far as picturesqueness of effect is concerned, is about tantamount to sketching the profile of a pyramid....Even Scoresby...[made miniature drawings of whales] with the microscopic diligence of a Leuwenhoek (Ch 56).

The inaccurate depiction of whales alluded to in *Moby-Dick* may represent an example of the uncertainty principle, or complementarity, of Niels Bohr. To Bohr, the concept of complementarity had a greater philosophical significance by suggesting that antithetical concepts of human experience might be controlled by an analogous 'uncertainty principle'; for example, the concepts of free will and determinism, or vitalism and mechanism as complementary pairs—if one is adopted, the other cannot exist. The validity of either depends upon what question is asked. In order to study the anatomy and physiology of a living animal it would have to be killed and dissected. The observer alters the nature of the specimen irrevocably. The observation of primitive cultures is influenced by the presence of the observer.[30]

Chapter 58, "Brit," compares the antithesis of sea and land; Ishmael disputes the naturalists who claimed all land creatures have their counterparts in the sea, criticizing comparative anatomists: "For though some old naturalists have maintained that all creatures of the land are of their kind [counterparts] in the sea," a concept of de Maillet discussed in *Mardi*, and which Melville disputes: "does the ocean furnish any fish that in disposition answers to the sagacious kindness of the dog? The accursed shark alone can in any generic respect be said to bear comparative analogy to him" (Ch 58). Furthermore, science can never understand the vastness of the sea:

> ...though we know the sea to be an everlasting terra incognita, so that Columbus sailed over numberless unknown worlds to discover his one superficial western one; though, by vast odds,...though but a moment's consideration will teach, that however baby man may brag of his science and skill, and however much, in a flattering future, that science and skill may augment; yet for ever and for ever, to the crack of doom, the sea will insult and murder him, and pulverize the stateliest, stiffest frigate he can make; nevertheless, by the continual repetition of these very impressions, man has lost

> that sense of the full awfulness of the sea which aboriginally belongs to it. (Ch 58)

The limit of science is a persistent theme of *Moby-Dick*, here stated succinctly. Cetacean research, with its many technical difficulties, reached the "mainstream" of science only in the 1980s.[31]

Ishmael elaborates on the treacherousness of nature, that nature is not all kind and nurturing:

> Consider the subtleness of the sea; how its most dreaded creatures glide under water, unapparent for the most part, and treacherously hidden beneath the loveliest tints of azure. Consider also the devilish brilliance and beauty of many of its most remorseless tribes, as the dainty embellished shape of many species of sharks. Consider, once more, the universal cannibalism of the sea; all whose creatures prey upon each other, carrying on eternal war since the world began. (Ch 58)

In commenting on the "universal cannibalism of the sea," he objects to the New England transcendentalists who claimed the benign and healing quality of nature, a remark based on his own observation and possibly borrowed from Lamarck, who said, "...it is the stronger and better equipped that eat the weaker, and that the larger species devour the smaller in 'the war of nature.'"[32] Lamarck, aware that the earth undergoes gradual change, postulated a mechanism by which life can adapt to change without extinction, and postulated the concept of 'inheritance of acquired characteristics.' He suggested that the animal's needs determine the organs its body will develop, allowing the organism to adjust to environmental conditions. Those parts of the body that are exercised the most will receive the most "nervous fluid," develop more complex tissue, and increase the size of the organ; disused organs will degenerate.[33] The sea sharks and air sharks pounce upon the whale carcass once it is cut loose from the ship: "Oh, horrible vulturism of earth! from which not the mightiest whale is free" (Ch 69).

Melville noted the dangers of whaling, especially in the whaleboat after the whale is struck and the whale line is taken out of the boat, "to be seated then in the boat is like being seated in the midst of the manifold whizzing of a steam-engine in full play, when every flying beam, and shaft, and wheel, is grazing you," perhaps a reference to Melville's *Journal* (1849-1850),[34] of the accident that occurred on the boat to France when a man lost his foot in mechanical gears. Like the cabin before the storm, "All men live enveloped in whale-lines. All are born with halters round their necks; but it is only when caught in the swift, sudden turn of death, that mortals realize the silent, subtle, ever-present perils of life" (Ch 60). In this and other examples, Melville doubts the worth of the power of the steam engine and locomotive, symbols of 'progress,' and feared that technology could be dangerous.

One of the harpooners cuts the blubber making "a scientific dash" at the mass (Ch 67), yet the beheading of the sperm whale is a "scientific anatomical feat," upon which experienced "whale surgeons" pride themselves. The exacting task of dissection of the whale required knowledge of the anatomy of the neck, and Stubb was the *Pequod's* skilled practitioner. The head of a sperm whale is hoisted on the side of the ship to remove the oily spermacetti from the case of the head; a smaller right whale's head is hoisted on the other side of the ship as a counter balance, providing a chance to study "practical cetology" (Ch 74). The sperm whale has a "mathematical symmetry" (Ch 74) lacking in the right whale. Melville notes the visual characteristics and absence of binocular vision in the sperm whale since the eyes are located caudally behind the great mass of the head. The whale may be able to concentrate his gaze on two opposite objects, "as if a man were able simultaneously to go through the demonstrations of two distinct problems of Euclid," a 3rd Century B.C. Greek mathematician influential in the development of geometry. His principles were accepted as doctrinal until new theories of geometry and the concepts of time and space developed in the early nineteenth century.

The whale's eyes are as "broad as the lens of Herschel's great telescope," yet its ears are "smaller than a hare's" (Ch 74). The great telescope of Herschel is mentioned in *Mardi,* Chapter 122, and again in *Moby-Dick.* The expansion of astronomical knowledge in the eighteenth and nineteenth centuries was largely due to the achievements of Sir William Herschel (1738-1822) and his sister Caroline. Through his art of advanced telescope construction, dedicated observations, and comprehensive cataloguing of stars and celestial objects, Herschel founded the study of galactic movement, forcing the study of stars outside the Solar System and outside our galaxy. Herschel developed the reflecting telescope to its highest form; his greatest achievement was a forty-foot instrument with a four-foot aperture—a technological wonder of the eighteenth century. His most important work was accomplished with a twenty-foot instrument having an aperture of 18.7 inches. After Herschel made the discovery of nebulae, or oval glowing discs, astronomers came from far away to see the celestial phenomena visible only in Herschel's telescope. He applied statistics to astronomy, discovered infrared rays in the sun's spectrum, and discovered the first new planet in the Solar System since antiquity, the planet Uranus, which made him an international celebrity and earned him membership in the Royal Society of London. Caroline Lucretia Herschel (1751-1848), an expert on comets, worked from 1775 until her death in 1848, aged 97, in the study of astronomy, winning many honors. At age 75, she completed her work in cataloguing 2500 nebulae. The Herschels did as much to widen the vistas of man's universe as did Darwin in a different field.[35]

The advent of the telescope enhanced, rather than weakened, the importance of the Solar System. The sun, moon and planets could be magnified, but the stars remained mere points of light in spite of the telescope. Astronomy was pursued not only for its scientific importance, but also for the pragmatic purpose of attempting to determine a ship's longitude for navigation. Even Newton's discoveries of gravitation did little to change the lack of interest in stars until Halley's spectacular success in predicting by the application of Newton's laws that the comet seen in 1682 would return in 1758. Thereafter, the laws of gravity were applied to every object in the universe, no matter how small. In spite of Laplace's *Mécanique Céleste,* which was devoted to the Newtonian motions of the Solar System, the stars were thought to be outside the field of productive study. When in 1718 Halley noted a shift in four bright stars from their position at the time of Ptolemy, the first change occurred in the concept of a fixed crystalline sphere of stars. The discovery of stellar movement in the "fixed stars," as opposed to the "wandering stars" or planets, opened the investigation of sidereal astronomy; Herschel proposed that the Solar System is but one of many star systems in the universe in *On the Proper Motion of the Sun and Solar System* (1783), and that the sun itself is in motion. With his twenty-foot telescope, he was able to show that the nebulae were composed of a myriad of individual stars. He conceived the stellar universe as three-dimensional, striving to show that the universe has another important dimension—immense depth. In 1785, he postulated the "disc theory" of the shape of the Milky Way, and that the Solar System is only one of many systems in numerous strata of stars and not at the center of all creation. The telescope mentioned by Melville is undoubtedly Herschel's forty-foot instrument completed in 1789, which required four years to build, and became famous in itself as a tourist attraction. However, the telescope did not improve his viewing because it was so difficult to use except to confirm some distant observations made with his reliable twenty-foot instrument.[36]

Ishmael contrasts the sperm whale's head and the head of a right whale which is used as a counterbalance: "So, when on one side you hoist in Locke's head, you go over that way; but now, on the other side, hoist in Kant's and you came back again; but in very poor plight" (Ch 73). The head may sideways be divided into "two quoins" which Melville says is not a "Euclidean term" (Ch 77), but is a wedge tapering from one side instead of mutually from both sides. Ishmael employs phrenology when he contrasts the heads of the two whales: "This Right Whale I take to have been a Stoic; the Sperm Whale, a Platonian, who might have taken up Spinoza in latter years" (Ch 75). "A sensible physiologist" must settle whether the sperm whale's head has the battering ram power alleged to it. Melville reviews the anatomy of the whale's head and it's peculiar properties, as though the forehead were paved with horses' hoofs, and full of the most delicate oil. Phrenologically, the sperm whale is an enigma which the capture and hoisting of the head permits Ishmael to examine: "To scan the lines of his face, or feel the bumps on the head of this Leviathan; this is a thing which no Physiognomist or Phrenologist has as yet undertaken" (Ch 79). Lavater may as well have "scrutinized the wrinkles on the Rock of Gibraltar," or Gall the "Dome of the Pantheon." Lavater not only studied "various faces of men" but the "faces of horses, birds, serpents, and fish....Nor have Gall and his disciple Spurzheim failed to throw out some hints touching the phrenological characteristics of other beings than man." Ishmael says he will attempt "the application of these two semi-sciences to the whale," but meets an obstacle: "Physiognomically regarded, the Sperm Whale is an anomalous creature. He has no proper nose" greatly affecting "the countenance of the whale." Yet, it has a "horizontal, semi-crescentic depression in the forehead's middle, which, in man, is Lavater's mark of genius." Ishmael says, "Champollion deciphered the wrinkled granite hieroglyphics. But there is no Champollion to decipher the Egypt of every man's and every being's face" (Ch 79). Jean Francois Champollion (1790-1832), French Egyptologist, made an exhaustive study of the Rosetta stone. He was the first to be able read more than a few words and proper names in Egyptian hieroglyphics. His studies of ancient Egypt met strong opposition for giving so much attention to a barbaric culture. Champollion is used as an adjective in *Mardi* (Ch 157).

Ishmael continues: "Physiognomy, like every other human science, is but as passing fable. If then, Sir William Jones [(1746-1794) British orientalist, linguist and jurist] who read in thirty languages, could not read the simplest peasant's face in its profounder and more subtle meanings, how may unlettered Ishmael hope to read the awful Chaldee of the Sperm Whale's brow" (Ch 79)? Dryden says science, like religion, is a fictive creation of man, derived of his attempts to penetrate beneath the surface of an enigmatic world symbolized by Ishmael in Egypt, birthplace of the gods and of hieroglyphic writing as well. Like the hieroglyph, the whale's "broad firmament of a forehead" is "pleated with riddles," and like the deified crocodile of the Nile, its "pyramidical silence" indicates that it is tongueless and cannot solve the difficulties of man.[37] Ishmael ponders:

> If the Sperm Whale be physiognomically a Sphinx, to the phrenologist his brain seems that geometrical circle which it is impossible to square....
>
> It is plain, then, that phrenologically the head of this Leviathan, in the creature's living intact state, is an entire delusion. As for his true brain, you can then see no indications of it, nor feel any. The whale, like all things that are mighty, wears a false brow to the common world. (Ch 80)

Melville acquired Lavater's *Essays on Physiognomy for the Promotion of the Knowledge and the Love of Mankind* in London in 1850. Phrenology had two basic tenets: the brain is divided into identifiable organs or faculties whose quality was proportionate to their size, and that suitable exercise would improve the quality of these organs. *Essays* claims that facial features reflect the character of man and animal. Lavater maintained that man's potential for divinity could be seen in the development of the face. Consequently, the fish, without a vertical forehead, arched mouth, and pointed teeth is "senseless, intractable, and void of passion or feeling; devouring without passion or satisfaction." Moby Dick, with an enormous head, was even more phrenologically deprived: "a dead, blind wall without a single organ of prominence whatsoever." A 'sub-pseudo-science' emphasized nasal classification, or nasology, further confounding understanding of the whale—the whale has no nose except the spout hole on the top of his head. The wrinkles in the forehead may indicate genius, but the whale has no forehead for the wrinkles of genius to crease. Melville refutes the pseudosciences of phrenology and physiognomy, yet he used phrenological characteristics in subsequent writings.

In Chapter 80, "The Nut," Ishmael examines the whale's brain. The enormous brow does not contain a twenty-foot brain, only a "ten-inch nut." The small anterior brain shows weak perception and lack of intellectual or moral maturity. Ishmael, looking at the rear view of the brain, finds no great attributes, because the whale appears to lack self-esteem, veneration or nobility, and religious devotion. Its best developed faculties are "Animal Propensities," organs governing procreation and self-preservation. Melville takes phrenology to an extreme carrying his inquiry "from the cerebellum through the spinal canal....Apply this spinal branch of phrenology to the Sperm Whale" (Ch 80). A phrenology craze swept America in the mid-nineteenth century. The chapter on the phrenology of the whale probably originated from *The Whale and His Captors,* by Henry T. Cheever, who wrote humorously on the discrepancy of the sperm whale's head and its brain.[38] After dispensing with physiognomy and phrenology, Ishmael presents his own 'mock-phrenology' on the contours of the whale's spine, saying the whale's superiority cannot be confirmed in its brain, but is affirmed in its spine—the symbol of power and muscularity. He says the whale's hump is the "Organ of Firmness or Indomitableness," supposedly indicating willfulness and stubbornness which "you will yet have reason to know" in the tragedy to follow. Ishmael concludes his phrenological assessment that the whale's character is a combination of attributes, and cannot be expected to carry forward some great work, for its unquenchable dynamism is yoked only to brutish stupidity. By arriving at this conclusion, he emphasizes Ahab's pursuit of Moby Dick is a self-deluded struggle against brute force, animal drives, sexual and self-preservation instincts. The pseudo-sciences have done little more "than cloak the mysteries of existence in elaborate hypotheses." Phrenology, like romantic transcendentalism, was a German optimistic philosophy.[39] In the following chapter, "The Pequod Meets the Virgin," Chapter 81, a German whaler asks to borrow oil, its own barrels for sperm oil are empty, and the lamp of German optimistic philosophy is also empty. Hillway says Melville, unlike other writers of the time, was not deceived by the claims of the phrenologists, instead he recognized their limitations. His literary skill makes the pseudosciences effective, but never quite serious.[40]

The study of gases and the study of the atmosphere led to greater understanding man's environment:

> We all know what an astonishing atmospheric weight we ourselves stand up under; even here, above-ground, in the air; how vast, then, the burden of a whale, bearing on his back a column of two hundred fathoms of ocean! It must at least equal the weight of fifty atmospheres. One whaleman has estimated it at the weight of twenty line-of-battle ships, with all their guns, and stores, and men on board. (Ch 81).

The atmosphere, or the ocean of air which surrounds and sustains the earth, has always fascinated and intrigued man. Aristotle's *Meteorologica* is the first systematic treatise of the subject. Important developments were the invention of the thermometer by Galileo (1607), the barometer by Evangelista Torricelli (1643), and the discovery of Boyle's Law in 1659. The 'atmosphere' is a unit of pressure of the normal pressure of air at sea level, about 14.7 pounds per square inch.

In Chapter 85, "The Fountain," Melville writes of the whale's intelligence; the spout signifies it is as "profound" as "Plato, Pyrrho, the Devil, Jupiter, Dante, and so on." That man and whale are closely related has greater import than may be apparent at first; the Great Chain of Being placed animals close together on the basis of similar physical characteristics, not mental capacity. The whale is too large to study, yet through study of the smaller porpoise, the whale's smaller brother, the *cetacea* have become reasonably well known. Though dissimilar in anatomy, man and whale are closely related intellectually. Ishmael says of the whale:

> Genius in a Sperm Whale? Has the Sperm Whale ever written a book, spoken a speech? No, his great genius is declared in his doing nothing particular to prove it. It is moreover declared in his pyramidical silence. (Ch 79)

Eiseley says the brain of the porpoise, a close relative of the whale, is forty percent larger than man's and is as complex in functional units, "man's position at the top of the hierarchy [of intelligence] begins to be questioned." The porpoise left the land to return to the sea millions of years ago, and is able to solve problems with amazing rapidity, much faster than the monkey. The *cetacea*, unlike man, their intellectual counterparts, may be more 'civilized' in that the whales and porpoises have a touching altruisms and friendliness in their attempts to aid injured companions. Through writing, man is able to record his thoughts for posterity. The whale, inscrutable as the Great Pyramids, philosophizes without leaving monuments.[41] Large brain size may be linked to a life strategy of great longevity, slow maturation, single births after a long gestation, and late weaning. A practical definition of intelligence (and its relation to brain size) still eludes science, but numerous other behavioral reasons may be related: the complexity of foraging strategies and the possible need for forming and remembering social relationships in complex societies that must avoid predators and secure food in a three-dimensional space. The sophisticated click-based echolocation may account for the large brain size. Dolphins are able to learn quickly and remember for long periods of time.[42]

A killed whale, due to its great buoyancy, usually floats with the body considerably elevated in the water. Occasionally, a whale will sink: "their pads of lard diminished and all their bones heavy and rheumatic" causing an "uncommon specific gravity" (Ch 81), but rises due to gases generated. The term "specific gravity" was first used by Robert Boyle (1627-1691), English naturalist and one of the founders of modern chemistry. Specific gravity compares the density, or weight per unit of volume, with a standard, usually water or air in the case of gases. The study of density led to the science of fluid mechanics which was important in the building of canals in England and France. In the early nineteenth century, accurate measurement of the density of gases and liquids was instrumental in the theories of molecular chemistry and the formulation of the Periodic Table of Elements by Dimitri Mendeleev in 1869. Mendeleev achieved his reputation on the classification of elements, and was called the "Linnaeus of chemistry." In fact, the greatest achievement of the physical sciences in the nineteenth century was taxonomic, bringing order to a formidable collection of facts.[43]

Melville describes the whale's anatomy and physiology of respiration in Chapter 85, "The Fountain," which is probably taken from Beale's *The Natural History of the Sperm Whale*. The spiracle located on the top of the whale's head allows breathing while the mouth remains submerged: "it withdraws from the air a certain element, which being subsequently brought into contact with the blood imparts to the blood it's vivifying principle, I do not think I shall err; though I possibly use some superfluous scientific words," by a remarkably "involved Cretan labyrinth of vermicelli-like vessels, which vessels, when he quits the surface, are completely distended with oxygenated blood" (Ch 85). The whale breathes a number of times on the surface during a few minutes and then dives for over an hour and to a depth of over 1 kilometer.[44] The necessity of rising to the surface for air makes the great whale vulnerable to attack by its predator man: "Not so much thy skill, then, O hunter, as the great necessities, that strike the victory to thee" (Ch 85)!

Ishmael discourses on the nature of the spout and superstition surrounding it; he concludes: "My hypothesis is this, that the spout is nothing but mist" and it is appropriate to the whale's "great inherent dignity and sublimnity,...both ponderous and profound," like the "semi-visible steam" about great men (Ch 85). He mentions an important scientific observation about the formation of the rainbow: "For, d'ye see, rainbows do not visit the clear air; they only irradiate vapor," a topic discussed in Chapter 9 of *Billy Budd*. From this discussion, Ishmael attempts to strike a balance between conflicting ideas:

> And so, through all the thick mists of the dim doubts in my mind, divine intuitions now and then shoot, enkindling my fog with a heavenly ray. And for this I thank God; for all have doubts; many deny; but doubts or denials, few along with them, have intuitions. Doubts of all things earthly, and intuitions of some things heavenly; this combination makes neither believer nor infidel, but makes a man who regards them both with equal eye. (Ch 85)

Ishmael implies understanding comes not from natural philosophy, but from intuitions or faith as a counterbalance to reason and science. Simultaneously holding conflicting ideas in the mind is particularly difficult when the mass of people hold one or the other.

The discussion of the anatomy, function, and beauty of the whale's tail in Chapter 86, "The Tail," is probably borrowed from Beale who quotes John Hunter, cited in "Extracts." He observes the Leviathan mating, sees a newborn whale, and the battles of the young males. In these chapters, Melville quotes almost directly from Bennett's *A Whaling Voyage Around the Globe*. [45]

The *Pequod* encounters a pod of eight whales swimming rapidly away in a close group, followed by "a huge, humped old bull...seemed afflicted with the jaundice" (Ch 81). The touching episode of the killing of the old whale probably had its origin from two short paragraphs in Beale's *Natural History of the Sperm Whale,* and from Browne's *Etchings*.[46] The aged and crippled whale with many infirmities magnifies the lore of the indestructibility of the White Whale. The humor of the whale's dyspepsia gives way to a physiological discussion of the whale's circulation, and a detailed account of the act of killing of the whaler's prey. In death, the old whale "over and over slowly revolved like a waning world," like the Cartesian vortex of the masthead, the sinking of a ship, or death of a star (itself a new concept as stated in *Mardi*). The indestructibility of the whale and the importance of time is illustrated by "the fact of a lance-head of stone being found in him, not far from the buried iron, the flesh perfectly firm about it. Who had darted that stone lance? And When? It might have been darted by some Nor' West Indian long before America was discovered" (Ch 81). He cites the "learned Fogo Von Slack, in his great work on Smells, a text-book on that subject" (Ch 92) which Hayford and Parker say is a comic reference to Scoresby.[47] Ishmael sums up his attempt to understand the whale in a restatement of one of the most profound themes in *Moby-Dick*—the inability of science to understand the meaning of life: "Dissect him how I may, then, I but go skin deep; I know him not, and never will" (Ch 86). Indeed, all his laborious scientific cetology only serves to underscore this final sense of bafflement in his attempt to understand the Leviathan.[48]

Stubb's after-oarsman sprains his hand, and Pip, the lowest ranking man aboard, takes his place in the whaleboat. Pip becomes frightened when the whale is struck and jumps out of the boat forcing Stubb to cut the line to save him. On the next chase, Pip leaves the boat again. In a dramatic account, Pip floats abandoned in the ocean until the Pequod, by the merest chance, finds and rescues him, nearly drowned in the "unwarped primal world":

> ...among the joyous, heartless, ever-juvenile eternities, Pip saw the multitudinous, God-omnipresent, coral insects, that out of the firmament of waters heaved the colossal orbs. He saw God's foot upon the treadle of the loom, and spoke it; and therefore his shipmates called him mad. So man's insanity is heaven's sense; and wandering from all mortal reason, man comes at last to that celestial thought, which, to reason, is absurd and frantic; and weal or woe, feel then uncompromised, indifferent as his God. (Ch 93)

In this deistic sentiment, Melville alludes to the Neptunian theory of creation from which were thrown the planets under the control of God, or the uniformitarianism of Hutton and Lyell—a fading nineteenth century concept of creation, mentioned earlier in the book at the masthead: "There is no life in thee, now, except that rocking life imparted by a gently rolling ship; by her, borrowed from the sea; by the sea, from the inscrutable tides of God" (Ch 35). When faced with death, reason is of no value. Similarly, the tranquilizing effect of squeezing the sperm becomes a metaphor for the failure of reason: "in all cases man must eventually lower, or at least shift, his conceit of attainable felicity; not placing it anywhere in the intellect or the fancy; but in the wife, the heart, the bed, the table, the saddle, the fire-side, the country" (Ch 94). The comforts of the home are as remote from the whaler as from the "head," or intellect alone.

Distortion of time and depersonalization in dreams counters the vivid reality of the peril of the whale hunt, the dream-like unreality of Chapter 96, "The Try-Works," is a place of "profound mathematical meditation," perhaps a derogation of mathematics and the illusion of scientific precision. In addition, he refers to an unusual mathematical problem—the cycloid: "It was in the left hand try-pot of the Pequod, with the soapstone diligently circling round me, that I was first indirectly struck by the remarkable fact, that in geometry all bodies gliding along the cycloid, my soapstone for example, will descend from any point in precisely the same time" (Ch 96). The cycloid (a curve generated by a point on the circumference of a circle which rolls without slipping along a straight line) was intensely studied in the seventeenth century by the most famous mathematicians, especially Galileo, Fermat, Wren, Pascal, Newton, and Christian Huygens. In 1658, Huygens discovered the principle cited by Melville: that an object released from the inside of a bowl in the shape of a cycloid would descend to the bottom in the same time independent of the height from which it is released, therefore, the cycloid curve is a *tautochrone*, i.e., the curve traced by a body moving without friction under the force of gravity such that the time required to reach a fixed point is the same regardless of the starting point—an observation of considerable importance to the art of horology, though never of much practical use.[49] He implies that natural objects and events have a symbolic, or spiritual meaning: "And some certain significance lurks in all things, else all things are little worth, and the round world itself but an empty cipher, except to sell by the cartload, as they do hills about Boston, to fill up some morass in the Milky Way" (Ch 99). It may also be considered a restatement of the Aristotelian idea of the potential in all objects and the moral significance of natural events.

Ishmael elaborates further on the anatomy of the *Cetacea* in Chapter 102 "A Bower in the Arsacides," claiming to have dissected a cub sperm whale, which is probably taken from a dull recitation in Beale's *Natural History of the Sperm Whale,* or from an entry in "Extracts": "John Hunter's Account of the Dissection of a Whale. (A Small Sized One.)." An adult whale skeleton transported to a native village became a chapel with new growth of vines about the ribs. He questions the "humming" of the activity of life; the mixture of the bower's green undergrowth and the white bones of the whale cannot settle whether life is a by-product of death or death is the product of life, a restatement of Chapter 47, "The Mat-Maker," (and a prominent theme in *Pierre*) and the relationship of freewill, chance, and determinism.[50] He attempts to measure the skeleton of the whale; the natives protest: "How dar'st thou measure this our god! That's for us," which is followed by a fierce dispute about feet and inches. He likens the whale skeleton with its growth of vines to a machine: "The weaver-god, he weaves; and by that weaving is he deafened, that he hears no mortal voice; and by that humming, we, too, who look on the loom are deafened; and only when we escape it shall we hear the thousand voices that speak through it" (Ch 102). The whale skeleton grew new life in the growth of new vines: "Life folded Death; Death trellised Life; the grim god wived with youthful Life, and begat him curly-headed glories" (Ch 102). Ishmael refers to the "Leviathanic Museum" in Hull, England, and similar ones in Manchester, New Hampshire, and Yorkshire, England (Ch 102). Though he attempts to measure the temple of faith by the tools of the scientist, the faithful are certain their god defies such manipulation. He concludes: "Only in the heart of quickest perils; only when within the eddyings of his angry flukes; only on the profound unbounded sea, can the fully invested whale be truly and livingly found out" (Ch 103).

Ishmael is overcome by the enormity of the whale: "Having already described him in most of his present habitatory and anatomical peculiarities, it now remains to magnify him in an archæological, fossiliferous, and antediluvian point of view":

> For in the mere act of penning my thoughts of this Leviathan, they weary me, and make me faint with their outreaching comprehensiveness of sweep, as if to include the whole circle of the sciences, and all the generations of whales, and men, and mastodons, past, present, and to come, with all the revolving panoramas of empire on earth, and throughout the whole universe, not excluding its suburbs. (Ch 104)

Fossils of whales had "within thirty years past, at various intervals, been found at the base of the Alps, in Lombardy, in France, in England, in Scotland, and in the States of Louisiana, Mississippi, and Alabama" (Ch 104). Excavations produced important new geological and anthropological information for the naturalists. Ishmael continues:

> Ere entering upon the subject of Fossil Whales, I present my credentials as a geologist, by stating that in my miscellaneous time I have been a stone-mason, and also a great digger of ditches, canals and wells, wine-vaults, cellars, and cisterns of all sorts. Likewise, by way of preliminary, I desire to remind the reader, that while in the earlier geological strata there are found the fossils of monsters now almost completely extinct; the subsequent relics discovered in what are called the Tertiary formations seem the connecting, or at any rate intercepted links, between the antechronical creatures, and those whose remote posterity are said to have entered the Ark; all the Fossil Whales hitherto discovered belong to the Tertiary period,

> which is the last preceding the superficial formations. And though none of them precisely answer to any known species of the present time, they are yet sufficiently akin to them in general respects, to justify their taking rank as Cetacean fossils. (Ch 104)

The idea of extinct species was a problem that could no longer be ignored. From the discoveries of William Smith, the geological strata yielded remarkable information of a systematic development in the history of life through successive periods of geological time. Cuvier knew that few mammalian remains were located below the Tertiary, and below them were a wide range of bizarre reptilian forms. In 1824, Buckland described the first known dinosaur, a giant carnivore he called *Megalosaurus*.[51] William Smith appears to be a probable source of Ishmael's geological credentials. Ishmael says of the Alabama fossil whale, "the most wonderful of cetacean relics":

> The Alabama doctors declared it a huge reptile, and bestowed upon it the name of Basilosaurus. But some specimen bones of it being taken across the sea to Owen, the English Anatomist, it turned out that this alleged reptile was a whale, though of a departed species. A significant illustration of the fact, again and again repeated in his book, that the skeleton of the whale furnishes but little clue to the shape of his fully invested body. So Owen re-christened the monster Zeuglodon; and in his paper read before the London Geological Society, pronounced it, in substance, one of the most extraordinary creatures which the mutations of the globe have blotted out of existence. (Ch 104)

Melville's knowledge of fossil whales is thought to have its source in Robert Hamilton's *Mammalia, Whales, etc.* (1843), published as the eighth volume of Jardine's popular reference, *The Naturalist's Library*. In 1832, Judge Bry of Louisiana found several fossil vertebrae which he sent to the Philosophical Society of Philadelphia to Dr. Richard Harlan, who determined that the bones were reptilian in origin, Mesozoic in age, and of the genus Basilosaurus. A few years later, Judge Jonathan Creagh found large fossil bones on his plantation in Clark County, Alabama, which Harlan also determined were Basilosaurus bones—a genus of large slender-bodied, extinct Eocene (40 to 60 million years of age) whales found most abundantly in Alabama and Florida rock deposits. Harlan took the bones to London in 1839 where Owen, England's greatest paleontologist, determined that they were from a seagoing mammal, giving it the name Zeuglodon, another name for

Basilosaurus. Whether the bones represented a new species or whether they were the remains of an ancient whale produced a lively controversy. Some of the bones were shipped to Albany, New York, in 1842, creating public interest when reported in the newspapers where Melville undoubtedly read about them. The Albany bones were later sold to Doctor John Collins Warren of Boston and are displayed in the American Museum of Natural History in New York.[52] Melville appears to have taken the information and expressed it in the same diction and syntax as Owen: "Observations on the Basilosaurus of Dr. Harlan (Zeuglodon cetoides, Owen)." *Transactions of the Geological Society of London* records Owen's concluding remarks, "...we cannot hesitate in pronouncing the colossal Zeuglodon to have been one of the most extraordinary of the Mammalia which the revolutions of the globe have blotted out of the number of existing beings." Moore says Melville most probably had Owen's discourse in hand when he composed the chapter.[53]

As expeditions crossed Siberia, corpses of mastodons were found preserved in the ice, but no live ones had ever been seen, yet fossil remains had been found in Africa. An animal so large could hardly be overlooked, therefore, the mastodon must be extinct. The doctrine that had supported the Great Chain of Being, that this is the best of all possible worlds and that its flora and fauna are unchanging, had to be abandoned due to the discovery of extinct animals.[54] World exploration brought many new species previously unknown to European scientists, however, the new species did not fill the gaps found in the Great Chain of Being, and produced more evidence of extinction of species rather than resolving the difficulty.

In Chapter 104, "The Fossil Whale," occur descriptions of horror reminiscent of "The Whiteness of the Whale": Ishmael obtains "dim shuddering glimpses" into the "Polar eternities" of "preadamite" time and is "horror-struck at this antemosaic, unsourced existence of the unspeakable terrors of the whale, which, having been before all time, must needs exist after all humane ages are over" (Ch 104). As Friedman states, "What Copernicus and Pascal stated of space, Ishmael here states of time: that man is not its center, that human life shrinks into itself in terror before the vision, preeminently accorded to modern man, of time stretching indefinitely into the past and the future."[55]

Ishmael's discussion includes contemporary interest in extinction of species, the time and antiquity of man, the pre-human era, glaciation of the earth, the universal flood, measurement of the circumference of the earth, and fossil layers:

> When I stand among these mighty Leviathan skeletons, skulls, tusks, jaws, ribs, and vertebræ, all characterized by partial resemblances to the existing breeds of sea-monsters; but at the same time bearing on the other hand similar affinities to the annihilated antechronical Leviathans, their incalculable seniors; I am, by a flood, borne back to that wondrous period, ere time itself can be said to have begun; for time began with man. Here Saturn's grey chaos rolls over me, and I obtain dim, shuddering glimpses into those Polar eternities; when wedged bastions of ice pressed hard upon what are now the Tropics; and in all the 25,000 miles of this world's circumference, not an inhabitable hand's breadth of land was visible. Then the whole world was the whale's; and, king of creation, he left his wake along the present lines of the Andes and the Himmalehs....
>
> But not alone has this Leviathan left his pre-adamite traces in the stereotype plates of nature, and in limestone and marl bequeathed his ancient bust; but upon Egyptian tablets, whose antiquity seems to claim for them an almost fossiliferous character, we find the unmistakable print of his fin. (Ch 104)

The whale must antedate man, like his God—topics of great scientific interest in the first half of the nineteenth century—and a more definitive statement of Neptunism when the earth was covered by water than in earlier works. In saying "In those Polar eternities; when wedged bastions of ice pressed hard upon what are now the Tropics..." (Ch 104), according to Foster, Melville's theories of the ice age probably came from Agassiz, who in 1840, and in his public lectures in 1845 in New York and Boston, said the earth had been covered with an immense sheet of ice extending as far south as the erratic boulders. Lyell and others, however, persisted for over two decades in believing that great floating icebergs had transported the large angular blocks of rock known as the drift, although in support of their theory they had to submerge northern Europe, northern North America east of the Rockies, and much of South America and Asia: "Melville adopted the iceberg rather than the glacial theory, and then with creative abandon sank all the continents completely." Foster objected to the image of the glacier "pressing hard on the Tropics" for the glacier stopped half a continent short of the tropics, concluding that Melville was interested in the general idea of the glacial period rather than the detail of where the glacier terminated. The cautious Agassiz had once said all of North America was covered with ice and may have been Melville's source for his overstatement.[56] Melville's remark on the circumference of the earth of 25,000 miles takes into account current interest in measurement of the globe and the practical application of progress in science. Eratosthenes (third century B.C.) in Egypt postulated that the earth is spherical and estimated its diameter to be similar to those present measurements erring by only 16 percent which he determined by measuring the angle of the sun at the same time of day from different locations.[57] Well into the Middle Ages, by cosmic standards the earth was considered a point with no appreciable magnitude, being much smaller than the smallest star. In the late Middle Ages, the earth was considered to be a globe, although the belief in a flat earth had proponents well into the nineteenth century. The most vivid description of a round earth is that in Dante's *Inferno* (xxxiv), with Lucifer at the center of the earth, embedded to his waist in ice. It is *down* to his waist and *up* to his feet, which Lewis says is the first science fiction effect in literature.[58] The first modern measurement employed a method of triangulation used by Jean Picard (1620-1682). During the eighteenth century, numerous measurements were conducted and accuracy of measurement was advanced in the nineteenth century. The new developments were applied to map making, which was necessary for world exploration.[59]

In Chapter 105, "Does the Whales Magnitude Diminish, etc.," Melville makes another specific reference to geological periods in *Moby-Dick* that received so much attention in *Mardi,* saying that present day whales are as large as the remains "found in the Tertiary system (embracing a distinct geological period prior to man)." He quotes the great naturalists: Pliny the Younger (A.D. 23-79), Roman naturalist, encyclopedist, and writer; Ulisse Aldrovandi (1522-1605), Italian naturalist, botanist, and physician; Sir Joseph Banks (1734-1820), English naturalist; Bernard Lacépède (1756-1825), French naturalist and writer; Cook's naturalists, and a Danish member of the Academy of Science (probably D. C. Solander who went with Cook to the South Seas), in an appeal to authority serving to establish the enormous size and permanence of the whale. Ishmael protests the possibility of the extinction of the whale, which is, in effect, an awareness of the extinction of other species:

> Wherefore, for all these things, we account the whale immortal in his species, however perishable in his individuality. He swam the seas before the continents broke water; he once swam over the site of the Tuileries, and Windsor Castle, and the Kremlin. In Noah's flood he despised Noah's ark; and if ever the world is to be again flooded, like the Netherlands, to kill off its rats, then the

> eternal whale will still survive, and rearing upon the topmost crest of the equatorial flood, spout his frothed defiance to the skies. (Ch 105)

Using fossil evidence and the emerging theories of geology, Ishmael insists on the immutability of the species of whale and that the idea of extinction of species over great spans of time does not apply to the Leviathan. The statement denies the idea of 'progress' and, through the use of science, lends religious significance to the whale as the truth of God. In *Moby-Dick*, geology gave the imagery of largeness and, with its suggestion of cosmic sweep and grandeur, sustains the sense of vastness, timelessness, and deeper significance that was discordant with the Christian faith of the special creation of man.[60]

In Chapter 107, "The Carpenter," the "omnitooled, open-and-shut carpenter" was little more than a "machine of an automaton": "...he had a subtle something that somehow anomalously did its duty....but only like an unreasoning wheel, which also hummingly soliloquizes" (Ch 107). Ishmael likens the carpenter to Prometheus:

> I do deem it now a most meaning thing, that that old Greek, Prometheus, who made men, they say, should have been a blacksmith, and animated them with fire; for what's made in fire must properly belong to fire; and so hell's probable....Hold; while Prometheus is about it, I'll order a complete man after a desirable pattern. (Ch 108)

Friedman says that Prometheus is a symbol of man not only in his knowledge and craft, but also his role as the extender of human potentialities and the father of human science. He is also the symbol of man as the "being in between, the one who is not all-powerful like Zeus yet knows and sees the future. He is man wrestling room for himself from a jealous creation....Prometheus is not simply the symbol of man's knowledge and science down through the generations. He is the very symbol of the ambiguity of science which extends man's dominion and at the same time brings him closer to *hybris* and self-destruction."[61]

During a gam [a meeting at sea] with the *Samuel Enderby*, Ahab damaged his artificial leg. The carpenter, who Ahab calls a "manmaker," makes a new leg out of whale bone. Ahab asks another perplexing matter of the carpenter—his phantom limb:

> ...put thy live leg here in the place where mine once was; so, here is only one distinct leg to the eye, yet two to the soul. Where thou feelest tingling life; there, exactly there, there to a hair, do I. (Ch 108)

The senses' observations of the natural world were thought to be infallible by naturalists and the positivism of Auguste Comte, but the senses mislead and confuse the logic of Ahab. Chase says Ahab perceives the "strange dualism" in the carpenter: creativity on one hand and "mechanicalness" on the other becoming a "pure manipulator."[62] The carpenter is made to seem mechanical by use of the negative affix in profusion, a negation of the life process.[63] The description of "Mechanical Man" in the chapter on Ahab and the Carpenter was probably based on Hawthorne's "The Minotaur," which is a retelling of the myth of Theseus.[64]

Queequeg is seized by a fever and insists a coffin be made for him like the coffin-canoes he had seen in Nantucket. Having made every preparation for death: "Queequeg suddenly rallied...at a critical moment, he had just recalled a little duty ashore, which he was leaving undone; and therefore had changed his mind about dying: he could not die yet, he averred." They asked him if to live or die is a matter of free will: "In a word, it was Queequeg's conceit, that if a man made up his mind to live, mere sickness could not kill him: nothing but a whale, or a gale, or some violent, ungovernable, unintelligent destroyer of that sort" (Ch 110). Wilkes described the coffin-canoe in *Narrative*.[65] After his recovery, Queequeg used his "coffin" for a sea chest, and spent spare hours carving the lid copying the "hieroglyphic" tattoos of his body:

> ...a complete theory of the heavens and the earth, and a mystical treatise on the art of attaining truth; so that Queequeg in his own proper person was a riddle to unfold; a wondrous work in one volume;... (Ch 110)

The superiority of the native in recovering from sickness defies the supposed higher place of the European in the scale of nature. The miraculous cure of sick Queequeg and the wisdom of the "natural" savage defies Ahab's sense of worldly logic and order, and he is driven to exclaim, "Oh, devilish tantalization of the gods" (Ch 110)! The tattoos of the native prophet make a theory of heaven and earth, and a means of attaining truth although wasted on the noble savage, who cannot understand though his heart beats against it, for knowledge and the heart are separate. The riddle remains unknowable by savage or civilized man, yet implies that order exists in the universe, and that the quest for the knowledge of order, mystical or rational, tantalizes and defies man.The quest, says Melville in other settings, is the only truth.

When Queequeg is near death, Pip holds his hand and "with soft sobbings" speaks nonsense. Starbuck, referring to Pip's bizarre ramblings, says:

> ...that in violent fevers, men, all ignorance, have talked in ancient tongues; and that when the mystery is probed, it turns out always that in their wholly forgotten childhood those ancient tongues had been really spoken in their hearing by some lofty scholars. (Ch 110)

Melville refers to persons in a delirium speaking in ancient languages in *Pierre,* where it has a greater significance in the story.

Ahab supervises the blacksmith in making a special harpoon for his attack on the White Whale. He insists the barb must be fashioned from the finest steel and gives the blacksmith his best razors, opposed to the usual practice of using soft iron so the harpoon can be easily reshaped and used again.[66] After he has welded the barbs to the shank, Perth asks for the water cask to temper the red-hot steel. Ahab insists he wants a "true death-temper" and calls the pagans Tashtego, Queequeg, and Daggoo: "Will you give me as much blood as will cover this barb?...Three punctures were made in the heathen flesh, and the White Whale's barbs were then tempered" (Ch 113). Ahab knew something about tempering steel unknown to the blacksmith. Damascus swords produced better steel if "death-tempered" in human blood, sometimes the sword was run through the body of a condemned criminal or slave. The rate of cooling as well as the medium is important in the hardening of the metal. However, blood probably has no greater tempering property than oil or salt water. The practice of tempering steel blades was probably known by the Hittites and the Greeks at the time of Homer. Although seemingly implausible, the madness of the blood quench has a long history in metallurgical practice.[67]

As the long search for the White Whale nears its completion, Ahab takes his readings with the quadrant, sighting the sun for the location of the ship; only the sun knows the location of both Moby Dick and the *Pequod*. Ahab calls the quadrant a useless toy, a plaything of haughty admirals, commodores, and captains: "thou insultest the sun! Science! Curse thee, thou vain toy" (Ch 118). He destroys the quadrant to navigate instead with "level" instruments—the level ship's compass, the level dead reckoning, and by log and by line—determined not to be dependent on the tools of science. In "The Quadrant," Chapter 118, Ahab, who has been defying the world of nature, wants to follow nature's way. Ahab's defiance is based neither on an order that will sustain him, nor on the mastery of "fire," i.e., the power stolen from the gods. Instead, in the case of the quadrant and the compass, Ahab discards science, which man has used to gain his greatest dominion over nature. Science, the very essence of man's Prometheanism in the modern world, the key symbol of man's unlimited power since the Renaissance, no longer suffices to assure Ahab of his victory over nature and the gods. As Ishmael says in "Brit" (Ch 58), "However baby man may brag of his science and skill, etc.," Ahab abandons the central belief of Bacon and Renaissance man that the way to the realization of one's humanity is through knowledge that gives one power over nature.[68]

The *Pequod* encounters a severe storm with vivid lightning, driving rain, and gale winds. Corposants, or coronal discharges called St. Elmo's fire, light the masts and yardarms. The reference to the Holy Trinity, "three tapering white flames," in natural phenomenon adds to the supernatural horror of the storm. Starbuck asks Ahab to drop the lightning rod chains overboard. Ahab refuses, for the chains will slow their progress. Ahab asserts his defiance of God and the terrors of nature. Starbuck tries to persuade Ahab to change his course and give up his mad quest for the White Whale. The episode of the corposants was probably taken from Melville's experience sailing to Liverpool; he recorded a fierce electrical storm in *Journal,* October 13, 1849:

> It was blowing horribly—pitch dark, & raining. The Captain was in the cuddy, & directed my attention to "those fellows" as he called them,—meaning several "Corposant balls" on the yard arms & mast heads. They were the first I had ever seen, & resembled large, dim stars in the sky.[69]

A similar scene occurs in Richard Dana's *Two Years Before the Mast,* and Melville was familiar with Hakluyt's *Navigations* (1598-1600), in which an electrical storm is vividly recorded. Wilkes described corposants in *Narrative,* "On the 24th, we had a remarkably severe storm of thunder and lightning; the ship appeared filled with the electric fluids; the points of the conductors, the mastheads, and yardarms were illuminated with Corpo Santos; and several of the officers declared that they had felt electric shocks." [70] The ambiguous symbol of the corposants probably was influenced by Robert Burton's *Anatomy of*

Melancholy.[71] In addition, corposants were discussed at length in a popular periodical regularly read by New Englanders, the *Penny Magazine,* March 22, 1845. "St. Elmo's Fire," known from antiquity, evoked both admiration and fear. The article describes at length the electrical nature of the corposants, "The experiment can be shown at the electric machine, as it is known as brush discharge."[72] In the passage, "to this hour I bear the scar," Ahab explains the scar down his face described in Chapter 27, "Knights and Squires," which becomes one of the many ambiguous statements on the symbolism of fire and Zoroastrianism. Zoroastrianism divides the universe between *Ahmazd,* the god of light, or 'good', and *Ahriman,* the god of darkness, or 'evil.' Fire paradoxically represents evil in Chapter 96, "The Try-Works," and virtually becomes the malignant force in nature that Ahab opposes. Walcutt points out the importance of Fedallah, the Parsee, as the agent of Ahab's evil self in the ambiguous meaning of fire. Ahab's acceptance of the Christian belief in the goodness and omnipotence of God gives way to the recognition of the presence of ubiquitous evil. From a quester for 'good-menaced-by-evil,' Ahab's conviction that evil lays at the heart of reality drives him to his tragic end, which by reasoning reaches a higher wisdom that man's fate must be tragic, or, on the contrary, in a perfect world, that man's existence would be no different than the existence of animals. Ahab says, "My malady becomes my more desired health" (Ch 119), a realization that the conflict between 'good' and 'evil' disappears, fusing in a reality that embodies both. At first, Ahab worshipped fire as the destroyer of evil, then he is disfigured by lightning; fire becomes a malignant force as well, he hates fire as he hates Moby Dick; as Walcutt states, "because he considers it essentially evil, alien to man and maliciously destructive." He calls the corposants a "clear spirit" and says fire is indifferent to man, unmoved by love or reverence, whose "right worship is defiance." Walcutt credits Ahab with a great intellectual and emotional development from the insane hatred of the White Whale to the realization that evil cannot be destroyed; man rises to greatness in struggling against it. He says, "Fire as destroyer and purifier, as in the phoenix myth, was an obvious complementary symbol to the whale." Ahab is not able to change his course and avoid his destruction, but must, like the phoenix, experience destruction in order to experience its purification. He is driven forward by the knowledge of the inscrutable being: "There is some unsuffusing thing beyond thee, thou clear spirit, to whom all thy eternity is but time, all thy creativeness mechanical" (Ch 119). Fire adds to the evidence Melville accumulates in opposition to the transcendentalist's assertion of the all-goodness of nature.[73] Ahab was 'branded' by lightning like a huge tree, as he is frequently described. He comes to realize his God is utterly implacable; he must fight fire with fire and ultimate defeat is certain. Ahab's defiance, which is incomprehensible to his crew, reaches its fullest expression in Chapter 119, "The Candles." He challenges the deity to do His worst and loses his fear of his God: "Thou cast blind; but I can then grope."[74] The mystery of Creation is as elusive as before the advent of faith or the beginning of science; it is deeper than the disfigured skin of man, behind the pasteboard mask, and beneath the surface of things that can do no more than reflect part of the whiteness of light. Canfield says, "In *Moby-Dick* the White Whale symbolizes the complex entity of Truth which Melville—and Ahab—had a passion to comprehend." Examine it how he may, the White Whale remains unknowable by either science or faith.[75]

When the Pequod was struck by lightning, a reversal of the magnetic compass occurred, "all its loadstone virtue being annihilated" (Ch 124). The superstitious crew thought it one of many evil portents. Ahab magnetized a sail maker's needle by hammering the steel of a lance, then placing the needle next to it, gently hammering it. The needle placed in the binnacle pointed north; Ahab retained his spell over the crew, "Look ye, for yourselves, if Ahab be not lord of the level-lodestone" (Ch 124)! On April 24,1850, Melville borrowed *An Account of the Arctic Regions, with a History and Description of the Northern Whale-Fishery* (1820), and five days later borrowed *Journal of a Voyage to the Northern Whale-Fishery; etc.* (1823), both by William Scoresby, Jr., which he held during the time of composition of *Moby-Dick*, returning them June 14, 1851. Heflin, studying the second book, demonstrated the similarity of the two in the matter of the loadstone. *Journal* contains learned discussions on magnetism, compass deviations, errors in nautical charts, etc. Scoresby described experiments on a method of developing magnetism in steel by the "elicitation of magnetic energy by percussion." He gives an account of a ship struck by lightning causing a reversal of polarity of the ship's compass. Heflin says reversal of polarity of compasses by electricity (the Leyden jar), was illustrated by Benjamin Franklin in 1750. The best known navigation books of the nineteenth century did not mention this method of inducing magnetism. However, it is mentioned in two lesser known books. Scoresby's matter-of-fact account provided a scientific experiment which Melville developed into dramatic effect, allowing Ahab to maintain control over the superstitious crew. They peered into the binnacle, convinced of his mastery, "one after another they slunk away....In his fiery eyes of scorn and triumph, you then saw Ahab in all his fatal pride" (Ch 124).[76] That is, the fatal pride of science.

References to the magnet occur frequently in *Moby-Dick*. William Gilbert of Colchester published *De Magnete* in 1600 and showed that the earth is itself a magnet by analogy to a lodestone sphere which he constructed. His method of experimentation greatly influenced Galileo and Bacon. He illustrated a method of making a magnet by hammering steel in the north-south meridian.[77] It was known in the early nineteenth century that both electrical and magnetic forces existed and exhibited very similar action at a distance effects to gravitational force. In the first three decades of the century, André Ampère, Christian Oersted, Jean Biot, and Felix Savart found that forces were created by moving electric charges or magnetic fields: a moving magnetic pole could produce an electric charge, and a moving electric charge could produce a magnetic field, demonstrating a relationship between the two which stimulated Faraday's investigations tended to undermine the Newtonian concept of forces acting at a distance, for the forces depended upon the pattern of the field lines, and were everywhere—even inside magnets and in a vacuum. His studies were extended by Maxwell, who produced a system of four equations in 1865 which expressed the interrelationship of electricity and magnetism—*electromagnetism*. This led to the development of the electric generator and electric motor, and became, to a considerable extent, the technological basis of modern society. Maxwell's equations went much further than Newton's laws by allowing far-reaching predictions about unexpected aspects of the world. The speed of propagation of electromagnetic waves was found to be the same as light; Maxwell concluded that electromagnetic waves were a form of light, which also showed some wave characteristics. In 1887, Heinrich Hertz discovered the existence of radio waves having a wavelength nearly a billion times longer than that of light. Later, the entire spectrum of electromagnetic radiation was revealed. Faraday's approach to science was entirely practical and non-mathematical, and the mathematics of Maxwell were beyond his understanding. The powerful image of mechanical explanation was virtually a definition of Victorian science. Maxwell saw the importance of Faraday's practical, mechanical experiments and realized that they could be translated into mathematical language, but suffered because they lacked concrete demonstration that could be easily seen, and led to many new questions. Hertz remarked that the new mathematical expression took on an existence of its own producing more than was originally put into them. Barrow comments: "Maxwell had found an expression of natural laws whose outworkings extended far beyond everything that had made their discovery possible. Explanations of the known would be but a secondary role for future laws of Nature to play." Maxwell's equations marked the end of the understanding of the laws of nature by *visualization*.[78]

Black Pip, the lowest ranking seaman on board, and Starbuck, the highest ranking next to Captain Ahab, one with madness, the other with humanity, unsettle Ahab who says: "I feel deadly faint, bowed, and humped, as though I were Adam, staggering beneath the piled centuries since Paradise." Ahab is doomed to pursue the White Whale. The conflict of fate versus free will, or predestination and volition, casts Ahab as the mechanical creature who rejects the healing quality of human kindness. Ahab asks Starbuck what drives him:

> Is Ahab, Ahab? Is it I, God, or who, that lifts his arm? But if the great sun move not of himself; but is as an errand-boy in heaven; nor one single star can revolve, but by some invisible power; how then can this one small heart beat; this one small brain think thoughts; unless God does that beating, does that thinking, does that living, and not I. By heaven, man, we are turned round and round in this world, like yonder windlass, and Fate is the handspike. (Ch 132)

Ahab attempts to reconcile deistic and theistic conceptions of God. Additional references to mechanicalness occur in the later chapters of the book: "For so revolvingly appalling was the White Whale's aspect, and so planetarily swift the ever-contracting circles he made, that he seemed horizontally swooping upon them" (Ch 133); "What soulless thing is this that laughs before a wreck? Man, man! did I not know thee brave as fearless fire (and as mechanical) I could swear thou wert a poltroon" (Ch 133); Ahab exhorts the crew to kill the White Whale:

> "D'ye feel brave, men, brave?"
> "As fearless as fire," cried Stubb.
> "And as mechanical," muttered Ahab." (Ch 134)

In this respect, Ahab is no longer the planning, rational man, for he abandons reason in his pursuit of Moby Dick:

> What a lovely day again! were it a new-made world, and made for a summer-house to the angels, and this morning the first of its throwing open to them, a fairer day could not dawn upon the world. Here's food for thought, had Ahab time to think; but Ahab never thinks; he only feels, feels, feels; *that's* tingling enough for mortal man! to think's audacity. God only has that right and privilege.

> Thinking is, or ought to be, a coolness and a calmness; and our poor hearts throb, and our poor brains beat too much for that. And yet, I've sometimes thought my brain was very calm—frozen calm, this old skull cracks so, like a glass in which the contents turn to ice, and shiver it. (Ch 135)

Reason has given way to Ahab's passion. He says God is the only being that reasons, i.e., a restatement of the concept of divine design. In addition, he employs basic physics of water that when it freezes, it expands, breaking its container.

At last, the White Whale is sighted by Ahab's scientific plotting of the charts. On the third day, in the fair breezes, the *Pequod* has oversailed the White Whale; the science of man has overstepped its mark. Again, Ahab rejects Starbuck's plea to quit the chase: "Ahab is for ever Ahab, man. This whole act's immutably decreed. 'Twas rehearsed by thee and me a billion years before this ocean rolled" (Ch 135), an estimate of time not conceived by physics until the twentieth century; no scientist had theorized anything near a billion years except Hutton's idea of unlimited time. Earlier in the book, he says, "yet lies Adam who died sixty round centuries ago" (Ch 7), the six thousand years of Biblical time, and later says, "That for six thousand years—and no one knows how many millions of ages before—the great whales should have been spouting all over the sea..." (Ch 85) Ahab darts his lance at Moby Dick, "Towards thee I roll..." (Ch 135) fulfilling the mechanical, Cartesian, deterministic fate of the chase. Ahab is caught in the whale line and taken from the whaleboat by Moby Dick. As the White Whale rushes toward the Pequod, the seamen "now hung inactive; hammers, bits of plank, lances, and harpoons, mechanically retained in their hands..." (Ch 135). Moby Dick stoves and sinks the *Pequod*; "And now, concentric circles seized the lone boat itself, and all its crew, and each floating oar, and every lance-pole, and spinning, animate and inanimate, all round and round in one vortex, carried the smallest chip of the Pequod out of sight." All hands of the crew are lost, except for Ishmael, the outcast, who was thrown out of Ahab's boat a distance far enough away to be spared from the vortex of the sinking ship. "Now small fowls flew screaming over the yet yawning gulf; a sullen white surf beat against its steep sides; then all collapsed, and the great shroud of the sea rolled on as it rolled five thousand years ago" (Ch 135)—a return to Biblical time: the time of the biblical Flood. The life buoy made of Queequeg's "coffin" floats to the surface and saves Ishmael.

In the "Epilogue," crazy Ahab, right-minded Starbuck, jolly Stubb, and the "whole anarchic crew" are destroyed, but the vortex spares Ishmael: "the man who has gone forth to look into the fire but who has turned back before 'the wisdom that is woe' could descend into 'the woe that is madness.'"[79]

Many of Melville's characters are based on people of the times, yet Captain Ahab is not well identified. Jaffe produces evidence that Ahab was based on the famous, or infamous, navy Captain Charles Wilkes (1798-1877), who earned a reputation for excellence in surveying, astronomy, and other nautical sciences such that he was assigned to head the new Depot of Charts and Instructions of the Navy Department. An expedition to the Pacific and Antarctica was formed that was to be one of the most ambitious voyages of exploration of all time. Earlier British, French, and Russian expeditions had entered the waters of the unknown continent, but had not sighted land. After two years of delay, President van Buren replaced the commander with Wilkes, a junior lieutenant, already known as inordinately ambitious and arrogant. Wilkes got the expedition under way in a matter of months, and set sail in August 1838. The expedition was to promote the whaling industry and perform numerous types of scientific research: "to extend the bounds of science, and promote the acquisition of knowledge." A corps of brilliant young scientists were assigned to Wilkes; many became famous for their work with the expedition. The expedition was an enormous success, returning to New York in June 1842 after crossing the Pacific Ocean three times and travelling over 87,000 miles. Wilkes expected a hero's welcome; instead, he faced a court-martial on a number of charges arising from his pride, willfulness, and extreme discipline, resulting in a public reprimand. After the trial, Wilkes began an ambitious and controversial plan to publish his report of the expedition. The first of five books, *Narrative of the U.S. Exploring Expedition...1838-1842,* was published in December 1844. Melville referred to *Narrative* in *Mardi*, in the "Extracts" in *Moby-Dick*, and drew some characters and scenes from it. Wilkes said the scientists were not aware of his instructions as to the purpose of the expedition, similar to Ahab's secret plan to search for the White Whale. He wrote of a mysterious white ocean, with cathedral-like icebergs looming over the vessels on all sides; of the white terror of an Antarctic gale, and death seemingly but minutes away. Ishmael says, "Nor, in quite other aspects, does Nature in her least palpable but not the less malicious agencies, fail to enlist among her forces this crowning attribute of the terrible. From its snowy aspect, the gauntleted ghost of the Southern Seas has been denominated the White Squall" (Ch 42). In Chapter 87,

"The Grand Armada," Melville writes that after the old whale was struck, the boat tore through the water "like a ship mobbed by ice-isles in a tempest, and striving to steer through their complicated channels and straits, knowing not at what moment it may be locked in and crushed." Wilkes persisted in the face of all these dangers, and at extreme risk to his ships and crew, explored 1500 miles of the coast of the mysterious continent, much of it now named Wilkesland, an area larger than the United States including Alaska. He was charged with scandalous conduct for making a false entry as to the date he first sighted Antarctica. Wilkes drove his men through arctic gales in constant danger of icebergs and the crew half-dead from fatigue and exposure; a letter signed by two physicians called for Wilkes to turn back. According to Jaffe, Melville probably recognized the conflict of ambition and duty in the official language of the report. In Chapter 16, "The Ship," Ishmael says, "For all great men tragically great are made so through a certain morbidness. Be sure of this, O young ambition, all mortal greatness is but disease." He may have decided Ahab should be like Wilkes, "able, unconventional, and great, but with a certain sickness of the soul." The basic traits of strong will, egotism, fierce independence, pride, defiance of authority, monomania, harshness, absence of humor, great energy, intellect, and conscientiousness apply equally to Wilkes and to Ahab. During the Civil War, Wilkes was court-martialed for insubordination and conduct unbecoming an officer, and suspended from duty.[80]

Melville's use of the vortex theory of Descartes has received considerable comment. Melville borrowed Ephraim Chambers's *Cyclopaedia: or, An Universal Dictionary of Arts and Sciences,* from Herman Gansevoort in 1846 and held it until 1872 when he gave it to Captain Thomas Melville. Hillway includes the *Cyclopaedia* in the list of the sources of Melville's scientific knowledge before 1851, the date of publication of *Moby-Dick.* Although many critics have speculated on the interpretation of the Cartesian vortex in *Moby-Dick,* Leonard examined the *Cyclopedia* for the references 'Cartesian' and 'Vortex'. The 'vortex' entry states:

> Such Vortices are the Grand Machines whereby these Philosophers solve most of the Motions and other Phaenomena of the heavenly Bodies.—Accordingly, the Doctrine of these Vortices makes a great part of the Cartesian Philosophy.[81]

The motion of each system is endlessly circular, and being three-dimensional, is endlessly vortical. As a result, everything in the material world is condemned to a "hellish circular flight" about its center and about the center of a central sun. He points out a number of vortical systems in *Moby-Dick*: Ahab is likened to the sun endlessly circling the earth, "For a long time, now, the circus-running sun has raced within his fiery ring, and needs no sustenance but what's in himself. So Ahab" (Ch 87); an agent greater than the sun moves both the sun and Ahab in endless circles: "By heaven, man, we are turned round and round in this world, like yonder windlass, and Fate is the handspike" (Ch 132); the crew is controlled by Ahab's vortex: "my one cogged circle fits into all their various wheels, and they revolve"; in the Grand Armada chapter, the whales form a separate vortex system, a microcosm of what Leonard calls a violent macrocosm: "in more and more contracting orbits the whales in the more central circles began to swim in thickening clusters... the entire host of whales came tumbling upon their inner centre" (Ch 87); and "concentric circles seized the lone boat itself, and all its crew, and each floating oar, and every lance-pole, and spinning, animate and inanimate, all round and round in one vortex" (Ch 135). Ishmael is drawn to the center of the vortex, "at the axis of the slowly wheeling circle, like another Ixion I did revolve" (Epilogue). Ixion was punished by Zeus for insolence, having him bound to a fiery wheel in perpetual motion. In addition, Ahab says, "toward thee I roll" as he darts the harpoon, as if controlled by fate. Leonard states, unlike the transcendentalists who view man as progressing toward God through nature, Melville in *Moby-Dick* finds man caught in a system of nature that is non-progressive and non-spiritual. The empiricism of Francis Bacon, "the prophet of science," and the rationalism of René Descartes, "the founder of science," combine to form a mathematical physics that would reorder and re-explain the universe. Melville considered the vortical motion a horror, as horrible as the White Whale. The "transcendental peace and calm" of Ishmael standing at the masthead is illusory, for at the bottom is a vortex whirling about in a chained orbit, a fiery hell, an ungodly colorless all color of universal motion. The Cartesian vortex replaces the optimism of the transcendentalists with the pessimism of a mechanism independent of human or divine intervention.[82]

Descartes is largely responsible for the idea that the universe is governed by mathematical laws, although nearly all of Descartes's theories have been discarded. He advanced the Copernican theory by displacing the earth even farther from the center of man's idea of the universe; in Descartes's cosmology, neither the earth nor the sun was the center of God's creation. He theorized the universe was originally in a state of 'primordial chaos'; the stars were created by the operation of natural laws in a deterministic way. He did not share the notion of his contemporaries that the world would soon come to an end, and was one of the first to advance the idea of progress in time. [83] According to Westfall, Descartes's God, like the God of Kepler, was a creator and sustainer at the expense of God the redeemer (Father Mapple's "deliverer God"), with a loss of a sense of wonder and worship. All things, including the miracles, could be explained by natural physical means; God revealed himself in the unchangeable laws He ordained, not in miracles or in altering natural events by the interference of angels. Yet, Descartes did not question the miracle of incarnation.[84] In *Discourse on Method,* written in the vernacular and devoted to the reason of man, Descartes, who after much thought and travail, decided that he must discard all ancient opinion and start out again by doubting all teaching with a dramatic rejection of inherited systems and theories in order to find a more firm basis for belief in a policy of methodical doubt.[85] The Cartesian scheme of nature sought to explain the origin of the universe in physical terms without reference to supernatural creation; God established the basic laws of nature and made them responsible for all future events. The planets were carried around the sun in a vortex or whirlpool of transparent ether, and it was possible for one vortex to run down and disappear while another formed elsewhere. Individual suns and planetary systems could be formed within the ceaseless motions of the universe.[86] The conflict between "pure" and "applied" science is illustrated by Thomas Shadwell's (1642?-1692) play, *The Virtuoso,* and expressed by Bacon, that experiment alone is not enough, but must also include *lumen siccum*, the light of understanding.[87]

Melville's use of the theory of light in several descriptive and emotional sections of *Moby-Dick* in addition to Chapter 42, "The Whiteness of the Whale," is similar to Eddington's account of "the two tables": one a common sense, solid table, but also a scientific table consisting almost entirely of empty space.[88] Galileo says in *The Assayer*: "that tastes, odors, colors, and so on as regards the objects in which they seem to reside are nothing but pure names and reside only in the feeling body, so that if the animal is removed, all these qualities are taken away and annihilated." Aristotle stated in *De Anima (On the Soul)*:

> Perception (1) of the special objects of sense is never in error or admits the least possible amount of falsehood. (2) That of the concomitance of the objects concomitant with the sensible qualities comes next: in this case certainly we may be deceived; for while the perception that there is white before us cannot be false, the

> perception that what is white is this or that may be false. (3) Third comes the perception of the universal attributes which accompany the concomitant objects to which the special sensibles attach (I mean e.g. of movement and magnitude); it is in respect of these that the greatest amount of sense-illusion is possible.[89]

The Assayer turned this hierarchy over. Galileo maintains "that if the sensible qualities exist only in sensation and in the material substance, then taste, odor, and color are mere names with respect to the substance in which they seem to reside." It granted as real the direct sense perception of color, etc., but not the perception of motion, size, and shape, which was radically changed by Galileo. The preoccupation with language in the seventeenth century included science, and Galileo proposed a new language in physics in a more elaborate, analytical, richer, and more rigorous language: "Many are the ways to tell the story of the book of nature—poetry, painting, and music—in which the senses are privileged. But if one wishes to read that book in the style of physics, one must use only words in the [mathematical] category." In this, Galileo preceded similar ideas a half-century later.[90]

The idea of the refraction of light interested other writers, including Goethe. Newton dispersed white light into a spectrum of different colors; Huygens conceived light as wave motions of a hypothetical medium called ether; finally, Maxwell interpreted wave motion as oscillation of electric and magnetic fields in empty space. In these theories, science sacrifices the 'living' phenomena perceptible by our senses to mathematical formulation. The observation that electric, magnetic, and optical phenomena are related to Maxwell's equations was a remarkable discovery of nineteenth century science. Newton's theory of light makes optical phenomena accessible to measurement and mathematical treatment turning optics into an 'exact science' and permitting construction of accurate optical instruments that opened parts of the universe to observation not normally accessible to our senses.[91] In twentieth century physics, the atom can only be symbolized by a mathematical equation in an abstract, multidimensional space. It is no longer correct to say the qualities of bodies have been reduced to the geometry of atoms. On the contrary, the knowledge of the color of a body is made possible at the expense of knowledge of the other qualities of the body. "Ernst Mach [1838-1916] was Einstein's original intellectual hero because he originated the positivist view that has been the sheet-anchor of observational science for most of the past century: reality is what you can measure, and what you cannot measure does not count."[92] One of the fundamental discoveries of twentieth century physics was the principle of uncertainty, or the principle of indeterminism, (1927) by Werner Heisenberg (1901-1976), which states that the exact velocity and the exact location of a body, indicated by light, cannot by determined simultaneously, only approximated. The deception of color, which science says reflects only the surface of things, becomes as horrible as the vortex.

Phrenology, employed in several of Melville's novels, became a quasiscientific cure-all in the mid-nineteenth century, luring some prominent people into its favor. Henry Ward Beecher, the most popular preacher of the day, converted to phrenology, adopting it during his student days at Amherst and preaching it from the pulpit of Plymouth Church in New York City in the 1850s. He acclaimed phrenology as the great American secular faith—an infallible index to human worth that would facilitate the scientific creation of a better race of men. Beecher, along with his classmate at Amherst, Orson Squire Fowler, America's foremost phrenological writer and publisher, made wildly exaggerated statements on the value of phrenology; that phrenology had established a truth greater than Newton's. Phrenology was endorsed by the New England transcendentalists whose greatest activity was from 1830 to 1855 as an explanation that man possessed an innate morality or intuitive sense of truth, as opposed to the tabula raza or need for experience of Lockian psychology.[93] For a time, phrenology was at the core of transcendentalism. Of all the 'occult' topics, none so caught the public fancy as phrenology. Later, it was denounced as a "barren Golgotha" and useless fad.[94]

Ahab's isolation takes on the characteristics of a gigantic, threatening machine through the use of mechanistic imagery. Arvin observes that next to the idyllic scenes of the whale at play occur images from nineteenth century industry or technology of drilling, blasting, cogged wheels, mechanical looms, magnetic wires, and even the Leyden jar of Ahab's "own magnetic life." The mechanistic carpenter and the blacksmith correspond to physicians and are the ones to minister to Ahab's bodily ailments. The carpenter regards heads as topblocks, men as capstans, and himself as a tool for repairing tools, "a pure manipulator," "like an unreasoning wheel" (Ch 107). Ausband comments that Ahab's leg is mechanical, artificial, a product of the "man-makers," the carpenter and the blacksmith: its failure foreshadows the breakdown or doom of Ahab's machine.[95]

The mechanistic view of the world commencing in the seventeenth century in the development of mathematical physics separates ancient from modern science. Beginning with Galileo's formula of acceleration,

Descartes's application of geometry to nature, Huygen's law of centrifugal force, and Newton's *Mathematical Principles of Natural Philosophy*, the seventeenth century increasingly and successfully described the world in terms of mathematics. In the process, the world concept of Plato replaced that of Aristotle as the prevailing view of natural philosophy. Aristotle's view had come to the fore in the fourth century when it was advocated by St. Thomas Aquinas, and dominated inquiry into nature from the thirteenth century. In Aristotle's view, matter was imbued with power to change, objects possessed inherent tendencies, and were capable of undergoing transformation and development not subject to mathematical description. In Plato's view, matter was defined in abstract mathematical terms, reducing objects to numbers and geometrical shapes. Aristotle's world was active and 'alive;' in Plato's world, matter was passive. The passive quality of matter, the fundamental assumption of the seventeenth century revolution of science, lead to the idea of the mechanical principle of nature and life: "In half a century, nature came to be seen as a machine, and the natural philosophy of Aristotle gave way to the new promise of mathematics." Science was thought destined to reveal the intricacies of creation and to improve the condition of man; science was endorsed "To the glory of God and the good of mankind," especially by the Puritans in England in the mid-seventeenth century. The chance association of atoms in a void was rejected for centuries because atomism was closely associated with atheism; random materialism offered no basis for rationality or a purpose in the world. Atomism became possible to seventeenth century philosophers by the introduction of God as providing the laws governing the behavior of atoms, thus creating an orderly universe and establishing a mechanical world view which removed the stigma of atheism. Newton's *Principia* (1686), included a description of the inverse-square law of gravitational attraction of bodies. Leibniz objected to Newton's law of gravity, claiming it attributed unseen properties to matter and was a reversion to Aristotelian inherent properties of matter. Newton disclaimed any explanation of the meaning or the purpose of gravity; he insisted he merely described its effects and left the explanation to posterity. Newton struggled with a solution to the problem of gravity, arriving at the idea of a 'passive' principle of matter and an 'active' principle that is God. Thus, the world is lifeless and mechanistic, but permeated by the life of God. In spite of Newton's reservations, gravity was seen by the theologians and popularizers of faith as a powerful tool against atheism. Newton's science demonstrated a need for a Creator who sustains a world incapable of sustaining itself: "The mechanical worldview, in their hands, became an uncompromising witness to the glory of God." At the same time, the assurance of religious salvation was exchanged for the assurance of scientific explanation.[96]

Many critics regard Chapter 96, "The Try-Works," as the thematic or central chapter in *Moby-Dick* because of the imagery of fire as the agent that produces machines. Ahab, burned by lightning, arms himself with artificial fire. Ishmael was once "welded" to Ahab's purpose; at the Try-Works, he is no longer under the spell of the mad captain. As the chase of Moby Dick progresses, Ishmael describes Ahab and the chase in mechanistic terms; his 'machinery' has overpowered the natural inclinations of the crew: "Like machines, they dumbly moved about the decks" (Ch 96). Ahab risks losing his mechanicalness in the humanizing influence of Pip and Starbuck. Stubb, the most unfeeling of the crew, jokes by the side of a wrecked whaleboat, startling Ahab, "Man, man! did I not know thee brave as fearless fire (and as mechanical)..." (Ch 132). The individuals of the ship of "all varieties were welded into oneness" (Ch 134). As the Pequod sinks, the "mechanical" arm of the submerged Tashtego still acts as a machine, hammering the flag to higher points on the subsiding spar and catches the wing of a skyhawk. (Ch 135). Among the many other complexities of the work, Ahab is a machine likened to mills, trains, generators, and the fires of industry that can both better man, and dehumanize and destroy him.[97]

Seventeenth-century natural philosophers accepted the idea, borrowed from Plato, that mathematics was the key to understanding nature; according to Galileo: "The book of nature is written in mathematical language" and mechanics, a branch of physics, became the premier science by viewing the universe as a gigantic clock put in motion by God and operating by the laws of mathematics and mechanics. The search was for how the 'clock' worked, not doubting that God had set it in motion. Nature's laws had been dictated by God to be obeyed by intelligent beings. Newton reasoned that it was not necessary to search for a scientific explanation of the system of the universe other than God, a theme of seventeenth century England: "the wisdom of God demonstrated by the marvels of Nature" allowing harmony among the scientists and theologians during the seventeenth century.[98] Polkinghorne declares:

> When [the Enlightenment thinkers] did not lapse into a detached deistic belief in a God who had set the world a-spinning but cared little for it thereafter, [they] adopted a coolly rational tone, placing great reliance on natural theology's supposed demonstrations from

> the intricate design of the world. In line with the spirit of the age, God had become the divine Mechanic.[99]

By the end of the eighteenth century the argument of divine design had become part of religious orthodoxy, but objections began to appear. The two philosophers with the greatest influence were David Hume and Immanuel Kant. Hume puzzled over the statement of Ovid, "whichever of the gods it was, says he, that dissipated the chaos, and introduced order into the universe," and finds no solution.[100] Hume concludes:

> The whole is a riddle, an ænigma, an inexplicable mystery. Doubt, uncertainty, suspense of judgment appear the only result of our most accurate scrutiny, concerning this subject. But such is the frailty of human reason, and such the irresistible contagion of opinion, that even this deliberate doubt could scarcely be upheld; did we not enlarge our view, and opposing one species of superstition to another, set them a quarrelling; while we ourselves, during their fury and contention, happily make our escape into the calm, though obscure, regions of philosophy.[101]

Hume did not accept that there is any unique lawfulness of the universe, or that it had been shown to be a mechanism any more than an organism, nor the logical connection assumed by Newton (set out in *Dialogues*), which aroused animosity, but stirred Kant.[102]

Kant initially doubted the interpretation of Newton's laws of nature as the only logical possibility of motion and gravity, but he was influenced by the writings of Hume. He argued that the physical world cannot be proved or disproved by reason alone. He had argued that the laws of nature are inevitably mental creations, and so are the metaphysical conclusions about design in nature, yet he was sympathetic to the design argument on other grounds, that the world was purposefully ordered and attempts to find mathematical formulas distort our vision, which is mistaken for reality. Kant, a Lutheran, said we never see "things in themselves," only our subjective representatives of them, which allowed him to reconcile the Newtonian view with the existence of free will. The writings of Hume and Kant had little effect in England since they did not counter the meticulous observations of nature that appealed to the argument of design in Newtonian physics and biological science. Man was no longer the center of the world, but Kant placed the mind of man at the center, which seemed like a step backward into the pre-Copernican era. Kant endeavored to lay philosophical foundations for Newtonian physics.[103]

In the early nineteenth century, Lamarck, a proponent of 'biological mechanism,' claimed a physical cause of life could be demonstrated by the mechanics of fluids and tissues, and dispensed with any spiritual influence. The new generation of German physiologists discarded divine influence on living beings and worked to reduce life to physicochemical processes, replacing the clockworks of Descartes with electricity, thermodynamics and chemistry, discrediting the concept of 'vitalism,' that living matter is different from nonliving matter. Vitalism was a spiritual philosophy, a concept destroyed in 1827 when Wöhler synthesized urea. In reaction, many religious leaders denounced science, especially biology, as a menace to religion and morality. God had been removed from life processes as well as natural events.[104] Bowler remarks, "If Lamarck's theory was the last of the Enlightenment's speculations on the origin of life, the work of his chief opponent [Cuvier] served as a new starting point for many nineteenth-century views." Cuvier detested Lamarck and used his scientific and political influence to ensure Lamarck's progressionism did not gain favor. In addition, his own investigations led him to believe that the internal structures of living organism were so delicately balanced that change was impossible, and that reconstructed extinct fossils remained in distinct species that could not be linked by transmutation. In 1812, Cuvier perfected the techniques of comparative anatomy from which came a new system of classification of animals emphasizing internal structures in the "correlation of parts." Improved knowledge of the internal structures of animals and their power of movement would be more important than external appearances, which meant putting great emphasis on the nervous system and the backbone and unified the Linnaean classes of mammals, birds, reptiles, and fishes. Such a division broke down the absolute hierarchy of the Great Chain of Being. Cuvier concluded that vertebrates were not necessarily superior to invertebrates, merely different—so different as to make ranking one above the other meaningless. Thus, fishes and mammals are different kinds of vertebrates adapted to different habitats. It was many decades before the majority of naturalists could accept this complete breakdown of the hierarchical view. The ability of the environment to effect change within a species was limited by the necessity of preventing a disturbance of the basic pattern of the species. Cuvier presented the fixity of species as a pragmatic necessity, rarely making reference to a supernatural designer, an attitude that was strongly resisted in Britain since it appeared to undermine religion.[105]

Laplace, a century after Newton, dispensed with the need for God to understand nature, causing him considerable torment. The announcement of the superfluity of God by a scientist was a significant change in the course of intellectual history. At the same time, new discoveries using the microscope gave evidence of the intricacies of nature and the wisdom of the Creator agreeing with Newton's concept of a world machine and belief in the design of God. After the mid-eighteenth century, the era of criticism and reassertion of design in nature gave way to attempts to establish a new philosophy of belief in a mechanical universe—a triumph of Newtonian views. Thus, Laplace's ideas grew in a new and different atmosphere from earlier philosophers, one where knowledge could progress without entering into metaphysical issues. In Laplace's world, God existed only as a human idea; if God exists, it is only as a philosophical mathematician, i.e., in the science of probabilities. Hahn asserts:

> In less than a century, both celestial mechanics and probability theory had been turned on their heads; they no longer served as an essential support for believing in the Deity, but were now put to work to confirm the brilliance of human effort to penetrate nature's secrets.[106]

In the gradual process that separated God from the physical universe, Laplace in 1796 took another step by advancing a hypothesis of the origin of the Solar System without the need of God in his "nebular hypothesis," incorporating the discovery of nebulae in astronomy by William Herschel. Free from religious censure and ancient superstition, the concept of a "first cause" or divine order became redundant in Laplace's revolutionary scientific theory. Laplace ridiculed Newton for his religious conviction, and he ridiculed Leibniz for trying to prove the existence of God by science. By the beginning of the nineteenth century, Laplace was thought to be the archetype of the dangerous, atheistic scientist. Laplace's views on the mechanical nature of the heavens, the origins of the Solar System, and probability theory were well known in the nineteenth century and their implications for science and religion were debated ardently by theologians, philosophers, and scientists, expanding intellectual discussion to a new dimension. Enormous advances in many areas of science and the inquiry into nature were made readily available to the populace providing potent arguments for both faith and doubt in matters of religion, yet nearly every advance of science was a loss for faith.[107] Melville, through Ahab, says he doubts his faith and doubts his doubt, undoubtedly because of his assimilation of science.

Ahab may have had a notable forerunner in pondering the relationship of faith and doubt to nature in Hugues Félicité Robert de Lamennais (1782-1854), French priest, philosopher and political theorist, one of the most honored and condemned figures in the French church rivaled among Catholic clergy only by John Henry Newman. Lamennais wrote in *Essays on Indifference in Matters of Religion* (1817-24), that in the attempt to discover the basis of certainty, two important truths are recognized: "the first is that all philosophical systems result in absolute doubt; the second, that absolute doubt is impossible for man. Hence when he consults reason alone, he is placed in an unnatural state; for while reason constrains him to doubt, nature compels him to believe."[108] The English translation of the book by de Lamennais, *Le Livre du peuple* (1838) or *People's Own Book* (1839), was in the ship's library of the whaleship *Charles and Henry* during Melville's voyage in the years 1842-1843.[109]

The difference in the length of time of composition of *Moby-Dick* from his earlier novels, taking sixteen months, remains unexplained. Olson maintains it is two books; Ahab and Moby Dick were not in the first book, but added later. Vincent concluded that the original story was a straightforward whaling voyage, and new material added after he was nearly finished that accounts for the delay. Howard claims a major change in the direction of the book occurred with the addition of the cetology chapters.[110] Stewart asserts the composition was in two main parts with a 'transition' section in Chapters 16 to 22. The book probably started in one direction, and as new ideas occurred, shifted in another direction as is evident in Melville's earlier works, but Stewart is no more clear on when the cetology and other science material were added.[111] Readers and literary critics alike objected to the long chapters on whaling and cetology, a blend of exposition and narration, "a chaotic melange of adventure, metaphysics, and amateur scientific investigation." Recent opinion, however, credits Melville with creating one of the most carefully crafted novels in American literature. Ward states, "Melville constantly attempted to arrive at an understanding of spiritual reality through an understanding of physical reality"; more specifically, an understanding of the natural sciences. In addition, the factual expositions give variety and expand time, for little happens during long, tedious stretches of time on a lengthy whaling voyage of three to four years' duration. By the time of the encounter with Moby Dick, the reader is familiar with the whale, the method of the chase, the dangers of whaling, and the strength and maliciousness of the White Whale. The sheer weight of scientific fact builds the metaphysical and spiritual meaning of Moby Dick on physical reality, balancing the ordinary with the extraordinary. The cetology chapters give the illusion of objectivity and contrast with the subjective beliefs of the members of the crew. Ward comments:

> In Melville's quest for absolute truth, no knowledge is adequate that stops at what the scientist considers the discernible limits of an object....With each analysis of each part of the whale, with each description of each operation in whaling, the scientific framework reveals itself to contain meanings that establish the whale as a creature immeasurable by science.[112]

Thus, the detailed scientific examination is unable to understand the magnitude of the whale—or any aspect of human existence—and heightens the need for spiritual understanding, which is equally elusive. Kazin declares: "through physical assault and then by scientific and industrial cunning, man finds his final relatedness to nature neither as a hero (Ahab) nor by heeding Father Mapple's old prophetic warning of man's proper subservience to God."[113] The introspection, or 'deep diving,' in the minute examination of the whale is reminiscent of the works of Robert Burton and Sir Thomas Browne who said we have "all the mysteries of Africa in us"; to know the universe one must examine the small part of the world he knows. The use of humor saves the cetology chapters from the dullness of a scientific treatise. In jesting about the whale, Melville paradoxically ennobles the whale by mocking it; the humor is directed not so much at the whale as to the scientific method. If Melville indicates the dangers of subjectivism as a means to knowledge, he is even more scornful of empirical science, which he associates with the land, the known side of reality; the knowledge science gives is only the reflected light of the surface of things; the deep, inner nature of reality lies beyond its power.[114] The inconsistencies in Melville's scientific references are consistent with the early nineteenth century because experts and scientists publicly argued and disagreed. As Kuhn contends:

> Because it demands large-scale paradigm destruction and major shifts in the problems and techniques of normal science, the emergence of new theories is generally preceded by a period of pronounced professional insecurity. As one might expect, that insecurity is generated by the persistent failure of the puzzles of normal science to come out as they should. Failure of existing rules is the prelude to a search for new ones.[115]

Nearly all theories and accepted practices of the eighteenth century were reexamined in the early nineteenth century and new theories came in profusion. The conflicts of the scientists and the developments of science were reported in the press to a curious and receptive audience. Melville, while rejecting the idea of nature as a benevolent goddess, did not regard it simply as the source of evil. Science provided him with a more harrowing paradox: Nature breeds both good and evil, but is equally indifferent to both! Melville attempted to reach through this paradox in his search for truth and found nature, as Pierre did in Melville's next book, "not so much her own ever-sweet interpreter, as the mere supplier of that cunning alphabet, whereby selecting and combining as he pleases, each man reads his own peculiar lesson according to his own peculiar mind and mood."[116]

Although Melville mastered no science and denied the competence of science to plumb the mysteries of life, in a layman's way, he kept well abreast of new knowledge, and for a time, received it as any other current news. The scientific discoveries, with their stark vision of the passionless impersonality of the unknown and unknowable, also played their part in dethroning the anthropocentrism of Melville's youth and in providing one of two poles of his thinking—naturalism and Christianity.[117] Watters concludes that the conflict in *Moby-Dick* is the drama of an individual, in the person of Ahab, who refuses to admit anything beyond human comprehension; Ahab asserts the superiority of intelligence, or science, to brute power, but receives death for his arrogant pride.[118] Ahab is ambiguous in his attitude toward science. On one hand, he is the agent of science in his study of the charts and in the mastery of the level loadstone. On the other hand, he defies science in destroying the quadrant. In Ahab, with understanding and knowledge, man lost 'paradise.' As Ahab says, "Gifted with the high perception, I lack the low, enjoying power; damned most subtly and most malignantly! damned in the midst of Paradise!" He asserts in the face of God, man, because of his understanding, has the right to guide has own way, that man has free will.[119] Melville declares of Ahab's purpose, "by its own sheer inveteracy of will forced itself into a kind of self-assumed, independent being of its own." He says man is intellectually not equipped to understand the universe in all its immensity; he discovered that man's imagination failed to see a single goal behind the cosmic process. But, through Ishmael, Melville made a positive philosophy of his failure; man could proceed in this world even though he could perceive no ultimate answer. He could be certain the universe was not surely meaningless or surely evil; it is unknowable. Vincent comments, "In reading the last chapter of *Moby-Dick*, at times the mind becomes bewildered by the accumulation of effects, the massing of meanings, if one approaches the book symbolically as well as literally."[120]

The seed of science begun in *Mardi* came to full flower in *Moby-Dick*. The sheer mass of science in *Moby-Dick* is unmistakable. Mumford declares that Melville is distinguished from other nineteenth century writers by his use of science; Hawthorne, for example, used little of contemporary developments in science.[121] Arvin contends, "No great poet has ever, before or since [Melville], brought zoology and poetry together in an even comparable way."[122] Even though man and whale may be more closely related than the Great Chain of Being might indicate, the many contrasts between man and whale dramatize the developmental break between the two. Melville was influenced by the science of the day, and, *Moby-Dick*, like science, has no clear position and reveals "a mind in transition."[123] Even doubt brought about by science leads back to faith: "But Faith, like a jackal, feeds among the tombs, and even from these dead doubts she gathers her most vital hope" (Ch 7). From "Etymology" to "Epilogue," Melville assimilated and incorporated enormous amounts of natural science into his story, struggled with the meaning and import of wrenching changes in the perception of man's place in the universe brought about by science, and, though seemingly inconclusive, produced a monumental, prophetic work at the single period in man's history when the vast Western society, through the hubris of intellect, for a time, perceived no need of God.

Notes

1. Frank Shuffelton, "Going Through the Long Vaticans: Melville's 'Extracts' in *Moby-Dick.*" *Texas Studies in Literature and Language* 25 (1983):528-540.

2. James William Nechas, *Synonomy, Repetition, and Restatement In the Vocabulary of Herman Melville's* Moby-Dick. Darby, Pennsylvania: Norwood Editions, 1980, p. 43-50.

3. Richard Chase, *Herman Melville: A Critical Study.* New York: Macmillan, 1976, pp. 75-77.

4. Euroclydon is a tempestuous wind that buffets Paul's ship, Acts 27.

5. David Jaffe, "Some Origins of *Moby-Dick*: New Finds on an Old Source." *American Literature* 29 (1957):263-277.

6. David Knight, *Ordering the World: A history of classifying man.* London: Burnett Book, Andre Deutsch, 1981, p. 116.

7. Thomas Vaughn, "On the Doctrine of Life after Death" *Parerga und Paralipomena II,* cited by Lovejoy, Arthur O. *The Reason, the Understanding, and Time.* Baltimore: Johns Hopkins University Press, 1961, pp. 145-146.

8. Homer W. Smith, *Man and His Gods.* Boston: Little, Brown, 1952, p. 23.

9. Richard Morris, *Time's Arrows: Scientific Attitudes Toward Time.* New York: Touchstone; Simon and Schuster, 1985, p. 169; *Encyclopædia Britannica* 19 (1971):323-326.

10. G. J. Whitrow, *The Natural Philosophy of Time.* Oxford: Oxford University Press, 1980, pp. 270-288.

11. James Robert Corey, *Herman Melville and the Theory of Evolution.* Ph.D. Dissertation, Washington State University 1968, pp. 72-75.

12. Howard P. Vincent, *The Trying-Out of* Moby-Dick. Boston: Houghton Mifflin Company, 1949, pp. 154-158.

13. Herbert Rothschild, Jr., "The Language of Mesmerism in 'The Quarter-Deck' Scene in *Moby-Dick.*" *English Studies* 53 (1972):235-238.

14. Charles MacKay, *Memoirs of Extraordinary Popular Delusions and the Madness of Crowds.* London and New York: Richard Bentley, National Illustrated Library, Farrar, Straus and Giroux, 1841, 1852, and reprinted 1932, pp. 319-334.

15. Bernd Würsig, "Cetaceans." *Science* 244 (1989) 1550-1557.

16. Herman Melville, *Moby-Dick: An Authoritative Text, Reviews and Letters by Melville, Analogues and Sources Criticism.*

Harrison Hayford and Hershel Parker, editors. New York: Norton, 1966, p. 117n.

17. Janez Stanonek, "Did Melville Ever See an Albino?" *American Literature* 43 (1971):637-638.

18. Stephen Toulmin and June Goodfield, *The Architecture of Matter*. Chicago and London: University of Chicago Press, 1982, p. 58.

19. R. W. Southern, *Robert Grosseteste: The Growth of an English Mind in Medieval Europe*. Oxford: Oxford University Press, 1986, p. 168.

20. F. Sherwood Taylor, *A Short History of Science and Scientific Thought: With Readings from the Great Scientists from the Babylonians Through Einstein*. New York and London: Norton, 1949, pp. 137-138.

21. Don Cupit, *The Sea of Faith: Christianity in Change*. Cambridge: Cambridge University Press, 1984, p. 138.

22. Vincent, ref. 12, pp. 182,184.

23. *Encyclopædia Britannica* 14 :1132, 1971.

24. Morris, ref. 9, p. 24.

25. Morris, ref. 9, pp. 61, 64; Szamosi, Géza *The Twin Dimensions: Inventing Time and Space*. New York, San Francisco: McGraw-Hill, 1986, p. 135.

26. Whitrow, ref. 10, p. 352.

27. Vincent, ref. 12, p. 217.

29. *The Advancement of Learning*, (1605), by Francis Bacon.

30. John D. Barrow, *The World Within the World*. Oxford and New York, Oxford University Press, 1990, pp. 139-140.

31. Würsig, ref. 15.

32. Loren Eiseley, *Darwin's Century*. Garden City, New York: Doubleday, 1958, p. 52.

33. Peter J. Bowler, *Evolution: The History of an Idea*. Berkeley, Los Angeles, and London: University of California Press, 1984, p. 81.

34. Herman Melville, *Journal of a Visit to London and the Continent 1849-1850*. Eleanor Melville Metcalf, editor. Cambridge, Massachusetts: Harvard University Press, 1948, p. 52.

35. Michael Hoskin, "William Herschel and the Making of Modern Astronomy." *Scientific American* February (1986):106-112; J. B. Sidgwick, *William Herschel: Explorer of the Heavens*. London: Faber and Faber, 1953, pp. 15, 102-103.

36. Sidgwick, ref. 35, pp. 109-127, 135-136, 214.

37. Edgar A. Dryden, *Melville's Thematics of Form; The Great Art of Telling the Truth*. Baltimore and London: John Hopkins University Press, 1968, p. 97.

38. Vincent, ref. 12, p. 266.

39. Harold Aspic, Phrenology and the Whale. *Nineteenth Century Fiction* 23 (1968):18-27.

40. Tyrus Hillway, "Melville's Use of Two Pseudo-Sciences." *Modern Language Notes* 64 (1949):145-150.

41. Loren Eiseley, "The Long Loneliness: Man and the Porpoise: Two Solitary Destinies." *American Scholar* Winter (1960-1961):57-64.

42. Würsig, ref. 15.

43. René. Taton, *Science in the Nineteenth Century*. New York: Basic Books, Inc., 1965, pp. 284-286; Knight, ref. 6, p. 139.

44. Würsig, ref. 15.

45. Vincent, ref. 12, pp. 300-302.

46. Vincent, ref. 12, pp. 268.

47. Herman Melville, *Moby-Dick*. Harrison Hayford and Hershel Parker, editors, New York: Norton, 1967, p. 344n.

48. Vincent, ref. 12, p. 298; Maurice Friedman, "The Modern Job: On Melville, Dostoevsky and Kafka." *Judaism* 12 (1963):436-455.

49. Carl B. Boyer, *A History of Mathematics*. Princeton, New Jersey: Princeton University Press, 1968, pp. 410-415.

50. Nechas, ref. 2, p. 125.

51. Bowler, ref. 33, pp. 115-116.

52. Vincent, ref. 12, pp. 348-350.

53. Elizabeth S. Foster, "Melville and Geology." *American Literature* 17 (1945):50-65; Richard S. Moore, "Owen's and Melville's Fossil Whale." *American Transcendental Quarterly* 26 supplement, 24, 1975.

54. Knight, ref. 6, p. 88.

55. Maurice Friedman, *Problematic Rebel: Melville, Dostoevsky, Kafka, Camus*. Chicago and London: University of Chicago Press, revised 1970, p. 70.

56. Foster, ref. 53.

57. Taylor, ref. 20, p. 43.

58. C. S. Lewis, *The Discarded Image: An Introduction to Medieval and Renaissance Literature*. Cambridge: Cambridge University Press, 1964, pp. 97-98, 140-146.

59. *Encyclopædia Britannica*.10:132-135, 1971.

60. Foster, ref. 53.

61. Maurice, ref. 55, p. 36.

62. Chase, ref. 3, pp. 46-47.

63. Nechas, ref. 2, p. 123.

64. Gerard M. Sweeney, *Melville's Use of Classical Mythology.* Amsterdam: Rodopi, 1975, p. 159.

65. Jaffe, ref. 5.

66. Vincent, ref. 12, pp. 373-374.

67. Joseph Jones, "Ahab's 'Blood Quench': Theater or Metallurgy?" *American Literature* 18 (1946):35-37; *Encyclopædia* Britannica, 15: 241-244, 1971.

68. Friedman, ref. 55, pp. 106-107.

69. Melville, ref. 34, pp. 7-8.

70. David Jaffe, *The Stormy Petrel and the Whale. Some Origins of* Moby-Dick. Baltimore: Port City Press, 1976.

71. Vincent, ref. 12, p. 379.

72. Kenneth W. Cameron, "A Note on the Corposants in *Moby-Dick.*" *Emerson Society Quarterly* 19 (1960):22-24.

73. Charles C. Walcutt, "The Fire Symbolism in *Moby-Dick.*" *Modern Language Notes* 59 (1944):304-310.

74. Paul W. Miller, "Sun and Fire in Melville's *Moby-Dick.*" *Nineteenth Century Fiction* 13 (1958):139-144.

75. Francis X. Canfield, "Moby Dick and the Book of Job." *Catholic World* 174 (1952):254-260.

76. Wilson E. Heflin, "The Sources of Ahab's Lordship over the Level Lodestone." *American Literature* 20 (1945):323-327.

77. Taylor, ref. 20, p. 90-92.

78. Barrow, ref. 30, pp. 90-96.

79. Friedman, ref. 55, pp. 76-77.

80. Jaffe, ref. 70; Nathan Reingold, editor, *Science in Nineteenth Century America: A Documentary History.* Chicago and London: University of Chicago Press, 1964, pp. 108-110.

81. Tyrus Hillway, "Melville's Education in Science." *Texas Studies in Literature and Language* 16 (1974):421-422.

82. David Charles Leonard, "The Cartesian Vortex in *Moby-Dick.*" *American Literature* 51 (1979):105-109.

83. Richard Morris, *Time's Arrows: Scientific Attitudes Toward Time.* New York: Touchstone; Simon and Schuster, 1985, pp. 71-72.

84. Richard S. Westfall, "The Rise of Science and the Decline of Orthodox Christianity: A Study of Kepler, Descartes, and Newton." in *God and Nature: Historical Essays on the Encounter between Christianity and Science.* David C. Lindberg, and Ronald L. Numbers, editors. Berkeley, Los Angeles and London: University of California Press, 1986, pp. 198-226.

85. Herbert Butterfield, *The Origins of Modern Science 1300-1800.* New York: Free Press, 1957, p. 123.

86. Bowler, ref. 33, p. 26.

87. Peter Medawar, *The Limits of Science.* Oxford: Oxford University Press, 1984, p. 8.

88. Stephen Toulmin, *The Philosophy of Science.* New York, Hagerstown, San Francisco, and London: Harper and Row, 1953, p. 12.

89. *The Basic Works of Aristotle.* Richard McKeon, editor, New York: Random House, 1970, p. 589.

90. Pietro Redondi, *Galileo: Heretic.* Translated by Raymond Rosenthal. Princeton, New Jersey: Princeton University Press, 1987, pp. 56-59.

91. Werner Heisenberg, *Philosophical Problems of Quantum Physics.* Woodbridge, Connecticut: Ox Bow Press, 1979, pp. 36, 61-65.

92. John Maddox, "Down with the Big Bang." *Nature* 340 (1989):425.

93. Aspic, ref. 39.

94. John B. Wilson, "Phrenology and the Transcendentalists." *American Literature* 28 (1956):220-225.

95. Hugh H. Ausband, "The Whale and Machine: an Approach to *Moby-Dick.*" *American Literature* 47 (1975):197-211.

96. Gary B. Deason, "Reformation Theology and the Mechanistic Conception of Nature," in *God & Nature: Historical Essays on the Encounter between Christianity and Science.* David C. Lindberg and Ronald L. Numbers, editors. Berkeley, Los Angeles and London: University of California Press, 1986, pp. 169-187.

97. Ausband, ref. 95.

98. Jacques Roger, "The Mechanistic Conception of Life," in *God and Nature: Historical Essays on the Encounter between Christianity and Science.* David C. Lindberg and Ronald L. Numbers, editors. Berkeley, Los Angeles, and London: University of California Press, 1986, pp. 292-293.

99. John Polkinghorne, *One World: the interaction of science and theology.* London, SPCK Holy Trinity Church, 1986, p. 3.

100. David Hume, *The Natural History of Religion.* Edited and Introduction by H.E.Root. Reprint. Stanford: Stanford University Press, 1956, p. 35.

101. Hume, ref. 100, p. 76.

102. J. L. Mackie, *The Cement of the Universe: A Study of Causation.* Oxford: University Press, 1980, p. 88.

103. Barrow, ref. 30, pp. 78-82; Mackie, ref. 102, p. 111.

104. Roger, ref. 98, pp. 277-293.

105. Bowler, 33, pp. 106-108.

106. Roger Hahn, "Laplace and the Mechanistic Universe," in *God and Nature: Historical Essays on the Encounter between Christianity and Science*. David C. Lindberg and Ronald L. Numbers, editors. Berkeley, Los Angeles, and London: University of California Press, 1986, p. 270.

107. Hahn, ref. 106, pp. 256-273.

108. Hugues Félicité Robert de Lamennais, "Authority in Religion," from *Essays on Indifference in Matters of Religion* (1817-1824) in *Religious Thought in the Nineteenth Century: Illustrated from Writers of the Period*. Bernard M. G. Reardon, editor. Cambridge: Cambridge University Press, 1966, p. 187.

109. Merton M. Sealts, Jr., *Melville's Reading*. Revised and enlarged edition. Columbia, South Carolina: University of South Carolina Press, 1988, p. 250.

110. Charles. Olson, *Call Me Ishmael.* New York: Reynall and Hitchcock, 1947, p. 35; Vincent, ref. 12, p. 26; Leon Howard, *Herman Melville*. University of California Press. Berkeley, Los Angeles, and London, 1952, p. 162.

111. George R. Stewart, "The Two *Moby-Dicks*." *American Literature* 25 (1953):417-448.

112. J. A. Ward, "The Function of the Cetological Chapters in *Moby-Dick*." *American Literature* 28 (1956):164-183.

113. Alfred Kazin, "Ishmael and Ahab." *Atlantic Monthly* 198 (1956):81-85.

114. Ward, ref. 112.

115. Thomas S. Kuhn, *The Structure of Scientific Revolutions*, 2nd edition, enlarged. Chicago: International Encyclopedia of Unified Science, 1962, pp. 67-68.

116. Tyrus Hillway, "Melville and the Spirit of Science." *South Atlantic Quarterly* 48 (1949):78-88.

117. Foster, ref. 53.

118. Reginald E. Watters, "Melville's Metaphysics of Evil." *University of Toronto Quarterly* 9 (1940):170-182.

119. Corey, ref. 11, p. 70.

120. Vincent, ref. 12, p. 375.

121. Lewis Mumford, *Herman Melville*. New York: Harcourt Brace, 1929, pp. 163-164.

122. Newton Arvin, "The Whale." in Moby-Dick *as Doubloon: Essays and Extracts (1851-1970).* Parker, Hershel and Hayford, Harrison, editors. Norton: New York 1970, p. 201.

123. Corey, ref. 11, p. 79.

Chapter 5

Pierre: nature's cunning alphabet

Contemporary issues in science, conflicting concepts of time, developments in geology, and other current debates on the natural world receive attention in Melville's next novel, *Pierre; or, the Ambiguities* (1852). Pierre lives with his mother at Saddle Meadows, a manorial estate in New York left by his father, who died when Pierre was twelve years old. Pierre, the only child of the manor, lives in a grandly idealized relationship with his mother, and he is engaged to be married to Lucy Tartan. In the midst of the serenity and security of the family, reminiscent of the whales in Chapter 87, "The Grand Armada," in *Moby-Dick*, time and tragedy are likened to a crumbling shaft:

> ...not less by Palmyra's quarries, than by Palmyra's ruins....these Time crushed in the egg; and the proud stone that should have stood among the clouds, Time left abased beneath the soil. Oh, what quenchless feud is this, that Time hath with the sons of Men! (Bk I pt 2)

Melville herein states one of the themes of *Pierre*: the importance of time and the conflicting philosophical and scientific examination of what seems both common sense and unknowable. He emphasizes time by capitalizing it. The antiquity of the ruins of Palmyra, an ancient city near the Euphrates River, also called Tadmor in pre-Semitic times dating from the nineteenth century B.C., becomes an archaeological metaphor for the fate of Pierre and the incompleteness of the works of man. The phenomenon of time is mentioned prominently in *Mardi* and *Moby-Dick*. The history of time is characterized by the opposing points of view of Archimedes and Aristotle, whose influence dominated medieval and Renaissance pioneers of modern science. Archimedes (287?-212 B.C.) 'eliminated' the importance of time by following the principles of Euclid which reduced much of physics to geometry and in which time plays no part. Aristotle, on the other hand, theorized a 'coming-into-being' of things, requiring time, and greatly complicating the study of physical nature. For most of the history of the physical sciences, the ingenious separation of space and time permitted great achievements by virtually ignoring the complications of time and subordinating the temporal to the spatial. In physics, Joseph Lagrange (1736-1813) advanced the notion that time was a fourth dimension of space by concluding that the laws of motion of Newton are reversible, thus eliminating time from dynamic theory. Beginning with Sadi Carnot (1796-1832), and later Rudolph Clausius (1822-1888) and Lord Kelvin in the mid-nineteenth century, scientists struggled with the problem of time in mechanics. Clausius's interpretation of the laws of thermodynamics argued that the universe was moving in one predetermined direction rather than a cyclic flux and eternal balance; all reactions are not reversible and, over time, are not the same, a concept difficult to accept because of its philosophical and cosmological implications.[1]

Melville examines the importance of time, whether cyclic or linear, and the phenomenon of the 'sublime of nature' in America in the mid-nineteenth century. The beautiful country around him recalls proud memories in the beauty of nature: "all its hills and swales seemed as sanctified through their very long uninterrupted possession by his race....the sacred Past hath no fixed statues erected to it, but all things irreverently seethe and boil in the vulgar cauldron of an everlasting uncrystallising Present." Political institutions in America seem to possess "the divine virtue of a natural law; for the most mighty of Nature's laws is this, that out of Death she brings Life." Green is the color of growth and renewal as well as the color of decay, a restatement of the idea expressed in Chapter 102, "A Bower in the Arsacides," in

Moby-Dick. Campbell comments that a system of myths and rites derived from the "reciprocities of death and life" has been identified from across the West African Sudan, across the Indian Ocean, and into Polynesia as far as Easter Island.[2] Cupit says Christianity renews itself by the process of death and rebirth. It is the nature of certainties to dissolve away. The deep existential thinker must "descend into the underworld, the primeval chaos, and there await the remaking of meaning and the emergence of a new reality."[3] Pierre continues, "And if in America the vast mass of families be as the blades of grass, yet some few there are that stand as the oak; which, instead of decaying, annually puts forth new branches; whereby Time, instead of subtracting, is made to capitulate into multiple virtue" (Bk I pt 3).

The 'sublime of nature' arose from a complex of seventeenth century scientific, theological, and philosophical developments that became a submerged aesthetic in the eighteenth century opposed to the Enlightenment, the opposite of the ordered and rational world of Cartesian science. The 'sublime' declined in importance in Europe in the early nineteenth century, but it remained vital through the middle decades of the nineteenth century in America. The upward direction of medieval mysticism was replaced by theological interest in an infinite universe, that spiritual omnipresence has a physical nature in the forests, deserts, mountains, sky, and wilderness. The most important writer to influence the advance of sublime nature was Locke, who said that all knowledge originates from sense perception causing a shift from reason to the imagination, and from knowledge to sensation. The mingled terror and exultation reserved for God extended to the greatest objects of nature.[4] Seventeenth century European and American views agreed that the city was of God, the wilderness was of the Devil and the abode of evil. Through the late decades of the eighteenth century, the concept of natural wilderness as a moral resource arose, as well as the idea of the corrupting influence of civilization on the virtuous life of the noble savage. In the eighteenth century, Newtonian philosophy caused a shift of the object of worship from God to nature.[5]

The Old Testament depicts God ordering the world out of a formless void. The early Hebrews forbade idols and 'graven images,' so that God was not in objects of the natural world. The external world was distinct from the ordering force of nature. Forbidding the casting of spells and divination prevented human willpower from altering the events of nature, emphasizing an abstract view of nature as aesthetic and celebrative rather than analytical or something that could be manipulated. The desert, for the ascetics as for the biblical Israelites, was at once the haunt of demons and the realm of bliss and harmony;

New Testament passages provide a reason for belief in creation's goodness and unity.[6] Nature was a 'signpost' pointing to God, but not a representation of God. Dominion over creatures was legitimized in the Garden of Eden, but not dominion over nature. Although nature was the work of God, understanding nature did not lead to an understanding of God: wisdom came not from "earthquake, wind, or fire," but from the voice of the spirit of God. Secular nature gods were anathema, including astrology, which attracted most primitive cultures. The Babylonian sun-god Marduk is described in the Gilgamesh creation-story as a law giver to some extent and able to control the stars. In the Old Testament, Yahweh is a divine lawgiver with power over natural phenomena such as separating the land from the sea, ordering night and day, seasonal change, and the winds and tides, without any other explanation or innate tendencies within objects. It was a faith in the rationality, intelligibility, and constancy of nature influenced from without from which the idea of natural law could develop. In addition, the early Jews may not have developed an interest in science because they had not developed a seafaring tradition which required the study of the heavens for navigation. Early nomadic life was tied to belief and agriculture with little stimulus to inquiry. Only Solomon took an interest in the natural world.[7] The ascetic ideal and ethos were powerful stimuli to an appreciation of the natural environment, which can be seen in the letters of Basil (d. 379), "it bears for me the sweetest of all fruits, tranquillity" and that "the contemplation of Nature abates the fever of the soul." St. Francis of Assisi (1181-1226) often drew moral allegorical parallels from Creation, which medieval people took to be the "Book of Nature."[8] At the beginning of the nineteenth century, American writers incorporated theological ideas of primitivism and sublime nature into their work; Americans turned to nature with an enthusiasm free of European influence. Europe had an established, complex cultural background as well as nature, but America had a vast, untouched wilderness equivalent to a new Eden and a divine covenant.[9] Pierre's family, the Glendinnings, appear at first to defy the law of nature of decay by transcending the effects of time, "the limbs of an oak," as if the family went forward in linear time rather than cyclic time of death and renewal (Bk I pt 3).

During the delirium just before death, Pierre's father spoke of his daughter born to a beautiful, mysterious French woman before he married Pierre's mother (Bk IV pt 2). The girl's existence was kept secret from the family becoming a major complication of the novel. The contrast of two portraits of his father—one painted before his marriage and one after marriage—gives evidence to Pierre of a change in his father by observing his "Physiognomy," the pseudoscience Melville used to advantage in earlier works. Pierre's cousin spoke of "a very wonderful work on Physiognomy" that could be used for detecting people's innermost secrets by studying their faces. The portrait revealed his father was secretly in love with the "French young lady" (Bk IV pt 4). The "very wonderful" book on physiognomy is most certainly Lavater's *Essays on Physiognomy,* which Melville bought during his European trip of 1849-1850.[10] The enthusiasm for the pseudoscience of phrenology and physiognomy is illustrated by one of its critics, David Meredith Reese, a New York physician, who wrote in the *Humbugs of New York* in 1828: "They have swallowed Maria Monk, abolitionism, and homopathia; and are now equally busy in bolting down Phrenology and Animal Magnetism."[11] The most famous physiognomist was Polemon Laodicensis (d. about 144 A.D.), a famous rhetorician and historian who flourished under Trajan and Hadrian. Physiognomical traits were closely linked with the principles of astrology. For Chaucer and every educated man of his time, physiognomy made it possible to judge the inner character of a man from a study of his form and features by interpreting every line of the face, the shape and color of the eyes, and every tone of voice. Chaucer emphasized the physiognomical features of his characters, especially the Pardoner.[12] During the intrigues of seventeenth century Rome, the "art of the gaze" for discovering without being discovered the intentions of the human spirit was an invaluable art.[13] One of the great hopes of the early nineteenth century was for a science of man; the first attempts were physiognomy and phrenology, but they appeared to be deterministic, undermining free will.[14] Melville used phrenology to demonstrate character, even as late as *Billy Budd,* but showed little confidence in it otherwise.

A servant girl at a neighboring manor house, Isabel, reveals the story of their father's relationship with her mother and presents vague evidence that they are brother and sister, greatly disturbing Pierre. In one of many philosophical digressions in the book, Melville expresses skepticism on the rational cause and effect of the scientific method, and argues that the human heart can not be defined by science:

> In their precise tracings-out and subtle causations, the strongest and fieriest emotions of life defy all analytical insight....Why this cheek kindles with a noble enthusiasm; why that lip curls in scorn; these are things not wholly imputable to the immediate apparent cause, which is only one link in the chain; but to a long line of dependencies whose further part is lost in the mid-regions of the impalpable air. (Bk IV pt 1)

Every event has a cause based on the principle of determinism, or fate, in a mechanical sense, yet unknowable by man. Scientific paradigms often induce a sense of an authoritative "truth-definition" response by defining the framework within which science works; its truth can be determined only when it is challenged by another, conflicting idea.[15] Hume asserts:

> We are placed in this world, as in a great theatre, where the true springs and causes of every event are entirely concealed from us; nor have we either sufficient wisdom to foresee, or power to prevent those ills, with which we are continually threatened. We hang in perpetual suspense between life and death, health and sickness, plenty and want; which are distributed amongst the human species by secret and unknown causes, whose operation is oft unexpected, and always unaccountable. These *unknown causes*, then, become the constant object of our hope and fear; and while the passions are kept in perpetual alarm by an anxious expectation of the events, the imagination is equally employed in forming ideas of those powers, on which we have so entire a dependance.[16]

Pierre becomes convinced that Isabel's story is true and accepts her as his sister. He is confused by the conflicts that "defy all analytical insight" of science.

Isabel tells her story of loneliness in a forlorn house, perhaps in France, cared for by an old man and woman who rarely spoke to her; she has a vague remembrance of "chattering in two different childish languages; one of which waned in me as the other and latter grew" (Bk VI pt 3). After a lengthy period of isolation with no human contact, Isabel recalls having a fever when a child and the effect it had on her memory and language:

> There seemed people about me, some of whom talked one [language], and some the other; but I talked both; yet one not so readily as the other; and but beginningly as it were; still this other was the one which was gradually displacing the former. (Bk VI pt 3)

The delirium incorporates the dominance of one language over the other suggesting a progression of language. The strange 'truth' of the unconscious, like the revelations of Pip in *Moby-Dick*, came to Isabel in a state of delirium in a simple "sparkling-gay, and lightsome" childlike, innocent language. Horne Tooke (1736-1812) and Etienne Condillac (1715-1780) theorized that language and thought are inseparable. Tooke attempted to make 'mental' philosophy into a natural philosophy after the model of Newtonian physical science. Sir William Jones, (mentioned in *Moby-Dick*), mastered Italian, French, Greek, and Latin while a student at Harrow, and after entering Oxford in 1764, studied Spanish, Portuguese, German, Arabic, and Persian, translated numerous Arabic and Persian poems into English, and wrote scholarly treatises on the Eastern languages to become the leading Orientalist at Oxford by 1774. He then studied law and resided in India from 1783 until his death in 1794. In an effort to enhance his mastery of Indian law, Jones began the study of Sanskrit in 1785 and recognized the similarity of the roots of verbs as well as the forms of grammar in Sanskrit with Greek and Latin. Jones concluded the antiquity of Sanskrit made it the basis of Greek, Latin, and Persian as a primitive, primary language. Whewell said (about 1832) that language was arranged like "geological layers" progressing from Sanskrit, to Arabic, to Latin. In 1844, Chambers's *Vestiges of the Natural History of Creation* made a sensation by suggesting what the earlier philologists had already said, that language arose from a simpler form and developed into more complex forms. He shocked the concept of the special creation of man with the outrageous suggestion that man had once been barbarous, and that animals had a gesture and sign language, i.e., a form of communication that became more developed in man; language was not a miraculous gift of God peculiar to man, but arose from man's physical and mental constitution. The impossibility of inventing language proved the existence of God, according to the axiom, "vox populi, vox Dei." The furor over *Vestiges* was a puzzling phenomenon, for Chambers had presented the conventional account of the natural history of language.[17]

Isabel bought a guitar from a peddler, a magical "spectral" guitar, which was a concept of spiritualism popular in the mid-nineteenth century. The guitar became "human" to Isabel and was a "loving" and "heart friend." The mystery of the guitar's "ringing silveriness" convinces Pierre of Isabel's claim of being his sister. His mother perceives a change in their closeness saying: "I feel my blood chemically changing in me." Pierre leaves the manor house and plunges deep into the woods to a remarkable, enormous stone balanced on a minute contact point which he calls the Memnon Stone. Pierre changes his mind and rejects the thought of Isabel as his sister, yet acknowledges his passion for her may be incestuous (Bk VII pt 8).

Isabel sits in the window casement with "mild heat-lightnings and ground-lightnings" flashing outside on a warm and noiseless summer night playing the magical guitar, She shows him the name "Isabel" written inside the guitar, present when she bought it. Isabel is certain it belonged to her mother and calls upon her mother's spirit from the instrument: "Again, after a preluding silence, the guitar as magically responded as before; the sparks quivered along its strings; and again Pierre felt as in the immediate presence of the spirit." The sparks illuminated the dark hair of Isabel and the entire casement of the window. The same words of mystery came from the guitar as the previous night, casting him under a preternatural spell told in the language of mesmerism: "Isabel seemed to swim in an electric fluid; the vivid buckler of her brow seemed as a magnetic plate," "an extraordinary physical magnetism in Isabel," "the sparkling electricity in which she seemed to swim," "She seemed moulded from fire and air, and vivified at some Voltaic pile of August thunder-clouds heaped against the sunset" (Bk VIII pt 2). Isabel becomes a spiritual medium calling upon the dead spirit of her mother with a generous amount of mesmerism, or animal magnetism, in "electric glory" in a more florid treatment of mesmerism than Melville used in Chapter 36, "The Quarter-Deck," in *Moby-Dick*. "Voltaic pile" is the name of the first operating battery invented by Volta, in 1800. It consisted of a series of silver discs, cloth or paper soaked in saline, and zinc discs in succession. Volta proved 'animal electricity' was the same as electricity generated from nonliving sources.[18] After the mesmeric spell is cast, she tells the rest of her story in an artless, peasant-like simplicity. A "heavenly magnet" has drawn them together. The reference to magnetism is equivalent to an unseen force, or field, as strong as the mechanical forces in *Moby-Dick*.

Melville generously utilizes the craze of spiritualism in America in the nineteenth century. Spiritualism, the communication between the living and the dead, began in America in 1848. During the following decades, spiritualism became a popular social fad and a vigorous heterodox religious movement becoming at once a subject of curiosity and a consolation to the bereaved. The mystical nature of the language related by Isabel is in keeping with spiritualism since spirits often manifested themselves in ancient and unknown tongues. During its peaks of popularity in the 1850s and 1870s, its practitioners were accorded celebrity or notoriety with national attention and criticism. Spiritualism promised a religious and social millennium as a demonstration of the soul's immortality in an age of growing doubt in the face of the advance of scientific discoveries. Hydesville, in upstate New York, was the obscure birthplace of spiritualism. On the night of

March 31, 1848, mysterious knocking noises began responding to the commands of thirteen-year-old Margaret Fox and her twelve-year old sister, Kate. Forty years later Margaret Fox confessed that she and Kate meant only to tease their superstitious mother by cracking their toe-joints against the bedstead. During the 1850s, spirits manifested themselves at seances overseen by a medium whose magnetism brought intelligible responses from the spirits. Spirits caused alphabetical rappings, movements in the medium's table or tabletipping, and music played on an accordion or guitar by unseen hands. Spiritualism incorporated the concepts and vocabulary of mesmerism as a scientific explanation for the trance, except that spirits activated the magnetic fluid instead of a mesmerist. The magnitude of the movement was partly an extension of popular ideas of the 'miracles' of science and technological progress. The pseudoscience of mesmerism explained the method of spirit communication, and table rapping was compared to the telegraph. The spirit world was considered a higher state of being, such as the spiritual essences of the Great Chain of Being. Men no longer needed to depend on the church and clergy for proof of the soul's immortality. It offered an alternative to the wrath of a Calvinistic God, and to the agonies of doubt in a period grown skeptical toward religious faith.[19]

Melville elaborates the inconsistencies of human existence that science cannot explain, such as Newton's "refracting of light," the "confounding effects" of astronomy, polar exploration "amid those treacherous regions," and the "directing compass of his mind" (Bk IX pt 1). The search for truth through the pursuit of science leads to the barren poles where all direction is lost: "it is not for man to follow the trail of truth too far." He describes the life of the genius, the lonely existence of a mind in advance of the times pursuing "the inroads of Truth into Error":

> ...only here and there some of its individuals do; and by advancing, leave the rest behind; cutting themselves forever adrift from their sympathy, and making themselves always liable to be regarded with distrust, dislike, and often, downright—though, ofttimes, concealed—fear and hate. (Bk IX pt 1)

The hazards of seeking the truth are very old, being found in Ausonius in 4th century A.D., and often repeated: *Veritas odium parit;* "Truth purchaseth hatred," attributed to Thomas Wilson (1592), and repeated by Robert Burton in *Anatomy of Melancholy*. Melville's statement resembles George Herbert's (1593-1633) remark, "Follow not truth too near the heels, lest it dash out thy teeth." The revelations of science gained the status of "truth" challenging faith. Pierre walks the night in profound meditation:

> But it is through the malice of this earthly air, that only by being guilty of Folly does mortal man in many cases arrive at the perception of Sense. A thought which should forever free us from hasty imprecations upon our ever-recurring intervals of Folly; since though Folly be our teacher, Sense is the lesson she teaches; since if Folly wholly depart from us, Further Sense will be her companion in the flight, and we will be left standing midway in wisdom....so that the Empire of Human Knowledge can never be lasting in any one dynasty, since Truth still gives new Emperors to the earth. (Bk IX pt 1)

To this point, twentieth-century physicist Werner Heisenberg quotes Barton Hoag:

> Newtonian physics used to provide an accurate enough description of the observed facts. Then we became acquainted with electromagnetic phenomena, and found that Newtonian mechanics was no longer adequate, but that Maxwell's equations did the trick. Finally, the study of atomic dynamics could account for the experimental evidence. And so, physicists had willy nilly to go beyond the old laws or equations. The result was quantum mechanics....Perhaps you make the mistake of treating the laws of nature as absolutes, and you are therefore surprised when they have to be changed. To my mind, even the term 'natural law' is a glorification or sanctification of what is basically nothing but a practical prescription for dealing with nature in a particular domain. I believe that once all absolutists claims are dropped, the difficulties will disappear by themselves.[20]

The provisional state of knowledge ran against the certainty of opinion of mechanics. Pierre doubts his intellect, but not his heart. The conflict of intellect in the advance of science over faith of the heart was the mood of the mid-nineteenth century and was the mood of Pierre in the early morning hours on his return to Saddle Meadows, causing indecision between the mind and heart. In order to resolve his conflict and preserve the name of his father, he decides he must publicly acknowledge Isabel. Pierre announces to his mother that he has secretly married Isabel, a sacrifice that would also protect his proud mother from the indiscretion of his father. Melville includes the controversy of fate and free will in the predicament of Pierre using the metaphor of billiard balls to illustrate Newton's third law of motion—for each action there is an equal and opposite reaction:

> So, through long previous generations, whether of births or thoughts, Fate strikes the present man. Idly he disowns the blow's effect, because he felt no blow, and indeed, received no blow. But Pierre was not arguing Fixed Fate and Free Will, now; Fixed Fate and Free Will were arguing him, and Fixed Fate got the better of the debate. (Bk XI pt 1)

Fate, in this example, becomes as mechanical as Ahab's purpose, as inevitable as a Cartesian vortex, as if the necessity of genetic inheritance is opposed to free will.

The portrait of his father painted before marriage which a likeness to Isabel, confirming her story: "by visible and uncontradictable symbols, the tyranny of Time and Fate. [He burns the portrait, family letters, and pours out] all my memory in one libation!" He is free of the idealized memory of his father:

> Henceforth, cast-out Pierre hath no paternity, and no past; and since the Future is one blank to all; therefore, twice-disinherited Pierre stands untrammeledly his ever-present self!—free to do his own self-will and present fancy to whatever end! (Bk XII pt 3)

By ridding himself of physical objects of his past and rejecting the past to live only in the present, Pierre encounters an obstacle in the awareness and the meaning of time. St. Augustine considered the mind as the ultimate source and standard of time; he did not account for physical external events, but recognized that the awareness of time is an internal mental process. Kant concluded that all knowledge comes from experience, but the awareness of time does *not* come from experience. Time is not inherent in objects, only in the mind, that it is a function of the mind, not of things; thus it is intuitive, closely connected with the development of speech—evocative speech pointing forward in time and descriptive speech pointing backward in time. Time and simultaneity (the psychological awareness of the present) was important in the repetition of mythical events, not duration or direction of time. The intermittent nature of time, such as lunar cycles, ultimately led to the division of time and the measurement of intervals of time. Primitive man regarded events in time as directed by arbitrary demonic or magical forces; by studying the movements of heavenly bodies, civilized man inadvertently directed his attention to a universal world order. Out of man's primeval awareness of rhythm and periodicity eventually emerged the abstract idea of world-wide uniform time, but it was not formulated mathematically until the seventeenth century. Throughout the medieval period, cyclic time and linear time were in conflict; cyclic time was emphasized by astronomy and astrology, and linear time was emphasized by man's work and material progress about him. Even in Christianity, with emphasis on the uniqueness of the incarnation, cyclic time still predominated in the minds of western scholars into the seventeenth century when cyclic time was replaced by the homogeneous, linear, scientific time of Newton. The invention of the pendulum clock in the middle of the seventeenth century had a tremendous influence on the acceptance of the concept of linear time, but linear time did not prevail in the general thinking of man until the mid-nineteenth century, a change largely due to the work of biologists.[21] Pierre returns to a primitive or animalistic state in an attempt to exercise free will.

Isabel pledges her loyalty to Pierre as they leave the 'natural sublime' of Saddle Meadows forever. They begin their journey in silence: "Silence is at once the most harmless and the most awful thing in all nature. It speaks of the Reserved Forces of Fate. Silence is the only Voice of our God" (Bk XIV pt 1). God does not reveal to man the nature of truth, man must find his own way and cannot find it in the examination of nature. In the silence of the long coach ride, a sense of the "positive falsity" of the world comes over him:

> ...at first the youth is apt to refuse the evidence of his own senses; ever as he does that same evidence in the matter of the movement of the visible sun in the heavens, which with his own eyes he plainly sees to go round the world, but nevertheless on the authority of other persons,—the Copernican astronomers, whom he never saw—he believes it *not* to go round the world, but the world round it. (Bk XIV pt 2)

A similar sentiment occurs in *Mardi* in relation to the global nature of the earth which must be taken on faith in the scientists instead of the senses of the individual representing a 'new faith' in science. Copernicus worked on a problem long a concern to the church—the calendar and the accurate prediction of holy days. The mathematical and physical aspects of astronomy complemented each other, i.e., the determination of the position and movement of the planets. Initially, the heliocentric

Copernican theory published in *De revolutionibus (*1543), was received hostilely because it conflicted with the literal meaning of certain biblical passages as well as with the Aristotelian doctrine of simple motion. Calendar reforms and natural philosophy were not important topics of the Council of Trent (1545-1563), and Copernicus' theory was not discussed. The council affirmed the Latin Bible as literally accurate leaving no room for an opposing interpretation of cosmology. Subsequently, the Copernican theory attracted little official notice; Catholic astronomers were under no prohibitions on Copernicus's new theory of astronomy since it was merely an hypothesis and not a serious scientific concept. The invention of the telescope in 1609 radically changed celestial natural philosophy for it provided conclusive evidence against the Ptolemaic system. A small group of Copernicans attempted to revise the conservative stance of the church, but were strongly opposed by powerful theologians. Galileo challenged theology by showing that the conclusion of the Council of Trent was incorrect in the matter of the natural science of astronomy, that physical astronomy is not a matter of faith. Galileo's ideas came at a time of intense struggle between traditionalists and reformers within the Catholic church. Copernicus' *De Revolutionibus* was suspended from the approved reading list. However, the book was available and could be read with the understanding that the doctrines were false.[22] Melville says the concepts of science opposed to common sense and observation advanced by unseen astronomers must be taken on faith as much as the concepts of religion. The 'center' of the universe is not so easily dismissed: according to Infeld and Einstein, if there is no absolute coordinate system, the sun cannot be said to rotate around the earth, nor the earth to rotate around the sun. If physical laws are valid in all coordinate systems, there would be no absolute, only relative motion. In an infinite universe, any point (or every point) can be considered the center of the universe and the rest revolving about each center.[23]

Melville chides the world's philosophers because their vain philosophies fade into practical oblivion: "That profound Silence, that only Voice of our God...for how can a man get a Voice out of Silence" (Bk XIV pt 2)? The absence of absolute knowledge pervades the novel. Absolute truth eludes the philosopher as well as the scientist and theologian. Pierre discovers a crumpled piece of paper in the seat of the coach; he reads and rereads the pamphlet before he grasps the intent of the author, introduced by saying man has difficulty in comprehending a new "theory and practice" because, to comprehend is to contradict himself which is "highly inconvenient and uncomfortable to a man." The pamphlet, the first of 333 lectures, titled "EI," meaning anguish or pain, by Plotinus Plinlimon, contains only the first lecture, "Chronometricals and Horologicals," subtitled: "Being not so much the Portal, as part of the temporary Scaffold to the Portal of this New Philosophy," putting some doubt on its meaning. He says life is a state of probation and worldly truth is "provisional," or we can know nothing with absolute certainty. However, certain rare people carry into the world "Heaven's own Truth" coming from God, the sole source of truth. Plinlimon uses the metaphor of time to illustrate by comparing the Greenwich clock tower as the giver of correct time to the sea-chronometers of ships passing down the Thames adjust to Greenwich time:

> ...and if heedfully kept, will still give that same time, even though carried to the Azores. True, in nearly all cases of long, remote voyages—to China, say—chronometers of the best make, and the most carefully treated, will gradually more or less vary from Greenwich time, without the possibility of the error being corrected by direct comparison with their great standard; but skillful and devout observations of the stars by the sextant will serve materially to lessen such errors. (Bk XIV pt 3)

The Royal Observatory at Greenwich, England, was established in 1675 for the purpose of improving navigation. According to Whitrow, a sense of time is produced by a "linear continuum of overlapping durations"; the intervals of duration of clock time depend on external physical phenomena; time corresponds to a state of the physical universe known as the principle of simultaneity; that time is a 'moving knife edge' covering all places simultaneously, similar to the threads in the swordmatt in Chapter 47, "The Matt-Maker," of *Moby-Dick*. According to Newton's *Principia*, "absolute, true, and mathematical time flows of itself, and from its own nature, flows equably without relation to anything external,"[24] which became a definition of *absolute time*. The idea of a single world wide time order is a highly sophisticated concept relating the microcosm of oneself to the macrocosm of the universe. Kant argued that a universal time depends on the principle of causality; i.e., if one event causes another, it must precede the other. We must with certainty be able to determine that one event definitely precedes the other. This can occur only in 'local time' where the interval needed to transmit the signal, i.e., sound, light, etc., is negligible; the farther away the event, the greater the discrepancy between the interval of received signals. The concept of simultaneity in universal, or world wide time, is an inferred concept, and depends on the relative position of the external event and the mode of connection between it and the observer's perception of it, particularly light. The first demonstration of the finite speed of light was in 1675 by Ole Christensen Roemer (1644-1710) at the Paris Observatory by observing a variation in the eclipse of Jupiter's satellites. The first experiment to demonstrate the speed of light carried out on earth (instead of astronomical observation) was performed in 1849 by French physicist Armand Fizeau (1819-1896). Consequently, all observations of distant events have some time lag. Whitrow comments:

> As Eddington once remarked, "Time, as we now understand it, was discovered by Roemer", for, as we have slowly come to realize over the intervening centuries, his investigations first revealed a fundamental physical difference between local time and time at a distance.[25]

The universal natural scale of time was measured by the movements of heavenly bodies, which Newton considered to be independent of other phenomena. Modern measurement has shown the moon and the sun vary slightly in their orbital movements and are not 'absolute' in time; atomic movements used since 1967 as a time standard may or may not be closer to an absolute unit of time. The ultimate scale of time depends on our concept of the universal laws of nature, and any estimate of duration of time must have an element of arbitrariness. A basic rhythm of the universe for establishing a unit of duration of time has not yet been discovered.[26]

Determining time at a distance is more complicated than merely reading a clock. Philosophers and scientists accepted as an intuitive, self-evident truth that all events could be brought into a single time sequence dependent on the electromagnetic nature of light. If the distance of the observer away from the event is known as well as the velocity of the signal (sound, light, etc.), the time of the occurrence of the event can be calculated. In 1905, Einstein in the Special Theory of Relativity assumed the velocity of light is a universal constant applying Maxwell's theory of electromagnetic waves. Later, Einstein developed the General Theory of Relativity to account for the observation that in the presence of a gravitational attraction, the speed of light is not uniform [although the local speed of light may be considered uniform]. Thus, in the General Theory of Relativity, space and time are influenced by gravitation; the speed of light is not uniform through the entire gravitational field of a body. Roemer's discovery of the finite nature of the velocity of light destroyed the common sense idea of simultaneous events. According to Whitrow, if a clock identical to a stationary clock is carried around the world, common sense would claim the two clocks would show identical time on its return. However, the circumnavigating clock will lag behind the stationary clock because of a difference in their respective relationships to the universe as a whole. The 'relational' or 'relative' theory of time arose from the work of Leibniz in opposition to the absolute theory of time proposed by Newton. Melville's example of a clock carried to the Azores or to China, although used in a metaphorical sense, becomes even more complicated. According to twentieth century theory removed from our commonplace observation, simultaneous events cannot occur. Melville says the soul of a man is farther removed from God and divine truth "than the chronometer carried to China, is from Greenwich." The most accurate chronometer will indicate midnight in Greenwich when its is noon in China:

> ...so the chronometric soul, if in this world true to its great Greenwich in the other, will always, in this so-called intuitions of right and wrong, be contradicting the mere local standards and watchmaker's brains of this earth.
>
> Bacon's brains were mere watchmaker's brains; but Christ was a chronometer; and the most exquisitely adjusted and exact one, and the least affected by all terrestrial jarrings, of any that have ever come to us. (Bk XIV pt 3)

According to the twentieth century theory of relativity, time changes according to the gravitational field of the clock; a clock in the gravitational field of the earth would keep a different time from a clock in the gravitational field of heaven, assuming heaven is not on earth.[27] If the velocity of light is the same in all coordinate systems, including heaven, then moving rods must change their lengths and moving clocks must change their rhythm; time is determined by clocks and space is measured by rods, and their measurements will depend on the behavior of the clocks and rods when in motion.[28] The mechanical view of the universe began to break down toward the end of the nineteenth century with the awareness of the importance of invisible 'fields,' such as gravitational, electromagnetic, etc., acting on objects, especially by the work of Maxwell. Pierre says Christ's teachings seemed folly because they are of heavenly truth and Jerusalem keeps its own earthly truth, not the truth of heaven: "Did he not expressly say—My wisdom (time) is not of this world" (Bk XIV pt 3)? No change has occurred from the time of Christ since heaven and earth keep their separate times and truths. He says both Greenwich time and China time are acceptable, or that both heavenly and earthly truths are correct:

> But though the chronometer carried from Greenwich to China, should truly exhibit in China what the time may be at Greenwich at any moment; yet, though thereby it must necessarily contradict China time, it does by no means thence follow, that with respect to China, the China watches are at all out of the way. Precisely the reverse. For the fact of that variance is a presumption that, with respect to China, the Chinese watches are right as to China, so the Greenwich chronometers must be wrong as to China. (Bk XIV pt 3)

With this lengthy and convoluted exposition, Melville, using the metaphor of time, illustrates the theme of *Pierre,* and one of the most important ideas of his works. He summarized by saying:

> And thus, though the earthly wisdom of man be heavenly folly to God; so also, conversely, is the heavenly wisdom of God an earthly folly to man. (Bk XIV pt 3)

This theme is apparent in the near drowning of Pip in Chapter 93, "The Castaway," in *Moby-Dick:* "So man's insanity is heaven's sense..." He says God does not expect man to keep His truth on earth; China time would be identical with Greenwich time, which would make Greenwich time wrong: "And yet it follows not from this, that God's truth is one thing and man's truth another; but—as above hinted, and as will be further elucidated in subsequent lectures—by their very contradictions they are made to correspond" (Bk XIV pt 3). Cyclic time is disturbed by the appearance of a "meteoric stone" which cannot recur in cyclic time; the same argument used by St. Augustine on the death and resurrection of Christ. If someone has in himself a "chronometrical soul" and attempts to force heaven's truth on earth, he will never succeed, but will "array all men's earthly time-keepers against him, and cause himself woe and death" (Bk XIV pt 3) as Plinlimon notes was the fate of Christ. To live in this world by heaven's truth, man is "apt to involve those inferior beings eventually in strange, unique follies and sins, unimagined before." Though man cannot practice both on earth, he by instinct knows that the impractical heavenly one cannot be wrong. Plinlimon criticizes the philosophers for not acknowledging the possibility of the infidel idea:

> ...that whatever other worlds God may be Lord of, he is not the Lord of this; for else this world would seem to give the lie to Him; so utterly repugnant seem its ways to the instinctively known ways of Heaven. (Bk XIV pt 3)

The truth of heaven, or faith, and the truth of this world, or science, are not the same. Melville says God is the master of heaven, but not the master of physical laws. He implies a separation of God from the world, the separation of faith and science which was the emerging conflict of the nineteenth century among scholars, but not ordinary people. Yet, the two in conflict are in "meridional correspondence"; perhaps God gave the laws of the universe, but does not interfere with physical laws once in force, i.e., he reiterates the concept of deism—that God created the world and set the law of nature in motion, but has since remained indifferent to it. Hawking notes, "These laws may have originally been decreed by God, but it appears that he has since left the universe to evolve according to them and does not now intervene in it."[29] The impossibility of living on earth according to the principles of heaven does not give license to acts of wickedness. His chronometrical and horological lesson gives "consolation to the earnest man" (Bk XIV pt 3). At this point, the pamphlet is torn and the remainder is missing in an "untidy termination." We are left with no further explanation, but surmise that 332 more lectures would not add clarity. Later, Pierre attempts to locate Plinlimon's book, but fails to find it.

The pamphlet of Plinlimon has received considerable literary comment. Cady says Chapter 83, "Jonah Historically Regarded," in *Moby-Dick* is similar to the ideas expressed by Plinlimon, i.e., "the foolish pride of reason."[30] Murray points out many possible sources for the argument presented, however, Bacon, the only philosopher mentioned in the pamphlet, is probably the most important. Bacon sought to improve man's condition by reason rather than faith. Although he made no lasting inventions or important observations of nature, Bacon more than any other, by eloquence and vision of the possibilities of man's intellect, caused a backward-looking culture to attempt to comprehend its future. Man could be rescued from the degradation of the Fall by the imaginative gifts of the mind, for the world was thought to be far gone in decay.[31] Bacon held that if man could understand nature, he could control it to man's benefit. Eiseley observes:

> Formal theology had been shaken by observations in continents unmentioned in the Bible. A second Book of

> Revelation, the book regarded as unclouded by human error and confusion—the book of Nature—was becoming increasingly respectable to devout minds.[32]

In *The Advancement of Learning* (1605), Bacon warned that studying the Bible or nature cannot be searched too far by either divinity or philosophy, "in the book of God's word, or in the book of God's works,"[33] but cautioned that science and religion should be kept separate. Things and ideas must be distinguished; to restore the cognitive harmony between mind and nature disrupted by the Fall of mankind, things must be studied in their own right. The doctrine of the 'two books,' nature and the Bible, was a compromise between the meaning of scriptural texts and the interpretation of nature, allowing freedom from harassment by interpreters of the Bible. For over two hundred years, the "Baconian compromise" became the basis of cooperation between naturalists and the church, the chief sanction for the growth and expertise of the scientific examination of nature, particularly in the English-speaking world.[34] Bacon reasoned that the function of science was to enhance man's control over natural forces, although the potential of science toward material welfare had been noted by the medieval empiricists and was part of the development of both science and magic. The scientific method cannot be attributed to any single origin or philosopher; the content of new information affected the form of investigation more than the reverse. Bacon was exceptional in recognizing the importance of accurate observation and the gathering of facts to the method of science.[35]

Higgins says the pamphlet has been taken by some to represent the religious attitude of Melville as well as a satire of the views he opposed. He notes the correspondence in many parts with Jonathan Swift's *A Modest Proposal*. That Plinlimon advocates a "virtuous expediency" and nominal Christianity from a god who remains silent is calculated by Melville to amuse. The compromise of the convenient Christian and Melville's awareness of the anti-Christ doctrine may, in part, reflect the Baconian compromise which allowed the growth of science without interference by the church.[36] Whether serious or satire may be inferred from the introduction to the pamphlet along with the first paragraph, that life and wisdom are "provisional." By introducing the pamphlet saying all human wisdom is merely provisional, Melville takes a stand opposed to the prevailing claim of the 'absolute' nature of the teachings of the church and the conflicting 'absolute' claims of science to understand nature. Man's truth is relative, not absolute, a concept of nature not formally presented until the twentieth century.

Even time cannot be known with certainty; Szamosi says no two clocks can be synchronized because simultaneity is observer-dependent: "Even less can you speak about it being 'the same time' everywhere....There are as many 'times' as there can be 'observers' moving relative to each other."[37] The Victorian frame of mind was one of certain knowledge and order: "A place for everything and everything in its place," tending to divide ideas and things into tight categories of true-false, good-bad, right-wrong, etc. Nevertheless, the framework of certainty of the conventional forms was beginning to break down.[38] Melville says that time, as well as truth, is provisional, or relative.

In Book XV, "The Cousins," Pierre denounces the shallowness and pretentiousness of Glen Stanley, Lucy's suitor:

> Pretensions and substitutions are only the recourse of undergraduates in the science of the world; in which science, on his own ground, my Lord Chesterfield is the poorest possible preceptor. (Bk XV pt 2)

In a short time, they have fallen from the grace of nature in the country to the meanness of the city. The intensity of events of the the few days before leaving Saddle Meadows produces a distortion of Pierre's time sense: "In ten days I have lived ten thousand years" (Bk XIX pt 2). When attention is concentrated on the present, we tend to be unaware of time; time seems short. In a situation causing the present to be related to the memory of past experiences or to consider the interval toward future events, time seems to have a greater duration and passes slowly; the more attention paid to time, the slower it passes. The sense of duration is lengthened by the amount of stimuli received and shortened if the amount of stimuli is reduced. Certain drugs may alter the sense of time, lengthening the duration relative to normal experience; Thomas De Quincey in *Confessions of an English Opium Eater* (1822), described the effect of opium producing a vast expansion of time so that he seemed to have lived 70 or 100 years in a single night. Similar distortions may occur during sleep. The psychological present is a "mental construct of overlapping durations" of perceptible time and is a logical abstraction like the straight line. Time sense is a late product of human development closely related to the development of language, and a sense that probably does not exist in any other creature.[39]

Pierre writes while Isabel resumes the role of a spiritual medium, playing her mystical guitar. A few spiritual mediums claimed to be able to call on the creativity of dead poets for literary purposes.[40] She plays the guitar "till Pierre felt chapter after chapter born of its wondrous suggestiveness" (Bk XXI pt 1) and reflects on his humblest childhood experiences and his metaphysical image.

As in most earlier works, Melville uses contemporary geological events in a metaphorical sense: in this case the puzzle of the formation of the Alps. Switzerland was especially appropriate because of Agassiz's *Etudes sur les glaciers* (1840), in addition to the great current interest in the discoveries in Egyptology:

> ...the Alps...their overawing extent of peak crowded on peak, and spur sloping on spur, and chain jammed behind chain, and all their wonderful battalionings of might...But, far as any geologist has yet gone down into the world, it is found to consist of nothing but surface stratified on surface. To its axis, the world being nothing but superinduced superfices. (Bk XXI pt 1)

By the time of the publication of *Pierre* in 1852, geology had made great advances leading to a workable theory of the formation of earth structures. The "onion-skin myth" of an earth entirely of successive precipitations of sedimentary rock originated with Torbern Bergmann (1735-1784), although often attributed to Abraham Werner. In the late eighteenth century, Hutton revived the theories of long-term erosion and deposition of sediment by abandoning biblical chronology of a few thousand years of age of the earth postulating vastly extended time. Each of his ideas was a repetition of theories developed in the seventeenth century held by Robert Hooke (1635-1703), and Steno—infinite time, cycles of erosion and deposition, and the long term power of these cycles to alter the earth's surface. In 1827, Pierre Louis-Antoine Cordier (1777-1861), ended the controversy over the origin of basalt—whether sedimentary or volcanic. By the discovery of a temperature increase in mines of one degree for each 30 or 40 meters of depth, he concluded the interior of the earth beyond 5,000 meters was liquid; that the earth was a cooled star with a molten liquid center, not an "onion" of endless rock strata. Hillway attributed Melville's error of earth strata to his sources of Oliver Goldsmith's *Animated Nature,* or John Mason Good's *The Book of Nature*. Foster says, "Melville's extravagant error lies in saying, as Goldsmith and Good do not, that the earth is stratified 'To its axis.'"[41] In earlier works, Melville made mention of the earth as a crust. The notion of the 'onion' formation of the earth's interior had been discarded by geologists by the time that Melville wrote *Pierre*. He later corrected the error in his poem "The Apparition."

Melville's metaphor of the formation of the Alps requires explanation. In 1831, Leonce Elie de Beaumont (1798-1874) claimed that not all change in the earth's crust was gradual as in Lyell's uniformitarianism, but at times change was abrupt. Fold mountains could not be the result of erosion alone; the conformable structure for great distances along the strike of a chain could not be explained by slow action, but were considered due to upthrust of mountains from horizontal strata as proposed by Leopold von Buch (1774-1853). His theory assumed the status of orthodoxy in France and was accepted by many geologists in Europe and North America from 1850 to 1875, attaining a greater importance than the theory of uniformitarianism of Lyell. The first detailed description and mapping of the Alpine range was reported in the 1830s and 1840s. James Dwight Dana (1813-1895) in 1847 advanced the theory of 'geosynclinal' formation, or the lateral pressure caused by a broad downfold of the ocean floor due to a contracting earth; the greatest mountains faced the greatest oceans, the source of the greatest lateral pressure. No adequate explanation of the subsidence was known except the irregular contraction of the earth during cooling of the globe, a theory that remained popular among geologists until 1900. The Alps, as noted by Melville, were made up of unusual rock formations and remained inexplicable. After seventeen traverses of the Alps between 1775 and 1796, Horace Benedict de Saussure, the first great Alpine geologist, abandoned them as a "hopeless jumble." Eduard Suess (1831-1914), after a quarter century of study, advanced the startling hypothesis of a lateral movement of an entire mountain system in a wide curve in a one-sided thrust from the south. Neither catastrophic nor uniformitarian, his theory had no counterpart in any other theory of mountain formation.[42] Alfred Wegener (1880-1930) published *Die Entstehung der Kontinente und Ozeane* (1915), and expanded it in 1920 and 1922, speculating on and presenting supporting evidence for continental drift. His theory enraged many scientists and gained little support over the decades. In 1961, R.S. Dietz published the concept of sea floor spreading that led to studies of "subducted fracture zones, magnetic evidence of subduction, the generation of abyssal hills, and...an association of the destruction of crust with the destruction of magnetic anomalies."[43] Melville's geological metaphor of heaped mountains "spur sloping on spur, and chain jammed behind chain" includes the essence of the geological debate of the mid-nineteenth century and suggests the late twentieth century concept in the rise of mountains by the upward and lateral movement of the margins of global tectonic plates, a revolution of geology, occurred in the 1970s and explained otherwise perplexing findings such as the presence of limestone and marine fossils at the peaks of the Alps and the peaks of the Himalayas. The new theory of plate tectonics was much like the theory proposed by Wegener in 1912, but dismissed by most American and European geologists.[44]

Pierre learns his mother is dead. In spite of his grief, he stays at his desk and works at writing his book through the summer and into the winter. Pierre is unable to ignore past time and cannot exercise free will; he must eventually come to grief: "In the midst of the merriments of the mutations of Time, Pierre hath ringed himself in with the grief of Eternity" (Bk XXII pt 2). The "revolving planet" or the fate of the author cannot be resisted any more than the Cartesian vortex.

Lucy writes that she is coming to live with him in the city. Her trunk arrives while the boorish Millthorpe, a lawyer, prates about "ten metaphysical treatises;" one a scientific work on "The Precise Cause of the Modifications in the Undulatory Motion in Waves." This notation was surely meant as satire of science. However, an investigation of the nature of waves was carried out by Newton, and subsequently by many scientists, especially Georg G. Stokes (1819-1903), in 1847. Stokes was Lucasian professor of mathematics at Cambridge and later president of the Royal Society. His major work was concerned with waves and the transformation imposed on them during their passage through various media,[45] and may have been Melville's source for this citation. Pierre ponders the god that made the banal, inane Millthorpe must be a greater god than made Napoleon or Byron saying: "Plus head, minus heart—Pah! the brains grow maggoty without a heart; but the heart's the preserving salt itself, and can keep sweet the head" (Bk XXIII pt 4). DeBakey says this illustrates Melville's belief that science stifles warm human feeling and deifies purely objective intellect.[46]

The intense work on the book causes Pierre great distress, both psychological and physical; he has so abused his eyes, that he is unable to write (Bk XXV pt 3). The reflexic refusal of his eyes is likened to fate; Pierre is losing the free will obtained in rejecting past and future time; illness is a matter of mechanical fate; blindness is equivalent to death, as in *Mardi*.

Melville makes several statements opposed to the position of absolute knowledge either in nature or in faith, but none as clear and emphatic as the next:

> Say what some poets will, Nature is not so much her own ever-sweet interpreter, as the mere supplier of that cunning alphabet, whereby selecting and combining as he pleases, each man

> reads his own peculiar lesson according to his own peculiar mind and mood. (Bk XXV pt 4)

Knowledge depends on the observer; observation is individual; truth is relative. By the end of the nineteenth century, physicists were saying that classical Newtonian physics had discovered all of the laws of nature and nothing remained for scientists except to refine measurements and their application to existing laws. The discovery of force fields of gravitation by Newton and the wave theory of light by Maxwell were found to be parts of the same electromagnetic field. Herbert paraphrased the attitude of the nineteenth century physicists:

> Second by second the universe, like a giant clockwork, ticks out Newton's inexorable laws, its future as fixed and immutable as its past....Classical physics in a nutshell: The universe consists of nothing but matter and fields—and we know the laws of both.[47]

The certainty of physical science was eliminated by Max Planck in 1900 with his observation of color emitted by a heated black body such as iron. Classical physics based on two sets of laws—Newton's motion laws and Maxwell's field laws—could not be reconciled with the fact that the velocity of light is constant in all directions regardless of the earth's movement as shown by Mickelson and Morley in 1887. The new physics lead to an entirely new approach to the nature of matter in the twentieth century. The work of Louis DeBroglie, Werner Heisenberg, Erwin Schrodinger, and Paul Dirac led to the quantum theory of matter which deals with the interaction of light with atoms based on the 'Copenhagen interpretation' (Copenhagen was the center of the new physics due to the enormous influence of Niels Bohr), based on the principle of uncertainty of Heisenberg and the theory of complementarity advanced by Niels Bohr in 1927.[48] Melville's statement predates the principle of complementarity by three-quarters of a century: there is no reality until that reality is observed, and there are as many realities as observers: "each man reads his own peculiar lesson" from nature's alphabet. In the quantum world, the observer plays a role in what is observed.[49]

Pierre dreams that the commonplace about him was replaced by the "phantasmagoria of the Mount of the Titans," a description of Mount Greylock in the Berkshire Mountains near Pittsfield, Massachusetts. He recalls walking in the meadow near the mountain and the effect of seeing the "igneous rock" face, a geological term for rock formed by cooling magma from the earth's molten interior. The Enceladus dream has stimulated considerable literary and psychological interpretation: 'Sublime nature' is threatening rather than spiritual. Pierre begins to doubt Isabel's story they are brother and sister. He receives a letter branding him a liar "in thy every lung-cell." The 'cell theory' (also mentioned in *Mardi*), was founded by Mathias Schleiden (1804-1881) and Theodore Schwann (1810-1882). In 1838 Schwann made the momentous discovery that the ovum is a cell, that the entire organism consists of cells thrown off by other cells, that each cell has a certain life of its own, and the cells are dependent on the life of the whole organism.[50] The discovery of 'cells' by Hooke in 1665 was not accepted as a structural, functional unit until the work of Schwann. Hooke contributed a new general insight into associating life with a particular arrangement of matter and stimulated the search for microscopically visible substructure of life. Hooke's contribution to the life-matter question consisted in considering the organism as a machine and life as a mechanical result of organization, a microscopically visible organization.[51] Virchow declared *Omnis Cellula e Cellula*, which was to become a fundamental axiom of cell theory—that objects in the world were either cellular organisms or noncellular 'nonorganisms.'[52]

The crisis in religion developing between the seventeenth and twentieth centuries became a slow process of secularization, with the impact of science, then the impact of biblical and historical criticism, the shift to a more man-centered outlook, the encounter with other faiths, and the "awesome and still incomplete transition to modernity." Other faiths, especially Islam, have tried to develop a science free from the skepticism of Western science, while in other instances the process of modernization has been so abrupt that it led to a retreat to the old faith in a period of great stress; the divine seemed to have withdrawn from the world, leaving the people vulnerable and religion extravagantly mystical. Science is so vast in scope and the engine of research and technical innovation which is value-neutral and independent of political or religious belief allows for the influence of nonreligious knowledge. No matter the beauty and stability of a traditional culture and values, the science-based secular society has produced enormous changes, and the traditional beliefs may seem less all-inclusive, immutable, and perfect. Scientific education teaches a method of arriving at truths (i.e., systematic skepticism) by a means opposite of truths sought in a religious manner—that all theories are merely man-made and provisional: "The great power and beauty of scientific knowledge lies in the fact that it is built on a firm foundation of doubt..." Natural science is the most visible product of the new ethic of knowledge, but the critical spirit underlies history, the arts, and faith during the

Enlightenment of the eighteenth century, especially in the investigations of Galileo and critical philosophy of Descartes, and vindicated by the discoveries of Newton.[53] Scientific advances or theories often induce an authoritative "truth-definition" response by defining the framework within which science works; its relative truth can be determined only when it is challenged by another, conflicting idea.[54] The conflict is summarized by Lovejoy:

> ...it seemed to Kant that there can be no moral responsibility without freedom, without something in the individual that is absolutely uncaused; but there can be no freedom in the spatio-temporal world. There all events are completely subject to the law of causality, and therefore every human act is simply the necessary effect of its antecedents. If, then, freedom is to be "saved...no other way remains to do so but to attribute it" to a non-temporal self—to the "intelligible character," good or bad which belongs, causelessly and eternally, to each noumenal Ego, yet somehow manifests itself in his temporal behavior as a whole, though without impediment to the determination of each moment of the behavior by antecedent natural causes.[55]

The meaning of *Pierre* may be summarized by Isabel's final statement, "All's o'er, and ye know him not!" restating one of Melville's most persistent themes: that the final nature of man is unknowable; knowledge is provisional. Prior to the nineteenth century, the 'man of genius' saw the universe as having an inherent significance in a perfect design, and as a manifestation of the wisdom and goodness that created it.[56] Pierre, like the modern 'man of genius,' confronts a reality whose significance he cannot know, or a reality that has no significance, or even if the question whether it has a meaning is meaningless. He must, by his own sensibility, discover it or give it significance from nature's "cunning alphabet" in what appears to be a meaningless cosmos.

Notes

1. G. J. Whitrow, *The Natural Philosophy of Time*. 2nd edition. Oxford: Oxford University Press, 1980, pp. 3-6.

2. Joseph Campbell, *The Masks of God: Primitive Mythology*. New York and London: Penguin, reprint. 1976, p. 201.

3. Don Cupit, *The Sea of Faith: Christianity in Change*. Cambridge: Cambridge University Press, 1984, p. 17.

4. Richard S. Moore, *That Cunning Alphabet: Melville's Aesthetics of Nature*. Amsterdam: Rodopi, 1982, p. 7.

5. Carl L. Becker, *The Heavenly City of the Eighteenth-Century Philosophers*. New Haven and London: Yale University Press, 1932, p. 63.

6. Roger D. Sorrell, *St. Francis of Assisi: Traditional and Innovation in Western Christian Attitudes toward the Environment*. New York and Oxford: Oxford University Press, 1988, p. 17.

7. John D. Barrow, *The World Within the World*. Oxford and New York, Oxford University Press, 1990, p. 33-34.

8. Sorrell, ref. 6, pp. 19-20, 46.

9. Moore, ref. 4, pp. 12-13.

10. Tyrus Hillway, "Melville's Use of Two Pseudo-Sciences." *Modern Language Notes* 64 (1949):145-150.

11. Taylor Stoehr, *Hawthorne's Mad Scientists: Pseudoscience and Social Science in Nineteenth-Century Life and Letters*. Hamden, Connecticut: Archon Books, 1978, p. 22.

12. Walter Clyde Curry, cites R. Foerster, I, lxxiv ff in *Chaucer and the Mediaeval Sciences*. Oxford: Oxford University Press, 1926, p. 56-57.

13. Pietro Redondi, *Galileo: Heretic*. Translated by Raymond Rosenthal. Princeton, New Jersey: Princeton University Press, 1987, p. 51.

14. David Knight, *The Age of Science: The Scientific World-view in the Nineteenth Century*. Oxford: Basil Blackwell, 1986, pp. 71-76.

15. Kevin J. Sharpe, *From Science To An Adequate Mythology*. Auckland, New Zealand: Interface Press, 1984, p. 52.

16. David Hume, *The Natural History of Religion*. Edited and introduction by H. E. Root. Reprint. Stanford: Stanford University Press, 1956, pp. 28-29.

17. Hans Aarsleff, *The Study of Language in England, 1780-1860*. Princeton, New Jersey: Princeton University Press, 1967, pp. 217-227.

18. René Taton, *Science in the Nineteenth Century*. New York: Basic Books, Inc., 1965, pp. 182-183.

19. Howard Kerr, *Mediums, Spirit-Rappers, and Roaring Radicals.* Urbana, Chicago, & London: University of Illinois Press, 1972, pp. 3-21, 51.

20. Werner Heisenberg, *Physics and Beyond: Encounters and Conversations.* New York, Evanston, San Francisco and London: Harper and Row, 1971, pp. 94-95.

21. Whitrow, ref. 1, pp. 51-59.

22. Robert S. Westman, "The Copernicans and the Churches." in *God and Nature: Historical Essays on the Encounter between Christianity and Science.* David C. Lindberg and Ronald L. Numbers, editors. Berkeley, Los Angeles and London: University of California Press, 1986, pp. 86-103.

23. Theo Theocharis. cites Infeld and Einstein. *The Evolution of Physics* (1938), p. 224, "Does the Earth really move?" *Nature* 341 (1989):100.

24. Florian Cajori, *Isaac Newton's Mathematical Principles of Natural Philosophy and His System of the World. Translated into English by Andrew Motte in 1729. The translations revised, and supplied with an historical and explanatory appendix.* Berkeley, Los Angeles, London: University of California Press, 1934, p. 6.

25. Whitrow, ref. 1, pp. 224-230.

26. Whitrow, ref. 1, p. 42.

27. Albert Einstein and Leopold Infield, *The Evolution of Physics: From Early Concepts to Relativity and Quanta.* New York: Touchstone, Simon and Schuster, 1938, p. 240.

28. John D. Barrow, *The World Within the World.* Oxford and New York, Oxford University Press, 1990, p. 103.

29. Stephen W. Hawking, *A Brief History of Time: From the Big Bang to Black Holes.* New York: Bantam Books, 1988, p. 122.

30. Edwin Cady, "Through a Glass Eye, Darkly" in *The Bible in American Arts and Letters.* Giles Gunn, editor. Philadelphia, Pennsylvania: Fortress Press, 1983, p. 39.

31. Henry A. Murray, "Introduction," *Pierre,* Hendricks House, 1949, pp. lxix-lxxix.

32. Loren Eiseley, *The Man Who Saw Through Time: Francis Bacon and the Modern Dilemma.* Revised and enlarged edition. New York: Scribner's, 1961, p. 40.

33. Francis Bacon, *The Advancement of Learning.* Arthur Johnston, editor. New York: Schocken, 1965, p. 24.

34. James R. Moore, "Geologists and Interpreters of Genesis in the Nineteenth Century." in *God and Nature: Historical Essays on the Encounter between Christianity and Science.* David C. Lindberg and

Ronald L. Numbers, editors. Berkeley, Los Angeles and London: University of California Press, 1986, pp. 322-324.

35. A. R. Hall, *The Scientific Revolution 1500-1800: The Formation of the Modern Scientific Attitude.* 2nd edition. Boston: Beacon, 1962, pp. 164-165, 184.

36. Brian Higgins, "Plinlimon and the Pamphlet Again." *Studies in the Novel* 4: 27-38, 1972.

37. Géza Szamosi, *The Twin Dimensions: Inventing Time and Space.* New York: McGraw-Hill, 1986, pp. 155-156.

38. Stephen Kern, *The Culture of Time and Space 1880-1918.* London: Weidenfeld and Nicholson, 1983, pp. 181-182.

39. Whitrow, ref. 1, pp. 64, 370-375.

40. Kerr, ref. 19, p. 16.

41. Elizabeth S. Foster, "Another Note on Melville and Geology." *American Literature* 22 (1950):479-487.

42. Mott T. Greene, *Geology in the Nineteenth Century: Changing Views of a Changing World.* Ithaca and London: Cornell University Press, 1982, pp. 121-164.

43. H. W. Menard. *The Ocean of Truth: A Personal History of Global Tectonics.* Princeton, New Jersey: Princeton University Press, 1986, pp. 22-26, 161.

44. Mott T. Greene, "History of Geology." *Osiris* 2nd series 1 (1985) 97-116.

45. *Encyclopædia Britannica.* 21: 269-270, 1971.

46. Lois DeBakey, "The Fictional Physician-Scientist of Nineteenth-Century America: Herman Melville." *Southern Medical Journal* 61 (1968):55-63.

47. Nick Herbert, *Quantum Reality.* Garden City, New York: Anchor Press/Doubleday, 1987, pp. 32-34.

48. Herbert, ref. 47, pp. 31-45.

49. Barrow, ref. 28, pp. 137-141.

50. Taton, ref. 18, p. 350.

51. Thomas S. Hall, *History of General Physiology: 600 B.C. to A.D. 1900,* Volume 1 *From Pre-Socratic Times to the Enlightenment.* Chicago and London: University of Chicago Press, 1975, pp. 303-310.

52. Stephen Toulmin and June Goodfield, *The Architecture of Matter.* Chicago and London: University of Chicago Press, 1982, p. 353.

53. Cupit, ref. 3, pp. 7-9.

54. Sharpe, ref. 15, p. 52.

55. Arthur O. Lovejoy, *The Reason, the Understanding, and Time.* Johns Hopkins University Press, 1961, p. 148.

56. C. S. Lewis. *The Discarded Image: An Introduction to Medieval and Renaissance Literature.* Cambridge and New York: Cambridge University Press, 1964, pp. 203-204.

Chapter 6

The Short Stories: man, the true God

Although the difference between science and technology is subtle, the blending of theoretical science into practical technology brought many changes in the lives of Western man. The application of science to technology resulted in the development of machines to do man's work. The Romans were excellent engineers, building bridges, pumps, aqueducts, machinery, and implements of war, but were not interested in theory. The Greeks were all theory and no practice; the Romans were the opposite, and it was only in the eighteenth and nineteenth centuries that these two aspects of science began to combine effectively,[1] which was expressly related in Melville's short stories.

In the first century A.D., Gall and the Rhineland became the centers for the craftsmen of Rome for pottery, glassblowing, bronze, and metallurgy. The development of harness for horses and the broad plow permitted the expansion of agriculture and the ability to raise new crops. In the Middle Ages, religious attitudes towards manual labor, mechanical arts, and Western monasticism were united as early as Benedict of Nursia who founded the monastery at Monte Cassino in 529

A.D. Work was no longer regarded as servility and given a new dignity. From Islam came a change in the status of the artisan: from slave to the life of a free laborer.[2] The church in some ways contributed to the "heresy" of trying to understand nature by the sanctification of work and its opposition to animism. But when saint replaced animistic sprite as the most important religious concern, man was free to exploit nature; the cult of the saints destroyed animism and allowed a naturalistic view of the world to develop. The urge to master nature grew while the opposition of the church declined in the face of triumphant materialism of early modern science that upset specific articles of religion and, in effect, discredited all traditional wisdom and authority. Science was the bridge between rationality and mastery, the application of reason to the understanding of nature, and a more effective response to manipulation of the natural and human environment.[3] The twelfth century was mid-way in the mechanical arts, from contempt to full acceptance.[4] The Latin Middle Ages produced the first civilization to evolve without dependence on slave labor; the fourteenth century showed the characteristics of modern European civilization by the utilization of natural resources through progressively more complex and efficient use of human labor. This led to a new attitude towards nature and technological proficiency that became overtly conscious in the writings of Bacon (1561-1626), but was not fulfilled until the nineteenth century.[5] Bacon understood the enormous importance of the new method, which he outlined in *The Advancement of Learning* (1603), and more fully expressed in *Novum Organum* (1620), *The New Instrument* (considering Aristotle's *Organon* as the 'old instrument'). He rejected all of the knowledge of ancient philosophy which, he asserted, hardly produced a useful discovery. Further, he stressed the importance of gathering reliable information, classification, and drawing up generalizations or laws which should lay a firm foundation for the growth of human power. Science was to minister to the arts—to medicine, navigation, and industry. Similarly, Descartes's *Discourse on Method* (1637), purports to be an account of a new method of discovering the principles of nature.[6] The essence of mechanistic philosophy in the seventeenth century was the idea that all natural phenomena could be reduced to a single concept: the motion of matter.[7] The age in which science became institutional was also the age of "Utopias," especially Francis Bacon's *New Atlantis* (1626), Tommaso Campanella's *City of the Sun* (1602), and Andreae's *Christianopolis* (1619), for the utopias depended to a great extent upon science-based technology, i.e., the improvement and melioration they thought science could provide.[8] The capacity of man had been limited to his own strength and his ability to control the strength of other men and animals. Beginning in the nineteenth century, however, man learned how to manufacture power and to distribute it to do work.[9] More systematic application of science was carried out in France in the period from 1780 to 1850 than in England, especially by military sponsorship, production of dyestuffs, and by the porcelain industry, leading to formidable growth.[10]

The main impetus of formal applied science to innovation came after 1850 on an ever-widening front. Scientific attitudes were more widespread than the understanding of science: traditional intellectual authority was challenged by observation, testing, and experimentation, leading to the development of empirical devices for better measurements to be used in industrial improvements. Until the nineteenth century, science learned as much from technology as technology learned from science in a society increasingly curious, seeking experiment and improvement manifested in the development of scientific institutions and societies in an intellectual milieu. Both science and technology were characteristics of that society, but one was not the consequence of the other.[11] Charles Babbage's *On The Economy of Machinery and Manufactures* (1832), a "hymn to the machine," analyzed the development of machine-based production and its social relations in industry. He concluded that the "whole of arithmetic now appeared within the grasp of mechanism."[12]

In the early decades of the nineteenth century, new organizations, lyceums, public schools, societies, and research institutions developed to explore many scientific fields. Scientists, though small in number, were in great demand as lecturers and advisers. National and state legislatures responded to the pressure for scientific knowledge with support for research in practical problems of natural history, geography, and astronomy. Although their interest was uneven and many promising investigations went unsupported, needed research was eventually financed by private funding through scientific societies, personal endowments, and lyceums.[13] The prospect of an immediate return on investment greatly influenced which and how many scientific projects were supported; pragmatic considerations governed the direction of American science. The discovery of Neptune in 1846 by observing aberrations in the orbit of Uranus and the prediction that a planet would be found at a certain location, proving that the force of gravitation spanned the universe, was one of the historic moments in science. The great potential of electricity was applied to the telegraph and electroplating. The Smithsonian Institute was founded in 1846 by a bequest from wealthy Englishman James Smithson for "the increase and diffusion of knowledge among men."[14] The first commercial locomotive began operation in 1833; the sewing machine and the Howe printing press were patented in 1846; mass production of wiredrawing became possible with the factory system supporting the development of the telegraph, which required vast amounts of wire.

The unreserved enthusiasm for science continued unabated through the mid-nineteenth century, paying homage to both science and technology, the successors of Prometheus. James Dana, addressing the Yale alumni in 1856 said, "Science is an unfailing source of good....Every new development is destined to bestow some universal blessing on mankind." Along with Carlyle and Hawthorne, Melville was among the few dissenters; Bruce says, "Melville realized better than Hawthorne how completely such factories would transform the social order as well as the landscape."[15] Melville's short stories disclose his skepticism of science and distrust of technology.

In Melville's first short story, "Bartleby, the Scrivener. A story of Wall Street" (1853), the narrator, a Wall Street lawyer, hires a new scrivener, Bartleby, ill with an incurable disorder, who writes "silently, palely, mechanically," like Ahab, as if free will were absent until the "machine" refuses to work. Initially, he sees Bartleby like the other scriveners, as mechanical functionaries in the same manner he regards other people. The attorney wonders if Bartleby was sent to him by providence "the predestinated purpose of my life." Bartleby is dehumanized, or machinelike, implying that death without feeling is the ultimate result of the machine. Patrick examined the two books cited in the story—Jonathan Edwards's *Inquiry into the Freedom of the Will,* and Joseph Priestley's *The Philosophical Doctrine of Necessity*—opened for examination by the narrator, both on the doctrine of necessity. The concept of limited free will alluded to in Chapter 47, "The Sword-Mat" of *Moby-Dick,* is similar to the view of the necessitarian philosophers cited in "Bartleby." That is, every act of volition has a prior cause or motive, just as the one before it had a cause or motive, in an endless chain of events leading back to the first link, which rests in the hand of God. A choice of action requires "the previous disposition of the mind" and "the view of the objects with the choice or resolution respects" or inclination of the mind. If the conditions presented to the predispositioned mind are the same, the choice will always be the same because the will acts in accordance to "a fixed law of nature"; Priestley says free will is a "perfectly mechanical thing" likened to the law of gravity. Patrick notes:

> Thus, while the God of Calvinism is an angry God, dooming all mankind but a select few to everlasting punishment, the God of Priestley's brand of necessitarianism is a benevolent God using evil and suffering as a means for effecting the greater good of all mankind.[16]

Bartleby arouses the attorney from complacency to a disturbing sense of compassion for the scrivener, away from his attitude of 'live and let live.'[17] The conflict of fate, free will, and necessity are present in nearly all of Melville's works, but mainly in an abstract sense; Bartleby's health and "mechanical death" become the focus of the conflict. Bartleby is presented with the aspect of an efficient office machine which the lawyer utilizes "without troubling over the eclipsed humanity that this quiet efficiency purports." Bartleby initially fits into a "satisfactory arrangement" with machinelike compliance, marred only by not being "cheerfully industrious" but writes "silently, palely, mechanically."[18]

Israel Potter: his Fifty Years of Exile (1855), was taken from an historical account of Israel Potter, a nineteen-year-old wanderer in the American Revolutionary War, whose numerous adventures and experiences produced "—hardships and privations unknown at the present day, when science has so greatly contributed, in manifold ways, to lessen the sufferings," one of Melville's few acknowledgements of the worth of science in bettering the condition of man. He carries secret messages to Benjamin Franklin in Paris, "Doctor Franklin," whose apartment walls are covered with diverse papers of history, mechanics, diplomacy, metaphysics, meteorology, geometry, maps, and "endless other surprising hangings and upholstery of science." Franklin lives on the side of the Seine that suits his worsted hose and "scientific tastes." At the same time, in the chambers overhead, a "clayey-visaged chemist" with a "soiled green flap over his left eye," was at work over "retorts and crucibles, discovering new antipathies in acids, again risking strange explosions similar to that whereby he had already lost the use of an optic." As mentioned elsewhere, the pursuit of science was, at times, a hazardous affair.

In 1841, Melville visited the Galápagos Islands, where Darwin had visited and studied the unusual fauna six years earlier. The islands were discovered in 1535 and named the "Encantadas" meaning "the bewitched." The most remarkable creatures on the islands are the iguanas, the enormous tortoises, and the unusual differentiation of the finches, along with other bizarre forms of life such as four-eyed fishes and a finch that uses a stick as a tool to obtain food. Darwin said his visit to the Galápagos Islands was by far the most important event in his life. Melville purchased Darwin's *Journal of Researches...Voyage of the H.M.S. Beagle* in 1847, and later wrote "The Encantadas or Enchanted Islands" (1854), ten sketches on the Galápagos Islands published serially in Putnam's Monthly in 1854, but which may have been written prior to *Moby-Dick*.[19] Melville refers to Darwin's account as one of the "barren, bootless allusions from some few passing voyagers or compilers" in what Franklin calls his "running quarrel" with Darwin.[20] Of Rock Rodondo, Melville says, "I know not where one can better study the Natural History of strange sea-fowl than at Rodondo. It is the aviary of Ocean." He introduces the sketch on the tortoise in verse after the style of Edmund Spencer in the *Fairie Queen*[21]:

> Most ugly shapes and horrible aspects,
> Such as Dame Nature selfe mote feare to see,
> Or shame, that ever should so fowle defects
> From her most cunning hand escaped bee;
> All dreadful pourtraicts of deformitee.
> Ne wonder if these a man do appal;
> For all that here at home we dreadfull hold
> Be but as bugs to fearen babes withall
> Compared to the creatures in these isles' entrall.

The tortoises are one of the most unusual creatures on the Galápagos Islands and are considered among the oldest living species on earth. The inter-island variation of the tortoise shells, some saddle-like and some dome-like, and the variation of the bills of finches in neighboring islands greatly influenced Darwin's views of nature.

"The Lightning Rod Man" (1854), tells of an overbearing salesman of lightning rods who travels through New England claiming remarkable protection by his rods. The story which was probably based on Benjamin Franklin's *Letters and Papers on Electricity* published in 1751-1753 and frequently reprinted and expanded thereafter. The salesman mentions the Leyden jar, a simple device for storing an electrical charge; Franklin was the first to perform detailed experiments with it; in addition, Franklin invented the lightning rod. Melville may have obtained additional technical facts from Lucius Lyon's *Treatise on Lightning Conductors* (1853). Emery regards the story, not as "fire-and-brimstone Christianity" but science "preached" by Lyon, Franklin, and other scientists, i.e., a dichotomy between science and religion rather than a symbolic combination of the two, or perhaps science as a new faith. The professional infighting between Canadian scientists, as noted in the story, calls into question the claims of all scientists. The scientists were forced to explain how well-protected homes and a church had been damaged by lightning, with the ironic implication that man cannot depend on scientific ingenuity for protection against the threatening forces of nature, which underscores science's confidence in its technology as well as its fallibility. The narrator prefers to see lightning as "portents of divinity," or Cotton Mather's "'covenental' symbol of grace" as in the Hebrew and Greco-Roman tradition of seeing heavenly occurrences as profound theological signs rather than mere electricity. Franklin's science, pretending to relieve human fear of the elements, worked to promote it: the narrator says, "For someone who would arm others with fearlessness, you seem unbeseemingly timorous yourself." At worst, Melville's scientists in the image of Franklin were paranoid technicians having discarded providence; the narrator was now troubled by the possibility that protective technology might fail him. That the evangelical salesman travelled in storm time implies that his unreliable science relies on fear.[22]

In "The Apple-Tree Table or Original Spiritual Manifestations" (1856), the narrator finds an old-fashioned table, "such a necromantic little old table as might have belonged to Friar Bacon" (i.e., Roger Bacon) in the attic of a house thought to be haunted. Late one Saturday night, the narrator hears a "faint sort of inward rapping or rasping—a strange, inexplicable sound." After great fright and searching, the noise is determined to arise from the apple-tree table. The sounds horrify his wife and his two daughters: "I bethought me of Democritus [mentioned in *Mardi*], and resolved to keep cool." Thus, Melville enlists science to resolve a mystery the narrator's wife and daughters would attribute to the witch-work of "Spirits! spirits!" A tiny bug works its way out of the wood of the table, the narrator stands over it with a poker unconsciously in hand and watches closely for another bug to appear while the rest of the family wants the table destroyed. The daughters suggests they consult Madame Pazzi, the conjuress, but his wife advises they consult Professor Johnson, a naturalist. The professor "manifested a cool, collected sort of interest, and gravely accompanied me home." His daughter asks the naturalist if it is not wonderful and the work of spirits. "Spirits? No," was the reply. In the end, the spiritualist dominates the scientist in Melville's satire of table rapping made popular by the Fox sisters. Table rapping was treated humorously by James Russell Lowell in *The Bigelow Papers*, Second Series (1867) and published "The Unhappy Lot of Mr. Knott" (1851) with mention of tale-spinning tables, prophetic armchairs, a pedantic footstool, and a dancing teapot. Lowell's "Kettelpotomachia," a satirical poem about a journalistic dispute in Virginia, was supposedly rapped out in the presence of an adolescent medium who was familiar with the works of a dead poet in a comic seance.[23] The idea for the story may have originated with finding an old table in a corn-loft of his uncle, Thomas Melvill, Jr., in Pittsfield, where Melville and his family stayed during the summer of 1850, but the story undoubtedly arose from an incident in David D. Field's *History of Berkshire County* in a passage marked by Melville. The same incident was mentioned by other writers including Timothy Dwight, president of Yale College, in *Travels in New England and New York* (1821). Three bugs came from the table; one of the bugs was preserved for a time in a tumbler. The table was used to iron clothes raising speculation that eggs laid in the wood were hatched by the heat of ironing.[24] Several readers have commented on the similarities between this story and Washington Irving's "Legend of Sleepy Hollow," citing Cotton Mather and satires on the Gothic supernatural tale. Nearly all agree the story is a humorous satire of religion leading to an inconclusive ending.[25] The incident, according to Melville's tale "happened long before the time of the 'Fox Girls.'" Spiritualism was on the wane by the time the story was published. The two most influential books on spiritualism were Judge John Worth Edmonds's *Spiritualisms* (1853, 1855) and Professor Robert Hare's, *Experimental Investigations of the Spirit Manifestations*. In addition, Melville used the recently republished *Marginalia* of Cotton Mather, bringing attention to the witchcraft trials of 1692. The eggs were 150 years old, the same length of time since the witchcraft trials.[26] Melville linked spiritualism with Puritanism, a belief in the doctrine rather than the person of Christ. Thoreau provided the source for the irony of "Apple-Tree Table," referring to the same incident in *Walden*. According to Davidson, Melville rejects Thoreau's optimistic view of the incident.[27] Spiritualism had a longer life than the bug (which expired the next day), for spiritualism returned with strength in the 1870s.[28]

In an era of great enthusiasm for science and technology of the mid-nineteenth century, America was perceived by Europeans as promising a renewed life in a fresh, green, unspoiled hemisphere, a realization of a poetic fantasy, a utopian scheme for a new beginning for Western society directing attention away from the city toward the country. Yearning for bucolic, rustic settings, and nostalgia for the forests and farms as 'closer to nature' in the pursuit of happiness produced a romantic simplemindedness. At the end of the eighteenth century, as early as 1780, at the beginning of industrialization, writers began to associate the new factory system with ugliness and suffering; the noise of the whistle aroused dislocation, conflict, and anxiety. The machine embodied the contrast of rural peace and simplicity with the urban power and sophistication of man's technology. The forces of industrialization have been the chief threat to the bucolic image of America with their greatest literary impact between 1840 and 1860, a time of acceleration of industry and economic development. The appearance of the steam locomotive in 1839, associated with fire, smoke, speed, iron, and noise, suddenly shattered the harmony of the country. The change from the rural ideal to industrial complexity brought by the steam engine's whistle is, in many ways, the greatest event of American history. Nothing quite like the steam locomotive and train in the woods had happened before. By the 1840's, the machine had captured public attention, but nothing like the excitement of the railroad in the 1830's, which had become a national obsession. The railroad embodied the age, an instrument permitting man to overcome natural obstacles— "the industrial revolution incarnate." In 1844, the invention of the telegraph added to the sanction of machines toward the progress of mankind bringing an unprecedented surge of energy in science, politics, and daily life. The myth of Prometheus, the fire-stealer, became a reality. The appearance of an efficient, powerful machine in the locomotive moving across the landscape proved to the common man the superiority of the present to the past, and was unmistakable and incontrovertible proof of progress. Man no longer feared nature, but felt a dominion over the earth in the march across the nation's wilderness, clearing swamps, changing the course of rivers, and the "annihilation of time and space"—a stock phrase of the age borrowed from Alexander Pope. The new pastoral ideal included the smoke stack, steamboat, and railroad tracks.[29] Yet the iron rails became a new kind of 'fate.'

The narrator's uncle in "The Happy Failure, A Story of the River Hudson" (1854), invents the Great Hydraulic-Hydrostatic Apparatus for draining swamps and marshes. The invention preoccupied his uncle who, convinced of his genius, would show a Roman emperor what can be done in "the present enlightened age." When the machine fails, his uncle says, "Boy, there's not much left in an old world for an old man to invent...take my advice, and never try to invent anything but—happiness." After working on the device for ten years leading only to failure, he says, "failure has made a good old man of me....Praise be to God for the failure!" Hillway says Melville met the great enthusiasm of the growing scientific movement with increasing skepticism; failure of the machine made the uncle a nobler man, one who recognizes the limitations placed by the Creator on man's intellect and achievements.[30] A study of the lives of inventors found that, in spite of the social benefit of their work, they were restless, itinerant, and lonely individuals dissatisfied with the comfortable bourgeois. Often they had worked as telegraphers or at other solitary occupations. In many respects, invention was a hostile act. To nearly every invention grew a militant resistance and sometimes the inventions were sabotaged or destroyed. After new machinery was accepted, men often continued in their familiar patterns of behavior, such as the farmer who cared for his team of horses after they had been replaced by a tractor, and worked at repairing the harness long after the horses had died.[31]

In "The Tartarus of Maids" (1855), the narrator travels to a paper factory in a remote mountainous area of New England on a cold, winter day. The quiet natural setting is disturbed by a large whitewashed factory: "Suddenly a whirring, humming sound broke upon my ear." Because his face is nearly frostbitten, he enters the factory. Inside sit rows of "blank-looking girls, with blank, white folders in their hands, all blankly folding blank papers... Machinery—that vaunted slave of humanity—here stood menially served by human beings, who served mutely and cringingly as the slave serves the Sultan." The pale, disheartened women could not create a new life with the machines: "So, through consumptive pallors of this blank, raggy life, go these white girls to death." The "iron animal" terrifies him: "but what made the thing I saw so specially terrible to me was the metallic necessity, the unbudging fatality which governed it." Melville's description of the dulling and dehumanizing effect of the factory, a product of scientific development, appalls and horrifies the reader in an explicit indictment of industrialism probably taken from reports of the mill girls in New England, particularly of Lowell, Massachusetts.[32] The first industrial revolution was based on the steam engine, built by practical men; the science of thermodynamics came a hundred years after the first use of working steam engines and theoretical understanding of steam led to fundamental understanding of heat, work, and changes of state.[33]

The purpose of invention from the earliest days of fire, iron, and the wheel was to give man some advantage over the natural environment. The advantage gained was occasional, local, and small scale, with little change in the domination of man by nature until the development of steam power. The development of steam power in the nineteenth century depended upon advances in related arts. The Greeks had a steam engine that did not lead to further development because there was no adjunct mechanical system for it to operate; in addition, work was performed cheaply by slaves. Centuries of experimenting with windmills and other devices had, by the eighteenth century, produced a sophisticated technology that could be operated by steam power.[34] The steam engine had been greatly improved since its invention in 1712 by Thomas Newcomen, particularly by the systematic studies of James Watt leading to the rotary steam engine, and later the small, high pressure engine and the expansive compound engine in 1804.[35] Andrew Ure's *Philosophy of Machinery* (1835), defined the factory:

> The term *Factory*, in technology, designates the combined operation of many orders of work-people, adult and young, in tending with assiduous skill a system of productive machines continuously impelled by a central power... But I conceive that this title [factory], in its strictest sense, involves the idea of a vast automaton, composed of various mechanical and intellectual organs, acting in uninterrupted concert for the production of a common object, all of them being subordinated to a self-regulated moving force.[36]

The French zoologist Henri Milne-Edwards formulated the most sophisticated metaphor of the machine as an organism, or animals as automata, in *Dictionnaire classique d'histoire naturelle* (1822-1831).[37] According to Morison, men perceived that a machine left to itself tended to establish its own conditions, create its own environment, and draw men into it:

> Since a machine, any machine, is designed to do only a part of what a whole man can do, it tends to wear down those parts of a man that are not included in the design.... By our developing instrumentation, and the set of ideas that lie behind it, we have slowly moved ourselves from a position of terrifying ignorance and dependence, frail beings in the hands of an angry God, to a place of knowledge and power in which we may think of becoming the measure of all things.[38]

Young says "...it is the machine itself—its 'unbudging fatality'—the narrator finds terrible."[39] In positive philosophy, human freedom and will were dissolved into natural laws that governed the inorganic and organic realms, as well as social and historical phenomena. Lenzer observes, "What the industrial revolution, the factory system and modern machinery had accomplished with regard to man's physical existence, the new philosophy and positive sciences were about to undertake for man's intellectual and emotional life: the elimination of human spontaneity and will."[40]

"The Bell Tower" (1855), which Morsberger classifies as "science fiction," tells of the genius of Renaissance scientist and mechanician Bannadonna who accidentally introduces a human fault into the mechanism of a bell tower that results in the death of its creator. Bannadonna's pride of science is fatal, like the pride of the artist in fifteenth and sixteenth century Italy, similar to the life of Benvenuto Cellini (1500-1572).[41] As the bell tower rises, it overtops walls, then trees—competing with nature, then surpassing nature. Standing at the top of his tower, Bannadonna views in equality with the gods the great works of nature—the Alps and the sea. According to Fenton, the power and energy of the tower controlled by reason becomes Melville's conception of man, "...American Man in particular, one would guess—attempting through science and mechanics to reestablish himself after the dislocations of the Copernican and scientific revelations."[42] Bannadonna fatally assaults the leader of the workmen, who are terrified by the boiling metals used for casting the bell, yet he goes untried for the crime; humanity is subordinated to science and technology as with the rise in fatal accidents in the factories of England, an unavoidable casualty and consequence of industrial progress. People throng about the site of the tower on holy days in celebration of the completion of the tower before the bell is first struck, a semireligious tribute to Bannadonna. He raises a draped figure to the top of the tower, the figure that was to strike the bell, but it slays Bannadonna. The mechanical figure was to further "the universal conveniences and glories of humanity; supplying nothing less than a supplement to the Six Days' Work;...All excellencies of all god-made creatures, which served man, were here to receive advancement, and then to be combined in one." It was to be called Talus, or Talos, son of the sister of Dædalus, who invented the saw, compass, and other mechanical instruments;[43] and also the name of a bronze giant in Crete who guarded the island by making himself red-hot and embracing strangers.[44] The mechanical creature was grotesquely disfigured with clubbed arms, although the finest creation of man's ingenuity, a human form designed to strike the hour more precisely than a man. Bannadonna relied not on divine guidance, but on sober reason and skepticism toward the possibility of a correspondence of mechanical forces and "the ruder animal vitality":

> As little did his scheme partake of the enthusiasm of some natural philosophers, who hoped, by physiological and chemical inductions, to arrive at a knowledge of the source of life, and so qualify themselves to manufacture and improve upon it. Much less had he aught in common with the tribe of alchemists, who sought,

> by a species of incantations, to evoke some surprising vitality from the laboratory. Neither had he imagined with certain sanguine theosophists, that, by faithful adoration of the Highest, unheard-of powers would be vouchsafed to man. A practical materialist, what Bannadonna had aimed at was to have been reached, not by logic, not by crucible, not by conjuration, not by altars; but by plain vice-bench and hammer. In short, to solve nature, to steal into her, to intrigue beyond her, to procure some one else to bind her to his hand; —these, one and all, had not been his object; but, asking no favors from any element or any being, of himself, to rival her, outstrip her, and rule her. With him, common sense was theurgy; machinery, miracle; Prometheus, the heroic name for machinist; man, the true God.

Friedman says Prometheus is a symbol of modern man, his knowledge and craft, the extender of human potentialities and the father of human science struggling for a place for himself in a "jealous creation":

> Prometheus is not simply the symbol of man's knowledge and science down through the generations. He is the very symbol of the ambiguity of science which extends man's dominion and at the same time brings him closer to *hybris* and self-destruction.[45]

The figure was not to be after human or animal pattern: "but equally in aspect as in organism be an original production; the more terrible to behold, the better." Those who found Bannadonna dead surmised that as he attended to his creation, he became absorbed in the intricacies of the mechanism and oblivious to its silent movement toward the bell, and it struck and killed him. The purposeless, undesigned pursuit of material progress through the invention of machines, thought to be unmistakable evidence of the advance of man and the hope of limitless improvement in man's condition, was potentially fatal. Traditional mythology implies a condemnation of the desire for scientific knowledge and technical control over nature as an expression of a presumptuous pride, ambition, and hubris. An example is the Tower of Babel that attempted to reach heaven, but angered God so that he "confounded" their language, and the Tower of Babel went unfinished. Similar stories occur in Greek mythology, including Prometheus and Daedalus. In the medieval tradition, the cosmos came before man, but with Descartes and Pascal, the individual has a "certain primacy." Man was integrated into nature which was thus perceived as full of value, meaning, and purpose. But the mechanistic philosophy secularized nature, and the human spirit withdrew into itself: alienation between the mind and the world became a common theme of the period.[46]

The narrator in "Cock-a-Doodle-do! or The Crowing of the Noble Cock Beneventano" (1855), likens his ill fortune to dreadful casualties caused by "locomotive and steamer." In a gloomy mood, he goes for a walk in damp, disagreeable air in the setting of the sublime of nature. He sits atop a hill overlooking the valley and reflects on what a slight work man makes on the earth and recalls a train wreck killing a friend and thirty people. Travel in the mid-nineteenth century involved considerable danger, such as boiler explosions on steamboats. By the 1850s, in addition to major train wrecks, so many people were losing life and limb under the wheels of trains that some states began to demand improved safety conditions, emergency care, and compensation for the injured.[47] Rev. Sydney Smith (1771-1845) told Lord Murray that every railroad accident seemed to lead to an improvement in standards, and all that was needed was "an overturn which would kill a bishop, or, at least, dean."[48] The railroad was made possible by the availability of cheap coal and cheap iron; it came from the coal mines themselves, since rails had been used there as far back as the fifteenth century.[49] The injustice of tragic deaths caused by the machine is inevitable and cannot be appealed to reason or God; "A miserable world!" he concludes:

> Great improvements of the age! What! to call the facilitation of death and murder an improvement!...that gigantic gad-fly of a Molock—snort! puff! scream!—here he comes straight-bent through these vernal woods, like the Asiatic cholera cantering on a camel.

Piercing the gloom of the day and his gloomy spirits, he hears the mighty crow of a Shanghai rooster, whose cry could scatter the fog from London. The hearty shrill lifts his spirits; he regains his appetite lost for the past week. He searches for the owner of the glorious crowing cock, and finally locates him—Merrymusk, the woodcutter. Merrymusk lives in a shanty with his four children; his wife is an invalid. All are sick and soon die. The narrator buries the family with the rooster "nigh the railroad track." In many ways, it is a caricature of Thoreau and a humorous treatment of transcendentalism.[50]

In 1847, Daniel Webster was foremost in bringing enthusiasm for the machine to the fore and urged that the psychic dislocations be ignored by rejoicing in the changes wrought by the machine. He made a "Ciceronian tribute" to the "mechanized sublime":

> I will not pretend, no one can pretend, to discern the end; but every body knows that the age is remarkable for scientific research into the heavens, the earth, and what is beneath the earth; and perhaps more remarkable still for the application of this scientific research to the pursuits of life. The ancients saw nothing like it. The moderns have seen nothing like it till the present generation....We see the ocean navigated and the solid land traversed by steam power, and intelligence communicated by electricity. Truly this is almost a miraculous era. What is before us no one can say, what is upon us no one can hardly realize. The progress of the age has almost outstripped human belief; the future is known only to Omniscience.[51]

Melville disagreed with the uncritical belief in the benefit of mechanism. A letter to Hawthorne in 1851 contains the theme of the short stories:

> It is a frightful poetical creed that the cultivation of the brain eats out the heart....I stand for the heart. To the dogs with the head! I had rather be a fool with a heart, than Jupiter Olympus with his head. The reason the mass of men fear God, and *at bottom dislike* Him, is because they rather distrust His heart, and fancy Him all Brain like a watch.[52]

Melville expresses distrust of the deistic, rational God of Descartes. From Bartleby to Bannadonna and the friend of Merrymusk, the machine competes with divine influence and is considered pejoratively by Melville as debasing humanity. Bannadonna like Prometheus, steals fire for man's inventions, becoming the "true god." The technological changes of the Industrial Revolution implied a far greater break with the past than anything since the invention of the wheel: the redistribution of investment and a revision of the concept of risk due to the lack of flexibility of fixed manufacturing plants. For the worker, the change was even more fundamental since his way of life now depended upon the machine. The worker, separated from the usual means of production, became a 'hand.' The machine imposed a new discipline. The worker no longer worked at home, but in the factory where a large team labored in unison under the eye of overseers: "The factory was a new kind of prison; the clock a new kind of jailer."[53] Only a few individuals like Babbage and Playfair could see the weaknesses and social implications in the growth of industry and laborsaving machines.[54] Science became a new faith:

> Our scientific marvels and technological gadgets parallel New Testament miracles in that they too are based on a mythic understanding of reality. We explain the success of our devices in terms of their interaction with what we see as reality; early Christians too explained the success of miracles in term of the relationship between the miracles and what they saw as reality, the most important characteristic of which was an *omnipotent* and loving creator who came to live among them....Scientific thinking is functionally the same as mythmaking in the way it enables control of reality, as well as with other things such as the way they are told or learned. Mythmaking is a basic human activity, the modern Western counterpart of which probably includes our science.[55]

The power of science has been placed in man's hands. With it, he can work his will with unprecedented speed, but "science has nothing to prepare him ethically for its use."[56]

Modern man considers that human knowledge is constantly increasing; therefore, we are wiser than the ancients. The discoveries of recent centuries are equally wonderful: the new world of unknown lands and animals, and new worlds revealed by science and psychology. The science of the ancients was surpassed, forgetting that Lucretius, Epicurus, and Democritus conceived matter constructed of atoms, inferred by thought alone that the planets revolved around the sun, and that Hippocrates laid the foundation of science. The conclusion was that civilized man has become better than the ancients, for the ancients differed in one major way: they never believed in the ideal of modern science—"that man can change and improve nature." The ordinary problems of men and women are no less difficult today than two millennia past, yet it would seem from the argument of scientific progress that we ought to have enough knowledge to enable us to solve the great complexities that troubled our forefathers. Highet speculates that life now with scientific progress may actually be more difficult:

> Now that we have learnt to change the world, the world has become less stable, so that it is more difficult to understand: new problems are constantly arising, for which no clear precedents exist. And our naïve confidence in applied science has to some extent dissuaded the common man from thinking out problems of conduct as earnestly

> as our forefathers did, in conversation, in public debate, in meditation, and in prayer.[57]

With scientific advance, much useful knowledge has been lost. Many of our secular values obey no final authority but critical reason, the belief in the authority of nature, and confidence in progress through science. The answers on how to control science (and technology) do not come from science itself.[58]

Notes

1. F. Sherwood Taylor, *A Short History of Science and Scientific Thought: With Readings from the Great Scientists from the Babylonians Through Einstein.* New York and London: Norton, 1949, p. 33.

2. Brian Stock, "Science, Technology, and Economic Progess in the Middle Ages." in *Science in the Middle Ages.* David C. Lindberg, editor. Chicago and London: University of Chicago Press, 1978, pp. 29-31.

3. David S. Landes, *The Unbound Prometheus: Technological Change and Industrial Development in Western Europe from 1750 to the Present.* Cambridge: Cambridge University Press, 1969, pp. 24-25.

4. Stock, ref. 2, p. 45.

5. A. R. Hall, *The Scientific Revolution 1500-1800: The Formation of the Modern Scientific Attitude.* 2nd edition. Boston: Beacon, 1962, p. 5-7.

6. Taylor, ref. 1, pp. 96-98.

7. Hall, ref. 5, p. 101.

8. Peter Medawar, *The Limits of Science.* Oxford: Oxford University Press, 1984, pp. 35-39.

9. Elting E. Morison, *Men, Machines, and Modern Times.* Cambridge, Massachusetts, and London, England: The M.I.T. Press, 1966, p. 2.

10. Peter Mathias, "Who Unbound Prometheus? Science and Technical Change, 1600-1900." in *Science and Society 1600-1900.* Peter Mathias, editor. Cambridge: Cambridge University Press, 1972, p. 65-66.

11. Mathias, ref. 10, pp. 78-80.

12. Anthony Hyman, *Charles Babbage: Pioneer of the Computer.* Princeton, New Jersey: Princeton University Press, 1982, pp. 103, 165.

13. Dirk J. Struik, *Yankee Science in the Making.* New York: Collier Books, 1962, pp. 238-239.

14. Robert V. Bruce, *The Launching of Modern American Science 1846-1876.* New York: Alfred A. Knopf, 1987, pp. 21, 74, 144, 187, 256.

15. Bruce, ref. 14, pp. 130-131.

16. W. R. Patrick, "Melville's Bartleby and the Doctrine of Necessity." *American Literature* 41 (1969):39-54.

17. Patrick, ref. 16.

18. Maurice Friedman, *Problematic Rebel: Melville, Dostoievsky, Kafka, Camus.* Chicago and London: University of Chicago Press, revised 1970, p. 83.

19. James Robert Corey, *Herman Melville and the Theory of Evolution.* Ph.D. Dissertation, Washington State University 1968, note 30, p. 45; George R. Stewart, "The Two *Moby-Dicks.*" *American Literature* 25 (1953):17-448.

20. H. Bruce Franklin, "The Island Worlds of Darwin and Melville." *The Centennial Review* 11 (1967):353-370.

21. Russell Thomas, "Melville's Use of Some Sources on the Entantadas." *American Literature* 3 (1931):432-456.

22. Allan M. Emery, "Melville on Science: 'The Lightning-Rod Man.'" *The New England Quarterly* 56 (1983):555-568.

23. Howard Kerr, *Mediums, Spirit-Rappers, and Roaring Radicals.* Urbana, Chicago, and London: University of Illinois Press, 1972, pp. 40-41.

24. Douglas Sackman, "The Original of Melville's Apple-Tree Table." *American Literature* 11 (1939):448-451.

25. Lea Bertani Vozar Newman, *A Reader's Guide to the Short Stories of Herman Melville.* Boston: G.K. Hall, 1986, pp. 3-14.

26. Jay Leyda, "An Introduction." in *The Complete Stories of Herman Melville.* New York: Random House, 1949.

27. Frank Davidson, "Melville, Thoreau, and 'The Apple-Tree Table.'" *American Literature* 25 (1968): 479-488.

28. Kerr, ref. 23, pp. 43-54.

29. Leo Marx, *Machine in the Garden: Technology and the Pastoral Ideal in America.* New York, Oxford: Oxford University Press, 1964, pp. 3-33, 190-215.

30. Tyrus Hillway, "Melville as a Critic of Science." *Modern Language Notes* 65 (1950):411-414.

31. Morison, ref. 9, pp. 10-11.

32. Johannes D. Bergmann, "Melville's Tales." in *A Companion to Melville Studies.* John Bryant, editor. New York, Westport, Connecticut, and London: Greenwood, 1986, p. 260.

33. David Knight, "Michael Faraday: The Use of Pure Science." in *Man Masters Nature: Twenty-Five Centuries of Science.* Roy Porter, editor. New York: George Braziller, 1988, p. 126.

34. Morison, ref. 9, pp. 8-16.

35. D. S. L. Cardwell, "Science and the steam engine, 1790-1825." in *Science and Society 1600-1900.* Peter Mathias, editor. Cambridge: Cambridge University Press, 1972, pp. 85-90.

36. Andrew Ure (1835), cited by Silvan S. Schweber, "The Wider British Context in Darwin's Theorizing." *The Darwinian Heritage.* David Kohn, editor. Princeton, New Jersey: Princeton University Press, 1985. p. 45.

37. Schweber, ref. 36, p. 46.

38. Morison, ref. 9, p. 119.

39. Philip Young, "The Machine in Tartarus: Melville's *Inferno.*" *American Literature* 63 (1991):208-224.

40. August Comte, *August Comte and Positivism: The Essential Writings.* Gertrud Lenzer, editor. Chicago and London: University of Chicago Press, 1983, p. lvi.

41. Robert E. Morsberger, "Melville's 'The Bell-Tower' and Benvenuto Cellini." *American Literature* 44 (1972):459-462.

42. Charles A. Fenton, "'The Bell-Tower': Melville and Technology." *American Literature* 23 (1951):219-232.

43. J. Lemprière, *Lemprière's Classical Dictionary.* London: Bracken, 1984, p. 655.

44. John Warrington, *Everyman's Classical Dictionary.* London, Melbourne and Toronto: J. M. Dent and Sons, 1970, p. 492.

45. Friedman, ref. 18, p. 36.

46. Don Cupit, *The Sea of Faith: Christianity in Change.* Cambridge: Cambridge University Press, 1984, pp. 50, 118.

47. James H. Cassedy, *Medicine and American Growth, 1800-1860.* Madison, Wisconsin: University of Wisconsin Press, 1986, p. 167.

48. Alan Bell, *Sydney Smith: A biography.* Oxford: Oxford University Press, 1980, p. 205.

49. J. D. Bernal, *Science and Industry in the Nineteenth Century.* London: Routledge and Kegan Paul, 1953. reprint. Bloomington and London: Indiana University Press, 1971, p. 21.

50. Egbert S. Oliver, "Cock-A-Doodle-Doo and Transcendental Hockus Pockus." *New England Quarterly* 21 (1948):204-216.

51. Marx, ref. 29, p. 214.

52. Herman Melville, *The Letters of Herman Melville.* Merrill R. Davis and William H. Gilman, editors. New Haven: Yale University Press, 1960, p. 129.

53. Landes, ref. 3, pp. 42-43.

54. Hyman, ref. 12, p. 224.

55. Kevin J. Sharpe, *From Science To An Adequate Mythology.* Auckland, New Zealand: Interface Press, 1984, p. 49.

56. Taylor, ref. 1, p. 1.

57. Gilbert Highet, *The Classical Tradition: Greek and Roman Influences on Western Literature.* Oxford: Oxford University Press, 1949. reprint. 1970, p. 266.

58. Sharpe, ref. 55, p. 59.

Chapter 7

The Confidence-Man: by chance or design

The Confidence-Man: His Masquerade (1857) is set aboard the riverboat *Fidèle* out of St. Louis bound for New Orleans. A series of strangers come aboard on April Fool's Day who ask other strangers to have confidence; each is swindled while demonstrating faith in his fellow man. A "grotesque negro cripple," whether "by chance or design" was able to raise a smile from the gravest (Ch 3). By 'chance or design' was the conflict so inflammatory in the nineteenth century; was God able to intervene in earthly affairs? Was the earth and all natural creation the product of a supreme being as maintained by theologians and many scientists, or were they the result of chance, a "fortuitous concourse of atoms?" a concept held mainly by atheistic, objective scientists. A Methodist minister denies the crippled negro his trust saying, "I suspect him for one naturally reprobate" (Ch 3). A man with a wooden leg approaches, he is a suspicious man who tells his story, then throws back his head, "and gave vent to a long, gasping, rasping sort of taunting cry, intolerable as that of a high-pressure engine jeering off steam" (Ch 6). The steam engine, with its great promise, is used here in a pejorative metaphor.

A distinguished man wearing a gray coat joins the conversation; he had exhibited a "Protean easy-chair" for invalids at the "World's Fair in London" (Ch 7), the Exposition of the Industry of All Nations at the Crystal Palace in 1851. Fairs and exhibitions had been held in Europe for centuries, but the age of science and technology, or the machine age, had its great exhibition of manufactures and inventions, the first great modern exhibition, which opened in Hyde Park, London, on May 1, 1851. It signaled England's shift from a distaste for industrialization to a confident acceptance of it. Dr. Lyon Playfair, who helped to organize the great exhibition, said that natural resources were no longer an advantage over other nations, and that industry must be supported by a "competition of intellects."[1] Prince Albert, the fair's sponsor, saw man as "approaching a more complete fulfillment of that great and sacred mission which he has to perform in this world, to conquer nature to his use, himself a divine instrument." The building was the main attraction, a great glittering cage of iron and glass 1,848 feet long with 293,655 panes of glass covering almost twenty acres: "...a gargantuan showplace of early Victorian Britain in all its confidence, prosperity, curiosity, and vulgarity."[2] Fourteen thousand exhibitors, including many foreign exhibitors, displayed more than 100,000 products. Among the American articles were McCormick's reaper, rubber boots, Colt's new automatic revolver, sewing machines, candlemaking machines, brickmaking machines, false teeth, soap, and false hair. Six million visitors attended the fair, making it one of most successful and one of the few profitable world's fairs.[3] At the exhibition, William Ragan, a manufacturer from Philadelphia, won honorable mention for a reclining chair promising some of the comforts described by the man with the gray coat.[4]

A grave American "savan," or savant, visiting London attended a party and observed and disdained a "certain coxcombial fellow"; the man was "no less a personage than Sir Humphry Davy" (Ch 13), brilliant English chemist and exponent of the scientific method mentioned in Melville's earlier works. Rev. Sydney Smith described Davy as "a very foolish coxcomb out of his crucibles."[5] The incident noted probably came from a memoir of John Quincy Adams, who met Sir Humphry at an evening party in June 1815. Adams remarked, "If modesty is an inseparable companion of genius, Sir Humphry is a prodigy." Foster says Adams's sedate and scholarly manner, unusual intellectual powers, and ardent interest in science suited Melville's grave American savant.[6] Davy's electrical theory of chemistry remains the basis of modern chemistry. Davy's genius was immense and often vulgar, pursuing "science and snobbery with equal vehemence."[7]

The merchant and Mr. Ringman, the unfortunate man with the weed in his hat, become sociable and drink wine together: "Ah, wine is good, and confidence is good; but can wine or confidence percolate down through all the stony strata of hard considerations, and drop warmly and ruddily into the cold cave of truth" (Ch 13), employing a geological metaphor similar to Jarl's tobacco pouch in *Mardi*. Later, he laments that pure wine is unpurchasable being "less the vintage of vineyards than laboratories" (Ch 29), and that bar-keepers are poisoners.

Melville digresses into a discussion of characterization, the inconsistencies of the novel, and the vagaries of life using an example from natural history: "When the duck-billed beaver of Australia was first brought stuffed to England, the naturalists, appealing to their classifications, maintained that there was, in reality, no such creature; the bill in the specimen must needs be, is some way, artificially stuck on" (Ch 14), leading to a revelation on human nature:

> Yet, as touching this point, it may prove suggestive, that all those sallies of ingenuity, having for their end the revelation of human nature on fixed principles, have, by the best judges, been excluded with contempt from the ranks of the sciences—palmistry, physiognomy, phrenology, psychology....The grand points of human nature are the same to-day as they were a thousand years ago....some mathematicians are yet in hopes of hitting upon an exact method of determining the longitude, the more earnest psychologists may, in the face of previous failures, still cherish expectations with regard to some mode of infallibly discovering the heart of man. (Ch 14)

The theme of the error of science, or the limit of science, is stated in many ways throughout Melville's works. A method for determining longitude had eluded the world's navigators, but its pursuit had become more important with increased ocean travel and world exploration. The most important advance in navigation in centuries was the use of chronometers by Thomas Hubbard Sumner (1807-1851), an American sea captain, son of a Boston architect and congressman. The use of chronometers was resisted by ship owners because of their great expense until Sumner developed an accurate method of determining a ship's position of longitude by sighting the sun coordinated with the chronometer known as "Sumner's line." The accuracy of the method was endorsed by Harvard mathematician Benjamin Pierce. Sumner published his method of determining longitude in 1843. It rapidly gained acceptance and a modification is still used.[8] The duck-billed beaver of Australia, the platypus, when first brought to Europe was thought to be fraudulent. The platypus, one of the most primitive of mammals, is confined to eastern Australia and Tazmania. Since it arrived in America by way of the orient, the specimen aroused the suspicion of scientists aware of "monstrous impostures" the artful Chinese had played on European voyagers, such as the "eastern mermaid" consisting of the forepart of a monkey stitched to the afterpart of a fish.[9]

The herb doctor skeptically says: "science is now-a-days so expert that, in consumptive cases [tuberculosis], as yours, it can, by prescription of the inhalation of certain vapors, achieve the sublimest act of omnipotence, breathing into all but lifeless dust the breath of life." He says a "great chemist in Baltimore" treated a patient for three weeks with a respirator, "a sort of gasometer," breathing vapors generated by burning drugs:

> Oh, who can wonder at that old reproach against science, that it is atheistical? And here is my prime reason for opposing these chemical practitioners, who have sought out so many inventions. For what do their inventions indicate, unless it be that kind and degree of pride in human skill, which seems scarce compatible with reverential dependence upon the power above? Try to rid my mind of it as I may, yet still these chemical practitioners with their tinctures, and fumes, and braziers, and occult incantations, seem to me like Pharaoh's vain sorcerers, trying to beat down the will of heaven. (Ch 16)

In his exhibition of pride, the physician is accused of being as atheistical as mechanician Bannadonna in "The Bell-Tower." The invalid tells the herb doctor "but I have heard of a book entitled 'Nature in Disease'":

> A title I cannot approve; it is suspiciously scientific. 'Nature in Disease?' As if nature, divine nature, were aught but health; as if through nature disease is decreed! But did I not before hint of the tendency of science, that forbidden tree? Sir, if despondency is yours from recalling that title, dismiss it. Trust me, nature is health; for health is good, and nature cannot work ill. As little can she work error. Get nature, and you get well. Now, I repeat, this medicine is nature's own. (Ch 16)

Nature in Disease: Illustrated in Various Discourses and Essays, to which are added Miscellaneous Writing Chiefly on Medical Subjects, published in 1854, was written by Jacob Bigelow (1786-1879), onetime president of the Massachusetts Medical Society. In the first essay, "Self-Limited Diseases," Bigelow gives a low estimate of the resources of the art of medicine when compared to those of nature, which is an extension of the concept of the natural sublime.[10] No one knew anything about the herb doctor, but suspected him of something:

> "Suspicion. We want knowledge."
> "Well, suspect first and know next. True knowledge comes but by suspicion or revelation. That's my maxim." (Ch 18)

Since revelation occurs only by faith, science amounts to no more than suspicion of nature or systematized doubt. The herb doctor says of the crippled man: "what a demoniac unfortunate, Regular Infernal machine" (Ch 19)! After the herb doctor departs, the miser is accosted by a bear-like man, the Missouri bachelor whose name is Pitch: "I stick to what I say." Spartan in his manner and sentiment, he had overheard their conversation:

> Yarbs, yarbs; natur, natur; you foolish old file you! He diddled you with that hocus-pocus, did he? Yarbs and natur will cure your incurable cough, you think.... Because a thing is nat'ral, as you call it, you think it must be good. But who gave you that cough? Was it, or was it not, nature?...Nature is good Queen Bess; but who's responsible for the cholera?...What's deadly-nightshade? Yarb, ain't it?...But who froze to death my teamsters on the prairie? And who made an idiot of Peter the Wild Boy? (Ch 21)

Peter the Wild Boy (1712-1785), also mentioned in Chapters 2 and 29 (also in *Mardi* Chapter 109, and Chapter 2 of *Billy Budd*), was a black-haired, dark-skinned boy about twelve years old, dumb and uncivilized, found naked in a field in July 1724, near Hamelin, Germany, walking on his hands and feet, climbing trees, and eating grass and moss. He was brought to town and called Peter with the speculation that a wild animal had nursed him. A year later King George I of England had him sent to Hanover and later to London to be studied. The controversy over innate ideas was at its height, and Peter was thought an appropriate subject for study. After he was examined by Dr. John Arbuthnot (1667-1735), Scotch mathematician and physician, Peter was found to be an idiot and no brilliant discoveries in psychology or anthropology could be expected. He had been lost in the woods for a time in 1723 and driven there again by his stepmother. Defoe was among the many who wrote about the subject, which enlarged into a controversy about the existence of innate intelligence; Linnaeus mentioned him in *Systema Naturae;* Buffon and others extolled him as the "true child of nature, the genuine unsophisticated man."[11] The "Confession of faith" in man's science, a confidence in the ability of man to understand the natural world and manipulate nature to man's benefit instead of seeking truth through revelation, is stated in a number of themes in the novel in that various characters suspect that the natural world is not created according to divine design. Some scientists in the nineteenth century began to think they were on the threshold of finding the complete works of nature, or the formula that would be God. Cook declares: "Suspicion and revelation might be said to constitute the epistemological method of the grotesque in the *The Confidence-Man*, and in Melville's other works as well."[12]

The Missourian distrusts the herb doctor and distrusts nature. He says he intends to find a machine to do the farm work his boys are supposed to do. The herb doctor gives the Missourian a box of medicine: "I am pained to meet with one who holds nature a dangerous character....Through her regularly-authorized agents, of whom I happen to be one, Nature delights in benefiting those who most abuse her" (Ch 21). The herb-doctor is probably based on the Thompsonian movement of botanical medicine prevalent in America in the nineteenth century.[13] Since the Missourian has no trust in man or boy: "then some sort of machine for you is all there is left." At this, the herb doctor disembarks at Cape Girardeau.

Soon after leaving Cape Girardeau, the Missourian meets the man from the Philosophical Intelligence Office (P.I.O.), an employment agency, who suggests the Missourian may need his services to hire a boy to work on his farm. The P.I.O. man's "analogical method" of reasoning "by analogy from the physical to the moral" probably comes from Emerson's *Nature* (1836), which states that "particular natural facts are symbols of particular spiritual facts." The P.I.O. man uses analogies of the physical and moral to defend an optimistic view toward human nature, that natural fact symbolizes spiritual fact.[14] The P.I.O. man says his office is founded on:

> "strictly philosophical and physio—"
>
> "Look you—come up here—how, by philosophy or physiology either, make good boys to order?" (Ch 22)

The Missourian is on the road to get a machine so he will never have to deal with boys or men to do his work:

> Machines for me. My cider-mill—does that ever steal my cider? My mowing-machine—does that ever lay a-bed mornings?...all faithfully attend to their business....shining examples that virtue is its own reward—the only practical Christians I know...Sir, a corn-husker, for its patient continuance in well-doing, might not unfitly go to heaven. (Ch 22)

The P.I.O. man protests: "Things incapable of free agency, to receive the eternal reward of well-doing—oh, oh, oh" (Ch 22)! The machine is supposedly free from sin, but cannot exhibit free will; nor does the machine suffer from natural depravity. The Missourian says he cannot trust servants, that for most work purposes man or boy is a losing animal: "Hence these thousand new inventions—carding machines, horse-shoe machines, tunnel-boring machines, reaping machines, etc." The bewildering array of new machines developed in the nineteenth century, such as exhibited at the Crystal Palace in 1851, threatened the natural setting of the wilderness as well as man's peace of mind. Melville's satire expresses one of his dominate themes, the distrust of the advance of the machine and man's technology. After considerable discussion on the worth of man, the agent explains the principles of his office that led to "a careful analytical study of man" resulting in the "state of boyhood scientifically viewed." The Missourian asks him to explain: "our theory teaches us to proceed by analogy from the physical to the moral." The Missourian strongly objects; the agent says, "Sir, if passion is to invade, surely science must evacuate." Even the devil could not have foreknown the downy-chinned child could grow a beard like a goat. The Missourian objects: "The devil is very sagacious. To judge by the event, he appears to have understood man better than the Being who made him." The agent claims noble quality in the boy will appear in time; like the beard, his theory requires confidence: "In the natural advance of all creatures, do they not bury themselves over and over again in the endless resurrection of better and better" (Ch 22)? The idea that creatures show progression over time was opposed to the concept of fixity of species. Melville's satire implies the uncomfortable notion of change in the natural order and design, that time alters and improves the creatures of the earth thought already 'perfect' by the work of God, an idea of Lamarck's advanced by Chambers in *Vestiges* and was denounced by clergy and scientist alike. The studies of the agent's office led to an enlarged study of mankind: "...that these studies directed always to the scientific procuring of good servants of all sorts, boys included," for their patrons. On inquiring the fee, the agent says it exceeds the charge of similar institutions, but promises that the boy supplied will be honest: "Such, at least, were the marginal observations on the phrenological chart of his head, submitted to me by the mother." The Missourian agrees to accept a boy from the agent "for the sake purely of a scientific experiment." He pays the money; the agent debarks at Cairo. The 'perfect boy' provided by the application of science becomes a satire of science being able to clarify philosophy, especially the issue of natural depravity and the exercise of free will.

The Missourian, with a Western dialect and manner of bluff uncouthness, lives in the natural sublime. Trimpi says:

> He claims to know Nature because he has lived with her and cannot be taken in by the Herb-Doctor's arguments for confidence in Nature....his austere Augustinian-Calvinist views of the natural depravity of boys and men...are pulled to pieces by the P.I.O. Man's "analogical theories" and his argument from the "physical to the moral," which are themselves a travesty of Plato's argument about the relationship of physical beauty to moral virtue.[15]

The Missourian expresses suspicion of the pride of science. The possibility of the 'perfectibility of man' arose in the later part of the eighteenth century with progress towards the idea of a perfect social order, and the advance of science began to gain a general audience. In the course of the nineteenth century, Western man grew more self-confident and hopeful about himself, that man is "naturally good." Theological writers alluded to the "total depravity" of man such that even outwardly good acts had hidden, evil motives. Man had been endowed by his Creator with the divine gift of reason, "it was the 'heart'—with a bad connotation—that controls the operations of the reason, but that in doing so the heart hides from itself, so that men are self-deceivers ever." Reason, with a belief in science, could elevate man's state from natural disgrace.[16] The P.I.O. man expresses the prevailing confidence in science to understand and improve upon human nature; the Missourian maintains his opinion on the natural evil of man and boy.

The shabbily dressed Missourian meets a gaudily dressed cosmopolitan. The Missourian says Marzetti, the African pantomimist, is a good performer: "plays the intelligent ape until he seems it. With such naturalness can a being endowed with an immortal spirit enter into that of a monkey. But where's your tail" (Ch 24)? Trimpi says Melville suggests that man is made in the image of an ape, not the image of God. Although used in a satirical sense, he anticipated events soon to occur.[17] The Missourian disdains several books including "Hume's on Suicide, as Bacon's on Knowledge; and, like these, will betray him who seeks to steer soul and body by it, like a false religion" requiring due confidence. Hume (1711-1776) argues in "Of Suicide" that it is superstitious, even blasphemous, to believe that a miserable man has no right to end his misery. "Bacon on Knowledge" could mean any of Bacon's works, particularly *The Advancement of Learning* (1605), *Novum Organum* (1620), or *De Augmentis Scientiarum* (1623).[18] Bacon, one of the earliest proponents of a faith in science, is also mentioned in Chapter 9 as an advocate of materialism: "My speculations, sir,...have been chiefly governed by the maxim of Lord Bacon; I speculate in those philosophies which come home to my business and bosom..." The cosmopolitan fails to convince the Missourian to show confidence in man. Shroeder says the Missourian is aware "nature is cursed for man's sake; that the natural evil of the universe—an evil which the confidence-man attempts to conceal—represents to man a perpetual emblem of his fall and consequent perilous spiritual state."[19]

In the puzzling chapters on "the metaphysics of Indian hating," he writes of the backwoodsman who by choice avoids man:

> Like the 'possum, the backwoodsman presents the spectacle of a creature dwelling exclusively among the works of God, yet these, truth must confess, breed little in him of a godly mind....Is it that he feels that whatever man may be, man is not the universe? that glory, beauty, kindness, are not all engrossed by him? (Ch 26)

Here again, Melville questions the position of man in the universe and in the eyes of an unseen god. Certainly his remark is opposed to the Renaissance view of an anthropocentric universe.

The cosmopolitan encounters a mystic who states a prevalent Melvillian theme: "I hold to the metempsychosis; and whoever I may be now, I feel that I was once the stoic Arrian..." (Ch 36), the last reference to the theory which was probably influenced by Melville's reading of Sir Thomas Browne.

While becoming intoxicated drinking wine, the cosmopolitan defends the press against the criticism of Charlie Noble: "I hold the press to be actually—Defender of the Faith!—defender of the faith in the final triumph of truth over error, metaphysics over superstition, theory over falsehood, machinery over nature, and the good man over the bad"

(Ch 29). Just how the press accomplished this feat is not disclosed, but it is clearly on the side of the new science and technological mastery over nature.

Melville makes a tangential reference to phrenology near the end of the book when the philanthropist challenges the barber: "...how does the mere handling the outside of men's heads led you to distrust the inside of their hearts" (Ch 43)? The error of perception again fools the judgement of human character. Melville elaborates the idea of an "original" character in fiction, a term the young or inexperienced are more likely to use: "Certainly, the sense of originality exists at its highest in an infant, and probably at its lowest in him who has completed the circle of the sciences" (Ch 44). He equates science with skepticism destroying creativity, the opposite of faith. Few originals must exist: "For much the same reason that there is but one planet to one orbit, so there can be but one such original character to one work of invention. Two would conflict in chaos" (Ch 44). That only one planet occupies an orbit is a Copernican concept that was proved by Newton, an example of 'order' demonstrating the design of God. "There would seem but one point in common between this sort of phenomenon in fiction and all other sorts: it cannot be born in the author's imagination—it being as true in literature as in zoology, that all life is from the egg" (Ch 44). He implies the innate ideas of Locke, possibly the concept of necessity, or more specifically, the current but fading theory of embryology—that all possibilities exist in the egg. That life came from eggs fascinated early Greek philosophers, illustrated by Aristotle's treatise on embryology, a large compendium of observation and argument; little was added to his theories for nearly 2,000 years. In 1827, exactly 150 years after Leeuwenhoek discovered sperm cells by use of the microscope, Karl Ernst von Baer (1793-1876) discovered the mammalian egg, or ova. Until about 1800, the general belief of the development of the embryo consisted of "preformation": either a preformed animal existed in miniature in the egg, needing only the stimulation of the sperm to develop, or a similarly preformed organism in the sperm enlarged once inside the egg.[20]

At night, the gentlemen's cabin is lit by "a solar lamp," creating strange images which "on all sides went rippling off with ever-diminishing distinctness, till, like circles from a stone dropped in water, the rays died dimly away in the furthest nook of the place" (Ch 45). Melville's use of the waves in water is the same metaphor used by physics teachers today to illustrate the nature of light: that intensity diminishes inversely as the square root of the distance from the source of light. The wave theory of light dominated the particle theory of light through the nineteenth century until Einstein theorized that light can behave as either wave or particle. Other lamps swung from the roof of the cabin had gone out, as if they were "barren planets" to the "solar lamp."

The cosmopolitan's sense of security is disturbed: "stories are told about steamboats and railroads fitted to make one a little apprehensive," yet, he is comforted by believing in a "Committee of Safety" guarding the night along rivers and streets, and he cites Proverbs 3:26: "Jehovah shall be thy confidence."[21]

The Confidence-Man went almost unnoticed in America; the few reviews it received were almost uniformly unfavorable. Like other books by Melville, twentieth century scholarship finds *The Confidence-Man* an astonishing work of literature.[22] Cawelti asserts:

> We find in this novel an attempt to grasp and structure human experience; to represent man's involvement in an inscrutable cosmos, where life is only a shimmering surface masking the impenetrable depths of ultimate reality. And man is masked; he changes suddenly, meaninglessly, from one role to another, his purposes and motivations always obscure. If there is any wisdom in such a universe it can only be that of seeing that there are at least two opposing sides to everything.[23]

Melville makes more explicit his attack on those who count on the goodness of nature. The romanticists, following Rousseau, thought that any person living in a state of nature must be blessed by beneficent and worthy influences. Nature was suspect, in spite of its great acceptance by the herb and root doctors and the transcendentalists. According to Foster:

> Western man has perhaps never seemed more safe and secure in the universe than towards the middle of the nineteenth century; Christian belief made him the child of an ever-loving Father and the inheritor of heaven, the scientists made him the confident master of nature and the inheritor of the earth. But as Melville saw it, man lives, like the Indian-hater, amidst a smiling, sly, circumambient, inscrutable malice.[24]

Friedman claims that *The Confidence-Man* is an "exercise in misanthropy, and his misanthropy is clearly linked to the distrust of Creation." He states that a century later, Martin Buber (1878-1965) said the same thing in the "eclipse of God":

> The existential mistrust is indeed basically no longer, like the old kind, a mistrust of my fellow-man. It is rather the destruction of confidence in existence in general...At its core the conflict between mistrust and trust of man conceals the conflict between the mistrust and trust of eternity.[25]

Until the mid-nineteenth century, the structure of the world was considered either an ordered cosmos or a disordered chaos. The laws of nature seemed to expose its inner workings convincing scientist and clergyman that the author of those laws was the essence of order and logic. Yet, Melville's confidence man observed human existence with wry, cosmic skepticism where nature, the representative of the divine, withstands the onslaught of science. Although Melville's utilization of science in *The Confidence-Man* is not as great as in other works, its completion only a few years before the culmination of centuries of conflict and cooperation between science and religion became open conflict makes it an especially significant book. The references cited are not only accurate, they also are succinct expressions of the turmoil of the times, and show Melville's remarkable awareness of current theories and controversies in science. The seemingly offhand remark in Chapter 3—"by chance or design"—has a greater significance than would appear to the casual reader because Melville was aware of the magnitude of the change in values. The controversy over chance versus design was little known outside academic institutions; the common man lived in a benevolent and ordered cosmos, but after the decade of the 1850s, all that changed forever. Man's confidence in religious faith was declining while his confidence in the faith of 'scientism' and materialism was gaining.

Mardi and *Moby-Dick* were expositions of nineteenth century science. In *Pierre* and the short stories, the threat of science in the form of technology and the machine—especially "The Bell-Tower" ("man, the true God")—became a reality. In *The Confidence-Man*, allusions to science have a new meaning—new theories in biology ("the natural advance of all creatures") would revolutionize philosophical attitudes as well as the minds of ordinary men. The decade of the 1850s was decisive in forming the outlook of Western civilization and the beliefs of modern man. *The Confidence-Man* marked the end of Melville's career as a novelist.

Notes

1. Peter Mathias, "Who Unbound Prometheus? Science and technical change, 1600-1900." in *Science and Society 1600-1800,* Cambridge: Cambridge University Press, 1972, pp. 60-61.

2. Annabel Walker, *Kensington and Chelsea: a social and architectural history.* London: John Murray, 1987, pp. 50-54.

3. Robert V. Bruce, *The Launching of Modern American Science 1846-1876.* New York: Knopf, 1987, p. 133; Dalzell, Robert F., Jr. *American Participation in the Great Exhibition of 1851.* Amherst, Massachusetts: Amherst College Press, 1960.

4. Herman Melville, *The Confidence-Man: His Masquerade.* Elizabeth S. Foster, editor. New York: Hendricks House, 1954, p. 307.

5. Alan Bell, *Sydney Smith: A biography.* Oxford: Oxford University Press, 1980, p. 94.

6. Foster, ref 4,, p. 315.

7. J. G. Crowther, *British Scientists of the nineteenth century.* London: Routledge and Kegan Paul, 1935, p. 66.

8. Dirk J. Struik, *Yankee Science in the Making.* New York: Collier Books, 1962, pp. 404-406.

9. Foster, ref. 4, p. 317.

10. Jacob Bigelow, *Nature in Disease.* Boston: Ticknor and Fields, 1854.

11. Herman Melville, *The Confidence-Man: His Masquerade.* Hershel Parker, editor. New York: Norton, 1971, p. 92n; Melville, ref. 4, p. 323.

12. Richard M. Cook, "Evolving the Inscrutable: The Grotesque in Melville's Fiction." *American Literature* 49 (1978):544-559.

13. Richard D. Smith, *Melville's Complaint: Doctors and Medicine in the Art of Herman Melville,* New York and London: Garland, 1991, pp. 157-161.

14. Helen P. Trimpi, "Three of Melville's Confidence Men: William Cullen Bryant, Theodore Parker, and Horace Greeley." *Texas Studies in Literature and Language* 21 (1979):368-395.

15. Helen P. Trimpi, "Harlequin-Confidence-Man: The Satirical Tradition of Commedia Dell'Arte and Pantomime in Melville's *The Confidence-Man.*" *Texas Studies in Literature* 16 (1974):147-193.

16. Arthur O. Lovejoy, *Reflections on Human Nature.* Baltimore: Johns Hopkins University Press, 1961, pp. 6-8.

17. Trimpi, ref. 15.

18. Foster, ref. 4, 329-330.

19. John W. Shroeder, "Sources and Symbols for Melville's Confidence Man." *PMLA* 66 (1951):363-380; Melville, ref. 11, p 308.

20. Leslie B. Arey, *Developmental Anatomy.* Philadelphia and London: W.B. Saunders, 1946, pp. 3-5.

21. Foster, ref. 11, p. 216n.

22. Richard Chase, *Herman Melville, A Critical Study.* New York: Hafner, 1971, p. 185.

23. John G. Cawelti, "Some Notes on the Structure of *The Confidence-Man.*" *American Literature* 29 (1957):278-288.

24. Foster, ref. 4, p. lxxxviii.

25. Martin Buber, *Pointing the Way: Collected Essays.* edited and translated with Introduction by Maurice Friedman, New York: Harper Torchbooks, 1963, cited by Maurice Friedman, *Problematic Rebel: Melville, Dostoievsky, Kafka, Camus.* Chicago and London: University of Chicago Press, revised 1970, p. 94.

Chapter 8

The Poetry and *Clarel*: The Years About 1859

The conflict of science and faith, expressed in most of Melville's works, beginning in the earliest records of man, erupted in controversy at the end of the decade of the 1850s just after Melville's major creative period from *Typee* in 1846 to *The Confidence-Man* in 1857. The main issue at the end of the decade was the question of divine design. Earlier, Hume had mounted a skeptical attack on the logical structure of many design arguments and on the rational basis of scientific inquiry. Hume did not accept the underlying order and rationality of the world. *Dialogues Concerning Natural Religion*, published posthumously, argues that the design argument is unscientific since there can be no causal explanation for the order of nature; analogical reasoning is too weak to give any sort of proof, and all negative evidence had been neglected. Hume maintained that one could argue as well for a disorderly cause if one concentrated upon the disorderly aspects of the world's structure. He not so much refutes the design argument as questions that divine design can be decided from available evidence: our position in the universe introduces limitations such that problems of design cannot be meaningfully posed. His argument was largely neglected; Samuel Johnson and Joseph Priestley thought he was merely being mischievous or frivolous; his writings were ignored and lay dormant for many years; yet a number of prominent men adopted his concepts, especially Eramus Darwin, who enthusiastically endorsed Hume's critical position. The most famous, however, was Kant.[1]

Kant read Hume's *Dialogues* in 1780 and later acknowledged his debt to Hume. Kant had tried to reconcile the mechanical and teleological views of Leibniz and Newton while maintaining a cautious respect for the design argument. In the *Critique of Pure Reason*, Kant deals with the "Physico-Theological Argument," outlines the evidence for design, then undermines its logical foundation, arguing that statements about the world can neither be proved nor disproved by reason alone; the system of empirical laws is adapted to the faculties of our own cognition in "self-created categories" which cannot be determined by observation—they are *a priori* conditions. Kant was enormously influential on German biologists in the first half of the nineteenth century. Mechanical, physical laws were expected to explain life at the chemical level without need of 'vital forces.' In spite of advances, especially in embryology, they felt that it was impossible for organisms to change their fundamental plan of organization from external influences. Kant had little effect on the movement toward the design argument growing in England where his ideas were eclipsed by Paley's *Natural Theology*, a minor classic in "the gospel according to anthropocentric design" of naive science. Paley achieved remarkable clarity of explanation where Kant's exposition was a model of obscurity. Paley brought to the attention of scientists the role of adaptation in the natural world. His work stimulated numerous similar works by the leading scientists in England, although Barrow and Tipler conclude most can be summed up by William Prout's statement, "The argument of design is necessarily cumulative; that is to say, is made up of many similar arguments!" However in Germany, Karl Ernst von Baer (1792-1876) remarked in 1834 on the possibility of organic change, and Goethe (1749-1832) commented on the bias of Man in thinking that everything on earth is "to serve his personal profit."[2] Whether the argument of design is ultimately proven or not, Paley remains important as a figure who refused to separate reason and faith; and showed that it is possible to retain empirical fact in the discussion of religion without forgoing logical consistency, even though we can no longer believe precisely what he believed.[3]

At the end of the eighteenth and the beginning of the nineteenth centuries, scientific emphasis shifted to geology and cosmology, as contained in most of Melville's works. Corsi claims that the debate which geologists and naturalists had launched in the early 1830s became of great relevance to laymen as well as religious philosophers: "The question of how to interpret natural operations or the relationship between the view of nature disclosed by science and the religious representation of creation was a problem which concerned the believer and the philosopher as much as the geologist..." The debate during the late 1840s and 1850s included the geographical distribution of organic forms, inquiries into the natural history of man, discoveries in embryology and physiology, the accumulation of paleontological data, and broad theological and natural theological considerations relevant to the puzzle of species, and a dissatisfaction on the mechanism of transmutation of species. The years 1855 to 1859 were characterized by a growing awareness that the transformist synthesis, i.e. the transformation of species, many had feared or hoped for since the late 1830s was now approaching.[4]

During the nineteenth century, science was still naive and innocent, which led to a belief that steady progress of civilization was possible. "Scientism," the belief that all human life is to be understood through science and that science can give us the values we need, was urged by various thinkers representing a major challenge to traditional Christianity, although many prominent scientists remained more or less orthodox members of churches.[5] Edward Hitchcock (1793-1864), a respected geologist and Congregational minister in Massachusetts and at one time president of Amherst College, was concerned that geology harbored dangers for traditional religion and devoted his life to the furtherance of natural, or scientific, theology that would make religion a branch of science. He became the leader of the movement, publishing his principles in *The Religion of Geology and Its Connected Sciences* in 1851.[6] Faith in a caring (theistic) God encountered the "nebular hypothesis" of Laplace; the earth and planets had coalesced from a cloud of diffuse matter surrounding the sun—an idea stated in 1795 but not appreciated by the American popular press until the 1840s after it had already been assimilated by eminent scientists. Some theologians sensed that geological uniformitarianism might be associated with biological development, removing God from the life of man to a time in the unimaginably remote past. Although fossil records left many gaps, natural explanations gradually took precedence over the supernatural accounts of Creation.[7]

Through the 1850s, led by Agassiz, scientists generally endorsed the view of progressionism, catastrophism, and the fixity of species, but the laity, surrounded by change, endorsed development and change.

Into this entente appeared Chambers's *Vestiges* (1844), bitterly attacked by theologian and scientist alike and restoring harmony between the two. Nevertheless, theologians had conceded jurisdiction of the interpretation of Genesis to scientists who would relegate God to a remote first cause, or even displace God altogether. An informed and interested public saw scientific knowledge based on dispassionate reasoning from verifiable data steadily gain in authority and material promise, while theological dogma was losing its credibility. Most theologians feared biological developmentalism, which would threaten the special creation of the human race.[8] The conflict of science and faith, and the remoteness of God "whose only voice is silence" was-well known to Melville, greatly influencing his major works. In 1859, the focus of theological and scientific attention dramatically shifted to biology. The progress in geology, stratigraphy, the study of fossil shells, fossil remains of vertebrates, linguistics, world exploration, technology, and social welfare was growing in public awareness. Ironically, the most influential scientist to disturb the detente of science and faith studied theology at Cambridge; the meaning of vast, diverse discoveries in the natural world were synthesized by the genius of Darwin.

Charles Darwin (1809-1882), the son and grandson of prominent physicians, attended Edinburgh University to study medicine, but found he could not tolerate the "ghastly" aspects of medical studies, and left to take a degree from Christ's College, Cambridge, in 1831, to prepare for the clergy. At both universities, he made the acquaintance of important scientists. His professor at Cambridge, John Henslow, arranged for Darwin to sail aboard the *H.M.S. Beagle* as a naturalist on a voyage of exploration from December 1831 to October 1836. Darwin published his observations in *Journal of Researches* (1839), read by Melville aboard the *United States* in 1843-1844. Two themes recur throughout Darwin's life: adaptation as both state and process, and continuity through transformation: both emerged in his early work on his theory of the formation of coral reefs.[9] By the late 1830s, Darwin had broken with the contemporary acceptance of natural theology. His mechanistic interpretation meant that natural selection would work whether or not one believed in the Creator since it operated on the everyday, deterministic laws of nature.[10] The earliest record of Darwin's theorizing about the transmutation of species was written in a notebook during March 1837, one of the most explored aspects of Darwin studies.[11] Definition of species was not entirely clear to the naturalists, nor was what constituted a variety, for "theory-laden definitions" were replaced with other "theory-laden definitions" and were necessarily arbitrary.[12]

Speciation is still a problem that remains unexplained in spite of great advances in genetics.[13]

The observation on the relationship of geographically separated animals, i.e., those living on the mainland compared with the same species on islands, and time separated animals, i.e., comparing extinct with living animals, led Darwin to doubt the long held view of fixity of species. Darwin's voyage on the *Beagle*, especially the visit to the Galápagos Islands, and the observation that closely related species replaced one another as he journeyed southward along the coast of South America, were particularly important in the development of his theory. He was influenced by Charles Lyell's theory of uniformitarianism and the notion of unlimited geological time. Malthus's *Essay on the Principle of Population* (1826), which Darwin read in 1838, along with his own observations, led him to the idea of competition among species for existence. Since all species show some variation, he reasoned those individuals with more favorable variations would have a better chance of survival than those with unfavorable variations, leading to a competition for existence resulting in the survival by natural selection; i.e., change in species without design—free from miraculous, divine intervention. In June 1858, Darwin received a manuscript from Alfred Russell Wallace (1823-1912), then at the Molucca Islands in Indonesia, containing an abstract of his own theory which was very similar to Darwin's. A joint presentation was read to the Linnean Society on July 1, 1858, "On the Tendency of Species to Form Varieties; and on the Perpetuation of Varieties and Species by Natural Means of Selection." Darwin quickly completed his remarkable work, *On the Origin of Species by Means of Natural Selection, or the Preservation of Favoured Races in the Struggle for Life*, and it was published November 24, 1859. The entire edition sold on the day of issue.

The outburst of shock and dismay at Darwin's theory of evolution by natural selection, called by some the "ape theory," denounced from the pulpit and by the press, culminated in a public debate the following year at Oxford. Darwinianism could not be dispassionately regarded; it became a creed to be accepted or rejected with religious vehemence and enthusiasm. The encounter of Thomas Huxley, English biologist, and Samuel Wilberforce, Bishop of Oxford, on June 30, 1860, has become a legend in the interaction of science and religion. The debate was on Saturday at the end of the week-long annual meeting of the British Association for the Advancement of Science, which was largely used to popularize science. Huxley was the the leading protagonist for Darwin, and Wilberforce the chief spokesman for the conservative stand of the church. The debate was not necessarily science against religion, but science against science in that Wilberforce had on his side the most eminent naturalists assembled at Oxford, including Sir Richard Owen, physician and comparative anatomist [mentioned by Melville in *Moby-Dick,* Chapter 104], and Sir Benjamin Brodie, surgeon [mentioned in *White-Jacket*]. Wilberforce handled the large and fractious audience better than Huxley and most gave him credit for winning the encounter, although the 'legend' accounts Huxley the winner with a resounding rejoinder to a personal remark by Wilberforce. Darwinians, in small numbers in 1860, grew into a dominant majority over the next twenty years, but never lost the sense of being persecuted, an effect of Huxley's personality. In fact, the Huxley-Wilberforce debate was one of many 'skirmishes' occurring at Oxford during the meetings of the British Association.[14] Outside of London, the British Association, whose first meeting was at York in 1831, was the chief agency for the spread of the message of the "Church Scientific."[15] Huxley, who became known as "Darwin's bulldog," gained his early experience as a naturalist aboard a British naval vessel, but his main interests were anatomy and paleontology. During the 1850s, he decided that science must be made free of theology; he ridiculed *Vestiges*, but on reading *Origin*, he immediately recognized a plausible hypothesis that opened the subject to scientific investigation. Huxley had been persuaded to attend the Oxford meeting of the British Association for the Advancement of Science by Chambers. Huxley went on to become a leading public figure, serving as an expert for the government on a number of scientific matters, and later becoming one of the men behind-the-scenes who shaped much of late Victorian science.[16] Darwin never used the term "evolution," but referred to "descent with modification."[17]

Although the principal cause of the hostility between Darwinians and orthodox religion was the destruction of the design argument, the relegation of the special status of man to that of animals was equally important. Charles Hodge said in *What is Darwinism* (1874): "It is, however, neither evolution nor natural selection which gives Darwinism its peculiar character and importance. It is that Darwin rejects all teleology, or the doctrine of final causes." Huxley saw that the mechanistic view of life must regard the later products of natural selection as a completely determined function of initial molecular configurations: "that things are as they are only because they were as they were." Huxley said, "Evolution has no more to do with theism than the first book of Euclid has."[18] Unlimited change and unqualified purposelessness were the philosophical implications of Darwinism that sent shudders through the nineteenth-century believer. These philosophical concepts had been equally implicit in every scientific advance since Galileo, but Darwin brought them into the open when he applied them to the hitherto sacrosanct topic of the origin and destiny of man. With *Origin,* the meaningless sea of endless, mindless nature seemed to darken man's existence.[19]

After returning from the voyage of the *Beagle* in 1836, Darwin became a semi-invalid recluse able to work no more than four hours a day and did not participate in the storm of controversy that arose about his theory, called "biological evolution." Nevertheless, he was well aware of the conflict with theology. Lyell wrote in *Principles of Geology* (1867):

> From the hour of its appearance it gave, as Professor Huxley truly said, 'a new direction to biological speculation,' for even where it failed to make proselytes, it gave a shock to old and time-honoured opinions from which they have never since recovered.[20]

In America, Asa Gray, who was originally strongly anti-evolutionary, tried to include the possibility of design in Darwin's theory; he never abandoned design throughout the controversy over evolution. Agassiz, on the other hand, was strongly anti-evolutionary. To Agassiz, the search for design was the purpose of science. Agassiz was joined by James Russell Lowell in criticizing Darwin, saying, "Such mush seems to me a poor substitute for the Rock of Ages." When Agassiz died in 1873, the main scientific opponent to evolution was lost. After the American Civil War, religion took little interest in evolution and scientists often had little interest in the implications of their work.[21] Melville was aware of the work of scientists as well as the work of philosophers; he cited important philosophers and scientists throughout his works, and faithfully reflected the conflict of science and religion in the pre-Darwin mid-nineteenth century. During the years following his European voyage (1856-1857), Melville was not occupied in any particular undertaking; he undoubtedly followed the dramatic events occurring in England as well as America involving the controversy over Darwin's theory and its implications on faith.

By any standard, the Darwinian revolution of 1859 was truly revolutionary. By destroying the anthropocentric design concept of the universe, it caused a greater upheaval of man's thinking than any other scientific advance since the rebirth of science in the Renaissance. Yet, the acceptance of evolution was remarkably long in occurring. According to Mayr: "The long time span is due to the fact that not simply the acceptance of one new theory was involved; as in some other scientific revolutions, but of an entirely new conceptual world, consisting of numerous separate concepts and beliefs. And not only were scientific theories involved, but also a whole set of metascientific credos": the age of the earth; refutation of both catastrophism (progressionism) and of a steady-state world; refutation of the concept of automatic upward development (or steady progress toward perfection in the living world); the rejection of creationism; and the abolition of anthropocentrism. In addition, it had far greater relevance outside of science than any of the revolutions occurring in the physical sciences. Even though a revolutionary climax occurred in 1859, the gradual development of evolutionary theory spanned a period of 250 years.[22]

Intense excitement occurred for a period after 1859; scientists spoke of philosophy, religion, and the cosmos in subjects remote from their areas of knowledge, but seldom achieving more than clumsy and inept speculation. Dupree says, "...talk of conversion to Darwinism was on everyone's tongue, and to the extent that conversion was from one scientific concept to another, one can speak of revolution." The "tree of life" became a metaphorical alternative to the Creation myth. Not everyone could qualify for the 'church scientific.' Huxley could lecture to the working man, but not evangelize him. Having learned the lesson of authoritarian absolutism in religion, the world after Darwin faced the problem of how not to repeat the tragedy with an authoritarianism based on the worship of science.[23] Charles Hodge (1797-1878) replied in *What is Darwinism?* (1875), that one had to choose between an intellectual process ruled by God or a material process ruled by chance: they were not compatible. He said *Origin* contained three components: evolution, natural selection, and natural selection without design. The first two were not new and could be traced to the work of William Wells and Patrick Matthew. Only the third, natural selection without intelligent cause, was new in Darwin's theory, its most important element, which was unacceptable in *Vestiges* saying, "The conclusion of the whole matter, is that the denial of design in nature is virtually the denial of God." Those who would try to reconcile evolution and religion did not realize Darwin's challenge was so fundamental. After Darwin's *Origin* of 1959, the relation between God, man, and nature could never again be as clear as it once had been.[24] In France, Darwinism aroused little interest. In Germany, it became a symbol opposed to traditional religion and a promise of progress in human affairs.[25] The remarkable advances occurring in the natural sciences, especially geology and biology, were included in the poetic works of Melville in the years following the period of his novels.

Melville corrects a statement in *Pierre* that the earth is stratified to its core in the poem, "The Apparition. (A Retrospect)." He incorporates the geological theory of Cordier (1827) on the molten state of the earth's interior, the rise of new volcanoes, and sinkholes:

> Convulsions came; and, where the field
>   Long slept in pastoral green,
> A goblin-mountain was upheaved
> (Sure the scared sense was all deceived),
>   Marl-glen and slag-ravine.
>
> The unreserve of Ill was there,
>   The clinkers in her last retreat;
> But, ere the eye could take it in,
> Or mind could comprehension win,
>   It sunk!—and at our feet.
>
> So, then, Solidity's a crust—
>   The core of fire below;
> All may go well for many a year,
> But who can think without a fear
>   Of horrors that happen so?

The upheaved, goblin mountain is probably a newly formed volcano. The appearance of a new volcano in modern times is a rare and remarkable event. The Jurullo volcano was born on September 29, 1759, about 150 miles west of Mexico City on the Pacific slope of the Mexican plateau; it is one of the best known volcanoes born in historic times. Accounts by eyewitnesses reported subterranean noises and earthquakes beginning in June 1759 until the appearance of the volcanic eruption in September 1759. A mass of fiery hot sand flowed nearly a mile down a creek obstructing neighboring streams, the "marl-glen and slag-ravine"; in addition, the volcano was accompanied by heavy rain, as often occurs with volcanic eruptions, causing extensive flooding and loss of domestic animals. The cone rose to a height of 380 meters above its base. No lava flow came from the crater until 1764, ceasing after about 15 years. Other 'new' volcanoes are Monte Nuovo near Naples, Italy, born in 1538, and most recently the Paricutin volcano, born in a corn field in Mexico in 1943. Volcanoes commanded respect by all civilizations. Greek mythology attributed volcanic eruptions to Vulcan, the god of fire. Virgil wrote that the giant Enceladus was buried under Mt. Etna, an active volcano, and his struggles to free himself caused frequent earthquakes in the area. Pliny the Younger described the eruption of Vesuvius in 79 A.D., the first account of volcanic activity free of supernatural meaning. According to early Christian teachings persisting well into the nineteenth century, hell was located somewhere near the center of the earth, and volcanoes were thought to be the gateway to the infernal regions. Little more was contributed to the understanding of volcanoes until they became part of the controversy of the neptunists and the plutonists in the eighteenth and nineteenth centuries. Charles Lyell devoted a large part of *Principles of Geology* (1830), to the question of volcanoes. Leopold von Buch (1774-1853), a student of Abraham Werner's, disagreed with Lyell on the formation of volcanic cones. Von Buch claimed that the earth rises like a 'blister' forming "craters-of-elevation," conflicting with Lyell's "craters-of-accumulation" resulting from the accumulation of ejected material. Monte Nuovo, born near Naples, Italy, in the volcanic area of the Phlegraean Fields in 1538, became an important subject in the debate on the formation of volcanic cones studied intensely by both geologists; the theory of accumulation is now considered so obvious the uplift theory seems absurd.[26]

Lyell traveled to Sicily to investigate Mt. Etna and found that the massive cone had been built up gradually through a long series of comparatively small eruptions, with only the last few recorded in historic times. Thus, the volcano must be immensely old, yet the cone rests on rocks that must be geologically very recent since they contain fossils of mollusks almost identical to those now living in the Mediterranean Sea. He concluded that the volcano had formed by the action of a series of earthquakes, not a single catastrophic upheaval, a process that must have taken an unimaginable period of time.[27] The reason catastrophism was adopted by virtually all of the leading geologists in the first half of the nineteenth century is that the available facts seemed to support it—breaks in fossil strata, the occurrence of vast lava flows, replacement of terrestrial deposits by marine ones and the reverse, and other phenomenon of a violent nature—all decisively refuted the gradual, uniformitarian view.[28]

Adding to Melville's observation of the impermanence of the earth's surface ("It sunk!—and at our feet.") is the occurrence of sinkholes, depressions in the earth's surface resulting from the collapse of limestone caves. Sinkholes occur in karst terrain, i.e., barren, rocky ground with caves, underground rivers, and the absence of surface streams and lakes. Karst occurs in many areas of the world and in the United States in southern Illinois, Indiana, and the Mammoth Cave areas of Kentucky. The underground rivers dissolve and carry away the limestone, which is readily soluble in slightly acidic water, leading to collapse. The poem gives strong evidence that Melville kept abreast of the rapid changes in geology occurring in the latter part of the nineteenth century.

"New Zealot of the Sun," which traces the sun from an object of worship to a promise greater than sunlight, concludes:

> But science yet
> An effluence ampler shall beget,
> And power beyond your play—
> Shall quell the shades you fail to rout,
> Yea, searching every secret out
> Elucidate your ray.

The idea that the sun and heavens gave signs of supernatural omens was being rapidly discredited by scientific inquiry.

The Malthusian theory of overpopulation that was so influential in Darwin's theory of evolution occurs in "The Ground Vine":

> O Rose, we plants are all akin,
> Our roots enlock; Each strives to win
> The ampler space, the balmier air.
> But beauty, plainness, shade, and sun—
> Here share-and-share-alike is none.

A year before *Origin of Species,* Darwin wrote of "the dreadful but quiet war of organic beings going on in the peaceful woods and smiling fields," while Melville wrote of the war of nature: "Consider once more, the universal cannibalism of the sea; all whose creatures prey upon each other, carrying on eternal war since the world began" (*Moby-Dick* Ch 58) and "And all the time, lo! that smiling sky, and this unsounded sea! Look! see yon Albicore! who put it into him to chase and fang that flying-fish" (*Moby-Dick* Ch 132).[29] The term "survival of the fittest" was coined not by Darwin, but by Herbert Spencer.[30]

Melville's satirization of science and exposition of pretense reach their culmination in his grand spoof, "The New Ancient of Days: The Man in the Cave of Engihoul." The high spirits of the poem resemble *Mardi,* but other evidence suggests composition at a later date. The study of rock strata, caves, and superficial deposits during the first half of the nineteenth century, particularly the Brixham cave near Torquay in Devonshire, England, in 1858, found evidence of a far greater antiquity of man than previously imagined.[31] The dominant goal of geologists at this period was to discover the true order of succession of rock strata and their fossils. Behind this enterprise lay the higher theoretical goal of reconstructing the main outlines of the history of the earth and the history of life on earth.[32] The Engis skull was found in 1835 by Professor P.C. Schmerling, anatomist and paleontologist, in Grotte d'Engis along the banks of the Meuse River near Liege, Belgium, beneath five feet of rock breccia in association with extinct Pleistocene fauna of the glacial period 10,000 to 1,000,000 years ago. The implications of the skull were argued in scientific circles and in the public press. Later, the skull was thought to be the first of the "missing links" proving evolution and threatening to displace the theory of Creation. The Engis skull and the Neanderthal fossils (found in 1856) were on the border of modern man, but were not convincing examples of a "missing link." The discovery of the Java man in 1891 by Eugene Dubois was the first fossil of man's ape-like ancestors to enhance the position of the evolutionists.[33] The title of the poem is taken from a scriptural term for the Almighty, "I beheld till the thrones set up and the Ancient of dayes did sit" (Daniel, 7:9), with the implication that science, or the discovery of a fossil man, is the new "god." The naturalist is the focus of his satire:

> The man of bone confirms his throne
> In cave where fossils be;
> Outdating every mummy known,
> Not older Cuvier's mastodon,
> Nor older much the sea:
> Old as the Glacial Period, he;
> And claims he calls to mind the day
> When Thule's king, by reindeer drawn,
> His sleigh-bells jingling in icy morn,
> Slid clean from the Pole to the Wetterhorn
> Over frozen waters in May!
> Oh, the man of the cave of Engihoul,
> With Eld doth he dote and drule?

Mastodon, coined by Cuvier in 1806, is the term for a large extinct mammal resembling an elephant and characterized by nipple-shaped tubercules in pairs on the crown of the molar teeth. The Glacial period (or epoch) occurred during the recent Pleistocene era, 10,000 to 1,000,000 years ago when the northern hemisphere was covered by a glacial ice sheet, a theory developed by Agassiz. Thule is the ancient Greek and Latin name for a land six day's sail north of Britain supposed to be the most northerly region of the world, first found in Polybius's (ca 205-123 B.C.) account of the voyage of Pytheas. "Eld" refers to the great age of the fossils of the Engihoul cave.[34] The first stanza establishes the importance of vast expanses of time and the antiquity of the fossil bones.

> A wizard one, his lore is none
>   Ye spell with A.B.C.;
> But *do-do* tracks, all up and down
> That slate he poreth much upon,
>   His algebra may be:—
> Yea, there he cyphers and sums it free;
> To all ages Indus met ocean's swell
> Addeth aeons ere Satan or Saturn fell.
> His totals of time make in awful schism,
> And old Chronos he pitches adown the abysm
> Like a pebble down Carisbrook well.
>   Yea, the man of the cave of Engihoul
>   From Moses knocks under the stool.

The wizard is probably Charles Lyell. The Carisbrook well, located in Carisbrooke on the Isle of Wight, England, is a medieval well 161 feet deep where the bucket is still drawn by a donkey. Indus, or indusial limestone, mentioned by Lyell in *Principles of Geology* (1833), is the limestone of Auvergne composed of encrusted larvae formed into rock.[35] By the middle of the nineteenth century, the idea of limitless time was assimilated into most of geological thought until the estimates of the rate of earth sedimentation and the determination of the rate of cooling of the planet more or less agreed on about 100,000 years as the age of the earth. Not until 1859 did the concept of time become important in scientific discourse when Darwin used an extravagant estimate of time for his theory. This allowed his adversaries to attack him at a weak point not supported by firm scientific evidence. The time of 100,000 years was not long enough to convincingly permit the changes in species Darwin proposed. Some attempts were made during the rest of the nineteenth century to return to the biblical time scale of 4,000 years, but Mosaic geology gradually lost ground, or was pitched "down Carisbrook well." Shorter periods of time, as brief as 50,000 years, were advanced later in the nineteenth century, placing further doubt on Darwin's theory.[36]

In *bas-relief* he late has shown
  A horrible show, agree
Megalosaurus, iguanodon
Palaeotherium Glypthaecon,
  A Barnum-show raree;
  The vomit of slimy and sludgey sea:
Purposeless creatures, odd inchoate things
Which splashed thro' morasses on fleshly wings;
The cubs of Chaos, with eyes askance,
Preposterous griffins that squint at Chance
And Anarch's cracked decree!
  Oh the showman who dens in Engihoul,
  Would he fright us, or quit us, or fool?

The griffin is a fabulous animal with head and wings of an eagle and the body and hind-quarters of a lion.[37] Possibly the reference to the griffin was taken from Lewis Carroll's *Alice in Wonderland*, if not, Melville and Carroll shared similar insights on evolution. The megalosaurus was a giant carnivorous lizard first mentioned by Buckland in 1824. The iguanadon, a large herbivorous lizard found in the Weaden formations, and the palaeotherm, an extinct tapir-like mammal fossil in the Eocene and Miocene strata, are mentioned by Lyell in *Principles of Geology.* Melville suggests "Anarch," i.e., chance or chaos without a head or chief, dominated nature rather than divine design. Stein says, "Investing dusty fossils in weighty scientific roots, the evolutionary theorists create the freaks for their imaginary environments, out of time and out of mind."[38] Geology was most important in Darwin's revolutionary concept of biology:

But, needs to own, he takes a tone,
  Satiric on nobs, pardee!
"Though in ages whose term is yet to run,
Old Adam a seraph may have for son,
  His gran'ther's a crab, d'y'see!
And why cut your kinsman the ape?" asks he:
"Your trick of scratching is borrowed from him,
Grimace and cunning, with many a whim,
Your fidgets and hypoes, and each megrim—
All's traces in the family tree!"
  Ha, the wag of the cave of Engihoul:
  Buss me, gorilla and ghoul!

The influence of evolution and the new discoveries and theories of geology are clear in this stanza. A "nob" is a head, a person of wealth or social standing,[39] or its covert meaning "by God."[40] A "pardee," or pardie, is an oath, as an asseveration.[41] "Old Adam" may have had a seraph, a fossil univalved shell, for an ancestor; a seraph is also an invisible member of the holy choir. This stanza is a statement of evolution and its critics. In 1864, Benjamin Disraeli, in a speech at Oxford, said of Darwinism: "What is the question now placed before society with glib assurance the most astounding? The question is this—Is man an ape or an angel? My Lord, I am on the side of the angels."[42] Melville's satire contains a certain fearfulness of the shock of the theory of evolution and its godless implications:

Obsterperous grown he's fain dethrone
  Joe Smith, and e'en Jones Three;
Against even Jos and great Mahone
He flings his fossiliffer's stone
  And rattles his shanks for glee.
  I'll settle these parvenu fellows, he-he!
Diluvian Jove of Ducalion's day—
A parting take to the Phocene clay!
He swears no Ens that takes a name
Commensurate is with the vasty claim
Of the protoplastic Fegee.
  O, the spook of the cave of Engihoul
  He flogs us and sends us to school.

The fossil skull has become "obstreperous," threatening to displace the comfortable Mosaic account of creation, including some of the prominent religious figures, possibly Joseph Smith (1805-1844), founder of the Mormon Church, who at age fourteen claimed to have received the word of God from engraved plates brought to America by ancestors of American Indians, and including Mahone, Mahoun, or Mahound, a 'false prophet' in the Middle Ages often vaguely imagined to be worshipped as a God. He puns the finding of the fossil bones as the "fossiliffer's stone" or the philosopher's stone, the alchemist's imaginary stone of absolute knowledge and health. Stein says, "A few scraps of a skull beget a brain, the projections of the brain's size a mind, then lo and behold the tables of taxonomy, aided by a geographical location, resurrect another hominoid ancestor," i.e., the process of "correlation of parts," a theory developed by Cuvier. Ducalion, a mythic hero of the Deluge with his wife saved by a tub, spawned a new race out of stones.[43] "Phocene," thought to be an imaginary word as a parody on the excavation, may be from Lyell's classification of geological time; due to Melville's nearly illegible handwriting, the letter "h" may be a combination or blurring of "li," which would read "Pliocene," agreeing with Lyell's nomenclature and the meter of the poem. The Pliocene era is now included in the Pleistocene era, the most recent and current period of geological time covering the time since the ordinary marine stratigraphic record with the present general distribution of land and sea, so that the material evidence of geology is chiefly from superficial land deposits of the Pliocene era. It happens to coincide with the Glacial period, the advent of man, a unique and highly peculiar faunal element, of about one million years. The term was introduced by Lyell in 1839 in a French translation of *Elements of Geology,* and adopted in the present sense in 1873.[44] Jove is the poetical equivalent of Jupiter, the highest deity of the ancient Romans.[45] No "Ens," an entity or something which has existed, is related to the "protoplastic," that which is first formed, archetype, or original, savage.

Hyena of bone! Ah, beat him down,
  Great Pope, with Peter's key,
Ere the Grand Pan-Jam be overthrown
With Joe and Jos and great Mahone,
  And the firmament mix with the sea;
And then, my masters where should we be?
But the ogre of bone he snickers alone,
He grins for his godless glee:
"I have flung my stone, my fossil stone,
And your gods, how they scamper," saith he.
  Imp! imp of the cave of Engihoul,
  Shall he grin like the Gorgon and rule?

Grand Pan-Jam, short for "Grand Panjandrum," probably refers to 'panjamdrum,' a pretentious, self-important official, the burlesque potentate of a nonsense story by Samuel Foote (1770).[46] Along with the other religious figures, "jos," pidgin English for the Portuguese deos, is overthrown and the mystery of the heavens mixes with the earthly ocean in his "godless glee." The "Gorgon" of bone, one of three mythical female personages with snakes for hair whose look turned the beholder to stone,[47] has scattered the divine order and tranquility of science and faith.

In *Principles of Geology*, Lyell relates an account of the work of Schmerling published in 1833-1834 on more than forty ossiferous caverns of the valleys and tributaries of the Meuse River. Schmerling found human bones having the same characteristics, color, etc., mingled with extinct animals including the cavebear, hyena, elephant, and rhinoceros, along with extant species, such as the wildcat, beaver, wild boar, wolf, and hedgehog. The human skeletons were incomplete in most caves, but in the Engis cavern, the remains of cranial bones of at least three human individuals were discovered. On the opposite side of the Meuse, in the cavern of Engihoul, the bones of man were similarly intermingled with the bones of extinct animals. The human remains were mostly extremity bones except for only two small fragments of a cranium. He discovered a number of flint instruments and polished needle-shaped bones causing Schmerling to conclude the caves were used for human habitation contemporaneously with the cave-bear and other extinct animals. Dr. Schmerling concluded, and Lyell concurred, that man had been introduced to the earth at a period earlier than the geologists of the time were willing to believe. Schmerling's unwelcome intelligence from the caves was not greeted warmly by his scientific colleagues or the by the public until twenty-five years after his researches. By 1860, the Engis cave and others had been quarried away for their limestone and nothing remains of the fossil record. The Engihoul cave was still intact, and Lyell explored it in 1860 with Professor Malaise, a naturalist in Liege. At a depth of two feet, Professor Malaise discovered three fragments of a human skull and two intact lower jaws in the same layer as extinct bears, large pachyderms, and other remains in the same state of preservation, placing them as living coexistently. The rock of the caves belongs to the mountain limestone mainly of the older Devonian formation.[48]

Corey says "Ancient" is a startling response to evolution and one of the earliest poetic comments on Darwinism to come out of America.[49] Melville added a note to the manuscript "(See Lyell's *The Antiquity of Man* and Darwin's *The Descent of Species*)" combining Darwin's two books, *The Origin of Species*, and *The Descent of Man*, the last published in 1871. Neither of Darwin's books mentions the Engihoul fossils while Lyell's *The Geological Evidences of the Antiquity of Man* (1863), covers the subject extensively. The quote "beat him down, Great Pope, with Peter's key," probably is a reference to *Syllabus of Errors* (1864) by the first Vatican Council under Pope Pius IX which reaffirmed the authority of the church to rule on the validity of scientific theory. During the 1870s and 1880s, the new science produced great internal conflict in American churches. Huxley and other scientists came to America confronting large audiences with their bewildering theories. Conner agrees that the poem satirizes the two incompatible books appearing at about the same time. Though the poem focuses on the discord between science and faith, it is not an attack by evolution on faith for it takes a non-committal attitude. Conner quotes Thomas Wentworth Higginson, who said at the Boston Radical Club, "The theologian is defunct as a power in the world; but I fear the despotism of science more than the despotism of theology."[50] Stein considers the poem as "logomachy," a war of words on the contradictions of mythology, religion, and scientific descriptions of human origins, in which the words of opposing beliefs ultimately collapse. In addition to the works of Lyell and Darwin noted in the manuscript, Stein says the poem is in the same style as the nonsense poetry of Edward Lear's *A Book of Nonsense* (1846), and *Nonsense Songs and Stories* (1871), as well as Lewis Carroll's *Alice in Wonderland* (1865), and *Alice Through the Looking Glass* (1872). Stein concludes:

> The millions of years so loosely applied to the geological changes in the surface of the earth decline to accommodate the once-upon-a-time wars in the heavens, both Christian and Pagan. Thus, these splits in time, scientific and mythological, posit the necessity of a reconciliatory system of chronometrics. But since no two system-makers ever agree in the definition of terms, Melville's mathematical wizard catapults the falsely deified emperor of time, "Chronos," into the pit of oblivion, there to perish with all his other deposed counterparts.[51]

Like the theme of "Time" in *Pierre*, the poetry includes the disturbing advances in the concept of the age of the earth and of man.

Stein further regards "The New Ancient of Days" to be "A post-Aristotelian assault" on the integrity of language, "its bestial conjurations allegedly confirm the superiority of the human race under the auspices of sacred reason."[52] The enormously expanded scale of time occurring in the early twentieth century revived the theory of Darwin, but by then, the religious implications of evolution had largely subsided.[53] In 1856 in Neanderthal, Germany, other remains were found possibly bordering on modern man. Experts were divided on their interpretation, but in 1891, a young Dutch army doctor made the remarkable discovery of the Java man, a much more convincing link between man and ape-like ancestors.[54]

The oceanic denudation of Weald, in southeast England, and the erosion of the Dover cliffs were used by Lyell as examples of the slow, time-consuming process of geological change. Darwin was convinced that marine action accounted for the shaping of the earth's surface, so an estimate of the time required for the denudation of Weald would allow an estimate of geological time, which he stated in *Origin*. His theory was simple but naive. In the second edition of *Origin*, appearing only a month after the first, he added a disclaimer on the length of time for this geological action. Thus, one of the main premises of biological evolution was under attack at the outset and it would prove to be a vulnerable point. By the time of the third edition of *Origin* in April 1861, all mention of the Weald had been deleted, quieting the critics for a time. By 1868, the unlimited time of Lyell had contracted to finite limits by Kelvin's physics. Further damage to the vast time scale required by evolution came from James Croll, a self-educated Scot, who concluded that the rate of deposit of the earth's crust during the glacial epoches was much faster than had been heretofore realized. Thus, the rate of geological change easily could have occurred in the time limits of Kelvin. However, Croll allowed for the possibility that limited time and natural selection were compatible. By the time of the sixth edition of *Origin*, Darwin was willing to accept that both geological change and biological change could have occurred much more rapidly than had been previously thought and in the future he was much more cautious.[55]

By 1869, Huxley began to withdraw his opposition to the views of Kelvin, and Huxley and Wallace gradually distanced themselves from Darwin's theory of natural selection. Darwin made some concessions in later editions of *Origin*, although he maintained confidence in natural selection, but he faced an insurmountable obstacle in the unknown age of the earth. In 1870, he wrote, "My theology is a simple muddle, I cannot look at the universe as the result of blind chance, yet I can see no evidence of beneficent design of any kind, or indeed of design of any kind, in the details." By 1871, in *The Descent of Man*, Darwin had retreated from his confident stand on natural selection of 1859 after the attack of Fleeming Jenkin criticizing the perpetuation of variations in offspring on the basis that a few variations would be "swamped out of existence" by breeding with the mass of individuals not possessing the altered trait. Only a mass variation at the same time could account for the appearance of a new species.[56] During the 1870s, the last ten years of Darwin's life, geology produced more and more evidence that overwhelmingly favored the limited time scale of Kelvin; at the same time, paleontology produced vast amounts of information supporting the gradual evolution of new species. The contrast of brevity of time and the extreme slowness of organic change remained as perplexing as ever. In the end, Darwin left the problem of geological time to younger scientists to solve, yet he remained convinced his theory would be vindicated.[57] As Darwin grew older, he abandoned the views of an orthodox member of the Church of England and became an agnostic; yet, the man whose sacrilegious ideas had been publicly assailed from the pulpit and press was buried in Westminster Abbey near the grave of Sir Isaac Newton.

In the early nineteenth century, the interpretation of Genesis was foremost in intellectual study; yet professional biblical criticism was slow in developing in England and excluded from Oxford and Cambridge except by a few nonconformists. At the same time, divinity students from Scotland studying in Germany in the 1840s returned with new and advanced ideas to teach in Edinburgh as early as 1847; similar studies did not begin at Oxford and Cambridge until 1869 and 1871. Germany was the principle source of biblical expertise because scholars functioned in an atmosphere of unprecedented academic freedom unknown in Britain and America. German scholars achieved a level of critical intensity matched only by the sciences in Britain and America: Genesis was studied as intently as geology. Parity between the two did not occur in the English-speaking countries until late in the nineteenth century. With the work of Benjamin Jowett (1817-1893) and Baden Powell (1796-1860), published in *Essays and Reviews* in 1860, German critical scholarship was adopted in that the Bible should be interpreted like any other book. *Essays* served the same purpose as Lyell's *Principles of Geology,* placing the two on equal basis to be studied and interpreted in whatever manner developed without need of a compromise with the traditional reading of Genesis.

Although the nineteenth century abounded in religious controversy, *Essays and Reviews* (1860), surpassed them all. The controversy raged for five years, then returned with violence in 1869. Seven essayists including Benjamin Jowett and Baden Powell, sanctioned a critical study of the Bible, arguing that the verification of Christianity no longer depends upon external evidences, especially miracles, but on the appeal to moral and spiritual experience. The essayists acknowledged their debt to Coleridge. Other essays suggested the Mosaic cosmogony should be regarded as a simple Hebrew creation myth, and another that since theology had grown in the past, it would continue to develop in the future. If *Essays* had a single theme, it was an acknowledgement of the need for new criticism, the same ideas that had occupied German theologians for half a century. Beginning in October 1860, *Essays* was bitterly attacked. Among the attackers was Samuel Wilberforce, who accused the essayists of "[s]carcely veiled atheism, open scepticism, laxity, and daring flippancy." The book sold enormously well and created a major stir, greatly upsetting the bishops of the Church of England to the point of seeking prosecution of the essayists.[58] The growth of experts or professionals in both geology and theology joined together against the meddlesome, censorious amateurs; rank and wealth yielded to merit and expertise. After 1860, the irrelevance of the scriptural geologists became apparent. Darwin had relieved the naturalists of the obligation of glorifying God. The principal harmonizers of religion and science had died. *Essays and Reviews* had precipitated the alliance, going through thirteen editions in five years and stimulating replies from over 400 books, pamphlets, and articles reaffirming the authority of the Bible. The conflict between science and religion was a social reality, but the professional scientist and the professional interpreters of the Old Testament supported each other. By 1890, scientists were free to interpret Genesis in their own manner with full approval of professional Old Testament scholars.[59]

In the years following the publication of *Origin*, the principle criticism was that Darwin's theory was not inductive; that it was based on assumptions instead of facts. Darwin was accused of deserting the true British scientific tradition inaugurated by Francis Bacon and exemplified by Newton. The theory of natural selection was also hypothetical; he postulated, but did not prove, that variations in nature were random in the selection of the fittest offspring. The inductive method was viewed as a uniquely British contribution, contrasted to the abstract and barren deductive methods of the Continental schools, especially the French. The English mind was down-to-earth, practical; thus, a departure into speculative theory was not only not scientific, but a betrayal of the British cause, if not also morally reprehensible. The critics were little interested in science, for science was the concern of a small minority, whereas the concern of the majority was the stability of society.[60] A few scientists adopted Darwinism readily. For example, Henry Baker Tristram, British ornithologist and canon of Durham, studied the birds of North Africa and was one of the first scientists to adopt evolution of species after the paper of Darwin and Wallace in 1858, even prior to the publication of *Origin*. However, he reconverted to orthodoxy following the Huxley-Wilberforce debate at Oxford in 1860.[61] The question of evolution is still debated. Sharpe illustrates the disquietude over Darwinianism:

> Evolution...is a myth, not a precise biological theory but a story providing an undergirding framework for understanding ourselves, our activities, values and hopes. The same is true for the use of the second law of thermodynamics to show the universe is 'running down', with a limited life expectancy, and various consequences (often pessimistic) of that.[62]

A more sardonic critic of the times put it this way: "Leave my ancestors in Paradise and I will allow you yours in the Zoological Gardens."[63]

By the end of the American Civil War in 1865, geology had irrevocably displaced the importance of theology and the Mosaic account of Creation causing changes and American social philosophy in a crisis of religious thought. According to Bezanson:

> Inherited beliefs were struggling especially with three successive developments in science: geology, with its implicit attack on Genesis and hence revelation; higher criticism, advocate of a new approach to Sacred History in keeping with scientific methods; and evolution, exponent of biological process as the explanation of man's history.[64]

The controversy was largely in Europe; the American Civil War diverted attention for a time, but the struggle was felt in America soon after the war ended. Leading popular magazines carried subjects on immortality, evolution, God, hell, and comparative religion. Melville recognized the potential danger in the growing dominance of science and technology.

During the 1860's, Melville developed an idea he had been pondering for some time leading to his next major work, a lengthy poem based on his travels to Europe and the Levant in 1856-1857: *Clarel: A Poem of Pilgrimage in the Holy Lands*, written over nearly twenty years, and published in 1876. He challenged popular nineteenth century notions of progress, optimism, and meliorism, and examined the promise of transcendentalism in which scientific investigations and conclusions produced a spiritual vacuum—the loss of faith in the advance of science.

The student Clarel journeys through the Holy Lands accompanied by the evangelist Nehemiah. Nehemiah is an "aged millenialist," innocent and childlike, who befriends Clarel in Jerusalem and joins the pilgrimage at Clarel's expense; he is orthodox, and carries an open

Bible. A number of fellow travelers journey with them for a time, somewhat similar to *Mardi* and *The Confidence-Man*. Rolfe is a roving American adventurer, the central figure among Clarel's companions, an experienced world traveler, mariner, and intellectual who assumes leadership of the group. An ideal union of "head and heart" with a wide range of qualities balanced by personal warmth; he is tolerant and non-sectarian, but feels the acute spiritual and institutional crisis of his time. Although he has the best knowledge of the past and a respect for the ancient world, he doubts that any one person, creed, or society can have final answers. "In the long run Rolfe is sure only that God exists, that good and evil are tightly braided together, and the world is undecipherable and will remain so, and that the tragic view is the only tenable one."[65] They meet Margoth, a German geologist; Rolfe says:

> "An Israelite, say, Hegelized—
> Convert to science, but for see
> The hammer; yes, geology."...(II,xix,55-57)

According to Bezanson, Georg Hegel (1770-1831), German philosopher, was cited for his dialectical materialism; he was actually an idealist, radically hostile to natural science—as Rolfe seemed not to know.[66] Margoth says:

> "Whereof I've taken strict account
> (Its first geologist, believe),
> And, if my eyes do not deceive,
> 'Tis Jura limestone, every spur;
> Yes, and though signs the rocks imprint
> Which of Plutonic action hint,
> No track is found, I plump aver,
> Of Pluto's footings—Lucifer." (II,xix,58-71)

The detail of "Jura limestone" lends credence to his use of geology, but the Jura Mountains lie between the Rhine and Rhone rivers in France and Switzerland and show evidence of extensive glaciation. He probably means the Jurassic period of 135 to 180 million years ago characterized by the presence of dinosaurs and conifers. Melville hints that the cause of the geologic formations is not the great Neptunian flood, but the coalesced fireball of Lucifer. "Uncouthly Margoth" denies the mystery of the volcano:

"Sirs, heed me:
This total tract," and Esau's hand
He waived; "the plain—the vale—Lot's sea—
It needs we scientists remand
Back from old theologic myth
To geologic hammers. Pray,
Let me but give ye here the pith:
As the Phlegraean fields no more
Befool men as the spookish shore
Where Jove felled giants, but are known—
The Solfatara and each cone
Volcanic—to be but on a par
With all things natural; even so
Siddim shall likewise be set far
From fable." (II,xx,45-59)

Scientists had determined the meaning of Jove, or Jupiter, the most powerful of the gods of the ancients. The Phlegraean fields were the mythical site of the great battle between the gods and the Titans, variously located, but most commonly at Solfatara outside Naples, the site of a dormant volcano with escaping steam and gases. Melville's *Journal* of 1856-1857 records "Went to the Solfatara—smoke—landscape not so very beautiful—Sulfurous & aridity, the end of the walk."[67] The Siddim Plain lies beside the Dead Sea and its importance in faith will surely give way to an examination by science. With scientific geological hammer, Margoth will dispel theologic myth, and develop Palestine:

"Stale is she!
Lay flat the walls, let in the air,
That folks no more may sicken there!
Wake up the dead; and let there be
Rails, wires, from Olivet to the sea,
With station in Gethsemane!" (II,xx,91-96)

Margoth and the Presbyterian elder, a dour, argumentative literalist, express the cold, harsh reason science brings to measure the claims of Scripture and history; abstract ideas have no reference to empirical truth. They accept the cult of scientism, blind to everything they cannot see, more a burlesque of reason than reasonable men; the confident promise of commerce, science, and progress contains no substance or comfort for Clarel.[68] Rolf speaks of Margoth, the geologist:

"Let him have his say,"
Cried Rolfe; "for one, I spare defiance
With such a kangaroo of science,"
"Yes; qualify though," Derwent said,
"For science has her eagles too."
Here musefully Rolfe hung the head;
Then lifted: "Eagles? ay; but few.
And search we in their aeries lone
What find we, pray? perchance, a bone."
"A very cheerful point of view!"
"'Tis as one takes it. Not unknown
That even in Physics much late lore
But drudges after Plato's theme;
Or supplements—but little more—
Some Hindoo's speculative dream
Of thousand years ago. And, own,
Darwin is but his grandsire's son." (II, xxi, 9-25)

Derwent would acknowledge the contributions of science, but Rolfe concedes little. Plato's theme, atomism and mathematical qualities of the natural world, is the growing achievement of science. Darwin his grandsire's, etc., refers to the grandson of physiologist Erasmus Darwin, a poet of science, as in his *Zoonomia*, or the *Laws of Organic Life,* and that is Rofle's point. Rolfe is the principal critic of science; he regards physics as merely conceptual and says Newton's system is not absolute.[69]

Modern physics, as Melville predicts, discovered exceptions to Newton's laws of physics, thought to be absolute and permanent:

"But Newton and his gravitation!"
"Think you that system's strong persuasion
Is founded beyond shock? O'ermuch
'Twould seem for man, a clod, to clutch
God's secret so, and on a slate
Cipher all out, and formulate
The universe." "You Pyrrhonist![70]
Why, no, perhaps you do not see—
Your mind has taken such a twist—
The claims of stellar chemistry."
"What's that?" "No matter. Time
runs on

And much that's useful, grant, is won."
"Yes; but more's claimed...." (II,xxi,1-38)

Stellar chemistry must refer to astral, or astronomical, spectroscopy. In 1814, Joseph Fraunhofer made the first map of the solar spectrum of light. Astrophysics is said to have its origin in 1859 when Gustav Kirchhoff reported the finding of sodium in the spectrum of the sun.[71] Stellar bodies proved to be composed of the same ordinary materials as the earth. Unlike other great scientists, Newton dramatically influenced an entire culture and created a new 'philosophy of nature' favored by the church, the crown, and government. He sought how phenomena occurred, not why. Descartes's rules or laws of nature did not seek a final cause, and were a forerunner of the mathematics of Newton, including Newton's first law of motion. Descartes's version was an error of observation. It implies that a body can be acted upon by *no* force, which no one could observe, but was a hypothetical model. Hypothetical models became increasingly useful in science, i.e., frictionless surfaces, ideal gases, perfect conductors of electricity, inelastic collisions, perfect insulators, perfect spheres, etc., sought by scientists towards the end of the century.[72]

The strong belief in the deterministic character of the world owed much to the religious thinking of the times. The Christian view of one God who laid down the laws of nature and upheld them by the word of his power led to a strong faith in the rationality, consistency, and predictability of nature. These laws had been pursued and found at least in part because a belief that a lawgiving deity existed. Part of Newton's quarrel with Leibniz was over these ideas, which Leibniz thought blasphemous because they did not allow the deity to intervene in nature after the initial act of Creation. Newton's mechanical view set the goal of science ever since: the reduction of everything to a visualizable mechanical picture. It was the greatest single contribution to human knowledge of the workings of the universe by an individual, and changed the thinking of the nonscientist as well in the creation of Newtonianism and the popularization of science. The Newtonian argument gave new impetus to the design argument that nature was contrived by an all-embracing divine plan appealing to universal laws of nature. The concept of meticulous environments that were especially for the inhabitants of the earth and secured by the laws of nature for human benefit was a major scientific enterprise which abruptly ceased with Darwin's *Origin*.[73]

Derwent, a worldly priest in the Anglican church, is mature in years and gracious in personal relations. He takes a benign view towards

God and nature as well as a relaxed view towards man and society; he postulates man's goodness and social progress with his optimism based in good health, natural sociability, and a comfortable sense of status. He is convinced of the benefits of truth and sees the recent findings of German higher criticism, comparative religion, and physical science in some general way lending support to his religion of the heart, able to compromise towards a hopeful future. Clarel admits his doubt to Derwent, who tells Clarel "Alas, too deep you dive" (III, xxi, 312). Derwent practices his profession so professionally as to endanger his response to experience, analogous to Surgeon Cuticle, the lawyer in "Bartleby," and Reverend Falsegrave.[74] That science threatens to achieve a dominance over faith is one of the major elements of the poem, for "more is claimed." Hillway says:

> And here, I take it, is Melville's principal criticism against the scientific spirit. Its claims are too large. Its endless burrowings after knowledge he describes as the mere widening of the areas of man's essential ignorance. While it presumably frees us from old and common superstitions, it also opens the door to other superstitions of its own creation. And in the religion of the scientist—horribly enough!—it is man who constitutes God.[75]

He expresses a sentiment similar to the mechanician Bannadonna in "The Bell-Tower." Science claimed too much; each advance brought a new round of exaggerated promises Melville refused to accept. Each claim for the superiority of human intelligence was a defeat for the faith of the heart. The travelers stop at Siloam grotto:

> Watching the fountain's troubled time
> Which after ebb began to flow,
> Gurgling from viewless caves. The lull
> Broke by the flood is wonderful.
> Science explains it. Bides no less
> The true, innate mysteriousness. (I,xxviii,106-111)

Edward Robinson, American sacred geographer and author of *Biblical Researches in Palestine* (1856), explored Siloam's Arch and the Fountain of the Virgin showing that the two are joined underground, thus explaining the intermittent flow of Siloam, a daring and widely reported finding of the new science of archaeology.[76] In spite of demonstrating the natural cause of the remarkable fountain, the "innate mysteriousness" remains. Vine speaks of the tragedy of an earthquake in Lima:

"Yea, long as children feel affright
In darkness, men shall fear a God;
And long as daisies yield delight
Shall see His footprints in the sod.
Is't ignorance? This ignorant state
Science doth but elucidate—
Deepen, enlarge. But though 'twere made
Demonstrable that God is not—
What then? it would not change this lot..." (I,xxxi,191-199)

Lima experienced an earthquake in 1746 that destroyed much of the city. Melville had been ashore in Lima in January 1844 when a member of the crew of the *United States*. Though science can aid in understanding, it cannot lessen fear, as Melville stated in his short story, "The Lightning-Rod Man."[77] Rolfe says, "Time, God, are inexhaustible" (I,31,271). By the latter part of the nineteenth century, Lyell's idea of unlimited time had been contracted to only 50 million to 100 million years. Although much longer than the estimates of time taken from the Bible, the span did not allow the observed changes found in geology or biology. Modern physics has not solved the question of the origin of time or the beginning of the universe.

Kenny says Clarel becomes the "man of sorrows," without destination, cut off from God and man who, paradoxically, constitute the very substance and radiance of his life. In recognition and acceptance, he asserts his worth as an integral part of elemental reality by casting aside lamentation and anger as unavailing emotions: "all is silence in the nameless universe. Peace lies only in acceptance of all the flux and processes of life 'twixt heaven and hell,' as the lilac replaces the willow and wildings grow over the fallen lilac." A part of nature's endless cycle, man ascertains his meaning and dignity when he recognizes how all things—even death—are a "part of the natural cycle of human destiny." This confidence in human resiliency and a faith in nature's balm are the only measures of peace and hope for civilization, but does not explain the purpose of human existence. Prevailing in a world where the answer is not forthcoming is an answer in itself: "It is the painful wisdom that turns a man into a hero."[78] Rolfe says of Jerusalem:

All now's revised:
Zion, like Rome, is Niebuhrized.
Yes, doubt attends. Doubt's heavy hand
Is set against us;...(I,xxxiv,18-21)

The history of the Greco-Roman world was rewritten by scholars of the nineteenth century. Barthold Niebuhr (1776-1831), a German historian, whose "constructive skepticism" was the basis of scientific method of criticism, rigorously revalued the classics, insisting on distinguishing between firsthand and secondhand information and skepticism of certain accounts of history.[79] Even the moon is made pedestrian by science:"Diana's moon / Affirming it a clinkered blot" (I,xxxiv,26-27), causing a great upheaval in man's perspective of himself and his relationship to God. Perhaps legends lead to truth better than man's contrivances:

The legends follow them and die—
Those legends which, be it confessed,
Did nearer bring to them the sky—
Did nearer woo it to their hope
Of all that seers and saints avow—
Than Galileo's telescope
Can bid it unto prosing Science now. (I,xxxvi,112-118)

According to Kenny, a man can tolerate mystery longer than strict formulas, and it is the reason Darwin quotes the poet Shelley rather than a scientist: "Legends, in fact, fill a greater need in man than science can, contrary to Margoth's arguments, for they appeal to the imagination and allow him to soar"[80]:

Darwin quotes
From Shelley, that forever floats
Over all desert places known,
Mysterious doubt—an awful one.
He quotes, adopts it. Is it true?
Let instinct vouch; let poetry
Science and instinct here agree,
For truth requires strong retinue. (II,xi,12-20)

Charles Darwin quotes Shelley in Chapter Eight of *Journal of Researches,* aboard the *H.M.S. Beagle* (1839): "None can reply—all seems eternal now. / The wilderness has a mysterious tongue, / Which teaches awful doubt." Melville appears resigned to the discoveries in geology and biology contrary to the biblical account of the nature of man and suggests that the two should cooperate in the search for "truth," although by all accounts, faith and science are immiscible. Rolfe says though "luminous on every hand," the "depths of Being moan":

> The breadths of shallow knowledge more expand?
> Much as a lightship keeper pines
> Mid shoals immense, where dreary shines
> His lamp, we toss beneath the ray
> Of Science' beacon. This to trim
> Is now man's barren office.—Nay,"
> Starting abrupt, "this earnest way
> I hate. Let doubt alone; best skim,
> Not dive." (II,xxi,97-105)

He finds the comfort of faith more satisfying to man than the illumination of science. Melville professed an admiration for those who "deep dive," or search for truth within themselves; however, in the case of science, "best skim" for the discoveries of the natural world and the nature of life by science are not satisfying. The Dominican, a French Catholic priest, says:

> "Science but deals
> With Nature; Nature is not God;
> Never she answers our appeals,
> Or, if she do, but mocks the clod....
> "Shall science then,
> Which solely dealeth with this thing
> Named Nature, shall she ever bring
> One solitary hope to men?
> 'Tis Abba Father that we seek,
> Not the Artificer...." (II,xxv,148-151,158-163)

Natural events do not demonstrate, nor argue for or against, the existence of God. Christ in his agony at Gethsemane cried out to "Abba, Father," to whom "all things are possible" (Mark 14:36), in contrast to the "Artificer," rationally apparent by the argument from design in the works of nature, and limited by natural law.[81] They find a cross traced in chalk, three stars in a row, the Southern Cross, and a poem carved in the stone:

Emblazoned bleak in austral[82] skies—
A heaven remote, whose starry swarm
Like Science lights but cannot warm— (II,xxxi,53-55)

Margoth climbs the side of the cliff and examines the writing carved in the stone:

A sledge or hammer as Thor's;
A legend lending—-this, to wit:
I, Science, I whose gain's thy loss,
I slanted thee, thou Slanting Cross.[83] (II,xxxi,100-103)

Hammer as huge as Thor's refers to the legend of the Norse god of thunder armed with a magic hammer that returned to him when thrown—a legend that is lost to science.[84] Margoth explores the coastline, Rolfe inquires if a stone the geologist has collected might be the "Stone of Moses"; they are standing on the site where great cities once stood. Margoth says:

"Tut, tut—tut, tut. Of aqueous force,
Vent igneous, a hake[85] or so,
One here perceives the sign—of course;
All's mere geology, you know." (II,xxxiii,48-51)

Although it is not clear who is speaking, the poem says the Fall of man is reenacted in each individual:

"Nearer the core than man can go
Or Science get—nearer the slime
Of Nature's rudiments and lime
In chyle before the bone. Thee, thee,
In thee the filmy cell is spun—
The mould thou art of what men be:
Events are all in thee begun—
By thee, through thee!—Undo, undo,
Prithee, undo, and still renew
The fall forever!" (II,xxxvii,97-103)

Science has its limits whether in geology or biology. Everything man needs to know is within himself, and cannot be made known by science, a sentiment expressed by Sir Thomas Browne.

After long travel, Nehemiah drowns in the Black Sea; the next morning the travelers discover his body and grieve his death, all except geologist Margoth who says, "czars, stars must go / Or change! All's chemistry" (II,xxxix,67-68). Mortmain, a self-exiled wanderer, says:

> Look! for his wake is here. O men,
> Since Science can so much explode,
> Evaporate in this God? (III,i,156-158)

In Mortmain, humanity dominates: "Precocities of heart outran / The immaturities of the brain" (II,iv,51-52). In the following passage, Melville recognizes the irresolvable conflict of science and faith:

> Science and Faith, can these unite?
> Or is that priestly instinct right
> (Right as regards conserving still
> The Church's reign) whose strenuous will
> Made Galileo pale recite
> The Penitential Psalms in vest
> Of sackcloth; which to-day would blight
> Those potent solvents late expressed
> In laboratories of the West? (III,v,64-72)

Galileo's advocacy of the Copernican system, branded heretical, forced his recantation before the Inquisition in 1616. Kenny says Melville did not categorically oppose science, but raised the question whether faith and science cannot come together: "its rigid attitude prevented a man from arriving at an intelligent point of view."[86] Science may dispel superstition, and in the process create new superstitions:

> In one result whereto we tend
> Shall Science disappoint the hope,
> Yea, to confound us in the end,
> New doors to superstition ope? (III,v,159-162)

Seeking indulgence and tolerance between science and faith, Rolfe says to Clarel:

> "Whether now in his priestly state
> He seek indeed to meditate
> 'Tween faith and science (which still slight
> Each truce deceptive) or discreet

Would kindly cover faith's retreat,
Alike he labors vainly....
"But none
Exceed in flushed repute the one
Who bold can harmonize for all
Moses and Comte, Renan and Paul...
Astute ones be though, staid and grave
Who in the wars of Faith and Science
Remind one of old tactics brave—
Imposing front of false defiance...
Indulgence should with frankness mate:
Fraternal be: Ah, tolerate!" (III,xvi,169-174,200-202,207-210,217-218)

Ernest Renan (1823-1892) was a major counterpart of David Friedrich Strauss (1808-1874), leader of the higher biblical criticism on the continent. Renan was a philologist and historian, author of *La Vie de Jesus* (1863), a heretic, idealist, scholar, and revolutionary.[87] He studied at Tübingen, where Melachthon, Kepler, Hegel, and Schelling had studied. The university was known for its advanced study and was in a great creative period, stressing historical change and the need for reformulation of faith. Strauss was influenced by Hegel's *Phenomenology of Spirit* (1807). Strauss's *Leben Jesu* (1835), more than 1500 pages long, dealt the literal interpretation of the Bible its severest blow. He was an acknowledged biblical scholar and exegete whose works were the definitive beginning of modern criticism of the New Testament. His book indirectly questioned the historicity of the Jesus of Mark, Matthew, and Luke.[88] *Leben Jesu* stimulated research into early Christian history and study of the four Gospels. He came to see Christianity as an expression of eternal truths, the historical setting was of secondary importance to the idea of humanity moving towards perfection. Strauss had attributed the Gospel narratives to the unconscious, mythologizing activity of the collective Christian imagination.[89] He refuted both schools of thought of interpretation of the Gospels: supernatural miracle and the rationalists who gave natural explanations of biblical events. Strauss gave a new, detailed mythological interpretation: he showed that Jesus was a Jewish teacher and martyr, imbued with apocalyptic ideas, whose followers accepted his claim to messiahship, ascribing to him supernatural attributes derived from the Old Testament: not history, but religious symbolism. The book caused an unparalleled uproar by its setting aside the Book of John as unhistorical with a merely human Jesus unable to sustain the traditional dogma and, especially, that divine revelations were "no more than creations of the human mythopoeic imagination." Liberal theologians seeking natural explanations were also uncomfortable. Were they also headed in the same direction, against orthodoxy? He was exiled from the university and the faith. The book was translated into English by George Eliot, *The Life of Jesus Critically Examined*, with the support of a group of liberal Anglicans, but it could be read only as an anti-religious work; after delays, it appeared in 1846. It was supported by a few theologians including Jowett.[90] Strauss, however, was convinced that historical criticism in no way detracted from the essential truth of Christianity.[91] In his last work, *Der alte und der neue Glaube* (1872), *The Old Faith and the New*, Strauss rejects Christianity in favor of scientific materialism. Melville writes in his *Journal*, February 5, 1857: "Heartily wish Niebuhr & Strauss to the dogs. — The deuce take their penetration & acumen. They have robbed us of the bloom. If they have undeceived any one — no thanks to them. — Pity that ecclesiastical countries so little attracted by nature."[92]

Comte, the founder of positivism, separated theory and practice in order to augment the power of existing forces and governing classes. Lenzer says, "Under the new positive system, observation of what exists is to replace the imagination, which hitherto had arbitrarily claimed freedom in the shaping of social and political affairs." Comte considered mathematics to be the cornerstone of positive philosophy and the positive method. Mathematical analysis is the logical instrument and supreme method of positivism, which in conjunction with observation of natural and social phenomena, would yield to the highest generalities and laws of phenomena. It is the most powerful instrument that the human mind can employ in the investigation of natural phenomena. Although Comte is little known and never developed a system of positive logic, his influence on J. S. Mill's *System of Logic*, particularly "Logic of the Moral Sciences," and much of Mill's sociology is enormous, even though his influence is largely forgotten. Comte's method was purely objective: he was a social scientist who claimed the study of man would yield to mathematical analysis alone.[93] Derwent says:

> And Faith's long dead. Attest that gold
> Which Bacon counted down and told
> In one ripe tract, by time unshamed,
> Wherein from riddle he reclaimed
> The myths of Greece. (III,xxi,202-206)

De Sapientia Veterum (1609), or *The Wisdom of the Ancients*, is a study of thirty-one Greek myths explained in terms of Bacon's philosophical views of inquiry into and the control of nature.[94]

Kenny says that the first three sections of "Jerusalem," "The Wilderness," and "Mar Saba" infuse the weary pilgrims with hope for rest and peace in Bethlehem. In the fourth section, their goal cannot be fulfilled, for Bethlehem is the spiritually bankrupt site of Christ's birth, a stopover on the way back to the wreck of Jerusalem they had left ten days before. Melville believed that all of the ingenious discoveries of science fail to relieve moral and physical evils, and the basic premise leads back to ignorance because the world contains mysteries undreamed of by scientists[95]:

> But solve the world! Scarce that he'll do:
> Too wild it is, too wonderful. (IV,iii, 114-115)

Rolfe was concerned that analysis by science and physiology would tend to undermine natural beauty:

> "Tell Romeo that Juliet's eyes
> Are chemical; e'en analyse
> The iris; show 'tis albumen—
> Gluten—fish-jelly mere. What then?
> To Romeo it is still love's sky:
> He loves: enough!" (IV,xviii,102-107)

Following the synthesis of urea by Wöhler in 1828, biochemistry made remarkable advances during the nineteenth century. He demonstrated the chemical behavior of living organisms to be the same as the ordinary laws of chemistry, leading to such diverse concepts as the nitrogen cycle and fermentation, aided by such minor discoveries as the Bunsen burner and a vacuum created by a common water pump.[96] The protein albumin coagulates on heating and dissolves in a dilute salt solution. Later, Rolfe says:

> Man disennobled—brutalized
> By popular science—Atheised
> Into a smatterer—' (IV,xxi,129-141)

That science debases humanity by its minute quantifying, a sentiment expressed by the character Oh-Oh in *Mardi*.

In the "Epilogue," the conflict of faith and science intensifies, though remains unsettled. Clarel's search for truth is unfulfilled, yet he must continue: "Unmoved by all the claims our times avow," the mysterious, unknowable shadow of the Sphinx retains its mystery, though despair scrawls on its stone forehead:

> If Luther's day expand to Darwin's year,
> Shall that exclude the hope—foreclose the fear?...
> Yea, ape and angel, strife and old debate—
> The harps of heaven and dreary gongs of hell;
> Science the feud can only aggravate—
> No umpire she betwixt the chimes and knell:
> The running battle of the star and clod
> Shall run for ever—if there be no God.
> Degrees we know, unknown in days before;
> The light is greater, hence the shadow more;
> And tantalized and apprehensive Man
> Appealing—Wherefore ripen us to pain?
> Seems there the spokesman of Dumb Nature's train. (IV, xxxv, 1-22)

He urges Clarel to "keep thy heart...the issues there but mind;" and illustrates a theme of many of Melville's works—the continuity of life and death: "And prove that death but routs life to victory" (IV,xxxv,27,28,34). In his examination of religion, Clarel realizes neither science nor the church can remove doubt, loneliness, and pain. Clarel finds no salvation and he must face the continuation of sorrow heroically and alone; the dilemma of faith and despair has no solution. Science was the hope of the nineteenth century, but, Melville says, science cannot satisfy Clarel's need and aggravates his distress. Conner points out that *Clarel* has as its theme the failing faith of the day, yet contains almost no comment on the theory of evolution and mentions Darwin only three times. He notes, "oscillation between hope and fear, faith and despair, is too deeply ingrained in human nature to be greatly affected by such a mere novelty in speculation as evolution." Science has not only failed to dissolve the mystery, but has deepened it. The conclusion is not one of doubt but of faith: "...even though the new science has shed no light on the eternal mysteries, neither has it extinguished the light of hope."[97] How to endure the shattered vision of the loss of faith is the basic theme of the poem. The scientists offered a cheerful and seemingly plausible explanation of man's evolution out of a dark existence into a 'paradise' of his own creation, but devoid of a divine creator. All similar illusion would be dispelled by greater scientific discoveries. To these claims in science and social order, Melville replied, "the greater the light, the more the shadow." He could accept neither the miracles nor the claims of science on blind faith.[98]

According to Dea, Melville concluded in *Clarel* that religion is an evolutionary process, a need for most men to provide a social and moral order. "Man's best hope" was deteriorating:

> There is no God, and the transcendental claims of religion are spurious; man's natural condition is one of misery, relieved only by his will to endure and survive; good and evil are not in categorical opposition but are natural phenomena controlled by the laws of physical exigency and of human rapaciousness and ignorance; man is an isolated creature.[99]

Clarel carries his intellectual searching to its conclusion of "atheistic existentialism" anticipating the twentieth century existentialists. The expression of hope in the "Epilogue" is intended for the mass of humanity, but not for Clarel. *Clarel* has greater meaning for the twentieth century realist than for the nineteenth century optimist. The "modern predicament" of contemporary western man is part of the lexicon, a factual condition peculiar to an age "restless without God and yet not content with faith in technology, a sterile state repeatedly prophesied in *Clarel*." Kenny maintains that, "Melville is saddened over nature's indifference, but he knows that human contentment comes only from imitating her neutrality."[100]

The theory of evolution was but one of many factors contributing to the destruction of the ancient beliefs, but it marked the beginning of the end of the era of faith.[101] Lamarck was probably the first author to propose the idea of gradual transformation of species. The idea was accepted by a considerable number of authors on the continent, but none developed it into a consistent theory. The theory of common descent was accepted with more enthusiasm than others because of its enormous power to explain what previously appeared to be chaos. Mayr declares: "The entire Linnaean hierarchy suddenly became quite logical, because it was now apparent that each higher taxon consisted of the descendants of a still more remote ancestor. Patterns of distribution that previously had seemed capricious could now be explained in term of the dispersal of ancestors."[102] Evolution completed natural cosmology, which was linked to the nebular hypothesis, a continuously developing arrangement of matter and energy from all previous time. Natural selection made organic change analogous to the nebular hypothesis of change of physical forms, or reduced modifications in organic structures to a rearrangement of matter and energy that required no supernatural agencies.[103]

The rapid development of the evolutionary debate in the 1840s and 1850s—not only biological, but philosophical, theological, and ideological—influenced readers to approach *Origin of Species* with a set of convictions outlined by the radical anthropological thought and theological debates of such diverse men as Chambers, Baden Powell, Lamarck, and Geoffroy Saint-Hilaire. In the debate over interpreting the succession of species, which concerned a wide audience, and whether providential care or rigid laws governed both nature and society, Baden Powell emerged as one of the key protagonists. He was at opposite poles from Strauss's *Leben Jesu.* By 1855, Powell believed that natural theology could no longer be regarded as the cornerstone of Christianity.[104] In 1857, he adopted an overtly deistic natural theological argument, yet revelation remained the basis of religious instruction; he denied there was unequivocal rational evidence of the truth of Christianity and the existence of the Christian God. Powell was the first British author to place the question of species in the context of an epistemology and natural theology favouring a naturalistic explanation of the succession of species. By the end of 1859 he had distinguished himself as a vociferous and enthusiastic supporter of Darwin. His sudden death on June 11, 1860, prevented him from entering into the great debates on science and theology.[105]

The decades following 1859 were especially troublesome for those who would seek to reconcile the conflict between science and faith. The publication of *Origin* in November 1859, changed western man's perceptions irrevocably. Copernicus demoted man from his central position, but Darwin's theory required a complete reinterpretation of man's spiritual role in creation.[106] Polkinghorne summarizes: "...people came to feel that they had no need of the hypothesis of God. The Enlightenment attitude had done its acid work and many people's faith dissolved away."[107]

In August 1859, nearly a decade after Melville began work on his masterpiece, *Moby-Dick,* and three months before the publication of *Origin of Species*, a Swedish whaler captured an enormous albino whale off the coast of Brazil. Old and worn-out, Mocha Dick succumbed quietly.[108]

Notes

1. John D. Barrow and Frank J. Tipler, *The Anthropic Cosmological Principle.* Oxford: Oxford University Press, 1988, pp. 69-72.

2. Barrow and Tipler, ref. 1, pp. 72-83.

3. William Paley, *Natural Theology.* (originally published in 1802 as *Natural Theology, on Evidences of the Existence and Attributes of the Deity collected from the Appearances of Nature*), Frederick Ferré, editor. Indianapolis and New York: Bobbs-Merrill, 1963, pp. xxxi-xxxii.

4. Pietro Corsi, *Science and Religion: Baden Powell and the Anglican debate, 1800-1860.* Cambridge: Cambridge University Press, 1988, p. 270-272, 284.

5. David Knight, *The Age of Science: The Scientific World-view in the Nineteenth Century.* Oxford: Basil Blackwell, 1986, p. vii.

6. Dirk J. Struik, *Yankee Science in the Making*. New York: Collier Books, 1962, p. 380.

7. Robert V. Bruce, *The Launching of Modern American Science 1846-1876.* New York: Knopf. 1987, pp. 119-122.

8. Bruce, ref. 7, pp. 121-123.

9. Howard E. Gruber, "Going the Limit: Toward the Construction of Darwin's Theory (1832-1839)." in *The Darwinian Heritage.* David Kohn, editor. Princeton, New Jersey: Princeton University Press, 1985, pp. 18-19.

10. Peter J. Bowler, *Evolution: The History of an Idea.* Berkeley, Los Angeles, and London: University of California Press, 1984, pp. 159-160.

11. Stan P. Rachootin, "Owen and Darwin Reading a Fossil: *Macrauchenia* in a Boney Light." in *The Darwinian Heritage.* David Kohn, editor. Princeton, New Jersey: Princeton University Press, 1985, p. 155.

12. John Beatty, "Speaking of Species: Darwin's Strategy," in *The Darwinian Heritage.* David Kohn, editor. Princeton, New Jersey: Princeton University Press, 1985, pp. 276-280.

13. Ernst Mayr, "Darwin's Five Theories of Evolution." in *The Darwinian Heritage.* David Kohn, editor. Princeton, New Jersey: Princeton University Press, 1985, p. 766.

14. J. R. Lucas, "Wilberforce and Huxley: A Legendary Encounter." *The Historical Journal* 22 (1979):313-330; I. Bernard Cohen,"Three Notes on the Reception of Darwin's Ideas on Natural Selection (Henry Baker Tristram, Alfred Newton, Samuel

Wilburforce)." in *The Darwinian Heritage.* David Kohn, editor. Princeton: Princeton University Press, 1985, p. 598.

15. Knight, ref. 5, pp. 128-129.

16. Bowler, ref. 10, pp. 183-184.

17. Michael Ruse, *The Darwinian Revolution: Science Red in Tooth and Claw.* Chicago and London: University of Chicago Press, 1979. p. x.

18. Barrow and Tipler, ref. 1, pp. 84-87.

19. Langdon Gilkey, "Evolution and the Doctrine of Creation." in *Science and Religion: New Perspectives on the Dialogue.* Ian G. Barbour, editor. New York, Evanston and London: Harper and Row, 1968, pp. 164-165.

20. Charles Lyell, "*Principles of Geology.*" in *Darwin*, 2nd edition. Philip Appleman, editor. New York: Norton, 1979, p. 243.

21. Philip Appleman, "Introduction" in *Darwin*, 2nd edition. Philip Appleman, editor. New York: Norton, 1979. p. xv-xvi; Sir Julian Huxley. "Evolution: The Modern Synthesis (1942-1963)." in *Darwin*, 2nd edition. Philip Appleman, editor. New York: Norton, 1979, p. 244-246.

22. Ernst Mayr, "The Nature of the Darwinian Revolution." *Science* 176 (1972) 981-989.

23. A. Hunter Dupree, "Christianity and the Scientific Community in the Age of Darwin." in *God and Nature: Historical Essays on the Encounter between Christianity and Science.* David C. Lindberg and Ronald L. Numbers, editors. Berkeley, Los Angeles and London: University of California Press, 1986, pp. 351-366.

24. Frederick Gregory, "The Impact of Darwinian Evolution on Protestant Theology in the Nineteenth Century." in *God and Nature: Historical Essays on the Encounter between Christianity and Science.* David C. Lindberg and Ronald L. Numbers, editors. Berkeley, Los Angeles and London: University of California Press, 1986, pp. 369-388.

25. Bowler, ref. 10, p. 186.

26. Fred M. Bullard, *Volcanoes of the Earth*, 2nd edition. Austin: University of Texas Press, 1984, pp. 11-29, 350-398.

27. Bowler, ref. 10, pp. 127-128.

28. Mayr, ref. 22.

29. Alfred Kazin, *An American Procession; The Major American Writers from 1830-1930—The Crucial Century.* New York: Vintage, 1985, p. 142.

30. John Durant, "Charles Darwin: Solving the Problem of Organic Diversity." in *Man Masters Nature: Twenty-Five Centuries of Science.* Roy Porter, editor. New York: George Braziller, 1988, p. 146.

31. Lyell, ref. 20, pp. 1-2.

32. Martin J. S. Rudwick, "The Devonian: a system born from conflict." in *The Devonian system, special papers in palaeontology,* vol. 23. London: The Palaeontological Association, 1979, pp. 10-11. cited by Sandra Herbert, "Darwin the Young Geologist." in *The Darwinian Heritage.* David Kohn, editor. Princeton, New Jersey: Princeton University Press, 1985, p. 483.

33. Ruse, ref. 17, p. 244.

34. OED.

35. OED.

36. Martin J. S. Rudwick, "The Shape and Meaning of Earth History." in *God and Nature: Historical Essays on the Encounter between Christianity and Science.* David C. Lindberg and Ronald L. Numbers, editors. Berkeley, Los Angeles, and London: University of California Press, 1986, pp. 296-318.

37. OED.

38. William Byshe Stein, "The New Ancient of Days: The Poetics of Logocracy." *Essays in Arts and Science* 5 (1976):181-192.

39. OED.

40. Stein, ref. 38.

41. OED.

42. James Robert Corey, *Herman Melville and the Theory of Evolution.* Ph.D. Dissertation, Washington State University 1968, p. 94.

43. Stein, ref. 38.

44. John Challinor, *A Dictionary of Geology.* Cardiff: University of Wales Press, and New York: Oxford University Press, 1962, p. 156.

45. OED.

46. Stein, ref. 38.

47. OED.

48. Lyell, ref. 20, pp. 63-75.

49. Corey, ref. 42, p. 81.

50. Frederick William Conner, *Cosmic Optimism.* Philadelphia: University of Pennsylvania Press, 1949, p. 141.

51. Stein, ref. 38.

52. Stein, ref. 38.

53. Rudwick, ref. 36, p. 317.

54. Ruse, ref. 17, p. 244.

55. Joe D. Burchfield, "Darwin and the Dilemma of Geological Time." *Isis* 65 (1974):301-321.

56. Loren Eiseley, *Darwin's Century*. Garden City, New York: Doubleday, 1958, p. 209.

57. Burchfield, ref. 55.

58. Alec R. Vidler, *The Church in an Age of Revolution: 1789 to the present day*. Hammondsworth and New York: Penguin, 1961, p. 126.

59. James R. Moore, "Geologists and Interpreters of Genesis in the Nineteenth Century," in *God and Nature: Historical Essays on the Encounter between Christianity and Science*. David C. Lindberg and Ronald L. Numbers, editors, Berkeley, Los Angeles, and London: University of California Press, 1986, pp. 322-350.

60. Alvar Ellegård, "The Darwinian Theory and Nineteenth-Century Philosophies of Science." *Journal of the History of Ideas* 18 (1957) 362-391.

61. Cohen, ref. 14, pp. 592-598.

62. Kevin J. Sharpe, *From Science To An Adequate Mythology*. Auckland, New Zealand: Interface Press, 1984, p. 53.

63. Vidler, ref. 58, p. 118.

64. Herman Melville, *Clarel: A Poem and pilgrimage in the Holy Land*. Walter E. Bezanson, editor. "Introduction." New York: Hendricks House, 1960, p. cvi.

65. Bezanson, ref. 64, pp. 543-546.

66. Bezanson, ref. 64, p. 600.

67. Herman Melville, *Journal of a Visit to Europe and the Levant October 11, 1856--May 6, 1857*. Howard C. Horsford, editor. Princeton: Princeton University Press, 1955, p. 180.

68. Vincent Kenny, *Herman Melville's Clarel: A Spiritual Autobiography*. Hamden, Connecticut: Archon Books, 1973, p. 168.

69. Bezanson, ref. 64, p. 601.

70. Pyrrho (ca 365-275 B.C.), Greek philosopher of skepticism and doubt, proclaimed that nothing can be known with certainty.

71. René Taton, *Science in the Nineteenth Century*. New York: Basic Books, 1965, p. 115.

72. John D. Barrow, *The World Within the World*. Oxford and New York, Oxford University Press, 1990, pp. 60-66.

73. Barrow, ref. 72, pp. 69-76.

74. Bezanson, ref. 65, pp. 535-536.

75. Tyrus Hillway, "Melville as a Critic of Science." *Modern Language Notes* 65 (1950):411-414.

76. Bezanson, ref. 64, p. 575.

77. Bezanson, ref. 64, pp. 578-579.

78. Kenny, ref. 68, p. 226.

79. Gilbert Highet, *The Classical Tradition: Greek and Roman Influences on Western Literature*. Oxford: Oxford University Press, 1949. reprint. 1970, pp. 472-473.

80. Vincent, ref. 68, p. 117.

81. Bezanson, ref. 64, p. 605.

82. Southern.

83. the Southern Cross appears at dawn.

84. Bezanson, ref. 64, p. 610.

85. hake is one of several related species of codfish.

86. Kenny, ref. 68. p. 167.

87. Bezanson, ref. 64, p. 588.

88. Homer W. Smith, *Man and His Gods*. Boston: Little Brown, 1952, p. 190.

89. Vidler, ref. 58, pp. 101-106.

90. Don Cupit, *The Sea of Faith: Christianity in Change*. Cambridge: Cambridge University Press, 1984, pp. 92-96.

91. Maurice Mandelbaum, "Philosophic Movements in the Nineteenth Century." in *Darwin to Einstein: Historical Studies on Science and Belief.* Colin Chant and John Fauvel, editors. Harlow, England: Longman, 1980, pp. 27-28.

92. Herman Melville, *Journal Up the Straits. October 11, 1856—May 5, 1857.* New York: Colophon, 1935. pp. 107-108.

93. August Comte, *August Comte and Positivism: The Essential Writings*. Gertrud Lenzer, editor. Chicago and London: University of Chicago Press, 1983, pp. xlv, li-lii, 88, 100.

94. Bezanson, ref. 64, p. 626.

95. Kenny, ref. 68, pp. 164, 223.

96. Taton, ref. 71, pp. 299-302.

97. Conner, ref. 50, pp. 146-147.

98. Kenny, ref. 68, pp. 7, 143.

99. Eugene Dea, "Evolution and Atheism in *Clarel*." Extracts: *An Occasional Newsletter* 26 (1976):3-4.

100. Kenny, ref. 68, pp. 176-177, 225.

101. Smith, ref. 88, p. 3.

102. Mayr, ref. 13, pp. 758, 760.

103. Frank Miller Turner, "Victorian Scientific Naturalism." in *Darwin to Einstein: Historical Studies on Science and Belief.* Colin Chant and John Fauvel, editors. Harlow, England: Longman, 1980, p. 60.

104. Corsi, ref. 4, p. 203.

105. Corsi, ref. 4, pp. 221, 272-274.

106. Bowler, ref. 10, p. 2.

107. John Polkinghorne, *One World: the interaction of science and theology.* London, SPCK Holy Trinity Church, 1986, p. 4.

108. Howard P. Vincent, *The Try-out of Moby-Dick.* Boston: Houghton Mifflin, 1949, p. 174.

Chapter 9

Billy Budd: according to Nature

Billy Budd, Sailor (an inside narrative),[1] written in the late 1880s and first published in 1924, contains a fusion of most of the themes of Melville's earlier novels including the conflict of science and religion, the limits of science, issues of free will, the natural sublime, and mechanistic theory. Billy Budd, a young, handsome merchant sailor on the *Rights-of-Man*, is impressed into military service on the *H.M.S. Bellipotent,* using terms of Calvinism in that only Billy was "elected" from the *Rights-of-Man.*[2] Simple, innocent Billy Budd, twenty-one-years old, serves in the foretop crew. What is admired in Billy inflames Claggart, the master-at-arms. In a conflict of fate and free will, he attributes the character of both Billy and Claggart to physiognomy: "The moral nature was seldom out of keeping with the physical make." With unpretentious good-looks and a genial happy-go-lucky air, Billy was everything a sailor should be in time of peril, except for a speech defect: "a stutter or even worse" (Ch 2). Melville implies that the defect, and Billy's fate, was God's plan. Claggart is about thirty-five-years old. His features are notable only for a "strange protuberant heaviness" of his beardless chin. "His brow was of the sort phrenologically associated with more than average intellect" (Ch 11). Little was known about Claggart prior to his entering the navy, no more than "an astronomer knows about a comet's travels prior to its first observable appearance in the sky." His facial physiognomy exposes a fault in an otherwise "high quality" man, or, Melville says, Plato's definition of "Natural Depravity":

> Toward the accomplishment of an aim which in wantonness of malignity would seem to partake of the insane, he will direct a cool judgement sagacious and sound.... Now something such an one was Claggart, in whom was the mania of an evil nature, not engendered by vicious training or corrupting books or licentious living, but born with him and innate in short "a depravity according to nature." (Ch 11)

Although he attributes the character of Claggart to the depravity of nature according to Plato, Thompson asserts that Melville slyly means depravity according to God: "Even as Billy's fateful impediment is God's birthright gift to Billy, so Claggart's 'natural depravity' is God's birthright gift to Claggart."[3] He also substitutes references to Plato for Calvin.

At the Synod of Dort, the Netherlands (November 1618-May 1619), a series of five canons were issued in language understandable to the unlearned laity that became the basis for what has been called "Calvinism." The synod was called principally by the followers of Jacobus Arminius (1560-1609), who presented five "remonstrances" against the movement of the followers of Calvin. The remonstrances were an enlightened, humane restatement of the Christian message of medieval conservative orthodoxy carried out in an atmosphere of a heresy trial; some of the remonstrant leaders who were viewed as a threat to the prevailing Calvinist orthodoxy were beheaded, banished, or imprisoned. One of the main assertions of the synod was the corruption of the innermost being of man due to Adam's fall from grace and propagated to all men through all generations. So deep is man's corruption that he is completely unable to perform any worthy act—even with a person in a state of grace, good acts are attributed to God alone. The synod left ambiguous whether nature and the material universe are also corrupt: "can one operate with a basic attitude of trust and calmness, or is the physical universe dangerous at every point, ready to destroy man's hopes and the spiritual values he seeks to realize?" Man is not free to attain grace; it is given or not given entirely by divine initiative. The synod also stated that Christ did not die for all men, but only for the limited number of the "elect." The elect cannot become reprobate because they will persevere, and the damned cannot achieve salvation. Shurr says that these decrees were so important in the American church that they were canonized as orthodoxy: total depravity, unconditional election, limited atonement, irresistible grace, and the perseverance of saints. The reaction of Jonathan Edwards as well as nineteenth century authors against Calvinism was a response to the meanings given at Dort. Even Thomas Jefferson, writing to John Adams (April 11, 1823), objected to Calvinism, saying it was "daemonism" and worshiping a false god; Hawthorne perceived it as a "diabolical malignity substituted for the Deity." Nevertheless, Calvinism, as formalized at Dort, was the predominate stance of Christianity in America in the nineteenth century as an object of national worship.[4] Calvin's doctrine held that "the world is so governed by God that nothing happens in it except by His secret counsel and decree" in the physical as well as the social institutions and minutiae of daily life—a contradiction of free will if God's will controls everything. However, believers devoted their lives to insure that what inevitably happened conformed to His will. This doctrine had a profound influence on historical developments and the form of politics, law, and most of the institutions of the New World. In the early nineteenth century, it was common sense in America to believe that all great historical achievements arose from a religious motive, and that they succeeded or failed depending on whether they corresponded to God's truth. Liberal Christians of the early nineteenth century celebrated the principles of honor and right affirming human dignity brought about by progress in science and social institutions; the Calvinists emphasized the ruin of man.[5] The "naturally depraved" puzzled the courts by concealing it; Melville suggested depravity is as readily assessed by the clerical profession as by law or medicine: "For this cause have our juries at times not only to endure the prolonged contentions of lawyers with their fees, but also the yet more perplexing strife of the medical experts with theirs" (Ch 12)? The clergy's vocation, which brings them into contact with many troubled human beings, sometimes in their least guarded hours, in interviews "more confidential than those of physician and patient," would qualify them to determine the intricacies of moral responsibility (Ch 12).

Theological writers developed the idea of the "total depravity" of man; even outwardly good acts had hidden motives. To maintain the doctrine, man's inner nature was at fault: "And it was precisely the corruption of 'the heart' of man, and not necessarily the invariable badness of his social conduct, that the dogma of his essential depravity usually maintained." Man had been endowed by his Creator with the divine gift of reason, "it was the 'heart'—with a bad connotation—that controls the operations of the reason, but that in doing so the heart hides from itself, so that men are self-deceiver ever."[6] Hume cites Diodorus Siculus (late 1st century A.D.):

> Fortune has never liberally, without envy, bestowed an unmixed happiness on mankind; but with all her gifts has ever conjoined some disastrous circumstance, in order to chastize men into a reverence for the gods, whom, in a continued course of prosperity, they are apt to neglect and forget.[7]

According to Lovejoy, man's greatest need, as expressed by religious writers through all ages, Greek, Hebrew, and Christian, is a need for knowledge about himself; man has had misgivings and self-distrust about himself in what he sees as his chief folly and primary sin—pride, and lives in perpetual self-abasement in his relationship with his deity "as frequently portrayed, might well have seemed more formidable than admirable":

> When the Hebrew prophet in the seventh century B.C. observed that "the heart is deceitful above all things, and exceedingly corrupt," (Jeremiah, 17:9) he was uttering a kind of psychological generalization which may have been already a commonplace, and at any rate remained one for more than two millennia; and the echo of it, and of Augustine, in that monument of Christian doctrine, the Westminster Catechism—"the heart of man is deceitful altogether and desperately wicked"—purported to be evident to the natural understanding even apart from any biblical authority or theological tradition.[8]

Shortly before his death, Jonathan Edwards (1703-1758) viewed with alarm the tendency beginning in the middle of the eighteenth century toward a too kindly view of the nature of man: "And no creature...can be found anywhere so destructive of its own kind as mankind are." The principle was stated by Plautus (2nd century B.C.), Pliny, Juvenal, and in 1769 by Voltaire. The seventeenth and eighteenth centuries were the great age of satire of both individual men and man in general, and the most frequent and vocal expression of the irrationality and inner corruption of man. In the course of progress noted during the nineteenth century, Western man grew more self-confident and hopeful about himself in the near and distant future, that man is "naturally good." At the same time, satire in literature went out of style and a faith in man through science assumed some practical and emotional function.[9]

Billy is secretly asked to join in mutiny, which disgusts Billy "like a young horse fresh from the pasture suddenly inhaling a vile whiff from some chemical factory and by repeated snortings tries to get it out of his nostrils and lungs" (Ch 16). Claggart falsely informs Captain Vere that Billy is involved in the plot: "Claggart deliberately advances within short range of Billy, and mesemerically looking him in the eye..." (Ch 20). Claggart's eyes undergo a remarkable change: "like the alien eyes of certain uncatalogued creatures of the deep. The first mesemeric glance was one of serpent fascination; the last was as the hungry lurch of the torpedo-fish." Billy is unable to speak due to his speech defect and strikes Claggart, "the blow had taken effect full upon the forehead, so shapely and intellectual-looking a feature in the master-at-arms," who fell like a heavy plank (Ch 20). Billy "mechanically obeyed" the captain's order to retire to a stateroom aft. The impulse of Billy's "heart" destroys Claggart's "head," consistent with Melville's sentiment expressed in his letter to Hawthorne: "I stand for the heart. To the dogs with the head!"[10]

The ship's surgeon is called; the captain exclaims, "Struck dead by the angel of God. Yet the angel must hang" (Ch 20)! The surgeon is "profoundly discomposed" at the incoherencies of the captain; to assume him mad "is not so susceptible of proof" (Ch 21). Melville comments:

> Who in the rainbow can draw the line where the violet tint ends and the orange tint begins? Distinctly we see the difference of the colors, but where exactly does the one first blendingly enter into the other? So with sanity and insanity. In pronounced cases there is no question about them but in some supposed cases, in various degrees supposedly less pronounced, to draw the exact line of demarkation few will undertake though for a fee some professional experts will. There is nothing namable but that some men will undertake to do it for pay. (Ch 22)[11]

Conflict over the colors and meaning of the rainbow occurs in the earliest records of man, in his art, and in early writings including the *Iliad* and an early Sumerian hymn. Iris, the goddess of the rainbow and messenger of the gods, appears in the *Iliad* as a harbinger of war and turbulence. Nearly every civilization attributes special significance to the rainbow, often both the messenger of peace and beauty and an omen of evil stimulating an elaborate mythology and folklore. Buddhists related the seven colors of the bow to the seven planets and the seven regions of the earth; in early Christianity, the seven colors were sometimes associated with the seven sacraments. Science and myth worked side by side in trying to unravel the mysterious bow in both fear and hope; the nonscientist looked upon the search for the causes of the rainbow as a pious effort to better know God, or a profanation of God's creation. In one of the earliest conflicts between science and faith, Anaxagoras (b. ca 500 B.C.) claimed the rainbow is merely a reflection of the sun from a spherical cloud; a theory to persist in various forms for nearly two thousand years. Aristotle noted the physical parts of the rainbow, its size and shape, and the origin of the colors which required a source of light, a dark rain cloud, and the eye of the observer. His explanation of the circularity of the bow is still acceptable in a general sense; it was the earliest geometrical theory to deal with an extraordinarily difficult measurement of a meteorological phenomenon. No new important theories developed until the rise of the Islamic civilization and its greatest scholar, Avicenna (980-1037), whose *Meteorology* contained a systematic treatment of the rainbow. He observed that the bow is located in a medium directly in front of the cloud, emphasizing the importance of the particles of moisture rather than the dark cloud. Melville must have known some of the physics of the rainbow because in *Moby-Dick,* Chapter 85, "The Fountain," he wrote: "For, d'ye see, rainbows do not visit the clear air; they only irradiate vapor." Avicenna found identifying the colors of the bow to be a difficult task and settled on three main colors. Robert Grosseteste's (ca.1175-1253) book on the rainbow *De Iride Seu die Iride et Speculo,* added refraction of light to the existing theory of reflection. Roger Bacon was the first to accurately measure the diameter of the bow at 42 degrees, differing only two degrees from the modern measurement of approximately 44 degrees. Theodoric of Frieberg (ca.1310) in *De Iride et Radialibus Impressionibus,* conceived the idea of a glass globe of water to represent a magnified raindrop, and the rainbow is the effect of an aggregate of raindrops. He said the number of colors in the bow was four, not three. Theodoric also advanced the concept of internal reflection of light rays within the drop at the rear, concave surface of the globe or raindrop. His model helped to explain the circularity of the bow, yet the origin of the colors remained unexplained. Theodoric's experimental model of the rainbow was one of the first 'laboratory experiments' investigating a remote phenomenon, and according to Bower, represents one of the greatest scientific accomplishments of the Middle Ages. Descartes's *Discourse de la Methode* (1637), made the greatest single contribution to the solution of the rainbow—the law of refraction. Descartes gave the rainbow scientific status by showing the quantitative agreement of theoretical calculations with the results of observation. Newton observed that the divergence of the incident ray of sunlight is about one half degree and the divergence of the refracted spectral colors is almost three degrees. The individual refracted colors passed through a second prism showed that each color has a separate angle of refraction, i.e., some light rays were bent more than others, or had a distinct "index of refraction." Newton's optics demonstrated that only colored light is pure and that sunlight is a composite of colors, a theory of light stated in *Moby-Dick,* Chapter 42, "The Whiteness of the Whale." In addition, Newton identified seven colors of the rainbow. Newton's discovery, presented to the Royal Society in 1672, was so severely criticized by Hooke and Huygens that he refrained from publishing anything further on optics until a year after Hooke's death in 1703. Thomas Young's discovery of optical interference in 1801 demonstrated the wave nature of light. Young applied his discovery to the rainbow, adding new insights such as the variation of the radius of the bow, and why the bow is brighter near the earth. His wave theory of light convinced few scholars, and his theories of light and the rainbow were largely disregarded. A new mathematical model of the rainbow was developed at Cambridge University through the work of a number of specialists under the leadership of George Biddle Airy (1801-1880), resulting in the "Cambridge theory." The theory states that the rainbow is a superposition of many bows of each color; the bright colors are limited by wave self-destruction to a narrow band, depending on the size of the raindrops. Airy's forbidding computations form the basis of the modern theory of the rainbow.[12] Nearly all new advances in the theory of the rainbow were tardily recognized. The development of a theory of the rainbow, including its colors, as Melville notes, was a long, contentious intellectual journey, but had arrived at a highly sophisticated state by the time he wrote *Billy Budd*.

A court-martial is called for the same night. No one can speak for the motives of dead Claggart; there is "a mystery of iniquity" or natural depravity of Calvinism: "a matter for psychological theologians to discuss" (Ch 22). Only the prisoner's overt act can be considered, yet how can a man innocent before God and innocent in the eyes of the court-martial be condemned to die? Vere ambiguously says, "It is nature":

> Though the ocean, which is inviolate Nature primeval, though this be the element where we move and have our being as sailors, yet as the King's officers lies our duty in a sphere correspondingly

> natural? So little is that true, that in receiving our commissions we in the most important regards ceased to be natural free-agents. (Ch 22)

In spite of living on the nature world of the sea where freedom of the individual surely exists, as in the sublime of nature in the New World, martial law requires the suspension of free will: "however pitilessly that law may operate, we nevertheless adhere to it and administer it." Although Captain Vere would acquit Billy for absence of intent of both mutiny and homicide, he warns, "But let not warm hearts betray heads that should be cool" (Ch 22). The statement is an inversion of Melville's earlier statement preferring heart over head. A sailor has struck and killed a superior in grade in time of war; sailors must obey orders without debating them, a suspension of free agency (Ch 17). The confrontation between Claggart and Billy was arranged to prove Billy's innocence, yet the result became a threat to the organized society of a warship and must be condemned, a conflict of military and "natural justice" (Ch 22). Noone says, "What is on trial is the competence of an exclusively mechanical reason to govern the affairs of man."[13] In natural justice, man ceases to be a natural free agent, he reflects Calvin's point of view that "natural impulses of 'natural man' were anathema."[14] Law is as mechanical and threatening, in this case, as the steam engine, the mechanistic fate of Ahab, and the machine of the short stories.

Within hours of the fateful meeting of Billy, Claggart, and Captain Vere, Billy is sentenced to hang at dawn. Vere's mechanistic values permeate and undermine the ship's crew. The court, in exercising its "free will," ironically reaches a decision predetermined by Captain Vere.[15] Billy is put in chains between two cannons "as nipped in the vise of fate" (Ch 25); yet, he is without fear of death, "a fear more prevalent in highly civilized communities than those so-called barbarous ones which in all respects stand nearer to unadulterate Nature" (Ch 25). Similarly, the sailors react to the execution "yielding to the mechanism of discipline" (Ch 28). Melville implies civilization, or the use of intellect and science, does not ease or reduce the fear of death. Billy's last words before hanging are "God bless Captain Vere." The crew reacts mechanically: "Without volition as it were, as if indeed the ship's populace were but the vehicles of some vocal current electric, with one voice from alow and aloft, came a resonant sympathetic echo—'God bless Captain Vere!' and yet at that instant Billy alone must have been in their hearts, even as he was in their eyes" (Ch 26).

Some days later, the purser at mess with the surgeon asks about the force of willpower, i.e., free will, and a phenomenon beyond scientific explanation. The surgeon, who supervised the hanging "scientifically conducted," says any movement of the body following the "completed suspension":

> ...such movement indicates mechanical spasm in the muscular system. Hence the absence of that is no more attributable to will-power as you call it than to horse-power—begging your pardon. (Ch 27)

The surgeon admits spasm is "more or less invariable." The purser asks the surgeon if he can account for the absence of spasm in the hanging of Billy Budd:

> Mr. Purser, it is clear that your sense of the singularity in this matter equals not mine. You account for it by what you call will-power, a term not yet included in the lexicon of science. For me I do not, with my present knowledge pretend to account for it at all. (Ch 27)

The surgeon admits its absence is "phenomenal" and "the cause of which in not immediately to be assigned." The purser inquires: "was the man's death effected by the halter, or was it a species of euthanasia?"

> *Euthanasia*, Mr. Purser, is something like your *will-power*; I doubt its authenticity as a scientific term—begging your pardon again. It is at once imaginative and metaphysical,—in short, Greek.... (Ch 27)

According to Noone, Melville satirizes the surgeon, the symbol of scientific reason, for dismissing the singularity of Billy's death as being an instance outside any known general law. He says, "An earlier digression on the possible competence of theologians as against lawyers and doctors, respective symbols of artificial and natural abstractions, testifies to Melville's belief in a world whose fulness is more than its rational reductions."[16] The surgeon says will-power, or free will, has no place in science, certainly not in the mechanistic scheme of Laplace or the philosophy of Schopenhauer. All three, Claggart, Billy Budd, and Captain Vere, die as the consequence of the "mechanism" of military discipline. In spite of Vere's intelligence and education, his free choice is constrained by the necessity of martial law. The reason for the lack of spasm must remain in Melville's metaphysical scheme for the sake of arguing the importance of free will and the inability of science to explain or deny it.

No work of Melville's debates determinism and free will to the same extent as *Billy Budd*. An historical conflict of long debate, it was brought to prominence in the eighteenth and nineteenth centuries by the advance of science. Pelagius, a British monk in Rome about 398 to 402 A.D., appalled by the lack of morality in the great mass of nominal Christians, stirred them to a sense of duty to God, later called the Pelagian heresy: that man has free will and the power to choose between good and evil. Because of its questioning of inherited sinfulness or guilt, it quickly met objections from the bishops, since it would have set reason above authority. Accordingly, if Adam sinned by free will, as do his children, death cannot be attributed to sinfulness. In that case, baptism is not necessary to virtue, and the redemptive power of the grace of Christ is not a requisite to salvation. Pelagius was denounced as heretic; the refutation of the Pelagian heresy was largely the work of Augustine, Bishop of Hippo, who was the greatest authority of the Christian church. He proved the existence of God by the presence of 'order,' that every cause is one of an endless chain of causes, and that God was the first cause. He endeavored to show God in the unity of things such as nature; beauty is evidence of perfect beauty and the unity of the whole; and the whole is God.[17]

A deterministic view—the conviction that all phenomena are subject to one set of natural laws—may be found in various religious and philosophical beliefs: the three fates of the Greeks, predestination and the eternal decrees of God of the Augustinians and the Calvinists, or the scientists' naturalism.[18] According to Thomas Aquinas, any meaningful concept of moral responsibility must be based on the assumption that a choice between good and evil is possible, and the will is free to choose. This produces the paradox of an all-knowing, all-powerful God foreseeing from the beginning of time how each life will be lived, yet individuals with freedom of will. Not until the Reformation of the sixteenth century did the conflict over freedom of will become a major issue in Christianity leading to the views of John Calvin (1509-1564). St. Augustine was the chief source of Calvinism, the main influence on the religion of the American colonies, especially man's utter inability, after the fall of Adam, to will not to sin; that man is completely dependent on God's grace to acquire the faith necessary for salvation; the irresistibility of God's grace when it is offered; and God's election of only a few persons upon whom to bestow His saving grace. The paradox was resolved by saying God would know in advance what choice the individual would make. Although the outcome was determined by God, the individual was not relieved of the need to strive to be righteous. According to Augustine and Calvin, the will is the instrument of achieving God's purpose. Calvinism paradoxically exalts the role of human will exhorting the damned to salvation even though it is entirely in the hands of God; the will of a converted man reflects the will of God. Even the efforts of the unregenerate serve God's mysterious purpose. The stubbornness and dogged determination of the Puritans resulted from knowing that they were doing the will of God. In the Thirty-Nine Articles of the Anglican Church (1571) and the Westminster Confession of Faith (1647) of the Puritans, the individual has nothing to do with his own destiny, salvation, or damnation. Nevertheless, for the next 200 years, Presbyterians and Congregationalists insisted man's choice was free and could achieve salvation by energetic exertions of the will. The critics of Calvinism claimed the natural depravity of Calvinism made God the author of sin.[19]

Locke's *An Essay Concerning Human Understanding* became the "psychological gospel" of the eighteenth century. "What Locke aimed at no doubt, what the eighteenth century acclaimed him for having demolished, was the Christian doctrine of total depravity, a black, spreading cloud which for centuries had depressed the human spirit." Hume wrote in *Dialogues* of the growing awareness that God had abandoned the world and left man with no one to care for his immortal soul: were they living in a world controlled by a beneficent mind, or by an indifferent force? Yet, the age of reason caused philosophers to admit the "feebleness of reason," and they turned to the study of useful, i.e., factual, subjects.[20]

By the beginning of the nineteenth century, sharp opposition developed between science and the concept of free will. For three centuries scientists had worked under the assumption that all observable events could be brought under a law of universal causation, and their work advanced continuously and unchecked. Everywhere, nature appeared to obey irresistible forces subject to exact scientific prediction; the cause of events was thought to be inevitable, especially in the case of inanimate matter. Beginning in the 1850s, Darwin, Marx, Pavlov, and Freud advanced deterministic causal explanations across all aspects of life and mind. Surely, life would soon be synthesized in the laboratory and human actions could be determined as readily as the elements. The scientific attitude distinctly changed in the twentieth century, with little reference to such ideas as 'irresistible forces,' and scientists abandoned the search for causation. The certainty of measurement gave way to the awareness that results could not be exact, only approximate, a theory expressed in *Pierre:* that knowledge is provisional, leading to the position that all scientific prediction is based on observed statistical irregularities and can not yield more than a probable result, which may allow for the possibility of free will or divine intervention. The essential features of the scientific method—measurement of certain characteristics, analysis by concentrating on certain features of an object, and repetition of similar sets of conditions rendering individual variation insignificant—all show considerable variability when applied to human behavior. The prediction of human behavior has shown a lower probability than in other fields of inquiry.

Schopenhauer, who was strong in natural philosophy, rejected God. He was pessimistic in his view of man locked into nature and the prisoner of natural forces.[21] The philosophy of Schopenhauer and the religion of Calvin appear as mechanistic as Laplace's demon, both having great influence on the composition of *Billy Budd*. Aquinas said a person governed by reason would chose rightly; the wise would be virtuous since their reason would make them choose to do good acts. The innate desire for happiness was expressed in the faculty of willing; questioning the possibility of free will undermined morality and was considered heresy. Free will was defended by noting that people could be persuaded to act differently—otherwise, council, reward, or punishment would be pointless. If free choice must be a rational choice, then reason would compel to moral logic; if irrational, choice is not free. Kant was unable to show that every change in the realm of common sense and science must be in accordance to some law; if determinism is discarded, it must be replaced by statistical laws of physics and the free will of human choices. Hume called the power or efficacy of causes, the necessity thought to reside in causal relations, one of the most sublime questions in philosophy. He endeavored to find an alternate method to induction in searching for how nature works. Mackie cites Hume in saying that the principles of association of events, or causation, are the 'cement of the universe'—the links that connect the ideas of unobserved things with impressions, that give rise to nonrational inferences.[22] Descartes brought about a revolutionary change in causal explanation and producing a new problem of free will by introducing a new explanation of natural occurrences: that physical events could be explained in terms of prior physical events according to fixed, immutable laws of nature ordained by God. He said man should seek to discover the laws of nature, not to seek God's purposes. Descartes's chance or mechanical account of the cosmos based on the argument that science had found evidence of God's design in the laws of nature is not compatible with Christianity. Most Christians thought Cartesian deterministic mechanism especially dangerous because it tended to minimize the importance of free will.[23]

The essential articles of the Enlightenment that saw the effect of science and reason on philosophy and society are: that man is *not* naturally depraved; that the purpose of life is life itself (the good life on earth instead of the beatific life after death), that by reason and experience man is capable of perfecting life on earth; and that man must free his mind from ignorance and superstition and his body from social oppression.[24] Westbrook asserts:

> By not regarding man as a machine—and no greater heresy could be imagined than to regard him as such—the Puritans...insisted that man had originally been created in the image of God and thus could not be devoid of will of some sort—especially after the image, defaced by Adam, had been restored by grace.[25]

American authors of the nineteenth century reflected the profound effect of Calvinism on the creative mind and the deepest levels of the American psyche; the predestinated will is pervasively present as a formative and thematic literary force. The Calvinism-influenced authors regarded the will as a mystery, "something that adds to the stature and dignity of man's life, not something to be explained chemically, physically, or biologically, or brushed aside as simple chance or fate."[26]

Billy Budd includes the language of mesmerism, physiognomy, and natural history. The conflicts of science and religion, fate and free will, as well as mechanism and divine design, and other theories of the workings of nature included in the work are remarkably current. Chaffee states:

> Despite the strong element of determinism in his final story, Melville never arrived securely at a committed acceptance of fatalism. Besides avoiding the bind of direct, unequivocal comment he fills *Pierre* with, he depicts, albeit faintly, the agony actually experienced in the process of choice. Vere's decision, however much predetermined, does indeed sadden him.[27]

Whether Captain Vere's decision represents free choice or determinism has stimulated considerable discussion with no consensus as to a final meaning. Hillway says Melville in *Billy Budd*, more than any writer of his time, searched the foundations of man's behavior: "he was probably a little too far in advance of his age to be understood and appreciated by his contemporaries."[28] The interaction of science, religion and philosophy in Melville's last story, though less obvious, is as disturbing and unsettling as in his florid use of science to illustrate philosophical principles in his earlier works. The issues discussed retain their importance a century after their composition.

Notes

1. Herman Melville, *Billy Budd*. Milton Stern, editor. Indianapolis: Bobbs-Merrill, 1981.

2. Lawrance Thompson, *Melville's Quarrel with God*. Princeton: Princeton University Press, 1952, p. 361.

3. Thompson, ref. 2, p. 379.

4. William H. Shurr, *Rappaccini's Children: American Writers in a Calvinist World*. Lexington, Kentucky: University Press of Kentucky, 1981, pp. 6-9.

5. T. Walter Herbert, Jr., "Calvinist Earthquake: *Moby-Dick* and Religious Tradition." in *New Essays on* Moby-Dick. Richard H. Broadhead, editor. Cambridge: Cambridge University Press, 1986, pp. 109-123.

6. Arthur O. Lovejoy, *Reflections on Human Nature*. Baltimore: Johns Hopkins University Press, 1961, pp. 25-26.

7. David Hume, *The Natural History of Religion.* edited and Introduction by H. E. Root. reprint. Stanford: Stanford University Press, 1956, pp. 31-32.

8. Lovejoy, ref. 6, pp 1-3.

9. Lovejoy, ref. 6, pp. 6-15.

10. Herman Melville, *The Letters of Herman Melville.* Merrell R. Davis and William H. Gilman, editors. New Haven: Yale University Press, 1960. 1[?] June 1851, p. 129.

11. The section "Lawyers, Experts, Clergy," is not included in the Hayford and Sealts text of *Billy Budd* (1962), cited here because it expresses Melville's views at the time of writing *Billy Budd*, and not intended to make a case for its inclusion or exclusion in the text. For discussion, see Hershel Parker, *Reading* Billy Budd. Evanston, Illinois: Northwestern University Press, 1990. pp. 169-173.

12. Carl B. Boyer, *The Rainbow: from Myth to Mathematics*. Princeton: Princeton University Press, 1987, pp. 28-35, 88-94, 294-310.

13. John B. Noone, Jr., "Billy Budd: Two Concepts of Nature." *American Literature* 29 (1957):249-262.

14. Thompson, ref. 2, p. 397.

15. Sacvan Bercovitch, "Melville's Search for National Identity: Son and Father in *Redburn, Pierre*, and *Billy Budd*." *College Language Association Journal* 10 (1967):217-228.

16. Noone, ref. 13.

17. Homer W. Smith, *Man and His Gods*. Boston: Little Brown, 1952, pp. 241-242.

18. Perry D. Westbrook, *Free Will and Determinism in American Literature*. London and Canberry, New Jersey, Associated Universties Presses, 1979, pp. ix-x.

19. Westbrook, ref. 18, pp. 1-8.

20. Carl L. Becker, *The Heavenly City of the Eighteenth-Century Philosophers*. New Haven and London: Yale University Press, 1932, pp. 64-65, 73-84.

21. Don Cupit, *The Sea of Faith: Christianity in Change*. Cambridge: Cambridge University Press, 1984, pp. 67-68.

22. J. L. Mackie, *The Cement of the Universe: A Study of Causation*. Oxford: Oxford University Press, 1980, pp. 231, 193-194, 296.

23. Jennifer Trusted, *Free Will and Responsibility*. Oxford and New York: Oxford University Press, 1984, pp. 30-32.

24. Becker, ref. 20, pp. 102-103.

25. Westbrook, ref. 18, p. 27.

26. Westbrook, ref. 18, p. 84.

27. Patricia Ann Chaffee, *The Lee Shore: Volition, Time, and Death in the Fiction of Herman Melville*. Ph.D. Dissertation, Indiana University, 1971, p. 51.

28. Tyrus Hillway, "Melville's Human Sacrifice." *Pacific Spectator* 6 (1952):342-347.

Chapter 10

Melville and Science: this strange mixed affair

The inclusion of science in literature expands and broadens the author's scope in the elaboration of events and climate of the times. Geoffrey Chaucer in the fourteenth century was one of the few English poets to combine science and poetry. The Doctour of Physik is a strictly scientific man who boasts that he relies little upon the Bible, finds rational causes of all maladies, and depends exclusively upon his own skill in manipulating natural laws for the working of cures.[1] The original legend of Faust, told by Christopher Marlowe in *The Tragical History of the Life and Death of Doctor Faustus* (about 1588), illustrates the conflict in the Renaissance passion for knowledge opposed to the medieval insistence upon salvation as the principal earthly concern, emphasizing the evil nature of purely human learning; the ambitious doctor of divinity, driven by a quest for knowledge, reason, and pleasure, is brutally destroyed.[2] Just as we get a perspective on the science of their times from the literature of Chaucer, Dante, Milton, Pope, and Diderot, Melville, more than any other author, gives us a view of science during the nineteenth century: the "Age of Science."

In Melville's early schooling, the curriculum included some natural history; the Albany Academy boasted of its library of "Natural Philosophy, Chemistry, and Astronomy" which may have stimulated Melville's interest in science during his subsequent years.[3] Since his formal education ended at an early age due to family circumstances, his education was haphazard. As he later put it, "the whale-ship was Yale and Harvard College." Except for elementary instruction in school, virtually all of his knowledge of science came from reading; his first sources were books and periodicals for laymen. Melville read extensively in certain fields when searching for material for his books; probably his earliest reading in science was aboard the frigate *United States*. Goldsmith's popular work, *Animated Nature* (1774, 8 volumes), which was mentioned in several of Melville's works, was regarded as a monument to the eighteenth century concept of a fixed, harmonious order in nature and the Great Chain of Being. Goldsmith's wit, geniality, and facility of expression gave it a place in literature long after its science was no longer current. In *White-Jacket*, he says that John Mason Good's *Book of Nature* was a "very good book." It was published by Harper's for a literary interest group, and is a collection of popular lectures in three series: the first is on the inanimate world, the second covers plant and animal physiology, and the third deals with the human mind. The book is largely derived from authoritative sources and its chief merit is popularization of scientific subjects. Robert Chambers's *Vestiges of the Natural History of Creation* was widely read in the intellectual circles of Melville's time; its main focus was centered on geology, and it attempted to find a scientific explanation for the creation of the earth. Although not directly mentioned by Melville, *Vestiges* was one of the most influential works of the mid-nineteenth century. In addition, William Jardine's forty-volume *The Naturalists Library,* and Lavater's *Essays on Physiognomy,* were important sources as were the periodicals of the day such as the *Edinburgh Review*. Comments made in his poetical works show that Melville was familiar with Darwin's *Origin of Species* (1859) and *Descent of Man* (1871). He also used more formal, scientific sources, such as Beale, Bennett, and Scoresby. From these authorities, he obtained information about other scientists such as Aldrovandi, Buffon, Cuvier, Hunter, Lacépède, Owen, Ray, etc., as though he were well acquainted with them. He was interested in the literary effect of science, using names of great scientists as an appeal to authority, often satirically more than respectfully. The piling up of scientific detail builds a solid basis for allegory and allusion. Hillway avows that Melville's awareness of the threat of scientific discoveries to religious faith makes his works more than romantic adventures, speculative allegories, or witty satires. After writing *Moby-Dick*, Melville's interest in science declined and his reading on scientific matters was largely confined to periodicals.[4] Nevertheless, some of his later poetry centers on geology and on science in a general sense.

One of the predominant influences on Melville's literary style was Sir Thomas Browne, seventeenth century English physician.[5] Beginning with *Mardi* and developing further in *Moby-Dick*, Doctor Browne's influence is apparent. Browne and Melville shared a love of antiquarianism and appeal to authority, as well as stylistic parallels. Both exhibit a hesitancy and tentative state of mind in some of their writings with neither able to make a definitive decision on his metaphysics, and both engage in pondering the 'unthinkable.' The ideas expressed by Browne were a fusion of the doctrine of faith and the new idea of proof by observation; as a result, he asserts that man should "tread softly and circumspectly in this funambulatory Track and narrow Path of Goodness." Browne's interest in the natural creation was stimulated by the enthusiasm for discovery during the seventeenth century and developed by his interest in science.[6] In Browne's lifetime, modern scientific method was gaining influence at the center of European intellectual life, and Browne reflected this. Whatever the topic, Browne turned it into a curious balance of faith and skepticism.[7] Browne declared: "*Natura nihil agit frustra* is the only indisputable axiom in Philosophy; there are no *Grotesques* in nature; nor any thing framed to fill up empty cantons, and unnecessary spaces." Browne was one of Charles Darwin's favorite authors.[8]

In 1776, British North America had one great investigator, Benjamin Franklin, and a few others who could be called scientists. De Tocqueville noted in *Democracy in America* (1835), that America was a technologically-oriented society of energetic people intent on acquiring wealth, but had no savants or devotees of abstract thought, which he believed required an aristocratic hierarchical order.[9] In the nineteenth century, Americans contributed little to science. The one exception was Matthew Maury, the founder of oceanography, mentioned in *Moby-Dick*. However, in the practical application of science by engineering, America became a leader in the early nineteenth century by producing such products as barbed wire, the reaper, and many other mechanical inventions. The application of scientific discoveries in physics and chemistry led to the invention of the telegraph and the development of photography. The first engineers were trained at West Point Military

Academy from 1812, explaining why the first railroads were laid out by army engineers—there were no other engineers except a very few trained in Europe.[10] In September 1823, a group of people, chiefly physicians, met to organize a society for the propagation of scientific knowledge, the Lyceum of Natural History of the Berkshire Medical Institution. The speaker was Reverend Edward Hitchcock, pastor and scientist who later became the president of Amherst College; his topic was on the "utility of natural history"—that a knowledge of science ought to increase respect for God.[11] America was a naturalist's delight: an entire continent of unclassified flora, fauna, and rocks. Popular lectures on chemistry and natural history drew large crowds. One in seven scientists had an M.D. degree during the mid-nineteenth century, but complexity and specialization caused medical training rapidly to lose its utility as preparation for a career in science.[12]

Throughout the Enlightenment of the seventeenth and eighteenth centuries, *reason* was the key word along with *nature*. If God could be known from His creation, the Bible was not necessary to prove the existence of God. Reason changed from formal logic to natural science; the laws of reason became identical with the laws of nature. In the seventeenth century, experiment became part of the "reasoned" approach to nature. Houyhnhem, in Jonathan Swift's *Gulliver's Travels* (1726), thought "Nature and Reason were sufficient guides for a reasonable animal." Spinoza (1632-1677) and John Toland (1670-1722) equated God with nature. Others (Denis Diderot, Julien Offray de La Mettrie, and Baron d'Holbach) denied the existence of any spiritual God, insisting that reason and nature were sufficient. The shift from reason as the perfect intelligence to reason as the law of nature was the major theme of the eighteenth century resulting in a paradox: the laws of nature could not give man guidance, but philosophers sought moral imperatives in nature; the laws of nature were thought to be deterministic and at the same time were able to set man free in "inalienable rights." Moral value could be assigned to science by attributing traditional values of purity to the pursuit of science in an unselfish search for truth in simplicity, humility, austerity, and love of nature with such stoic virtues as fortitude, duty, courage, and resolution. In literature, history lost its "providential character" and historians presented an objective account of past events. Seventeenth century philosophers felt they knew what the ancients knew in addition to the knowledge of recent times. The Enlightenment tended to make heroes of natural philosophers. Science, in natural philosophy, dealt with the existence of the soul, the activity and passivity of matter, the freedom of the will, and the existence of God.[13] Descartes concluded that

God had produced the same result that would have been produced by a Godless cosmic machine.[14]

Philosophers from Plato to the present have impugned the cognitive worth of common sense, considering it of negligible import. The greatest importance was given to "primary qualities" of the senses and measurement. Yet, in more recent times, Eddington has argued that physics reveals the structural world to be radically different from what the senses perceive—that a belief based on sense perception cannot possibly show the correct make up of the universe.[15] Although molecules have no color, make no noise, have no taste nor odor (a concept explored in *Moby-Dick*), the contents of the physical world are understood by our senses, i.e., by the accumulation of "sense-data" through their conversion to qualities the senses can interpret, and by this means only in positivism. Do sensible objects, or *sensibilia*, persist when we are not sensible of them? or do they require inference?[16]

In spite of many conservative theologians and conservative revivals of the French Romantic reaction and the Oxford movement, in spite also of the persisting tradition of metaphysical idealism, the most influential strand in nineteenth century thought was the attempt to divorce science and religion and maintain the value of each. Positivism merged with idealism to limit the domain in which science had authority, and once these limits were generally agreed upon, all schools relinquished the view that religion could intrude into that domain. On the other hand, the scope of religion had been broadened, not narrowed: in giving up its claim to the possession of any literal knowledge, religion came to be identified with whatever ranges of feeling and moral aspiration were of the most significance to man.[17] Polkinghorne, in concert with Melville, observes: "Science has been very ready to destroy religious beliefs, without trying very much to offer anything emotionally satisfactory to society in return."[18]

Melville's novels (1846-1857) just predate Darwin's *Origin of Species* (1859), and illustrate the difficulty of trying to reconcile science and faith in the mid-nineteenth century. Subsequently, Darwin's ideas were not only accepted rapidly, they were practically embraced. In 1866, Joseph Hooker reported that the theory of Darwin was approved by the British Association, and it was taken by the public with equal enthusiasm, notwithstanding objections from the church. The Victorian period was an age of intense interest in science, with eminent scientists lecturing to working-class audiences, and scientific treatises such as Lyell's *Principles of Geology*, read widely by the general public. The idea of biological evolution grew as a result of material progress which people saw around them as a result of the Industrial Revolution.

Progress had become an almost religious phenomenon, an outgrowth of the concept of Descartes's laws of nature: the universe was a great machine that would operate according to fixed principles of Laplacian determinism indefinitely into the future. Belief in divine intervention diminished, and belief in miracles was viewed with skepticism. The idea of indefinite future time made progress—social, intellectual, technological, and biological—possible. Time no longer constrained the works of man as was the case in medieval times. The present idea of almost limitless time began with the transformation of man's thinking brought about by the theories of Descartes. Some have suggested that technological society developed in the West because only the West had the concept of progressive, linear time. British philosopher Herbert Spencer (1820-1903) elevated the concept of evolution to a cosmic principle. To an even greater extent than Darwin, Spencer was the prophet of evolution and progress.[19]

The Darwinian controversy was propelled beyond science by religion because it was thought that Darwin's theory impinged on religious truths. In the 1860s, the conflict over evolution was part of a huge religious controversy resulting from the appearance of the German higher criticism in England. *Essays and Reviews* was published in 1860 just after *Origin of Species* by Anglican liberals appealing for a less dogmatic and less conservative Christianity with less dependence on the literal acceptance of miracles. Its appeal for reason in understanding Scripture caused a tremendous outcry by the public and conservative clergy. A correspondent wrote from Oxford, "The book [*Origin*] I have no doubt would be the subject still of a great row, if there were not a much greater row going on about *Essays and Reviews*."[20] Darwin's writings unsettled the relationships between fiction, metaphor, and the material world, in part as a result of his voluminous reading. In addition, evidence of Darwin's influence on literature has been demonstrated in George Eliot's *The Mill on the Floss,* and Robert Browning's poem "Caliban upon Setebos," written shortly after the publication of *Origin*.[21] Eliot read *Origin* soon after its publication and initially considered it "not impressive," but soon called it "an epoch," a scientific authentication of *Vestiges*, the essays of Herbert Spencer, and others on biological development. However, in her later works, *Middlemarch,* and *Daniel Deronda*, Eliot responded to the complex implications of Darwin's theory. Beer writes: "Like Darwin, George Eliot brought into consciousness the dismaying sense of hidden violence and irremediable waste associated with development....She transposed Darwin's concerns into the area of the human and its medium, and brooded on his conflicts." Her later books troubled Darwin by their contemplation of the unresolved dilemmas of the relationship between individual and species, of struggle, survival, extinction, and biological development. Similar sentiments were expressed by Melville; the universal cannibalism of the sea in *Moby-Dick* is an example.[22] The conversion to Darwinianism was as much philosophical as scientific, and was taken beyond the realm of science by its implications on religion, especially the interpretation of Genesis and the mathematical accuracy of the Old Testament. The mid-nineteenth century was characterized by tension and struggle; even a struggle for existence by humans did not seem farfetched. The conversion of scientists to evolution occurred at a remarkable rate. By 1865, and possibly as early as 1862, British biology had become evolutionary with very few exceptions, although many had reservations about Darwin's theory of natural selection.[23]

The publication of *Lux Mundi* in 1889 marked a new era in English theology which began in 1875 at Oxford with essays on the complete range of Christian faith. The essayists believed that historic Christian faith, reasonably interpreted, would satisfy reasonable men in a progression of God's revelation to man, allowing acceptance of biblical criticism and bringing enormous relief to educated Christians, especially with regard to the Old Testament which had been the chief battleground in the conflict between religion and science. The early chapters of Genesis were accepted as mythology and poetry: the history of Israel was seen as a slow ascent from savage beginnings to monotheism of the prophets which culminated in the faith of the incarnation, with its sequel in the sacramental life of the Christian church.[24]

When the early Victorian cleric-scientists died, younger clergymen came to regard science as the enemy rather than the helpmate of religion. Many were influenced by the Oxford movement which called for the Anglican church to become more autonomous, free itself from outside ecclesiastical and theological influences, and especially to liberate the church from domination by the secular state. In addition, they endeavored to redirect the church to define doctrine and the foundation for religious practice, not to surrender part of the intellectual and theological autonomy to nonreligious authority: "Science, especially as defined by the professional man of science and as accepted by the contemporary liberal or Broad-Church theologian, was part and parcel of the liberalism rejected by the Tracterians and their followers." Combining priesthood with science became increasingly difficult: a clergyman-scientist confronted the choice of perpetuating traditional natural theology and risking ridicule by scientists, or attempting further rationalization of theology with science and encountering persecution by fellow clergymen. The Roman Catholic church in *Syllabus of Errors* (1864), epitomized the most extreme exercise of religious authority for control of intellectual life, and specifically condemned the theory, methods, conclusions, and practice of modern science. In 1874, John Tyndall, in an address opposed to Catholicism in Ireland, declared that science "shall wrest from theology, the entire domain of cosmological theory." It was followed by one of the greatest furors in the conflict of science and faith. The internal ideology of much of early Victorian science had been related to the presence of the Creator in the Creation, but in the second half of the century professionalized science became the glorification and strength of the nation and its wealth. By World War I, most Christian theologians had abandoned natural theology, and the clergy no longer seriously attempted either to rival or complement scientists as interpreters of nature. The efforts of scientists to establish themselves in independent social and intellectual sphere had largely succeeded. Yet, the catastrophe of World War I shattered the idea of inevitable social progress through intellectual enlightenment and moral endeavor.[25]

During the 1870s, the issue of spontaneous generation (mentioned several times by Melville) was restricted to the beginnings of life and the origin of microorganisms. The discovery of endospores in bacteria (which resist extremes of heat) threw the matter of spontaneous generation into confusion by casting new light on previously contradictory experimental results. The connection between evolution and abiogenetic origin made by Haeckel and others in Germany was so strong that the vitalists were forced to abandon spontaneous generation. By 1880, scientists ceased to discuss the origin of life in Britain or on the continent; most considered the matter beyond scientific investigation, and considered that life either came from outer space or by abiogenesis only in the remote past. The discovery of nuclear mitosis (or division) by Walther Flemming in 1878 proved the continuity of cell and nucleus of the fertilized egg to the adult organism, and later nuclear continuity from generation to generation in plants and animals. The dictum *omnis cellula e cellula* of Virchow was refined to *Omnis nucleus e nucleo* by Oscar Hertwig in 1893. Despite the nearly universal rejection of spontaneous generation, and undercurrent of doubt remained.[26] However, spontaneous generation has returned in the latter twentieth century with the theory of self-organizing matter: the tendency of complex dynamic systems to fall into an ordered state without any selection pressure whatsoever. Evolution would not be just a series of accidents, but may be a combination of natural selection and spontaneous order, or a collection of self-reinforcing reactions.[27]

Ironically, while science and evolution challenged faith, the most important figure to the theory of evolution was a clergyman whose scientific contribution was at least as great as Darwin's. Father Gregor Johann Mendel (1822-1884), an Augustinian monk, on February 8 and March 8, 1865, read a paper to the Brunn Society for the Study of Natural Science titled "Experiments in Plant Hybridization" to a small audience in a school house in Brunn, Austria, published in 1866. Mendel noted that if certain characteristics of the garden pea, such as height, color of stems and blossoms, seed shape, form of pods, etc., were crossed with its opposite, only one type would occur in the offspring, but in the next generation, both characteristics reappeared in the ratio of three-fourths of one and one-fourth of the other characteristic. From his observations of the variations of the garden pea, he deduced the basic genetic laws of inheritance, i.e., dominate and recessive traits. Mendel was barely a footnote in the history of science until 1900 when he came to share the honors in nineteenth century biology with Lamarck and Darwin. Eiseley maintains that Lamarck and Darwin attempted to explain variation; Mendel searched for the explanation of biological stability. The theory of alteration of species was also studied by Hugo De Vries (1848-1935), Dutch botanist and geneticist, who in 1886 noted a change in the evening primrose which he termed a "mutation." He concluded that mutations were the explanation of the appearance of diversification of species. In 1900, Mendel's paper was discovered independently by three biologists: K. E. Correns, Eric von Tschermak, and De Vries. Darwin might have attributed biological variation to climate or soil; Mendel discovered that variations were due to the fluctuating expression of biological units, or genes, controlled by mathematical laws of assortment transmitted independently. In each successive generation, the two primal characters remain distinct and unaltered; heredity and variation in the Darwinian sense are not synonymous, for the units had a constancy the Darwinians did not discover.[28] The discovery of radioactivity and its application to the problem of geological time in the early years of the twentieth century established the age of the earth as five billion years, and the age of the universe at fifteen billion years, reviving interest in evolution which had waned towards the end of the nineteenth century. Evolution did not occur gradually as Darwin theorized, but in two bursts of diversification 200 million and 450 million years ago with a period of great extinction prior to the most recent burst. In the end, Mendel's work was more fruitful than the work of Darwin. Not until 1930 did it become apparent that important heritable variations are small, and that Mendelian genetics and Darwinian selection are complements, not rivals.[29]

The struggle between science and religion in the eighteenth century centered on whether the universe was governed by "immutable" laws or subject to free interference by a deity in the design argument: a recurrent theme in Melville's works. In the early nineteenth century, geology in conflict with the Mosaic account of Creation was the main issue, with the historical accuracy of the Deluge as a second controversy; each important in the overall problem of "design."[30] William Whewell said in the Bridgewater Treatise, *Astronomy and General Physics Considered with Reference to Natural Theology* (1833), that all the great scientific discoverers believed in an intelligent maker of the universe, while the doubters contributed little to science.[31] He states what was the generally accepted view of design from the Renaissance into the nineteenth century, even though the movement was underway that would destroy the concept of divine design:

> Law implies a Lawgiver, even when we do not see the object of the Law; even as Design implies a Designer, when we do not see the object of the Design. The Laws of Nature are the indications of the operation of the Divine Mind; and are revealed to us, as such, by the operations of our minds, by which we come to discover them. They are the utterances of the Creator, delivered in language which we can understand; and being thus Language, they are the utterances of an Intelligent Spirit.[32]

Evidence of divine design appeared to be everywhere and demonstrated the presence of God, until 1859 when Darwin's natural selection made evolution of species the product of atheistic chance.

The design argument and an anthropocentric universe have received even more attention in the twentieth century. The idea that humanity is important to the cosmos, or the 'anthropic principle,' appears to be nearly universal, occurring not only in Judeo-Christian culture, but also in non-Western religion and philosophy, including ancient Egyptian, Sumerian, Islamic-Persian, Chinese, Bantu, Mayan, and many American Indian traditions. The Persian philosopher al-Biruni (ca 1,000 A.D.) said that everything in nature is ordered according to God's plan and He "created everything for the best....there is no waste or deficiency in His Work," which is similar to Leibniz saying that this is the best of all possible worlds.[33] During the past few decades, the 'anthropic cosmological principle,' a collection of ideas relating mind and the observer to the phenomenon of the physical sciences has occupied scientists, philosophers, and cosmologists. That man was expelled from the center of nature by the Copernican principle, is now assumed as axiomatic in all scientific investigations. In 1974, Brandon Carter sought to limit the Copernican principle by the anthropic principle in that "our location in the Universe is necessarily privileged to the extent of being compatible with our existence as observers." Barrow and Tipler go on to say:

> The basic features of the Universe, including such properties as its shape, size, age and laws of change, must be *observed* to be of a type that allows the evolution of observers, for if intelligent life did not evolve in an otherwise possible universe it is obvious that no one would be asking the reason for the observed shape, size, age and so forth of the Universe.[34]

Though appearing trivial at first, it has far-reaching implications for physics: properties of the universe that may initially appear astonishingly improbable are necessary prerequisites for the evolution and existence of any observers at all. The measured values of the qualities that define our universe are determined by the necessity that we observe from a site that supports biological evolution of life—what scientists call "selection effect." The universe is fifteen billion light years in size because it is fifteen billion years old, and must be as old and as large as it is to evolve a single carbon based life-form such as exists on earth; other non-carbon based life forms may exist elsewhere. Our optical instruments are able to make observations only in the visible band of electromagnetic energy whereas the visible part of the electromagnetic band is relatively small. Thus, visible observations are self-selecting by not taking into account radiation from the nonvisible ranges that may give quite different information. The retrograde motion of planets that puzzled the ancient astronomers is due to the anthropocentric selection effect of observing the apparent retrograde motion from the moving earth. The realization that the possibility of biological evolution is strongly dependent upon the entire structure of the universe leads to the consideration that the existence of life on earth may be no more, but no less, remarkable than the existence of the universe itself. The sizes of stars, planets, and people are neither random nor the result of Darwinian selection from a myriad of possibilities, but are the consequences of 'necessity' in the manifestations of equilibrium states between competing forces of attraction and repulsion determined by the 'pure numbers' of the *constants of nature* such as the ratio of proton and electron masses, etc. If the relative strengths of the nuclear and electromagnetic forces were slightly different, carbon atoms could not exist and carbonbased life would not have evolved. The unlikely coincidence of numerical constants of enormous magnitude appear at first to be quite unrelated, but they occur so frequently that they suggest that the Universe *must* be such as to admit the creation of observers within it at some stage, and implies that the universe could not have been different—that the numerical constants could not be other than what we observe. Since the time required for cooling of the universe to allow formation of carbon atoms has been calculated to be ten billion years, life on earth must be connected with the size and age of the universe. The laws of nature must be such that life can exist, which leads to multiple interpretations, including the continuation of the traditional design argument in that one possible universe exists 'designed' with the goal of generating and sustaining 'observers': a position subject neither to proof nor disproof, and is religious in nature and implicit or explicit in most theologies. Observers are necessary to bring the universe into being which is closely related to the possibility that an ensemble of other universes is necessary for the existence of our universe. The anthropic principle is a modern manifestation of the traditional tendency to frame design arguments on successful mathematical models of nature, that order must have a purpose, that order must have a planned cause, to prove the existence of a deity from the apparent purpose or harmony of the workings of the machinery of nature, and that order can develop spontaneously in a biological population.[35] Thus, in the importance of man's point of view, as noted in a number of examples in *Mardi*, that of the oyster in Chapter 7 of *Moby-Dick*, and numerous other instances throughout his works, Melville anticipated the most modern views of the cosmos.

In the nineteenth century, the belief existed that by sense-experience, aided by instruments, through the idiom of mathematics, man could know ultimate physical reality, and that mathematics represents concrete physical reality. Quantities enormously large or infinitesimally small could not be visualized, but could be calculated; i.e., mathematics is the nearest to reality that is possible. Difficult concepts in science and mathematics have their limitation in how they can be communicated to the ordinary person: "Without a parable modern physics speaks not to the multitudes." Mainly in biology and astronomy did the medieval model of the universe experience the most serious alteration. The old astronomy of Ptolemy was not refuted by the telescope, but it added more complications to the economical use of the existing scheme.[36] In that magic was the forerunner of modern science, Keynes maintains that Newton was not the first of the age of reason, but he was the last of the magicians: "the last of the Babylonians and Sumerians, the last great mind which looked out on the visible and intellectual world with the same eyes as those who began to build our intellectual inheritance rather less than 10,000 years ago."[37] The triumph of Newtonian physics put science on a dogmatic foundation of materialism for two centuries, replacing the dogmatism of the medieval scholasticism.[38] Ampère's mathematical equations were not bound by the need to depict physical reality: "they cannot, and do not profess to, portray the forces of nature in a way that can be comprehended by the intellect of man."[39] This change in the point of view of science in the nineteenth century was already expressed by nonscientists: Wagner, Keats, Goethe, and others. The idea of 'progression' was stated by Robinet in 1786.[40] The demand for a new model grows first, as stated by C. S. Lewis:

> ...when it is full grown the scientists go to work and discover the evidence on which our belief in that sort of universe would now be held to rest. There is no question here of the old Model's being shattered by the inrush of new phenomena. The truth would seem to be the reverse; that when changes in the human mind produce a sufficient disrelish of the old Model and a sufficient hankering for some new one, phenomena to support that new one will obediently turn up. I do not mean that these new phenomena are illusory. Nature has all sorts of phenomena in stock and can suit many different tastes.[41]

Lewis cautions us to regard all physical models in the correct manner, respecting each and idolizing none. Not only does the prevailing idea of the universe affect the human mind, but the model is influenced by the prevailing temper of mind. The change in ideas cannot be regarded as movement from error to truth; none is a catalogue of ultimate realities: the new model will not be set up without evidence, "but the evidence will turn up when the inner need for it becomes sufficiently great. It will be true evidence. But nature gives most of her evidence in answer to the questions we ask her."[42] This is a sentiment akin to Melville's in Chapter 58, "Brit," saying, "...however baby man may brag of his science and skill, and however much, in a flattering future, that science and skill may augment; yet for ever and for ever, to the crack of doom, the sea [nature] will will insult and murder him..." and more explicitly in *Pierre*, "Say what some poets will, Nature is not so much her own ever-sweet interpreter, as the mere supplier of that cunning alphabet, whereby selecting and combining as he pleases, each man reads his own peculiar lesson according to his own peculiar mind and mood."

The scientific revolution overturned the authority of science, not only the science of the Middle Ages and of the ancient world since it eclipsed scholastic philosophy, but it also caused the destruction of Aristotelian physics: "it outshines everything since the rise of Christianity and reduces the Renaissance and Reformation to the rank of mere episodes, mere internal displacements within the system of medieval Christendom."[43] The result of the loss of faith was profound. Religion in Europe and America has been in gradual decay, and is tending to degenerate into a formula for a comfortable life.[44] Annie Wood Besant (1847-1933), married at a young age to a clergyman, suffered a loss of faith due in part to an awareness of science: "No one who has not felt it knows the fearful anguish inflicted by doubt on the earnestly religious soul. It seems to shipwreck everything. Is all blind chance, is all the clash of unconscious forces, or are we the sentient toys of an Almighty Power that sports with our agony?"[45] Beatrice Webb (1858-1943) said the scientists of the nineteenth century were the leading British intellectuals and men of genius "who were routing the theologians, confounding the mystics, imposing their theories on philosophers, their inventions on capitalists, and their discoveries on medical men; whilst they were at the same time snubbing the artists, ignoring the poets, and even casting doubts on the capacity of the politicians."[46] The process by which European philosophy became anthropocentric, developing since Luther and Descartes, was completed by Nietzsche, who announced the death of God.[47]

Science appeared to produce a demythologized, miracle-free religion. Berry observes: "Miracles are not inherently impossible or unbelievable, and acceptance of their existence does not necessarily involve credulity, but does involve recognizing that science has limits."[48] Only a few authors in the nineteenth century dealt with the effect of science on religion, because they did not see the important role of science in modern thought. Melville agreed with Carlyle in fearing science as a power that would mechanize human life and bewitch and entrap man just as the priesthood had bewitched and entrapped him with mystery.[49] Hillway contends science provides a harrowing paradox: "Nature breeds both good and evil but is equally indifferent to both. Melville attempted, presumably, to reach through this paradox in his futile search for truth."[50] Toward the end of the nineteenth century, Sir William Osler cautioned: "...one and all of you will have to face the ordeal of every student in this generation who sooner or later tries to mix the water of science with the oil of faith. You can only keep them separate. The worry comes from attempts at mixture."[51] Whitehead writes: "The dogmas of religion are the attempts to formulate in precise terms the truths disclosed in the religious experience of mankind. In exactly the same way the dogmas of physical science are the attempts to formulate in precise terms the truths discovered by the sense perception of mankind."[52] According to Coleridge in *Aids to Reflection* (1825), the reasoning of science "is the faculty of concluding universal and necessary truths from particular and contingent appearances"; his method of thought is described as 'inductive' and was long assumed to be the method of science.[53] But, biologist Medawar states:

> The truth is that there is no such thing as "scientific inference." A scientist commands a dozen different stratagems of inquiry in his approximation to the truth, and of course he has his way of going about things and more or less of the quality often described as "professionalism"—an address that includes an ability to get on with things, abetted by a sanguine expectation of success and that ability to *imagine* what the truth might be which Shelley believed to be cognate with a poet's imagination.[54]

Science has dispensed with the importance of trying to understand anything that might be an "underlying agency." Becker asserts, "It is one of the engaging ironies of modern thought that the scientific method, which it was fondly hoped would banish mystery from the world, leaves it every day more inexplicable."[55] Physics, which was thought to have eliminated the need for metaphysics, has become the most metaphysical of all the sciences: "A little science leads away from God: more science leads back to [God]."[56] The substantial world of Newtonian physics has dissolved into a complex phantom of "radiant energies"; the world cannot be fully understood in terms of mechanics. The modern position is factual rather than rational, although the facts are often contradictory: "So long as we can make efficient use of things, we feel no irresistible need to understand them. No doubt it is for this reason chiefly that the modern mind can be so wonderfully at ease in a mysterious universe."[57]

Medawar is of the opinion that the limit of science is due to the questions science cannot answer and that no conceivable advance of science would allow it to answer; i.e., the questions children ask: "How did everything begin? What are we all here for? What is the point of living?" Positivism dismissed all such questions leaving emptiness and dissatisfaction. We cannot look to science for these answers because there is a *prima facie* case for a limit to scientific understanding.[58] In 1936, Bridgman says of the extrapolation of vast expanses of time to the order of 10^9 light years and greater:

> It seems to me that one cannot take such extrapolations seriously unless one subscribes to a metaphysics that claims that laws of the necessarily mathematical precision *really* control the actual physical universe. For such a metaphysical claim I can find no operational meaning that would give one the faintest confidence in applying it in any concrete situation.[59]

The question of plurality of worlds and extraterrestrial life remains unsolved and just as fascinating today as in the mid-nineteenth century.[60] Even the basic ideas of Darwin have come under attack—that natural selection is a "tautology": if in the survival of the fittest, the fittest are defined as the survivors then the next stage becomes the "survival of the survivors."[61]

Melville's art is characterized by the ambiguous conflict of ideas and contradictions: the mineral versus the herb doctors, natural sublime versus the machine, the wisdom of mad Pip, doubt versus faith, heaven's sense versus earth's insanity, and many others. Watters notes, when King Media in *Mardi* asks the philosopher what is the ultimate meaning of life, he is told that the question is more final than any answer, and is as much of the 'truth' as man can achieve:

> It implies that consciousness, desire for knowledge, unceasing speculation about life and the universe, are the very meaning, the essence of life, and that the complete answer will differ in degree, not in kind. For once man strives to perceive values in the universe, he is on the road towards creating those values and thus answering the questions his intelligence propounds.[62]

He echoes Browne's statement: "I hold that God can doe all things, how he should work contradictions I do not understand, yet dare not therefore deny."[63] Neither absolute faith nor absolute knowledge through science is fulfilling; in *Moby-Dick*, Ahab cannot believe in God, but doubts his doubt as well. The truth must lie beneath the surface of things and beneath the skin of man, like tattoos, a pasteboard mask, disfigurement, and crippling. Absolute knowledge, a persistent Melvillian theme, cannot be attained:

> Scientific knowledge is always provisional, and despite the great support that Darwinian theory has received over the last hundred years there is always the possibility that it might go the way of other syntheses highly effective in their time, like Daltonian atomism or Newtonian mechanics, which have had to be highly modified so that while they have their uses they can no longer be believed in....Even 'laws of nature' are overtaken by the march of science: Boyle's Law is now only held to apply strictly to 'ideal' gases rather unlike real ones, and Bode's Law of planetary distances has been given up. In the same kind of way, classifications we suppose to be natural, or anyway more natural than their predecessors, may well turn out to be artificial, ready, like the Linnean system, to be abandoned in due course.[64]

We cannot achieve absolute knowledge in faith or science. As Melville noted in *Pierre*, all knowledge is "provisional."

According to Bernal, the greatest achievement of the physical sciences in the nineteenth century was the doctrine of the conservation of energy and the interchangability of its various forms, i.e., the science of thermodynamics and electrodynamics which originated from the practical study of sources of power and arose from the needs of transportation and communications.[65] It explained the operation of the vast mechanical structure of nature and established limits to science and the possibilities of nature.[66] The concept of mechanics played a critical role in the development of scientific thought: it was the first branch of knowledge in modern times to achieve the status of a scientific theory with wide application; and mechanical explanation was, until recently, largely considered as the standard for scientific explanation. The limits of mechanics was apparent as early as Hume who said, "Many principles of mechanics are founded on very abstruse reasoning; yet no man, who has any pretensions to science, even no speculative skeptic, pretends to entertain the least doubt with regard to them."[67] However, Newton's theory of gravitation was assailed immediately from several directions. Descartes objected to the theory as physics; Leibniz accused the theory of universal gravitation as being opposed to common sense, and Berkeley criticized the theory on the basis that its implications were impious if not atheistical.[68] Ernst Mach (1838-1916), Austrian physicist and philosopher who wrote *The Science of Mechanics* (1883), was a vigorous critic of Newton's *Principia,* regarding it as a "purely a thought-thing" devoid of experience that sought to remove metaphysics from science.[69] Subsequently, the basic principle of mechanics, that all physical processes are reversible, was negated by the second law of thermodynamics; the assumption that all physical processes are continuous was proved untrue by Planck's quantum theory; but the most dramatic challenge as to whether scientific laws are causal laws came from Heisenberg's uncertainty principle.[70] Life remained a mystery to physicist Lord Kelvin:

> Mathematics and dynamics fail us when we contemplate the earth, fitted for life but lifeless, and try to imagine the commencement of life upon it. This certainly did not take place by any action of chemistry, or electricity, or crystalline grouping of molecules under the influence of force, or by any possible kind of fortuitous concourse of atoms. We must pause face to face with the mystery and miracle of the creation of living creatures.[71]

Though science routed faith, scientists, as predicted by Melville, were left with a sense of failure.

In 1876, the centennial of the United States of America was celebrated by the Centennial Exhibition in Philadelphia. Corlisses' massive four-story high steam engine dominated the scene, but little attention was paid to more important technical exhibits that included new applications of electricity in motors, the telephone, and an early incandescent lamp. Visitors to the exhibits in London's Crystal Palace Exhibition of 1851 (noted in *The Confidence-Man*) could appreciate the inventions with little knowledge of science; however, by the time of the exhibition of 1876, the exhibits were too sophisticated for most visitors to comprehend.[72] In spite of the accomplishments of machines, the enthusiasm for the mechanical system to explain nature began to break down toward the end of the nineteenth century. The philosophy of mechanism assumes at all levels, all qualitative changes, and all chance fluctuations will eventually be reduced completely, perfectly, and unconditionally to fixed and limited schemes of purely quantitative physical law, yet the concept of mechanism does not follow from any specific scientific developments and can be no more than a philosophical assumption. By the end of the nineteenth century, physicists contended that all important laws of the universe had been discovered in a "deterministic mechanism" theory of causality—only the details remained to be found; that the future behavior of everything in the universe could be deduced from current differential equations and would never have to be amended. Only two problems remained unresolved: the failure of the Mickelson-Morley experiment to demonstrate the existence of ether, and the failure of the Rayleigh-Jeans equation to predict the distribution of radiant energy of a black body—

both heralded twentieth century revolutions in science and philosophy: relativity and quantum mechanics. The theory of relativity brought important modifications of causal theory to classical mechanics, but did not go outside existing theory. On the other hand, quantum theory of the micro-system of the atom was revolutionary in that it was the first example in physics based on laws giving only a statistical prediction of events in the behavior of individual atomic systems. The uncertainty principal of Heisenberg (1927) led physicists to renounce for a time causality in quantum theory. Thus, Newton's laws of motion, regarded as absolute and final for more than two hundred years, were found to have a limited domain of validity—limits as predicted by Melville in *Clarel*. The limits are expressed in the theories of relativity and quantum electrodynamics. Bohm suggests a "qualitative infinity of nature," stating that other systems and theories may extend or limit those of mechanism, relativity, and quantum dynamics. The laws described within a limited context are influenced by forces external to a limited test system since no system can be entirely isolated. Over infinite time, even the determination of essential features of an effect are not purely mechanical due to an infinite number of changing contingent factors, qualities, properties, and laws of connection.[73] In 1931, Sir James Jeans summarized the import of the new theories in physics: "The world begins to look more like a great thought than a great machine."[74]

John Stuart Mill in his essay *On Liberty* (1859) argued for intellectual and religious tolerance because we can never be so sure we are right as to be justified or prudent in repressing other opinions; all grasp of truth is "provisional and imperfect." Religion cannot be a closed system of immutable revealed truths, defined in doctrine whose meaning is not altered by the passage of time. Instead, faith is a continuous, evolving, living stream of community, devotion, thought, and debate interacting with each other and borrowing from each other. In other words, religion evolves over time. Cupit observes, "Thus, the modern argument for religious toleration is based on the recognition that religion is human, historical, multifarious and ever-changing."[75] Polkinghorne agrees: "Yet science and theology have this in common, that each can be, and should be, defended as being investigations of what is, the search for increasing verisimilitude in our understanding of reality."[76] Duhem claims that the laws of science are symbolic, neither true nor false, but approximate, making them provisional and relative subject to future interpretation and disagreements between laws and experiment; new observations modify laws in order to more faithfully represent the "facts" balancing precision and certainty: "one cannot be increased except to the detriment of the other."[77]

Although most hold religious faith and secular science as being separate, they are in fact a division of mythologies. Science and religion went separate ways at the end of the nineteenth century; as stated by Louis Pasteur about 1880, "Only a misguided mind tries to introduce religion into science; more misguided still is he who attempts to introduce science into religion."[78] Yet, science and religion have remarkable similarities. The scientist is elevated to a shaman-like role, the tellers of truths, that resembles the role given to the myth-teller, the shaman or witch doctor. Sharpe points out that organized science and organized religion are similar in that both are pursued by passionate and often dogmatic adherents who work diligently toward system-specific goals, and that science involves worship and various form of ritualistic behavior, dogmas and hierarchy, gatekeepers of truth, its own shrines; it is a thoroughly persuasive enterprise, makes ambitious claims about the nature of reality, and its attempts at proselytizing are no less energetic in its temples—the classrooms. The myths of science include that all things are possible with scientific man.[79]

Contemporary scientists and cosmologists have not fared any better than their predecessors, and they may be even more critical of science and more aware of its limitations. Recently, Subramanyan Chandrasekhar (1910—), the great twentieth century astrophysicist and one of the most productive and esteemed scientists of the century, says of his experience in science, "It does not seem to me that the [quest] of science results in the feeling of contentment or peace after years of pursuit."[80] In addition, physicist Steven Weinberg (1933—) remarks, "It is very hard to realize that [the entire earth] is just a tiny part of an overwhelmingly hostile universe.... The more the universe seems comprehensible, the more it also seems pointless."[81] In Chapter 49, "The Hyena," of *Moby-Dick*, Ishmael's skepticism is remarkably current:

> There are certain queer times and occasions in this strange mixed affair we call life when a man takes this whole universe for a vast practical joke, though the wit thereof he but dimly discerns, and more than suspects that the joke is at nobody's expense but his own.

The nineteenth century heroic image of the scientist gave way to the twentieth century image of the psychotic horror movie scientist in the 1930s; the line dividing madness and genius is unclear with only a qualified admiration for scientific inquiry, reflecting the promise and terror of science.[82]

According to Cupit, the Western Christian must work out his own faith based on a personal vision of Christ which, the Western Christian has always known, is tragic—it is the image of the cross. It is not a guided pilgrimage toward a certain destination, but a creative framing of one's life as a spiritual project, to live a new life that has lost the fear of death with little basis on supernatural facts. The new focus of religion has raised us out of the dark, chaotic unconsciousness of nature and has made us human; for religion, just as our values expressed in our social institutions and our practices, focuses on self-realization: "But the historic task of religion, of embodying our values, witnessing to them, conserving them, setting them forth in symbols and securing their realization in human life, remains unchanged." Is spite of material progress brought about by science and technology, Cupit is in concert with Melville saying: "We are still promoted to religious dread and longing by the thought of our own death, our own littleness, and the precariousness of human values in the face of Nature's vast indifference."[83] Sir Arthur Eddington said in his Swarthmore lecture (1929), "In science as in religion the truth shines ahead as a beacon showing us the path; we do not ask to attain it; it is better far that we be permitted to seek,"[84] a restatement of Melville's assertion in *Mardi* that the question is more final than any answer.

Today, it is generally held that the Genesis Creation story is intended to show the power of God rather than the structure of the cosmos: the Bible speaks of God's word, command, law, truth, knowledge, justice, mercy, righteousness, holiness, and glory. Ancient Jewish thought was a demand for allegiance, with little emphasis on the interpretation of nature, except that Yahweh was also the God of nature and of all natural phenomena. The development and evolution of philosophies of Judaism encountered and dealt with issues similar to those that troubled Christian churchmen: causality and free will, natural philosophy, reason versus revelation, and the rise of the scientific method, reflected in works of esteemed Jewish philosophers, such as *The Faith of the Synagogue Considered as an Exact Science* by Solomon Ludwig Steinheim (1789-1866), and *The Religion of Reason Drawn from the Sources of Judaism* by Hermann Cohen (1842-1918).[85] The tension between science and religion is due mainly to the efforts of theologians to regiment science and extend their influence beyond its limits, and the growing authoritarianism of science, which seemed to explain everything and appeared to make the supernatural out-of-date.[86] Science also has its presuppositions, though often unrecognized;

science is not based on facts alone, and scientific laws develop because of a personal element involved in their formulation.[87] Bush describes "Christian humanism" as a religious, ethical, rational, and largely unmystical view of God, man, and the world. Its basis was "right reason" of the moral will, the divine faculty in man with certain absolute values in alliance with God making those values the goal of human effort. The rift between humanism and science began in France prior to Francis Bacon, but Bacon was the principal influence in sacrificing inward values to machines and material progress.[88] The disintegration of science into highly developed disciplines in the latter nineteenth century did not result in a convincing view of nature. Melville would agree with Popper who said in 1968:

> Science is not a system of certain, or well-established, statements; nor is it a system which steadily advances towards a state of finality. Our science is not knowledge (*episteme*): it can never claim to have attained truth, or even a substitute for it, such as probability.[89]

Twentieth century scientists have objected to the separation of God from the universe, including Heisenberg, Schrodinger, de Broglie, Planck, Einstein, Jeans, etc., who were the pioneers of quantum theory. Sir Arthur Eddington (1882-1944) claims the exploration of the external world by the methods of physical science leads not to a concrete reality but to "a shadow world of symbols, beneath which those methods are unadapted for penetrating":

> If to-day you ask a physicist what he has finally made out the aether or the electron to be, the answer will not be a description in terms of billiard balls or fly-wheels or anything concrete; he will point instead to a number of symbols and a set of mathematical equations which they satisfy....[physics] has no means of probing beneath the symbolism.[90]

Twentieth century physics searches for new theories of cosmology, such as the grand unified theory, superstrings, non-linear dynamics, and other concepts.[91] Maddox asserts that mathematicians have so far failed to provide a finite solution to the some of the simplest, mundane problems and concludes, "the need to survive without full understanding is perpetual."[92] According to Campbell, much of the complexity and vitality of Western heritage must be attributed to conflicting claims—

both of which are accepted—the advocates of what is offered as the word of God, and of the rational individual:

> All, according to this vision, though in apparent tumult, is harmony at root, as a manifestation of the all-supporting, all-suffusing mystery of being, which transcends thought, imaging, and definition; that is to say, transcends the search of science.[93]

Though science and faith have parted ways, neither is secure in their separate search for understanding, yet the division remains wide. Twentieth century science and technology have greatly enhanced material comfort and health, but leave unanswered the age-old conflict of faith and doubt.

Melville rightly interpreted the exaggerated claims of the scientists and properly recognized the threat of Newtonian materialism with its implicit threat of destruction of religious faith occurring in the middle decades of the nineteenth century. It is no wonder that his works are somewhat diffuse and at times lack a clear focus while centering on intensely debated matters of the day. In his later works, he even calls for a rapprochement between the two which Pasteur, Osler, and others claim is impossible—that science and faith are entirely separate. Yet, beginning with quantum theory, twentieth century science makes no claims to the certainty expressed by the hubris of Humphry Davy or others of the seventeenth, eighteenth, and nineteenth centuries, and many parallels exist between the seemingly opposite positions of theologian and scientist. Hillway contends that Melville's broad interests and intellectual independence placed him far ahead of his literary contemporaries in the appreciation and understanding of the implications of science. He possessed the intellectual integrity to see that neither the enthusiastic, nature-worshipping romanticism nor the stubbornly anti-science Christianity of his time could stand up to scientific realism: "On the other hand, he saw in science, though objective and realistic, something cold and even threatening."[94]

Although Melville pondered the conflict of science and faith, it is difficult to determine his own sense of faith. According to his *Journal* to London in 1849, Melville attended religious services all but one Sunday while in Europe. After 1850, he seldom attended church, and according to Melville's granddaughter, on rare occasions went to All Souls' Church on Fourth Avenue in New York. However, for many years during the latter part of his life he attended no religious services.[95] Melville's works reflect the threat of the advance of science to long held doctrines and religious faith of the mid-nineteenth century, yet "he remained to the end crusty, defiant, and humorously iconoclastic about religious orthodoxy."[96] In the ceaseless debate over science and its encroachment upon faith, modern clergymen, philosophers, and scientists, like Ahab viewing Queequeg—his savage, noble heart beating against the science of the natural world "a complete theory of the heavens and the earth, and a mystical treatise on the art of attaining truth" tattooed on his chest—searching for the meaning of man's existence and purpose in this "funambulatory Track and narrow Path of Goodness," may alike exclaim of man and his science: "Oh, devilish tantalization of the gods!"

Notes

1. Walter Clyde Curry, *Chaucer and the Mediaeval Sciences.* Oxford: Oxford University Press, 1926. Revised and enlarged edition, New York: Barnes & Noble, 1960, pp. xi, 29-30.

2. Homer W. Smith, *Man and His Gods*. Boston: Little Brown, 1952, pp. 268-269; *The Norton Anthology of English Literature.* Third edition. M.H. Abrams, general editor. New York: Norton, 1974, p. 768-769.

3. William H. Gilman, *Melville's Early Life and Redburn.* New York: New York University Press and Oxford University Press, 1951, pp. 54, 103.

4. Tyrus Hillway, "Melville's Education in Science." *Texas Studies in Literature and Language* 16 (1974.):421-422.

5. F. O. Matthieson, *American Renaissance: Art and Expression in the Age of Emerson and Whitman.* Oxford: Oxford University Press, 1941, p. 124.

6. Egon Stephen Merton, *Science and Imagination in Sir Thomas Browne*. New York: Octagon, 1969, p. 73.

7. Brian Foley, "Herman Melville and the Example of Sir Thomas Browne." *Modern Philology* 81 (1984):265-277; Frank Livingstone Huntley, *Sir Thomas Browne. A Biographical and Critical Study.* Ann Arbor: University of Michigan Press, 1969; Jeremiah S. Finch, *Sir Thomas Browne: A Doctor's Life of Science and Faith.* New York: Henry Schuman. 1950.

8. Gillian Beer, "Darwin's Reading and the Development of Fictions of Development." in *The Darwinian Heritage.* David Kohn, editor. Princeton, New Jersey: Princeton University Press, 1985, p. 543.

9. Nathan Reingold, "200 years of American science: Reflections on 200 years of science in the United States." *Nature* 262 (1976) 9-13.

10. I. Bernard Cohen, "Some Reflections on the State of Science in America During the Nineteenth Century." *Proceedings of the National Academy of Science.*" 45 (1959) 666-677.

11. Tyrus Hillway, "Melville and the Spirit of Science." *South Atlantic Quarterly* 48: 78-88, 1949.

12. Nathan Reingold, "The World of the Natural Historians." in *Science in Nineteenth Century America: A Documentary History.* Nathan Reingold, editor. Chicago and London: University of Chicago Press, 1964, p. 29-31.

13. Thomas L. Hankins, *Science and the Enlightenment.* Cambridge: Cambridge University Press, 1985, pp. 3-8; Michael J.

Buckley, *At the Origins of Modern Atheism*. New Haven and London: Yale University Press, 1987, pp. 225-291.

14. Thomas S. Hall, *History of General Physiology: 600 B.C. to A.D. 1900. Vol. 1 From pre-Socratic Times to the Enlightenment.* Chicago and London: University of Chicago Press, 1975, p. 263.

15. Arthur Danto and Sidney Morgenbesser, "Introduction" to Section I "Science, Language and Experience." in *Philosophy of Science.* Arthur Danto and Sidney Morgenbesser, editors. New York: Meridian, 1960, p. 23.

16. Bertrand Russell, "The Relation of Sense-data to Physics." in *Philosophy of Science.* Arthur Danto and Sidney Morgenbesser, editor. New York: Meridian, 1960, p. 35.

17. Maurice Mandelbaum, *History, Man and Reason: a Study of Nineteenth-Century Thought.* Baltimore: Johns Hopkins University Press, 1971, pp. 35-36.

18. Fred Hoyle, "Articles of Faith," review of John Polkinghorne, *Science and Providence: God's Interaction with the World.* London: SPCK, 1989. in *Nature* 339 (1989): 23-24.

19. Géza Szamosi, *The Twin Dimensions: Inventing Time and Space*. New York: McGraw-Hill, 1986, pp. 127-128; Richard Morris, *Time's Arrows: Scientific Attitudes Toward Time.* New York: Touchstone; Simon and Schuster, 1985, pp. 81-83.

20. Michael Ruse, *The Darwinian Revolution: Science Red in Tooth and Claw.* Chicago and London: University of Chicago Press, 1979, pp. 239-240.

21. Beer, ref. 8, p. 543.

22. Beer, ref. 8, pp. 582-587.

23. Ruse, ref. 20, pp. 234-240, 205, 229.

24. Alec R. Vidler, *The Church in an Age of Revolution: 1789 to the present day.* Hammondsworth and New York: Penguin, 1961, pp. 190-194.

25. Frank M. Turner, "The Victorian Conflict between Science and Religion: A Professional Dimension." *Isis* 69 (1978): 356-376; Vidler, ref.24, p. 212.

26. John Farley, *The Spontaneous Generation Controversy from Descartes to Oparin.* Baltimore and London: Johns Hopkins University Press, 1977, pp. 135-150.

27. M. Mitchell Waldrop, "Spontaneous Order, Evolution, and Life." *Science* 247 (1990) 1543-1545.

28. René Taton, *Science in the Nineteenth Century.* New York: Basic Books, 1965, p. 483; Loren Eiseley, *Darwin's Century.* Garden City, New York: Doubleday, 1958, pp. 208, 224-231.

29. Roger Lewin, "A Lopsided Look at Evolution." *Science* 241 (1988):291-293; Ruse, ref. 20, pp. 231-232.

30. Dirk J. Struik, *Yankee Science in the Making*. New York: Collier, 1962, p. 373.

31. Yehuda Elkana, "Introduction." in William Whewell, *Selected Writings on the History of Science*. Yehuda Elkana, editor. Chicago and London: University of Chicago Press. 1984, p. xi-xv.

32. Whewell, ref. 31, p. 377.

33. John D. Barrow and Frank J. Tipler, *The Anthropic Cosmological Principle*. Oxford: Oxford University Press, 1988, pp. 92-95.

34. Barrow and Tipler, ref. 33, pp. 1-2.

35. Barrow and Tipler, ref. 33, pp. 3-6, 18-23, 109; Marek Abramowicz and George Ellis. "The elusive anthropic principle." *Nature* 337 (1989) 411-412.

36. C. S. Lewis, *The Discarded Image: An Introduction to Medieval and Renaissance Literature*. Cambridge: Cambridge University Press, 1964, pp. 218-220.

37. John D. Barrow, *The World Within the World*. Oxford and New York, Oxford University Press, 1990, p. 30.

38. A. N. Whitehead, *The Function of Reason*. Princeton University Press, 1929. reprint. Boston: Beacon Press, 1958, p. 4.

39. Harold I. Sharlin, *The Convergent Century: The Unification of Science in the Nineteenth Century*. London, New York, Toronto: Abelard-Schuman, 1966, p. 17.

40. Peter J. Bowler, *Evolution: The History of an Idea*. Berkeley, Los Angeles and London: University of California Press, 1984, p. 219.

41. Lewis, ref. 36, p. 221.

42. Lewis, ref. 36, pp. 222-223.

43. Herbert Butterfield, *The Origins of Modern Science 1300-1800*. New York: Free Press, 1957, p. 7.

44. A. N. Whitehead, *Science and the Modern World*. New York: Macmillan, 1925, p. 188.

45. Don Cupit, *The Sea of Faith: Christianity in Change*. Cambridge: Cambridge University Press, 1984, p. 172.

46. F. M. Turner, "Victorian Scientific Naturalism," in *Darwin to Einstein: Historical Studies on Science and Belief*. Colin Chant and John Fauvel, editors. Harlow, England: Longman, 1980, p. 50.

47. Cupit, ref 45, pp. 208-213.

48. R. J. Berry, "What to believe about miracles." *Nature* 322 (1986):321-322.

49. Tyrus Hillway, *Herman Melville.* Indianapolis: Bobbs-Merrill, 1979, pp. 143-144.

50. Hillway, ref. 11.

51. Charles C. Roland, "Introduction." *William Osler's Masterwords in Medicine: A Study in Rhetoric.* Springfield, Illinois: C. C. Thomas, 1972.

52. A. N. Whitehead, *Religion in the Making* Cambridge, Cambridge University Press, 1926, p. 57, cited in John Polkinghorne, *One World: the interaction of science and theology.* London: SPCK Holy Trinity Church, 1986, p. 28.

53. Peter Medawar, *The Limits of Science.* Oxford: Oxford University Press, 1984, pp. 13-14.

54. Medawar, ref. 53, pp. 17-18.

55. Carl L. Becker, *The Heavenly City of the Eighteenth-Century Philosophers.* New Haven and London: Yale University Press, 1932, p. 24.

56. Charles A. Coulson, "The Similarity of Science and Religion." in *Science and Religion: New Perspectives on the Dialogue.* Ian G. Barbour, editor. New York, Evanston and London: Harper & Row: 1968, p. 61.

57. Becker, ref. 55, pp. 20-28.

58. Medawar, ref. 53, p. 66.

59. P. W. Bridgman, *The Nature of Physical Theory.* Princeton: Princeton University Press, 1936. cited by F. Sherwood Taylor, *A Short History of Science & Scientific Thought: With Readings from the Great Scientists from the Babylonians Through Einstein.* New York and London: Norton, 1949, p. 357.

60. Frank J. Tipler. "Extraterrestrial Intelligence: A Skeptical View of Radio Searches." *Science* 219 (1983) 110.

61. John Maddox, "Is Darwinism a thermodynamic necessity?" *Nature* 350 (1991) 653; Michael Weale and Coel Hellier (letters) *Nature* 351 (1991) 600.

62. Reginald E. Watters, "Melville's Metaphysics of Evil." *University of Toronto Quarterly* 9 (1940): 170-182.

63. Sir Thomas Browne, *Religio Medici* in *Sir Thomas Browne: Selected Writings.* Chicago and London: University of Chicago Press, 1968, p. 34.

64. David Knight, *Ordering the World: A history of classifying man.* London: Burnett Book, Andre Deutsch, 1981, pp. 200-201.

65. J. D. Bernal, *Science and Industry in the Nineteenth Century.* London: Routledge and Kegan Paul, 1953. reprint. Bloomington and London: Indiana University Press, 1971, p. 6.

66. F. M. Turner, "Victorian Scientific Naturalism," in *Darwin to Einstein: Historical Studies on Science and Belief.* Colin Chant and John Fauvel, editors. Harlow, England: Longman, 1980, p. 59.

67. David Hume, *Dialogues Concerning Natural Religion* (1779). reprint. Norman Kemp Smith, editor. Indianapolis and New York: Bobbs-Merrill, 1947, pp. 137-138.

68. Stephen Toulmin, *The Return to Cosmology: Postmodern Science and the Theology of Nature.* Berkeley, Los Angeles, and London: University of California Press, 1982, p. 30.

69. Gerald Holton, "Mach, Einstein and the Search for Reality." in *Darwin to Einstein: Historical Studies on Science and Belief.* Colin Chant and John Fauvel, editors. Harlow, England: Longman, 1980, p. 237.

70. Danto and Morgenbesser, ref. 15, pp. 315-321.

71. Lord Kelvin (William Thompson), "The age of the earth as an abode fitted for life," *Philosophical Magazine* series 5, volume 47, p. 89, cited by Claude C. Albritton, Jr., *The Abyss of Time: Changing Conceptions of the Earth's Antiquity after the Sixteenth Century.* New York: St. Martin's Press, 1986, p. 185.

72. Robert V. Bruce, *The Launching of Modern American Science 1846-1876.* New York: Alfred A. Knopf, 1987, pp. 339-340.

73. David Bohm, *Causality and Chance in Modern Physics.* Philadelphia: University of Pennsylvania Press, 1957, pp. 62-69, 132-136, 158-160.

74. James Jeans, *The Mysterious Universe.* New York: Macmillan, 1931, p.158. cited by Annie Dillard, *Living by Fiction.* New York, Cambridge, Philadelphia, San Francisco, London, Mexico City São Paulo: Harper and Row, 1982, p. 56.

75. Cupit, ref. 45, pp. 163-164.

76. John Polkinghorne, *One World: the interaction of science and theology.* London: SPCK Holy Trinity Church, 1986, p. 42.

77. Pierre Duhem, "Physical Law," in *Philosophy of Science.* Arthur Danto and Sidney Morgenbesser, editors. New York: Meridian, 1960, pp. 182-197.

78. Samuel Devons, "Optics through the Eyes of the Medieval Churchmen." *Annals of the New York Academy of Sciences.* 441 (1985):205-224.

79. Kevin J. Sharpe, *From Science To An Adequate Mythology.* Auckland, New Zealand: Interface Press, 1984, pp. 32-33, 48.

80. George Field, *Chandra: A Biography of S. Chandrasekhar* by Kemeshawar C. Wali. Chicago: University of Chicago Press, 1991. Review in *Science* 251 (1991) 455-456.

81. Steven Weinberg, *The First Three Minutes: a modern view of the origin of the universe.* New York: Basic Books, 1988, p. 154.

82. Andrew Tudor, "Seeing the worst side of science." *Nature* 340 (1989) 589-592.

83. Cupit, ref. 45, pp. 32, 272-273.

84. Sir William McCrea, "Arthur Stanley Eddington." *Scientific American* June (1991): 92-93.

85. Don Cupit, ref. 45, p. 57; W. O. E. Oesterley and T. H. Robinson, *Hebrew Religion: Its Origin and Development.* London: SPCK, 1930, pp. 196-197; Julius Guttmann, *Philosophies of Judaism: The history of Jewish philosophy from Biblical times to Franz Rosenzweig.* translated by David W. Silverman. New York, Chicago, and San Francisco: Holt, Rinehart and Winston, 1964.

86. Ernan McMullin, "Science and the Catholic Tradition," *Science and Religion: New Perspectives on the Dialogue.* Ian G. Barbour, editor. New York, Evanston, and London: Harper and Row, 1968, pp. 34-35.

87. Charles A. Coulson, "The Similarity of Science and Religion," in *Science and Religion: New Perspectives on the Dialogue.* Ian G. Barbour, editor. New York, Evanston, and London: Harper and Row, 1968, pp. 71-72.

88. Douglas Bush, "Two Roads to Truth: Science and Religion in the Early Seventeenth Century." *English Literary History* 8 (1941):81-102.

89. Karl R. Popper, *The Logic of Scientific Discovery.* New York, Hagerstown, San Francisco, and London: Harper Touchstone Books, Harper and Row, 1965, p. 278.

90. Ken Wilber, *Quantum Questions.* Boston and London: New Science Library, 1984, pp. 181-182.

91. P. C. W. Davies, "Inflation and time asymmetry in the Universe." *Nature* 301 (1983):398-400; John Ellis, "The superstring: theory of everything, or of nothing?" *Nature* 323 (1986):595-597; Itamar Procaccia, "Universal properties of dynamically complex systems: the organization of chaos." *Nature* 333 (1988):618-623.

92. John Maddox, "Should technology be scorned?" *Nature* 326 (1987):737.

93. Joseph Campbell, *The Masks of God: Occidental Mythology.* New York: Penguin Books, 1964, p. 5.

94. Hillway, ref. 49, pp. 26-27.

95. William Braswell, *Melville's Religious Thought: An Essay in Interpretation.* New York: Pageant, 1959, pp. 7, 52-53.

96. Edward Wagenknecht, "Our Contemporary: Herman Melville." *English Journal* 39 (1950) 121:128.

Index